dicious. Based on three years of research, examination, and observation,
and written by a man sympathetic to
the antipoverty effort, the book provides an appraisal that will be of in-
estimable value to those involved in
planning and operating programs to
fight poverty.

Sar A. Levitan is Research Professor
of Economics and Director of the Center for Manpower Policy Studies at
The George Washington University.
He is also a consultant to several government agencies and congressional
committees, including the General Accounting Office, which prepared its
own evaluation of the antipoverty programs. He is the author of **Federal Aid
to Depressed Areas** and co-author
(with Garth L. Mangum) of **Federal
Training and Work Programs in the
Sixties**.

The Great Society's Poor Law

THE GREAT SOCIETY'S
POOR LAW

A NEW APPROACH TO POVERTY

Sar A. Levitan

The Johns Hopkins Press
Baltimore

Copyright © 1969 by The Johns Hopkins Press
Baltimore, Maryland 21218
All rights reserved
Manufactured in the United States of America
Library of Congress Catalog Card Number 74-82450

Standard Book Number 8018-1070-1

This book was prepared under a grant from the Ford Foundation.

The photographs in this book are reproduced by courtesy of
the Office of Economic Opportunity, and of the individual
photographers: Paul Conklin (pages 2, 48, 206, 246, 262),
Fletcher Drake (pages 108, 308), Stephen Feldman (page 190),
Ralph Matthews, Jr. (page 176), Michael Sullivan (page 132),
and Deborah Wager (page 226).

Contents

Preface

The Economic Opportunity Act, more than any other piece of legislation, is identified with the Great Society's commitment to our nation's poor. In the typical rhetoric of the day, it was heralded as a "total war on poverty." Its announced aim was not only to eliminate poverty but to restructure society by giving the poor a chance to design and administer antipoverty programs.

Poverty has not been eliminated. Society has not been restructured. And clearly the "total war" has died aborning. Expenditures under the Economic Opportunity Act have accounted for only a small part of total federal assistance to the poor. In fiscal 1969 appropriations of nearly two billion dollars under the Act's provisions constituted only eight percent of all federal antipoverty dollars.

Although the Act has fallen far short of its promises, this does not mean it has been a failure. Achievements must be judged not by inflated anticipations but rather by reasonable expectations that take account of the limited resources available under the Act and the enormous problems it sought to attack. What, then, has been the record of the Economic Opportunity Act and its composite programs? This study is intended as one answer to the question.

In addition to charging OEO with the planning and coordination of federal antipoverty efforts and the mobilization of antipoverty resources, the Act established a number of experimental and conventional programs. To mobilize and coordinate community resources to combat poverty, the Act called for the creation of Community Action Programs to improve and expand the social and educational services available to the poor. On the assumption that self-help was the most effective way to escape poverty, the poor were to be involved in the planning and administration of these programs. Recognizing that many of the poor could not obtain jobs in the competitive labor market, the Act provided jobs and training aimed at improving their employability. Separate programs were enacted to provide jobs for impoverished young people and to offer work relief with training to adults, particularly needy, unemployed parents. To give a "last chance" to youths who had failed to obtain a rudimentary education in school and who were unprepared for work, the Act established Job Corps centers where they could acquire a basic education and learn marketable skills. Finally, the Act provided for separate loan programs to foster self-employment for impoverished rural residents and small business owners.

This book traces the development of the Economic Opportunity Act, describing the organizational structure created to administer the legislation and evaluating its performance. Separate sections of the study analyze the major antipoverty efforts initiated under the Act. Part II is devoted to the Community Action Program. An over-all review of CAP is followed by more detailed analyses of Head Start, Upward Bound, community health centers, birth control, legal services, and VISTA. Technically, VISTA was not part of the Community Action Program, but because the bulk of VISTA volunteers worked on CAP-funded projects, I have considered it along with CAP programs. And though many rural programs were an integral part of CAP, they have been presented separately in Part III. An analysis of the manpower programs of the Economic Opportunity Act has been presented elsewhere by the author, jointly with Garth L. Mangum (*Federal Training and Work Programs in the Sixties*, Institute of Labor and Industrial Relations, University of Michigan, 1969); but in order to present a more complete picture of OEO operations, I have included a discussion of the Job Corps in this volume.

The Economic Opportunity Act has been revamped annually during its first three years of operation, and OEO has therefore remained in a constant state of flux. As a result, completion of this study has been repeatedly postponed to permit the inclusion of the latest developments. Finally, however, a cut-off date, the end of the fiscal year 1968, was established; the retirement of the Great Society provides a particularly appropriate point to take stock of the program, as the new Administration and the 91st Congress seek to chart its future scope and direction.

An evaluator's life is not an easy one, and the obstacles to assessment of programs initiated under the Economic Opportunity Act are especially formidable. These difficulties have placed very definite limits on the degree of analytical precision which could be attained. A brief exposition of the difficulties—which may be taken as both an evaluator's lament and an explanation of his work—is in order at this point.

While it is not uncommon for an investigator to point to an inadequacy of data, the plaint is more justified in the case of OEO programs than for many other governmental efforts. A number of factors have contributed to the paucity of information. For many of OEO's programs it is simply too early for meaningful data to have been assembled. The economic benefits of Head Start, for example, may not be apparent for years, because even the senior members of this group have not yet passed their tenth birthday.

The data-gathering process itself has been the source of many problems. Expectedly, evaluation was given low priority by administrators concerned with initiating and consolidating new programs. OEO programs required project-by-project approval, and the small federal staff, preoccupied with daily administrative chores, could not enforce systematic data retrieval. The problem was compounded by the sheer number and variety of school systems, welfare agencies, and other organizations to which projects were delegated. Local project administrators rarely developed the sophisticated research capability necessary for evaluation of the programs. In many cases project administrators placed an even lower priority than federal officials upon collection of data, and they were likely to gather only data needed for their own operations.

Paradoxically, the development of computerized data processing, designed to improve data collection capability, proved to be an impediment in the case of OEO programs. To simplify data preparation, OEO sent out uniform instructions for its collection and processing. When not ignored by the CAA's or delegate agencies, the instructions for preparing reports were frequently misunderstood or interpreted differently by project administrators. Thus, the information submitted was often of no use to the programmed computers.

Difficulties of data gathering are matched by difficulties in handling the data. These may be mechanical—for several computerized collection systems have undergone long periods of shake-down—but basically the problems are conceptual. Where data are available, one conceptual technique for handling them has been cost-effectiveness analysis, which seeks to determine the cheapest way to accomplish goals and to receive maximum advantage from expenditures. By attempting to measure the dollar-and-cents value of programs, and by relating these to program costs, an attempt is made to calculate the return on the government's investment.

The major limitation of this approach is that it invites unwarranted comparisons among dissimilar programs. As applied to the Economic Opportunity Act, the approach might be used, for example, to determine the most economic means of helping poor youths escape poverty. This study presents comparable costs on the Job Corps and Upward Bound, and it might at first appear to be a matter of simple calculation to determine the cost effectiveness of these education and training programs for young people. One might too hastily conclude that the Job Corps is more expensive than Upward Bound, for it costs several times as much to maintain a youth for a year in the Job Corps as it does to provide him with an education through Upward

Bound. The products of these two youth programs, however, are not necessarily interchangeable. Job Corps clients may never qualify for Upward Bound.

If a cost-effectiveness analysis did provide persuasive evidence that an alternative to an existing program was desirable, would the responsible officials be able to admit failure? Past experience has shown that such humility is rarely found. Shifts in program emphasis require either new appropriations or reallocation of available funds, both of which are difficult to achieve.

Each antipoverty program has attracted advocates within the federal establishment and a clientele outside the government, a fact which renders it hazardous for administrators to drop a going program, even if they are so inclined. And even if these obstacles within the executive establishment could be overcome, approval of changes in programs, or the substitution of alternatives, still requires congressional approval. Each program has its congressional sponsors and supporters, who may present insurmountable impediments to change. There is no guarantee, therefore, that programs of proven cost effectiveness will be implemented. The Office of Economic Opportunity has concluded, for example, that family planning is probably the most cost-effective antipoverty measure. Nevertheless, OEO has been most timid in funding birth control projects.

Moreover, the bases for calculating benefits and the assumptions necessary for placing price tags on the presumed benefits are arbitrary, so that almost any cost-benefit ratio can be fabricated. Only when two programs have the same type of benefits, and when their cost-benefit ratios can be calculated under the same assumptions, are the comparative ratios likely to be meaningful.

For these reasons, the study does not contain a single cost-benefit analysis. An earlier draft of Part IV included an evaluation of the Job Corps on the basis of cost-benefit calculations. The judgment that the Job Corps was justified on the ground that benefits to society would exceed costs had to be discarded when subsequent examination revealed that the data used by OEO were faulty. By the same token, to condemn the Job Corps on the basis of currently available data would probably be equally premature.

A final deterrent to adequate information is the tendency of some administrators to opt for "evaluation" based on a few selected anecdotes rather than risk rigorous objective analysis which might be unfavorable. Too frequently there has been a credibility gap in OEO statistics; and many of OEO's public statements have been sprinkled with such imprecise words as "reached," "affected," and "served." For example, testifying on the accomplishments of CAP, the OEO director asserted that the program had "affected the lives of four million impoverished Americans. . . ." The statement failed to specify the ways in which the poverty program had "affected" these people. Thus, "affected" could mean anything from giving a word of encouragement to providing a job or a place to live.

To point up all these difficulties in the evaluation of antipoverty programs perhaps overstates the case. Adequate data are available for some programs, and improved data will be available as antipoverty efforts mature. Bertrand M. Harding, OEO's director since March 1968, and other OEO officials have recognized the problems and have made continuous efforts to improve data needed for effective management and to help outside observers better understand their efforts.

Acknowledgments

During the three years that I have closely followed the antipoverty program, officials of the Office of Economic Opportunity have been most cooperative. Almost all of the top OEO officials gave generously of their time and shared their knowledge and insights in helping me to prepare an evaluation of the program, although the occasionally excessive commitment of program administrators made them somewhat defensive of their efforts and sensitive to criticism. The analysis of each program has also had the benefit of critical review by the administrator responsible for the program, but this does not necessarily mean that the officials share my conclusions.

I am indebted to my associates in the study. Professor Roger H. Davidson co-authored an earlier version of chapter 2 and has offered valuable critical suggestions on the entire volume. Ethel W. Brandwein, Jeffrey Burt, Judith LaVor, Geraldine Storm, and Robert Taggart III provided research assistance and counsel during various stages of the study. Only Mrs. Brandwein served from the beginning to the end of the study, but all have made valuable contributions toward its completion. Mrs. Ivis B. Steele and Mrs. Barbara Ann Pease served as administrative assistants for the project and saw the manuscript through the various drafts, from tape to the final proof. Lowell Glenn and Arnold Nemore have also contributed to the preparation of this volume. My colleague Garth L. Mangum contributed to the book in more ways than can be stated in a formal acknowledgment.

Finally, Brita Ann Levitan, after listening patiently to the travails of the antipoverty warriors and their evaluator, helped to resolve differences and indicated options to difficult situations.

Earlier versions of chapters 1, 6, and 9 appeared in *Poverty and Human Resources.* The consent of the editor to use this material is gratefully acknowledged.

This study was prepared under a grant from the Ford Foundation. In accordance with the Foundation's practice, complete responsibility for the preparation of the volume was left to the author.

SAR A. LEVITAN

Center for Manpower Policy Studies
The George Washington University
January 20, 1969

Part I

Design and Administration

1.

THE DESIGN OF STRATEGY[1]

To every man his chance, to every man regardless of
his birth, his shining golden opportunity—to every man,
the right to live, to work, to be himself and to become
whatever thing his manhood and his wisdom can combine
to make him—this . . . is the promise of America.

Thomas Wolfe

The Vision

On August 20, 1964, Lyndon B. Johnson signed the Economic
Opportunity Act, the most dramatic and highly publicized of the
Great Society's programs. Five months earlier, when the President presented his antipoverty message, he urged the American people as
"citizens of the richest . . . nation in the history of the world" to declare war on poverty. "Having the power," he exhorted Congress and
the nation, "we have the duty." In signing the bill the President declared that the passage of the Economic Opportunity Act was a commitment of a "great nation . . . to eradicate poverty among its people."

The aspiration of eliminating poverty is not new. Though the
Bible tells us that "ye have the poor with you always," the hope of
eliminating widespread poverty has been often expressed. And this was
not a dream cherished by social reformers alone. Two generations ago
the influential British economist Alfred Marshall expressed the belief
that "poverty and ignorance may be gradually extinguished . . . during
the present century."[2] Herbert Hoover anticipated an early victory
over poverty when, in accepting the presidential nomination in 1928,
he declared: "We shall soon, with the help of God, be in sight of the
day when poverty will be banished in the nation."[3] Even the slogan
"war on poverty" is not new: David Lloyd George requested funds
from the British Parliament to wage "warfare against poverty" six
decades ago.[4]

The Welfare System

The antipoverty programs enacted in 1964 are part of a public
policy that began with the Poor Laws of 1601 and has received increasing attention from policymakers since the early days of the Industrial

3

Revolution. In the United States, local governments and private charities traditionally have assumed responsibility for relief of the poor. In recent decades, however, the federal government, under pressure to alleviate the more visible shortcomings of the American social and economic system, has engaged in a variety of activities that bear on the plight of the impoverished. Since the Great Depression the United States has developed an intricate (though far from comprehensive) welfare system. This system is composed of programs that range widely in techniques and objectives but whose underlying assumption is that specialized programs are needed to take care of the more pressing and diverse needs of the poor.

In our society the state has assumed the responsibility of providing many social services to its citizens, and it provides most of these benefits without regard to the recipients' level of income. Governmental expenditures for education are almost twice as large as direct outlays on behalf of the poor. Many public services, in fact, tend to favor the more affluent members of society. An authoritative foreign observer of the American scene, Gunnar Myrdal, has aptly stated: "In almost all respects—minimum wages, social security, agriculture, housing, etc.— American economic and social policies show a perverse tendency to favor groups that are above the level of the most needy."[5]

Our welfare system for the needy can be divided into two distinct categories:

1. Programs that offer cash assistance. The major programs in this group are old-age, survivors, and disability insurance; public assistance programs, which also fall under the Social Security Act; general assistance, which is financed exclusively by states and localities for needy persons not covered by the Social Security Act; and pensions for needy veterans.

2. Programs that provide services and goods to the poor on the basis of need. Included in this category are the programs that were initiated under the war on poverty, as well as subsidized housing, several forms of food distribution, and health services.

Cash Support

The Social Security Act, now the product of more than three decades of evolution, is the basic instrument for providing income for the poor. This act creates two groups of beneficiaries: those who receive payments regardless of their economic resources and those who qualify for benefits only upon the determination of individual need. The distinction between the two groups is made on the basis of prior contributions. Those who have made payroll contributions qualify for benefits

for themselves and their dependents—or, alternatively, their survivors—
as a matter of right. On the other hand, those who qualify for public
assistance must first establish personal need.

The insurance features of the Social Security Act are partially
based on government fiat rather than cash contributions. Benefits under the act are heavily weighted in favor of low earners, and only
minimum qualifications are needed for a person to receive benefits.
According to a Social Security Administration special study, almost
half of the $18 billion benefits paid in 1965 either went to persons be-
low the poverty threshold or helped raise the recipients' income above
that threshold. The benefits would have been reduced by about a
third if the formula had not favored low earners. Thus the federal insurance system has a pronounced welfare bias.

Despite the heavy weighting of benefits in favor of low earners,
two of every five aged persons who receive social security benefits live
in poverty. In fact, aged beneficiaries residing in urban areas live in
poverty if they depend upon social security payments as their sole
means of support. The current contributions to the system clearly are
inadequate to permit millions of beneficiaries to escape poverty if the
system is to be kept on an actuarially sound basis. One obvious solution would be to add the government as a third contributory partner
to social insurance, as in the Medicare program. At present, whatever
subsidy goes to low earners is contributed mostly by middle-income
groups, whose contributions are identical to those of the most affluent.

Another cash support program under the Social Security Act is
unemployment insurance. The object of the program is to provide
essential income—about half of take-home pay—during spells of
enforced idleness. It limits the loss of income of those who become temporarily unemployed, and it staves off poverty for many. But unemployment insurance has only limited applicability to many of the working poor. Industries in which the working poor tend to concentrate
—agriculture, domestic service, and firms with three or fewer workers—are not protected by the law. Moreover, to receive unemployment
benefits, a person must have a recent history of work and be available
for work. A large percentage of the idle poor are not available for
work because of disability, illness, or home responsibilities.

The most significant effort at direct income support for the poor
is public assistance that provides aid to four impoverished groups: old
persons, the blind, the permanently and totally disabled, and families
with dependent children. The federal government contributes more
than half the funds, and the balance is made up by the states and
localities. In addition, most states provide some measure of general
assistance for destitute persons who fail to qualify under any of the

four categories. Although the states' eligibility criteria vary widely, public assistance recipients are among the most destitute groups in the population. The public assistance programs provide minimal income to one-third of the poor.

Veterans and their dependents have historically been singled out for preferential income support on the basis of need. Although the present programs may not permit all veterans and their dependents to escape poverty, major steps have already been taken to provide for their basic needs, particularly among older veterans and surviving dependents. There are about twenty-two million married veterans with thirty-three million children in the United States.

Veterans' benefits are as old as the nation; indeed, the first veterans' pension law was passed in 1776. The present law provides two types of cash benefits: compensation and pensions. Compensation is paid to veterans who have incurred an injury or disability while serving in the armed services. Pensions are paid to veterans who served during wartime, if their annual income is below a specified level and if they are permanently disabled. In practice, the disability qualifications are relaxed as the veteran advances in age. They are stringent for veterans below the age of fifty-five, but veterans aged sixty-five and over qualify for a pension on the basis of need.

The income criteria that qualify a veteran or his surviving dependents to receive a pension are liberal compared with other income support programs. A veteran whose income exceeds the official government criteria denoting poverty may nevertheless qualify for a pension. The widows and dependent children of deceased war veterans also qualify for pensions. Under the present law, the number of veterans or their surviving dependents who qualify for pensions will continue to increase with the age and mortality rate of the veteran population. Most veterans who receive pensions, and their survivors, also qualify for social insurance benefits. It can therefore be assumed that poverty has largely been eliminated among aged veterans and their survivors.

Services, Goods, and Rehabilitation

Provision for various social welfare services is now an integral part of governmental responsibilities. Few would question, for example, the desirability of free education or medical research supported by public funds. Though available to all, such governmental welfare services are particularly relevant to the poor. While there is some merit in the argument that the best way to assist the poor is to supply them with cash, realization of the full potential of individuals and families in our society requires that the state provide the needy with an opportunity to acquire education, health care, adequate nutrition, shelter, and essential social services.

Programs to aid children were the earliest social welfare services provided by the federal government; they date back to the Taft Administration. Federal contributions to child welfare programs have been increasing in recent years, and legislation enacted in 1967 made provision for expanded services for children.

Although these service programs are not aimed exclusively at the children of poor families, most beneficiaries of maternal and child health services come from low-income families. A government brochure explains that the child welfare services program is designed "for troubled children and children in trouble." Problems of child neglect, abuse, and emotional disturbance are not limited to impoverished homes, but it is not at all surprising that "poor children" have more than their share of such problems. Consequently, children from impoverished homes are likely candidates for the assistance offered by child welfare programs.

The admonition of a social worker from an earlier generation is still applicable today: "Social services never filled an empty stomach." While outright starvation may be rare in the United States, millions of persons do not have the means to purchase food to provide a well-balanced and adequate diet. To help improve the diet of needy persons and dispose of surplus foods, the federal government introduced the food stamp program and also operates a direct food distribution program. In addition, the national school lunch program and the special milk program contribute to the nutritional well-being of all children.

The law requires schools participating in the lunch program to provide free or reduced-cost meals for needy children. Ironically, however, many children from impoverished homes are not offered free lunches, either because the schools they attend do not participate in the program or because school authorities in poor neighborhoods lack the funds to serve all those in need. This gap is one of the many "costs" of poverty: Because many needy children are concentrated in impoverished areas, they are denied free lunches, while students in more affluent areas receive the benefit of government-subsidized meals.

The food stamp and direct food distribution programs are aimed exclusively at supplementing the diet of needy persons. Under the food stamp plan, eligible needy families may exchange money they would normally spend on food for food coupons that have greater purchasing value. The coupons may then be exchanged in retail stores for domestically produced food (imported caviar is out!). The value of the bonus coupons decreases as the recipient's income increases.

A major criticism of the food programs, aside from their expense, is that they tend to make the recipients dependent upon the government and thus destroy self-reliance. But the alternative—a deficient and debilitating diet—is also, unfortunately, destructive to self-reliance.

The federal government is deeply involved in the housing business. The extent of this involvement is reflected in the 1965 and 1968 Housing Acts, which carried multibillion-dollar price tags for insured loans, grants, and subsidies that were to be expended over a number of years. Several housing programs are designed exclusively to provide adequate shelter for the poor, but here again, although the government effort has been successful in helping millions of middle-income and affluent families acquire suitable housing, relatively little has been done for the poor. Because private enterprise cannot profitably provide adequate housing to low-income groups, the poor are largely confined to housing that is dilapidated, lacks plumbing, or is overcrowded.

A major barrier to the construction of public housing is the limited availability of sites. Even where sites are available, organized community groups have frequently raised effective opposition to locating public housing for impoverished families in the midst of relatively affluent neighborhoods. Racial prejudice is another obstacle to construction inasmuch as a large proportion of public housing residents are Negroes.

To improve upon the unimpressive record in public housing, President Johnson pressured Congress in 1965 to approve legislation that would subsidize the rent of impoverished families. The major impact of the new program would be to enable impoverished families to live among more affluent neighbors. If a family's income increased, its rent subsidy would decline; but in contrast to the current public housing practice, a family would not be compelled to move if its income rose above the subsidy level. The idea of a special provision to cover the costs of housing is hardly new; it is part of the federal tax structure that permits income tax deductions for mortgage interest. The mortgage-guarantee program for homeowners is another subsidy for the more affluent. The rent subsidy legislation has remained a promise, however; Congress failed to appropriate funds to implement the law.

In addition to food and shelter, various medical services are now considered by our society to be essential ingredients of a minimum standard of living. Public assistance programs include medical services as part of a basic-need budget. Since 1960 the federal government has contributed directly to the cost of medical care for indigent aged persons. States participating in this program are required to provide hospital and other medical care for qualified beneficiaries.

The federal government expanded its subsidies of health care in 1965. Although public attention has centered upon Medicare (the health insurance plan for the aged that went into effect July 1, 1966), the legislation also provided for Medicaid, which broadens the medical assistance given to relief recipients and other "medically indigent" persons. As in the case of other federally subsidized public assistance programs, it was left to the states to spell out the eligibility criteria. Congress did not anticipate that, in our welfare-oriented society, the term "indigent" would be broadly interpreted. The federal antipoverty warriors consider a family of four with a weekly income of $60 to be above the poverty threshold, but a number of states chose a much more liberal definition of "medically indigent." Two years later, Congress decided that cutting costs was more important than the right of states to determine Medicaid standards, and it limited federal contributions to families whose income does not exceed the aid to families with dependent children payments by more than one-third.

The Economic Opportunity Package

"War on poverty" is clearly an inflated description of this recent effort to help the impoverished. Even a casual inspection of the legislation reveals that its accomplishments could not meet the President's expectations. By the time the Economic Opportunity Act was passed, society was allocating about $15 billion annually to welfare programs on the basis of need criteria. The exact cost of the welfare system cannot be determined because many of the programs are closely interwoven with general government activity. Although the programs inaugurated under the Economic Opportunity Act have received major public attention in recent years, the Bureau of the Budget has estimated that in fiscal 1968 the total federal expenditure to assist the poor amounted to $23.9 billion (Table 1–1). Although the relevancy of some of the components of this total figure might be questioned, the OEO programs probably represent less than one-tenth of the total federal antipoverty effort. In a four-year period the Great Society nearly doubled its outlays in aid of the poor, and the Economic Opportunity Act accounted for about one-fifth or one-sixth of the total amount, depending on who is counting and what is included in the count. The Economic Opportunity Act may therefore be viewed as a supplement, albeit a significant one, to the welfare programs listed above. The Act added some $1.5 billion annually for welfare expenditures during the first four years of the "war," even though there were some 26 million poor people in the country in 1967. Obviously, this amount fell far

Table 1–1. Federal Aid to the Poor, Fiscal 1964 and 1968

Agency and Category	1964	1968
	(Billions)	
Total	$13.4	$23.9
Cash Benefit Payments	11.3	14.7
HEW-OASDI	5.8	7.9
Public assistance	2.5	3.5
Railroad retirement	.3	.4
Labor—unemployment benefits	.7	.5
VA—compensation and pensions	2.0	2.4
Education and Training	.1	2.8
HEW—elementary and secondary education	—	1.2
OEO–NYC, Job Corps, CAP, etc.	—	1.2
Labor–MDTA	a	.3
Interior	.1	.1
Health	1.0	4.1
HEW—health insurance for the aged and disabled	—	1.7
Public assistance medical care	.5	1.4
Other	.2	.3
VA—hospital and domiciliary care	.3	.6
OEO–CAP	—	.1
Services, Economic and Community Development, etc.	1.0	2.3
Agriculture—food programs	.2	.4
Other	.1	.2
Commerce—EDA and Appalachia	.1	.3
OEO–CAP and other	—	.4
HEW–SRS	.2	.4
HUD—public housing and rent supplements	.1	.2
Urban renewal and other	—	.1
Interior—services to Indians, etc.	.2	.3
Labor—employment, youth and other services	.1	a

a Less than $50 million.
Note: Figures may not add because of rounding.
Source: Bureau of the Budget.

short of the President's commitment to an "unconditional war on poverty."

In rejecting income support to the poor, the President indicated disdain for the "hand-out." This was in harmony with traditional American economic values. "The days of the dole in our country are numbered," the President declared upon signing the law. "Our American answer to poverty is not to make the poor more secure in their poverty but to reach down and help them lift themselves out of the ruts of poverty." It may not be entirely irrelevant, however, to suggest that hand-outs were rejected because they are costly: a meaningful program, based on cash payments, would run into billions of dollars. Indeed, it was soon commonly conceded that even the most successful implementation of the Economic Opportunity Act, at its current levels of funding, could not eliminate poverty, and that some income maintenance schemes would be needed to achieve this end.

Nevertheless, it was hardly surprising that despite its limited funds the new legislation was sold as a "total war on poverty." Such salesmanship follows the Washington habit of assuming a priori that every new piece of legislation will resolve the problem it is designed to attack. Thus the legislation enacted in 1962, providing various work projects for persons on relief and limiting the expansion of social services to the poor, was hailed by President Kennedy as a new approach to combating poverty. In keeping with this tradition, the claims made for the Economic Opportunity Act were quite understandable.

In effect, the Economic Opportunity Act is a series of programs, some experimental and others conventional. Reflecting the complexity of the causes of poverty, the new legislation concentrated on the needs of some groups but passed over the needs of others. Meaningful help for the five million aged poor, for example, was precluded by budgetary constraints. Obviously the aged could not be motivated, trained, or "rehabilitated." Legislating income maintenance and health care provisions would have been the only effective way to aid these poor, and such provisions were left out of the program. Other legislation planned by the Administration did seek to meet the needs of the elderly, and a year later Medicare and Medicaid were enacted by Congress.

The Economic Opportunity Act thus concentrated on helping young people. The hope was to "break the chains of poverty," which would be achieved, in the words of President Kennedy, through "rehabilitation instead of relief." Accordingly, the antipoverty programs focused on providing employment and services that, hopefully, would help motivate the poor to escape their poverty.

Poverty Becomes a Federal Issue

It is not easy to explain why a war on poverty was launched in 1964, nor why it gained such immediate and widespread support. Although unemployment remained at about 5 percent, general prosperity prevailed. For the third consecutive year the economy showed rapid expansion, and incomes for the bulk of the population were the highest in history. This was hardly a propitious atmosphere for inaugurating a war on poverty. The social welfare legislation of the thirties, in contrast, had been stimulated by a deep depression and mass unemployment. If the over-all economic conditions were not conducive to new social legislation, the explanation must be found elsewhere.

The problem of poverty was largely ignored during the post–World War II years. Widespread fear that the end of the war would bring mass unemployment led to the passage of the Employment Act in 1946, which committed the government to maintaining high employment and high purchasing power. This legislation remained largely an exhortation in the general prosperity that prevailed during the postwar years, and the Employment Act was not implemented. Social welfare legislation held low priority during the years following World War II and no important laws were enacted during the period, the exceptions being modification in minimum wages, extension of coverage under unemployment insurance, and Old-Age, Survivors, and Disability Insurance. The eight years of Eisenhower's Great Crusade put the stamp of respectability upon the New Deal programs but produced very few innovations of their own.

In this climate it was not really respectable to talk about poverty. When Hubert H. Humphrey announced his initial candidacy for the Democratic presidential nomination in 1959, he declared that he would be the "poor man's candidate." The press simply regarded this as an unsubtle reminder that Humphrey's three major rivals for the nomination were multimillionaires. Even candidate Kennedy's call for a "war against poverty" during the 1960 campaign went largely unnoticed.[6] Such talk was taken as normal campaign rhetoric.

Rediscovery of Poverty

Herman P. Miller observes: "A myth has been created in the United States that incomes are gradually becoming more evenly distributed. This view is held by prominent economists of both major political parties. It is also shared by the editors of the influential mass media."[7] This view was nourished by influential economists, including Arthur F. Burns, chairman of President Eisenhower's Council of Economic Advisers (later counsellor to President Nixon), and Paul Samuelson, one of President Kennedy's leading economic advisers. It was taken for granted that in a "laboristic" or welfare state this was a natural trend.

There were a few who dissented from this optimistic view, however. Most prominent in the 1950's was John Kenneth Galbraith, who deplored the failure to take steps that would lead to the reduction of poverty.[8] In 1950 and again in 1955, Senator John J. Sparkman of Alabama documented the persistence of rural poverty during extensive hearings of the Joint Economic Committee.[9] Beginning in 1955, Senator Paul Douglas of Illinois continuously pointed to the anomaly of depressed areas and pockets of deprivation in an economy of abundance.[10] An attempt by Governor Averell Harriman in 1957 to focus upon problems of poverty in the Empire State did not advance beyond the research stage;[11] when Harriman was defeated for reelection in the next year, the effort was dropped by his successor. In 1959 a Special Senate Committee on Unemployment, headed by Senator Eugene J. McCarthy of Minnesota, disclosed serious economic deprivation in many areas of the country.[12] Systematic statistical analyses of the incidence of poverty were developed by Robert J. Lampman of the University of Wisconsin in a 1959 study made for the Joint Economic Committee of Congress.[13] These findings were supplemented by a group of University of Michigan economists and the Conference on Economic Progress which prepared a popularized version of the data three years later.[14]

The evidence of economic imbalance piled up but few paid attention to the congressional hearings or the scholarly monographs. Even the impassioned argument of Michael Harrington's *The Other America* for an "integrated and comprehensive program [to] overthrow America's citadel of misery" was at first hardly noted.*

The first item to create a noticeable stir was an article by Dwight MacDonald that appeared early in 1963 in *The New Yorker*.[15] The article, "Our Invisible Poor," reviewed the major literature on poverty. It reached the White House and was read by Theodore Sorensen, and presumably by the President himself. Harrington's book was also given to the President by Walter Heller, then chairman of the Council of Economic Advisers, although it is not known whether the President read it. Thus the notion of the persistence of poverty continued to spread, and the phenomenon of mass poverty received increased attention. The next step was to place the problem on the agenda of the federal government's policymakers.

Poverty Reaches Kennedy's Attention

Every good story must have its hero, and it was Robert Lampman, then a staff member of the Council of Economic Advisers (CEA), who performed the role of catalyst in bringing poverty to the attention of

*The story of this book (New York: Macmillan, 1962) offers an excellent barometer of the interest in poverty. The book was published in March 1962 and sold only a few thousand copies during the balance of the year. After a review by Dwight MacDonald in *The New Yorker*, some 7,000 copies of the second printing were sold. The paperback reprint of the volume, released in the fall of 1963, sold several hundred thousand copies.

the "highest governmental level."* Lampman, in turn, had found CEA Chairman Walter Heller a sympathetic and encouraging ally. In a series of memoranda Lampman called the attention of Heller and his colleagues to the fact that New Frontier had failed to live up to its promise to aid the poor. Lampman stressed the fact that the investment tax credit of 1962 and the then pending massive income tax cut were of little help to large groups of the poor. He predicted that even if the pending income tax cut could bring the economy back to full employment, additional programs would be needed before the aged poor, the disabled, and the fatherless families could rise above the threshold of poverty.

Similarly, the social welfare legislation enacted under the Kennedy Administration was of little help to these groups. The Area Redevelopment Act, which provided aid to depressed areas, the Accelerated Public Works Act, which pumped development money into the same areas, and the Manpower Development and Training Act were of aid, at best, only to the poor who were *in* the work force. The limited data that were available at that time suggested that these programs were helping very small numbers of the poor.

Another staff paper prepared by Lampman demonstrated that after 1956 a decline of poverty had been sharply arrested. During the decade 1947–56 the proportion of families living in poverty—families with a total annual income of less than $3,000—declined by about 1 percent a year, from 33 percent to 23 percent. But in the following five years the proportion of poor families declined by only 0.4 percent annually while the number of people living in poverty increased. In transmitting this information to President Kennedy, Heller commented that he found the data "distressing." This memorandum, dated May 1, 1963, started the discussion within the Administration of what later became the "war on poverty."

The recognition of poverty was a long way from the design and implementation of a program aimed at combating this social ill. The facts supplied by the intellectual community were necessary to help identify and focus on the problem, but political forces were necessary to weld a program together. The most potent of these forces was the civil rights movement. In 1958 John Kenneth Galbraith asserted, with much justification, that there was no political payoff in fighting poverty: "Any politician who speaks for the poor is speaking for a small and inarticulate minority."[16] However valid this observation may have been in 1958, it certainly did not hold true five years later. To be sure,

---

*As long as the "war on poverty" remained popular, those who claimed to have originated the program could be numbered in the scores.

the civil rights struggle was initially waged in terms of social and political rights—spurred by increasing numbers of black and white militants, aided by an activist Supreme Court, and after 1960 supported by a sympathetic Administration. Yet the issue of civil rights inevitably led to the problem of poverty, for economic deprivation was an integral part of the over-all discrimination and injustice suffered by Negroes.

The increasing amount of statistics generated on the "Negro question" made it transparently clear that a disproportionate number of Negroes were to be found in the ranks of the unskilled, the unemployed, and the poverty-stricken. Most significant were the data developed by Herman P. Miller, an acknowledged expert on income distribution. On the basis of an exhaustive analysis of the 1960 census data, Miller concluded that, contrary to popular belief, the income gap between Negro and white had not narrowed during the post–World War II period. He estimated that the lifetime earnings of non-whites were about two-thirds those of whites in the same occupation with similar educational attainment.[17] The close relationship between economic and political discrimination was expressed succinctly by President Kennedy, who insisted (in a message to Congress on June 19, 1963) that equal employment opportunities must be included among the Negro's civil rights. "There is little value," the President stated, "in a Negro's obtaining the right to be admitted to the hotels and restaurants if he has no cash in his pocket and no job."

Thus the civil rights movement, which had become a potent power by 1963, could have supplied the political pressure for a program in aid of the poor. And the Administration was responsive and sympathetic to this pressure.

The President's Economists Take the Initiative

Early in the summer of 1963, when Heller and Lampman initiated the CEA's discussion on poverty, there was little public interest in a comprehensive governmental antipoverty program. In June 1963 Heller tried the idea before a presumably sympathetic audience at the annual convention of the Communications Workers of America. His address hammered at a double theme: the need for a tax cut and for policies "to open more exits from poverty."[18] Although the minutes of the convention indicate that Heller received the predictable applause at the end of his address, CWA President Joseph Beirne, in thanking Heller for his address, indicated his support for the tax cut but made no reference to the antipoverty program. Heller's own reaction was that the union members were interested in the tax cut but that he had lost his audience when he spoke about poverty. Later that same summer Heller tried to interest various newspaper reporters in the topic. Except for one press association story, the reporters seemed uninterested. One reporter, from a newspaper that publishes "All the news that's fit to print," took special pains to collect information and background data but returned to inform the CEA's staff members that the topic would have no appeal.

Even the Administration's advisers were divided about the wisdom of mounting an antipoverty program. In the summer of 1963 Heller called together a group of White House aides and other executive officials to discuss the feasibility of including new measures in aid of the poor as part of the Administration program for the coming year. The reaction was mixed, ranging from outright opposition to lukewarm support. Although none of the participants objected in principle to an antipoverty program, several questioned the wisdom of raising the issue so close to the 1964 election campaign. The time to have raised the issue, according to one Cabinet secretary, was 1960, when the Democrats were out of office and were not campaigning for reelection. A nationally known economist of unimpeachable liberal credentials, who was in the White House dining room where the meeting took place, joined the discussion and rejected the idea of a program so ill timed and politically unsound. (He later claimed credit for being an initiator of the antipoverty program.) But the idea had supporters, including presidential aide Theodore Sorensen, who thought the antipoverty program was both morally sound and a good political issue for 1964, Charles L. Schultze (Bureau of the Budget), and Wilbur J. Cohen (Department of Health, Education, and Welfare).

In the early fall of 1963 the notion of launching an antipoverty program received a temporary setback with the widespread talk about "white backlash" as a reaction to the civil rights movement. Apparently some outside advisers had reached President Kennedy and urged him to inaugurate a program focusing on the problems of suburbia as a central campaign theme for 1964. For a while Kennedy seemed to question the political wisdom of making an antipoverty program a theme of his reelection campaign. But the problem of poverty could not be ignored. On October 20, 1963, the New York Times published a penetrating survey of deprivation and want in eastern Kentucky.[19] The report described the region as "a vast ghetto of unemployables" where children went hungry and schools were "unfit for cattle." It is known that Kennedy read and was deeply moved by this article.

Heller and his staff persisted with the development of an antipoverty program. Although he encouraged their efforts, Kennedy refrained from committing himself to such a program until his last meeting with Heller, on November 19, 1963. At that time he instructed his chief economic adviser to formulate legislative proposals for the following session of Congress. Heller, meanwhile, had begun a series of consultations with key officials whose departments or agencies were responsible for the administration of welfare programs—at the same time keeping top White House aides advised of his activities. To augment his small staff, he involved the Bureau of the Budget in helping to design a program of action for 1964.*

During the summer and early fall of 1963 the Council of Economic Advisers–Bureau of the Budget task force concentrated on informational and analytical needs in designing "an attack on poverty." No attempt was made to devise specific programs, and in the absence of an explicit commitment from the White House the task force had no basis upon which to estimate the magnitude of the program that might be launched. It is apparent, however, that the staff people were not disposed to "think big." Although they raised the right questions, the general trend of their thinking was in the direction of pilot projects. In their defense, it must be remembered that there was no indication that the White House would favor a major new program.

Heller's goal was to submit a tentative program to the White House by Thanksgiving. On November 5, 1963, with this target date in mind, he circulated a memorandum to the heads of the major departments and agencies involved in administering welfare programs and requested suggestions for a 1964 legislative program aimed at "widening participation in prosperity"—the tentative title for the program to attack poverty.† Heller invited the administrators to suggest "imaginative new programs," to comment on redirection of existing programs, and to indicate, where necessary, the budgetary implications of the proposals. But Heller was looking primarily for new ideas; budgetary constraints would be considered later.

Capron and Weisbrod, the two CEA staff members assigned by Heller to coordinate the agency proposals, were inundated with proposals that were obviously too ambitious for the Bureau of the Budget. One staff aide commented that the combined departmental proposals

*The key people during the summer and early fall were Theodore Sorensen and Myer Feldman from the White House staff; William M. Capron, Robert J. Lampman, Burton A. Weisbrod, and Rashi Fein (who left the CEA in September 1963) from Heller's staff; and William B. Cannon, Michael S. March, and Charles L. Schultze from the Bureau of the Budget.

† The memorandum was addressed to the Secretaries of Agriculture, Commerce, Labor, and HEW, the Director of the Bureau of the Budget, and the Administrator of the Housing and Home Finance Agency. The Secretary of the Interior, whose department includes the Bureau of Indian Affairs, was apparently omitted by oversight and was solicited later.

were enough to keep Congress busy for a decade, though many hardly deserved consideration. Encouraged by Kennedy's commitment to include an antipoverty program in his 1964 legislative proposals, the CEA–BOB task force was in the process of examining and analyzing the departmental proposals on Friday, November 22, when they received the news of the President's assassination.

Johnson—"That's My Kind of Program"

The tragedy of Kennedy's death did not stop development of the program. Two days after he took office President Johnson met with Heller, and the first item on their agenda was the pending antipoverty program. The idea immediately received Johnson's unequivocal endorsement. As related by Heller, the new President's comment was, "That's my kind of program. It will help people. I want you to move full speed ahead on it."[20]

The first task was to reduce the program to manageable proportions. Although there was as yet no agreed-upon price tag for the program, an initial multibillion-dollar program obviously was not in the cards. The Agriculture Department's "laundry list" of previously rejected measures for raising the income level of the poor in rural areas was rejected as unrealistic. HEW's income maintenance programs were similarly dismissed because they would have been too costly. The task force was also unsympathetic to the proposals from the Housing and Home Finance Agency (now the Housing and Urban Development Department), except for approving additional funds for the long-established public housing program. A proposal for rent supplements and relocation allowances for families displaced by urban renewal was also rejected outright at this stage, only to be adopted in principle by Congress less than two years later.. The Labor Department's programs received the kindest treatment, probably because Labor's memorandum included a list of priorities. Practically all of the items at the top of Labor's list had won prior approval by the Bureau of the Budget, and some were already pending in Congress.

The CEA–BOB task force found that imaginative proposals could be very costly. One of the department heads indicated the difficulty of developing a low-cost "realistic" package that would not constitute merely a collection of a few miscellaneous small programs. His solution was to emphasize long-run programs and at the same time convey a sense of urgency about starting a war on poverty. He failed to indicate how this sense of urgency would help the poor, a problem that has plagued the antipoverty warriors ever since.

A Coordinated Community Action Concept

The solution to the task force's dilemma came from an entirely unexpected source and evolved from the combined experience of the Ford Foundation and the President's Committee on Juvenile Delinquency and Youth Crime. In the late 1950's the public affairs department of the Ford Foundation embarked on a search for ways to help rejuvenate slum areas in large cities. Under its resulting "gray areas program," a euphemistic title for aid to slum areas, the foundation helped sponsor community improvement projects that were initiated and implemented by local organizations. Underlying the gray areas program was the notion that the rehabilitation of slums requires institutional changes, including governmental reorganization. The needed transformation of slum communities could not be accomplished by "gobs of giving," according to the director of the public affairs program, Paul N. Ylvisaker. "It is not dependency we want to encourage," he explained, "but independence and choice."[21]

The need to attack problems that normally fall within the purview of the government imposed restraints upon the gray areas program. As a private organization, the foundation lacked the democratic mandate to impose its will upon public institutions; at the same time it wanted assurance that its funds would achieve maximum results. In a pluralistic society, this dilemma was not insoluble. The foundation acted as a catalyst by establishing local private organizations that shared its views on slum rehabilitation and that would have sufficient local support to continue their work after the foundation withdrew its aid. Thus the foundation insisted that private local agencies applying for funds must have the broad support of community leaders and that the agencies must either raise or promise contributions that would match the foundation's grant. To assure compliance, the foundation withheld part of each grant, releasing it as acceptable programs were submitted and the conditions of the grant were met. However, the design and the initiation of specific programs were left to the communities. A major aspect of these programs was an attempt to attack the problem of juvenile delinquency.

Closely related in concept and function to the Ford Foundation's gray areas program was the work of the President's Committee on Juvenile Delinquency and Youth Crime. The committee was established in 1961 and was chaired by Attorney General Robert F. Kennedy. Its goal was to reduce juvenile delinquency by developing the employment capacities of slum youth by organizing communities to improve themselves. Needless to say, effective programs for combating juvenile delinquency and making underprivileged youths employable required the coordination of diverse public and private institutions— welfare agencies, school systems, police, employment agencies, and employers, among others. Because the committee's appropriations were limited, ranging between $6 million and $8 million annually, it confined itself to making grants for the planning of community programs; the financing of these programs was left to local agencies or to state and federal sources. By the end of 1963 the committee had funded programs in more than a dozen cities. Its experience indicated that once communities succeeded in developing effective plans they encountered difficulties in obtaining federal funds, which were distributed on a fragmented basis, each under different criteria, and not easily adaptable to the multipurpose approach of the juvenile delinquency program.

The Ford Foundation program and the President's committee shared the goal of attacking the complex causes of poverty with the nascent antipoverty program. David L. Hackett, executive director of the committee, felt that the techniques developed by his program might be adapted to fight poverty on a broader scale. He believed that an effective antipoverty effort would require a coordinated approach which was not feasible under the existing single-purpose federal programs. William B. Cannon of the CEA–BOB task force was persuaded of the soundness of this approach and converted others to it. Soon it became the focal point in the antipoverty planning.

Key people on the task force favored the proposal for a number of reasons. Not only did the newly proposed approach appear to have substantive merit, it also lent itself to budgetary flexibility. The program could be sold as a comprehensive attack upon poverty that allowed experimentation and adaptability to local situations. Any number of communities could play, depending on the extent of budgetary allocations. (At this stage the planners failed to consider the usual tendency of federal programs to spread themselves thin. This occurred later.) The approach also provided a new area of experimentation for the coordination of general-purpose federal grants in line with the President's later stress on "creative federalism."[22] Charles L. Schultze hit upon the name for this aspect of the poverty program—Community Action Program.

This design for a conceptual framework was an important advance, but the edifice was far from complete; crucial problems remained to be resolved. For one thing, the emphasis on coordinated community action did not preclude single-purpose programs. Also, the advocates of expanded funding for education, housing, welfare services, and training—to mention a few major groups—presented persuasive arguments for their favorite programs. Spokesmen for federal funding of education argued, for example, that the antipoverty program presented an excellent opportunity to bypass the church-state controversy and provide federal aid for elementary and secondary education. This analysis was proved correct with the passage of the Economic Opportunity Act, which in turn opened the door for the passage of the Elementary and Secondary Education Act of 1965.

Another question arose over the components of the community action programs. Spokesmen for the Department of Labor and Health, Education, and Welfare, the two agencies whose traditional activities would be targets of a coordinated approach, were concerned that the new proposal would absorb their existing programs or serve as substitutes for their pending legislation. HEW officials even argued that no new legislation was necessary for planning coordinated community action programs. This objective could be accomplished, they said, under a 1956 amendment to the Social Security Act that authorized HEW to make grants for coordinated community services programs.[23] However, annual appropriations for these demonstration and research projects averaged less than $1 million out of a $5 million annual authorization—a fact that led a member of the CEA–BOB task force to observe that HEW "would make a molehill out of what is really a mountainous problem." On the other hand, representatives of the Department of Labor opposed the inclusion of a youth work component in the community action programs lest it serve as a substitute for the pending Youth Employment Act.

Overriding all these substantive and parochial controversies was the realization that the program was going to be too small to satisfy all the competing and complementary needs. And regardless of the size of the program, agency representatives were not inclined to surrender their domains even if they were persuaded by the soundness of the community action approach. Moreover, while the task force was trying to hammer out the antipoverty program, the President continued to preach and practice economy. At least one agency chief perceived a contradiction between the promises to cut the budget and the planning of new programs. Logically enough, he hesitated to propose expansion of his department's activities.

Finally, there was the problem of the administrative structure of the new program. This turned out to be the hardest-fought battle since it touched on the innermost preserves of those involved. Some wanted to run the entire show; others fought for only a piece of the action; but everyone wanted something. Because Cabinet-level departments were involved, only the President himself could ultimately resolve this controversy.

Dividing a Small Pie

The dialogue—some would say squabble—over these difficult issues continued within the executive branch until the very moment the President sent his bill to Capitol Hill on March 16, 1964. But some aspects of the controversy could not be delayed too long. Each January the President is required by law to submit to Congress his proposed budget for the ensuing fiscal year. If the fiscal 1965 budget was to contain any reference to the war on poverty, a specific line item had to be provided early in January. The amount could be changed later, but a tentative decision on the magnitude, if not the scope, of the effort could not be postponed.

During the month of December, Budget Bureau analysts were actively engaged in "costing out" the alternative proposals. These estimates, some of which were sent to Theodore Sorensen in the White House, called for new expenditures in fiscal 1965 ranging from $389 million to $629 million, with projections of three to four times this range for fiscal 1969. All the proposals carried a uniform amount of $100 million for the implementation of ten community action programs, with $25 million for development and administration. The other funds were to be allocated to work projects for youth and medical care for needy children and to raising the federal share of AFDC. At least one departmental representative, after being consulted by the task force, urged that the program should equal or exceed $1 billion to be "really dramatic."

The decision to ask Congress for an appropriation of $500 million was reached by January 4, 1964, and the budget contained a single-line item for this amount. But in a memorandum to the Secretaries of Agriculture, Commerce, HEW, Interior, and Labor, and the Administrator of the Housing and Home Finance Agency, Heller and Gordon elaborated that the $500 million for the financing of community action programs should be allocated as follows: (1) development and administration of local CAP's, $50 million; (2) assistance to local communities in providing summer work projects for youth, vocational rehabilitation, diagnostic care and health services, and funds for experimental programs, $275 million; and (3) supplementary funds for existing and new programs, $175 million.

The last-mentioned amount was judiciously distributed among the six agencies with a proviso that the funds be used only in conjunction with approved community action programs. Agriculture, HEW, and Labor were to receive $40 million each; Commerce and HHFA, $20 million each; and Interior, $15 million. HEW was to use its money for adult work training, vocational rehabilitation, community health programs, and child care. Labor's funds were to be allocated mostly for the expansion of training, employment services, and aid to migrant labor. Agriculture was to use its funds for the expansion of food distribution, loans to farmers, and grants for housing rehabilitation. HHFA was to direct its funds to experimenting with rent subsidies, coordination of services in public housing, and urban planning. Commerce was to expand the area redevelopment program; and Interior was to allocate its $15 million entirely to the Bureau of Indian Affairs. In addition, Heller and Gordon proposed that the five departments and HHFA allocate $625 million from existing programs or from proposed programs already included in the 1965 agency budgets to help carry out approved community action programs. In brief, the Heller-Gordon memorandum of January 6, 1964, outlined the substance, though not necessarily the detail, of what later became the Economic Opportunity Act.

Once the inclusion of the $500 million item in the budget was settled, at least as far as the federal officials were concerned, the debate over the magnitude of the new program began. Departments and agencies intensified their lobbying for the responsibility of implementing the proposal, and for the maximum feasible share of the program for their respective clienteles.

The Agriculture Department maintained that because almost half of all impoverished families are located in rural areas, half of the antipoverty money should be allocated to the rural poor. Agriculture particularly urged a grant program for subsistence farmers on the ground that most of these farmers are middle-age or older and lack adequate education or training to obtain and hold jobs in an urban environment. The department did not show how these subsistence farmers could be helped to escape poverty with a few thousand dollars or how they would be able to compete effectively in an agricultural economy that is increasingly mechanized and concentrated. For that matter, no information was supplied as to how the proposal would mesh with national policies in an era when agricultural production had outpaced demand. Lowering its sights somewhat, Agriculture subsequently appealed for parity with Commerce, arguing that since Heller and Gordon proposed to allocate $20 million to the Area Redevelopment Administration for stimulating investment in commerce and industry, at least an equal amount should be allocated for investment in farmers.

Commerce, on the other hand, was happy with the proposed $20 million allocation and promised to expand ARA from the thousand counties already in its domain to the entire country. Apparently no thought was given to the fact that ARA had already spread itself thin, or to how the Commerce Department expected to distribute the funds, $10,000 per additional county, for the purpose of offering technical assistance, loans for commercial and industrial facilities, and loans and grants for public facilities. Of course, all these funds were to be used to fight poverty, but the department supplied no information on the availability of entrepreneurs among the poor.

Interior also assured Heller and Gordon that it would have no difficulty in spending the proposed $15 million to combat poverty among the Indians—though the department conceded that it had no specific plans at the moment. Interior also indicated a willingness to play a larger role in the program by offering the use of its facilities to provide summer camps for youths.

The sharpest conflict seemed to exist between the Departments of Labor and Health, Education, and Welfare. The former made it quite clear that it resented the encroachment of the newly proposed program upon its established domain. Labor was concerned that the proposed summer work projects would overlap with the provisions of the pending Youth Employment Act (passed by the Senate in 1963) and that the proposed community work and training programs would compete with those of the Manpower Development and Training Act (MDTA). The department ignored the fact that only a handful of relief recipients had qualified for training under MDTA courses. In addition, the Labor Department urged that the war on poverty emphasize the extension of minimum-wage coverage to retail, service, and agricultural occupations, that it enact legislation to aid migrant labor, and that it strengthen unemployment insurance.

The Department of Health, Education, and Welfare made the broadest claims upon the proposed $500 million. In fact, it indicated its willingness to spend *all* the money, although it conceded $50 million for creating summer jobs for high-school-age youths to the Department of Labor, which for good and sufficient reasons did not want this program. HEW would have spent the bulk of the funds for community action programs and used the balance for supplementing the department's existing programs.

All the departments nominally endorsed the community action concept. With the wisdom of hindsight, Daniel P. Moynihan has suggested that at this stage of the legislative planning all that the concept meant to the federal officials involved was a coordinated effort in disbursing funds.[24] An examination of agency responses (including Moynihan's Labor Department) to the Heller-Gordon memorandum discloses significant reservations about even this narrow interpretation of the approach. HEW, which had traditionally operated programs through grants allocated to the states, wanted state agencies to be included in the planning and execution of community projects. The involvement of the states was considered necessary and desirable not only because they might contribute funds to community action programs but also bceause they could provide technical expertise which many communities lacked. HHFA, which thought that the principle of coordinated community action was good enough at the local level but not for the federal establishment, recommended that each participating agency administer its own traditional programs. In this approach, the coordinator of the local action program, the chief executive of the locality, would be required to apply separately to the several federal agencies for funds to implement the local antipoverty program. HHFA also believed that although it would take some time to plan community action programs, there should be no delay in implementing these programs; it therefore recommended that planning and action be funded simultaneously. It would appear that this agency did not believe that such action required prior, coordinated planning. Agriculture and Commerce also came close to denying the community action approach by arguing that the leadership of some localities would be either weak or indifferent to the whole program. These departments therefore urged a more activist federal role in some areas. The fears expressed by Agriculture proved correct in later experience, for many rural areas failed to apply for OEO funds.

Taken together, it would appear that much of the support for the community action approach among executive agencies was more lip service than a full understanding of what the concept meant.

Administrative Structure

The most heated discussion focused upon the organizational structure of the proposed program. In their January 6 memorandum, Heller and Gordon indicated that no decision had been made on this point and had declined to suggest any preference. This may have been a tactical move to focus on substantive proposals rather than administrative problems; or possibly they had not made up their minds. They indicated, however, that two alternative organizational arrangements were being considered. One alternative would turn the administration of the antipoverty program over to the Department of Health, Education, and Welfare, which would have required the appointment of a new assistant secretary in the Department who would be responsible for the day-to-day administration of the program. This approach was similar to the one taken three years earlier in connection with the Area Redevelopment Administration, whose functions also cut across traditional departmental lines. The second alternative would be to establish a new agency, headed by a council composed of Cabinet members under the chairmanship of a presidential appointee who was not himself a Cabinet officer. The chairman of the council would be responsible for administering the program.

Not surprisingly, there was no agreement on the suggested approaches, and new alternatives were suggested by the departments. Although quite naturally pleased with the first alternative, HEW urged the creation of an interdepartmental committee, chaired by the Secretary of HEW and consisting of heads of the agencies, that would have program responsibilities. To establish close ties with the White House, HEW also proposed that a special assistant to the President be assigned to maintain White House participation and liaison. For all practical purposes, however, this plan would have given HEW the responsibility for the antipoverty program.

Labor opposed handing over the responsibility for the program to a sub-Cabinet official and urged that a single Cabinet officer be placed in charge. Needless to say, Labor was quite willing to assume that responsibility. Like the true mother in the biblical story, however, Labor opposed cutting up the disputed babe and indicated that its second choice was HEW. Labor also conceded the need for program coordination and suggested that this function be assigned to a staff assistant of the President who would be responsible for the general direction of the program.

HHFA, on the other hand, believed that each agency should administer its own program. The presidential assistant would have field representatives who would be directly responsible to him for coordinating purposes, but they would have no power to direct local programs. Otherwise, HHFA argued, lines of responsibility among the participating departments and agencies would become confused and this would hamper the program. Because HHFA favored comprehensive community action programs, it suggested that the responsibility for funding such programs be vested in the presidential assistant but that the funding of components in implementing the plans remain the responsibility of the separate departments, each supplying the money for the "piece of the action" in its own domain. HHFA reasoned that coordinating the funding of comprehensive programs at the federal level would delay implementation of the programs.

Agriculture and Commerce favored vesting responsibility for the program with a Cabinet-level council chaired by a special presidential appointee—the second alternative suggested by Heller and Gordon.

From the interdepartmental dialogue a consensus emerged on the substantive aspects of the proposed program: the attack on poverty would be coordinated at the local level under the umbrella of the comprehensive community action programs. The President's requested $500 million in new appropriations would be divided as follows: $50 million for the planning and administration of community action programs, $275 million for their implementation, and the balance, $175 million, to supplement existing antipoverty programs which would be coordinated with community action programs. The supplementary funds were allocated to the various departments as Heller and Gordon had proposed, except that Labor lost $5 million in the process, which was allocated to the National Service Corps (later incorporated as VISTA in the Economic Opportunity Act). It was expected that another $500 million or more would be transferred from existing departmental programs to the community action programs.

No such agreement was reached for the administration of the program. Instead of the two alternatives proposed by Heller and Gordon, three distinct alternatives emerged, and each alternative had potent support within the executive establishment. There was, however, unanimous agreement that the central functions of the proposed program would be vested in the director of a new community action agency. Special appropriations would be made to him for grants to local communities or for allocation to participating agencies in accordance with the local community-action programs he approved. A Human Resources Council, chaired by this director and composed of the heads of the participating agencies, would be established to advise on policies and programs. But beyond this basic agreement, the three major alternatives for the organization of the program were:

1. An independent agency. Proponents of this alternative argued that it would dramatize the Administration's commitment to the war on poverty. Opponents countered that this arrangement would place the program at a disadvantage because the administrator of a single program is in a weaker bargaining position with Congress than is a department head. It was also suggested that the establishment of an independent agency would delay launching the war on poverty because of the time required to recruit an adequate staff.

2. A new unit in the Executive Office. Proponents of this approach argued that, in addition to the advantages of an independent agency, the program would gain even more prestige if it were located in the Executive Office, which presumably would help its director in his dealings with the heads of other agencies. Opposition to this plan was centered in the Bureau of the Budget, which has traditionally opposed the assignment of operating responsibilities within the Executive Office.* The Bureau of the Budget was concerned that placing the

*The major recent precedent for locating an operating agency in the Executive Office was that of the Office of Civil and Defense Mobilization (OCDM), established during the Eisenhower Administration. But President Kennedy had transferred the major operating functions of OCDM to the Defense Department and retained in the Executive Office only the Office of Emergency Planning.

operating functions of the antipoverty program in the Executive Office might create a precedent for other interest groups who might try to push their projects to the same lofty position. Also, it was feared that opponents of the pending bill to establish a Department of Housing and Urban Development would be led to urge the establishment of an Office of Urban Affairs in the Executive Office as a substitute for a new department.

3. Assigning the programs to the Department of Health, Education, and Welfare. The major advocates of this approach were of course from HEW. They argued that because HEW would have the major responsibility for carrying out the antipoverty programs, it would be most efficient to place the programs in that department. Opponents saw this fact as their strongest argument *against* placing the programs in HEW, arguing that the department's "old line" bureaucracy would oppose the new approaches envisioned in the antipoverty program. Another argument against having the antipoverty program in HEW was that it would preclude effective coordination of community action programs at the federal level.

Only the President was in a position to resolve this conflict among his major lieutenants. Accordingly, all the chief protagonists and the Attorney General were summoned to the White House on January 23, 1964, to present their arguments, after which the President was to make his decision. On February 1, 1964, eight days after the White House meeting, the President, to everyone's surprise, announced that he was appointing R. Sargent Shriver to plan the war on poverty.

Several factors may have accounted for postponing the decision. Any final determination would have displeased some, if not a majority of the Cabinet officers, and the new President may have wanted to defer such a potentially divisive decision. Another explanation is that the President wanted to give the future administrator of the program a chance to shape the program he would administer. There was also a chance that another review of the issues would produce some fresh ideas or approaches. This was in line with Heller's recommendations to the President.

Finally, tactics may have suggested the wisdom of postponing the presentation of a bill to Congress. As long as the Council of Economic Advisers and the Bureau of the Budget were planning the program, little was reported about it in the public news media, though there were a few news leaks—inadvertent or perhaps contrived. Nevertheless, the President's call for a war on poverty in his State of the Union message, together with the Council of Economic Advisers' report, were generating considerable public interest in the poverty problem. The appointment of a presidential aide to take charge of the program (inevitably, the public news media called him a "poverty czar") created an opportunity for educating the public and Congress about the problem of poverty and thereby generating support for the contemplated programs.

The Shriver Task Force

A brother-in-law of President Kennedy and a former Chicago businessman with a record of public service (he had been chairman of the Chicago Board of Education), Shriver had acquired an enviable reputation in dealing with Congress as the director of the Peace Corps from its inception in 1961. He was reported to be the only foreign-aid administrator who was able to obtain "not just almost as much as he wants but almost as much as he asks for the Peace Corps."[25] His effectiveness was not accidental. According to the same reporter, Shriver would absorb the public attack of a Congressman "and then at night he will call up some power figure from [the Congressman's] district and the next morning [the Congressman] is unexpectedly slapped on the back of the head."[26]

Upon assuming his new assignment (he retained the directorship of the Peace Corps), Shriver created the impression that he was looking for new ideas. "I come into this with an open mind," he declared; "I have been learning, sifting, and consulting."[27] A member of the task force, James L. Sundquist, then Deputy Under Secretary of Agriculture, remarked on Shriver's open-mindedness: "I've never known anyone as open to ideas as Shriver is. If a man came in with an idea, he would seem to accept it right away and, if you objected, Sarge would say 'What's wrong with it?' and the burden of proof would be on the one who objected instead of the one who suggested the idea."[28] But another observer of Shriver during the "task force period" was unimpressed by his apparent search for new ideas and held that his seeming tolerance of new approaches was simply an inability to sift sound suggestions from crackpot ideas. This observer described Shriver as a "dilettante with a propensity for schoolgirl enthusiasm."

Whatever Shriver's intellectual capacity for understanding the problem of poverty, he succeeded in fostering the image of bold innovation. Old welfare ideas were definitely out, and planning operations carried an almost mystic aura. The notion was conveyed that even jaded bureaucrats expected new ideas to emerge from the task force. Within six weeks after his appointment Shriver claimed to have consulted 137 different people about the formulation of the poverty program. The list included leaders in agricultural, business, labor, and civil rights groups; officials of federal, state, and local governments; an assorted group of college professors and administrators; and representatives from foundations. Social workers and welfare officials were conspicuously absent from the list—apparently there was nothing to be learned from the "old ways" of doing things.* There is little evidence that the "consultations" produced any usable ideas, or even that ideas were genuinely sought. It is quite apparent that some advisers were brought in primarily to be seen, not heard, in order to win their support and to indicate to the public that all sorts of "creative" personages were involved in designing the program.

Shriver was particularly interested in advertising the fact that the business community supported the poverty program. Among the business and agricultural leaders mentioned above were the names of one farm group leader and 30 corporate executives. According to a participant who was commissioned to carry the message of the antipoverty program to the business community, most of the business proposals dealt with tax cuts and removal of government restraints upon business enterprises. This might be one way of fighting poverty, but Sargent Shriver was not appointed to his post to reduce taxes. On the contrary, his mission was to find useful ways of spending public money.

Old Ideas, New Slogans

The scope and direction of the poverty program were determined during the two weeks that followed Shriver's appointment. Most of the ideas came from old government hands (sub-Cabinet officials and their advisers); only a few outside kibitzers or advisers participated in the process.

Within three days of his appointment, Shriver asked the Council of Economic Advisers, the Bureau of the Budget, departmental representatives, and a few personal associates to brief him on the state of the program and to explore other alternatives. Heller opened the meeting by describing in detail the proposed community action concept. Secretary of Labor Wirtz attacked this approach as too limited in scope and appeal and advocated an aggressive job-creation-and-training program as the most effective way to fight poverty. Of course the community action concept did not preclude emphasis on job-creation (presumably each community could determine its own program, based on local needs), but in their planning, the Council of Economic Ad-

---

*The President recommended that Shriver speak to a leading national authority on social welfare, a person whom the President had consulted in the past. Shriver obliged but terminated the conversation after a few minutes.

visers and the Bureau of the Budget had laid heavy emphasis upon its education, health, and social service components. It was also argued that adoption of the CAP approach would be time-consuming and that two years could elapse before most communities would develop operating programs. Several others in the meeting sided with Wirtz, and a consensus emerged: community action programs would be only part of the war on poverty, and the design of the legislation should stress the breadth of the approach.

Advocates of the broader approach were able to show that this could be accomplished with a minimum of extra funding. Instead of limiting the war on poverty to community action, therefore, the bill would include all the programs that focused on aiding the poor and had already been approved by the President. This course had been considered by Heller, Gordon, and their associates, but in deference to the established departmental jurisdictions they had not included these programs as part of the new package. By transferring a few items from other budgetary requests, however, the war on poverty could be increased by $350 million without raising the proposed administrative budget by one penny. Included in the transferred programs were Labor's Youth Employment bill (later transformed into the Job Corps and the Neighborhood Youth Corps), HEW's Community Work and Training bill (work for persons on relief), and "special education projects" (later part of the adult basic education and work experience programs). The need to include a special youth program in the poverty program was accentuated by a widely circulated report which demonstrated that the high rejection rate of draftees by the armed forces, particularly among Negroes, was due to causes associated with poverty.[29]

Nor was this all. To create the image of a broad attack on poverty, something had to be provided for everybody—or nearly everybody—as long as the costs were kept low. Although the community action programs were intended to aid rural as well as urban poor, an explicit program for impoverished rural residents and subsistence farmers seemed politically desirable.

Within two weeks of this first meeting, Shriver reported to the President on the progress of his undertaking in a memorandum his newly acquired staff had prepared. Although the statement was not intended for public consumption, it contained many of the slogans and clichés that have become the poverty war's stock in trade. The memorandum informed the President that the "war cannot be either limited or cheap" and that "in the coming war, we *can* make a reconnaissance in force" (italic in original). The ambitious prose of the memorandum indicated that Shriver planned to propose the following expenditures for the first year of the program: $400 million for youth programs, $300 million for community action programs, $50 million for rural grants and loans, and $50 million for adult work and training programs. Apparently the remaining $50 million had not been allocated.

The actual amounts recommended to Congress one month later were either the same as, or close to, these projections. As it turned out, the antipoverty bill proposed by the President requested $962.5 million instead of the $850 million envisoned by Shriver early in February. The major alteration was expansion of the work experience program from $50 million to $150 million, which qualified needy persons who were not on public assistance rolls to participate in a work relief program. Though the phrase was coined later, this was a modest effort on the part of the federal government to assume the responsibility of acting as an employer of last resort. A small-loan program was also added, with the theme of enabling the poor to help themselves, but this title of the Act cost nothing because the loans were to come from the Small Business Administration's revolving fund. The general framework of the bill, therefore, had already taken shape during the first two weeks of the existence of the task force. The distinguished citizens "from all walks of life" who trooped through Shriver's office to share their wisdom may have contributed to his education, but they added very little of substance to the legislation.

Shriver did alter his position on one substantive point. In his memorandum to the President he suggested that the National Service Corps (popularly termed the Domestic Peace Corps) which the President had already proposed be withdrawn "so that prospective volunteers might be staged into the other projects." However, the bill that went to Congress retained this program under a new title, Volunteers for America. Shriver did not have to go far to seek advice on this point. Another brother-in-law, Attorney General Robert F. Kennedy, persuaded him to include this provision.

All this is not to conclude that Shriver and his associates did not seek or welcome new ideas from outside, but it indicates the paucity of approaches, at least within the predetermined budgetary restraints. It is also clear that the Shriver task force was receptive to new ideas, a point that later self-righteous critics of the legislation who participated in shaping the bill might well consider. When good ideas were offered they were gladly received. For example, early versions of the bill required that Job Corps centers be administered only by federal, state, or local agencies. When John H. Rubel, one of the corporation officials whose advice was sought, suggested that this restriction be removed so that private companies engaged in developing new techniques and approaches in adult education or job training might contribute to the success of the Job Corps centers, his advice was accepted and became an important element in the later administration of the centers.

Drafting the Bill

Agreement on general principles is only the first requisite for legislation. Significant policy decisions are made at every step in the drafting process, and in the case of the antipoverty bill this process was especially crucial because the legislation dealt with uncharted areas that involved new substantive provisions and the coordination of established departmental jurisdictions. The drafting process was entrusted to old hands in the federal bureaucracy who, as usual, neither expected nor received adequate credit for their labors. Because the task force was subject to considerable turnover in personnel it is difficult to identify all those who played a role in hammering out the legislation. Few had clearly identifiable tasks, and even within the short span of time their roles changed; some were called in to perform specific chores and others because they were recommended to Shriver or one of his key aides. Many found that no one had a clear idea of the functions they were to perform, and many departed without making a discernible contribution to the course of history. In this amalgam, some stayed on and played definite roles, and others who came for only a brief time made significant contributions. But since no record was kept of who did what, memories fade and individual recollections differ over the roles played by the different participants. Any listing of the dramatis personae is therefore somewhat subjective.

As special assistant to the President for the war on poverty, Shriver was able to secure cooperation from the various departments that assigned representatives to his staff. Adam Yarmolinsky, a civil rights expert and special assistant to the Secretary of Defense, was installed as unofficial chief of staff. It became quite clear that important decisions had to be cleared with Yarmolinsky if Shriver was unavailable. Needless to say, there was no table of organization,* and only one task force member had a formal title; as befits a command post in charge of a war, the task force had an executive officer, Hyman Bookbinder. The role of the other departmental representatives was

* A *post facto* table of organization was constructed by Roger H. Davidson; see n. 1 in notes to Chapter 1, p. 233 of Davidson's book.

somewhat ambiguous; it was not clear whether they were there to present and defend parochial departmental interests or to strike off on their own. Included in this group were Harold W. Horowitz, a lawyer from HEW; Daniel P. Moynihan, Assistant Secretary of Labor; and James L. Sundquist, Deputy Under Secretary of Agriculture. Bookbinder was assigned to the task force by the Department of Commerce, where he was serving on a consulting basis, and therefore he was not a departmental representative but rather an assistant to Shriver. A former staff member of the AFL–CIO, Bookbinder also performed liaison functions with the labor movement. Finally, Richard Boone of the White House staff played an important role in shaping the Community Action Program.

The actual drafting of the bill required not only a substantive understanding of the proposed antipoverty program but a thorough knowledge of the executive establishment. To head the team of lawyers, Shriver secured Assistant Attorney General Norbert Schlei, who was assisted by Harold Horowitz of HEW, Ann Oppenheimer of the Bureau of the Budget, and others. Christopher Weeks, a former Peace Corps official who had moved on to the Bureau of the Budget, was put in charge of preparing the congressional presentation. The title for the bill, Economic Opportunity Act, was one of Sundquist's contributions to the legislation.

In addition, a group of nongovernmental technical advisers and kibitzers played the role of critic and performed such other chores as the hectic situation required. Included in this group were Paul Ylvisaker, initiator of the Ford Foundation gray areas program, Frank Mankiewicz, a Peace Corps official, and social reformers Michael Harrington and Paul Jacobs.

Substantive Issues

Of the many technical and substantive issues that were raised in drafting the legislation, the most stubborn related to the Community Action Program and the coordination and administration of the several new programs. One problem arose in specifying the types of assistance to be included in the catch-all, comprehensive community action approach. The first complete draft version of the bill (February 24, 1964) listed fourteen activities as falling within the scope of the Community Action Program. These included development of new employment opportunities, rehabilitation of the physically and mentally handicapped, diverse educational and counseling programs, and health services. Though the bill stated that the list was only illustrative, several agencies urged that their pet programs be included. Agri-culture alone urged the addition of nine specific programs. Obviously, only a limited number of activities could be mentioned in what be-came known as the "CAP laundry list." Moreover, it was feared that any list might be further extended on Capitol Hill and might also suggest to some congressmen the idea of making some of the programs mandatory, thus limiting administrative flexibility and local initiative. It was therefore decided to omit all reference to specifically eligible activities.

Early thinking about the community action concept assumed that these programs would be limited to ten to twenty urban and rural areas. The federal money would not only stimulate a coordinated approach to the diverse welfare, health, education, and other services offered the poor but would make a significant contribution to the total available resources of the community. Such a pilot approach did not fit in with the "total war on poverty" envisioned by the Shriver task force. The proposed bill therefore imposed no limit on the num-ber of communities that would be eligible to receive assistance. This expansion process has often occurred in public programs. For example, the depressed areas program at first contemplated aid for a few score communities, but restrictions on the number of communities were dropped in the legislative process. Within two years after the depressed areas legislation was enacted, more than a thousand different areas made up the "depressed area list." CAP would later experience the same kind of expansion.

No doubt the most frequently quoted provision of the Act relates to the role of the poor themselves, Section 202(a)(3), a portion of the definition of a community action program. One of the three criteria states that the program must be "developed, conducted, and adminis-tered with the maximum feasible participation of residents of the areas and members of the groups served." In light of later experience and the controversy generated by this phrase, it may be surprising that this language appeared in the first draft of the bill and was neither questioned nor commented upon by any of the departments that sub-mitted detailed criticisms of the various versions of the bill. Nor was it considered significant enough to be mentioned in the official sum-mary of the bill which was released, as is customary, when the bill was submitted to Congress. The advocates and planners of the com-munity action concept were concerned, and some were determined, that the program would not exclude minority groups. A version of the bill prepared by the Department of Health, Education, and Welfare just prior to Shriver's appointment required that community and neighborhood groups must be represented on CAP governing bodies. It was expected that this would overcome the problem of discrimination and would produce integrated community action boards. But this was considered inadequate by some of Shriver's task force members.

During the first meeting of the task force on February 4, 1964, Richard Boone, who had served on the Ford Foundation's gray area program and the President's Juvenile Delinquency Committee staff, urged that the poor be assigned a more definite responsibility in implementing community action programs. The final language of Section 202(a)(3) was the result. Whether anyone fully appreciated the implications of the language or the stir it might create is not known. To most of the task force participants "maximum feasible participation" represented a nice sentiment and a means of giving the administrator of the program power to prevent segregation in community action programs. According to Sundquist: "The clause ... relating to participation of the poor was inserted with virtually no discussion in the task force and none at all on Capitol Hill. ... I cannot say that I was aware of the implications of the clause. It just seemed to me like an idea that nobody could quarrel with."[30]

The federal government's share of the funding, not only in community action but in such other programs as the Neighborhood Youth Corps, was another major problem area. In the task force's original draft bill, the federal government was to contribute from 25 to 50 percent of the total cost of NYC programs (depending upon the income level of the community) and two-thirds of the total cost of CAP (with the proviso that the administrator could increase the federal share when this was deemed necessary). Most departments felt that state or local contributions would be of such magnitude as to constitute a serious obstacle to the program and that the communities most in need of help would not be able to participate at all. The federal share was therefore raised to 90 percent of the total cost, with the local contributions to be made either in kind or in cash.

Agriculture's proposal calling for the establishment of a new loan and grant program to low-income rural families was included in the bill. - Many participants on the task force had reservations about singling out low-income rural families for special treatment, but apparently Agriculture's lobbying was sufficiently persuasive and this provision was retained—on the argument that few rural areas would participate in community action programs. The program was yet another triumph for the department in winning special treatment for rural areas, and it appeared to have political appeal.

As expected, the most heated arguments centered upon organization and the division of administrative responsibility. Because neither Shriver's persuasiveness nor the passage of time served to resolve this controversy, it finally had to be referred to the President.

The Shriver task force managed to obtain agreement on the need for a new agency; there was no consensus, however, on the role the new agency would play. Shriver, who was destined to supervise the new program, favored operating responsibility rather than merely a coordinating role. The question then became how much of the total program should be placed in the new agency and how much delegated to the established departments and agencies. Health, Education, and Welfare relinquished its claim on the Community Action Program, and in the absence of other claimants it was assigned to the new agency. Locating training and job-creation programs was not so easy. Secretary of Labor Wirtz took a firm position that everything relating to work and training was within his department's domain; HEW held that the training of persons on relief was within its jurisdiction; and Shriver was bent on gaining control over the Job Corps, anticipating that it would yield quick results and favorable publicity. Knowledgeable Labor Department officials, foreseeing the difficulties in administering the Job Corps, did not share Wirtz's desire to have it assigned to Labor. The President finally divided the work and training programs three ways: the Job Corps went to Shriver, work relief and training to HEW, and the Neighborhood Youth Corps to Labor.

The status of the new agency was a final problem. Shriver insisted that it be placed in the Executive Office, on the assumption that this would provide the leverage needed to coordinate the program. Objections came from the top echelon of the Bureau of the Budget, though some of the bureau's subordinate officials thought there was merit in Shriver's position. Again, the President sided with Shriver.

The major problems having been resolved, the legal aides lost little time in completing the draft bill. The total cost of the legislative package approved by the President was $962.5 million. On March 16, 1964, Johnson sent the bill to Congress, reminding the solons that "Congress is charged by the Constitution to 'provide ... for the general welfare of the United States.'. . . Now Congress is being asked to extend that welfare to all our people."

Congress Reacts and Disposes

The President did not leave the fate of the antipoverty program to the whims of Congress. After sending the bill to Congress, he launched a successful campaign to persuade the public and Congress of the urgent need for the proposed legislation. The enlistment of outside support through the Shriver task force, the emphasis on traditional American values, and favorable publicity through the mass media all helped to generate public awareness of and support for the proposed program.

In general, Johnson cultivated the image of fiscal responsibility. Early in his Administration he asked Defense Secretary McNamara to cut defense costs, and he called for an over-all reduction in federal jobs. Pursuing this theme, he assured the country that the proposed expenditures for the antipoverty program would be absorbed from "savings" in other governmental activities. Ironically, in light of later developments, the savings were to be achieved largely by trimming defense expenditures.

Johnson also used direct personal methods to sell the bill. In a series of visits to depressed areas he emphasized the persistence of poverty and its debilitating effects upon individuals and communities. On a more pragmatic basis, he alluded to the prospect of the federal funds to communities and states that would result from the enactment of Great Society legislation. A number of communities—particularly several large cities that had participated in the gray area and juvenile delinquency programs and were geared to expand their activities— began to press for quick passage of the legislation on the assumption that poverty funds would be distributed on a first-come first-served basis. Congressional constituencies thus became aware of their stake in the poverty program. The efforts were so effective that only five months after the bill's submission to Congress it was the law of the land, an exceptionally short time for a novel piece of major welfare legislation.

Congressional Structure and Processing

The progress of the Economic Opportunity Act through Congress presented special problems. When a bill is drawn up by the executive branch, senior members of committees and/or their staffs usually are consulted about its general provisions and may also help in the drafting process. The poverty bill, however, was generated and drawn up by the executive branch without congressional participation. It was not even clear which committee in each house would consider the bill. Because the measure cut across jurisdictional lines—at least four committees in each house had jurisdiction over some part of the bill—the designers of the legislation did not know whom to consult in Congress.

During the drafting stage it was assumed that each affected committee might claim jurisdiction over at least part of the bill, but the expected jurisdictional difficulties did not materialize. Before the bill went to Congress, the leadership agreed to assign it to the House Committee on Education and Labor and the Senate Committee on Labor and Public Welfare. The chairmen of the other committees raised no objections to this. Inevitably, the two relevant committees were unable to assess all parts of the bill thoroughly. Like the executive branch, Congress was structurally ill prepared to process the bill efficiently.

Some parts of the bill had of course been proposed in earlier legislation, but various provisions, notably the community action section, represented unfamiliar approaches or were in the domain of other committees. Congressmen and Senators often acquire a background during their tenure on committees that helps them appraise legislation embodying new ideas. In this case, however, few members of the Senate and House committees possessed the needed expertise to deal with the bill. Indeed, the fact of poverty had been buried for a long time before it suddenly burst into the limelight. It is not surprising, therefore, that few if any legislators had reflected on appropriate strategies for fighting poverty. Congress, therefore, had to "play it by ear" in dealing with the Act.

The Administration's draft bill was introduced in Congress on March 16, 1964, and the next day hearings were begun by an ad hoc House Education and Labor Subcommittee on Poverty. Though the subcommittee was chaired by Adam Clayton Powell, chairman of the parent committee, Phil Landrum of Georgia was asked to sponsor the legislation (H.R. 10440) in order to give the bill an aura of conservative support. In addition to the 1,741 pages of testimony, Chairman Powell commissioned preparation of a volume of facts relating to poverty by technicians in the appropriate executive departments.[31]

The Administration's strategy was to portray the bill as a thoughtfully conceived, comprehensive, and integrated approach to combating poverty, even though it was really a series of compromises among various executive departments. Appearing as the lead-off witness, Shriver outlined the program and defended it as responsible, comprehensive, and representative of a consensus of many individuals and groups. He stressed that the bill's sections were "designed to complement one another" and warned that defeat of any part could "jeopardize" the entire program.[32] For the next two weeks a parade of the Administration's top brass appeared to nail down the case for the bill. The Secretaries of Defense, Labor, Interior, Commerce, Agriculture, and HEW, as well as the Attorney General, all testified in the same vein as Shriver.

Charges that the proposed authorization was too small to wage an effective war on poverty were cavalierly countered with the assertion that more funds could not be intelligently spent, at least during the first year. "We think this is a substantial first step," Shriver observed.[33]

Republican committee members found the hearings a frustrating experience. The great majority of witnesses favored the bill and were hesitant to criticize it. Of the sixty-nine primary witnesses who testified, only nine opposed the bill. Also, Chairman Powell's demeanor caused Republicans to complain that they were not being fairly treated. On one occasion, when government specialists testified on the extent of poverty in the United States, the Republicans on the committee tried to show that additional information was needed before effective legislation could be drafted. Powell cut short the hearings, responding to complaints by Republicans: "I am the chairman. I will run this committee as I desire."[34] Republicans consequently charged that the hearings were structured in the Administration's favor and that the opposition was gagged.

There appears to be little substance to the claim that the bill was rushed through Congress without giving the opposition an adequate chance to present its views. The fact that Congress approved the Administration proposal with relatively few major changes appears to be due rather to the paucity of alternative ideas and approaches. Even the three academic witnesses who testified in opposition to the Administration bill failed to offer constructive alternatives. One deplored the CEA's definition of poverty, another asked that a research design be built into the program, and a third criticized the bill for what he considered its welfare state aspects. As a result of this dearth of constructive alternatives, the criticism tended to degenerate into negativism. One need not argue in favor of the Administration proposal to acknowledge that outright opposition was difficult. No witness wanted to argue against helping the poor.

As the debate progressed, Republicans indicated that they were ready to meet the Administration part way, and if they had been given any encouragement by Powell and the Administration, the antipoverty program might have gained bipartisan support and the legislation might have been improved. As it turned out, the Republican alternative (H.R. 11050, introduced by Peter H. Frelinghuysen) was an ineffectual substitute that authorized the expenditure of $1.5 billion over a three-year period. The bill embraced the community action concept but placed emphasis upon education and training programs by requiring that 50 percent of the states' funds during the first year, and a third of their funds during the subsequent years, be spent on education

and training programs. The money would have been distributed to
states in grants by the Secretary of Health, Education, and Welfare,
with each state submitting its own plans subject to authorization by
the Secretary. H.R. 11050 would have required states to contribute
one-third of the total funds during the first year and one-half during
the following two years, a provision which probably would have deterred many states from taking advantage of the proposed legislation.
The Republican bill was repected by a 295 to 117 vote. Not a single
Democrat voted for it, and 49 Republicans opposed their party's bill.[35]

Once the hearings were completed, Powell caucused with his
Democratic colleagues on the committee. The purpose was to reach a
majority consensus and to present the Republicans with a final bill on
a take-it-or-leave-it basis. By suppressing Republican criticism in the
hearings and by excluding Republicans from the caucus, which considered a number of amendments, the Democrats prevented the Republicans from sharing credit for the bill. More tender treatment of
the feelings of the minority members and a willingness to permit them
to share credit for its enactment might have given the bill bipartisan
support.

Two years earlier, when the same committee considered the Manpower Development and Training bill, the majority actively sought
Republican support and gave the minority full credit for its contributions in drafting and passing the legislation. With remarkable bipartisan support, the Manpower Development and Training Act has been
amended four times during the subsequent six years, and spokesmen
for both parties consider the legislation "their" creation. Powell's deliberate exclusion of the Republicans from participation in shaping the
poverty legislation may have provoked Republican hostility toward the
Economic Opportunity Act which still persists. The winning of
broader bipartisan support for the antipoverty bill would also have
required some substantive changes in the legislation. It is useless to
speculate about the nature of these changes, but in light of later experience it would appear that proponents of the bill might have
welcomed some revisions.

Administrative Changes

The opposition directed much of its fire at the formal structure of
the proposed war on poverty. Such criticism is sometimes valuable, but
in this case alternative ideas were lacking. The consequence was an
undistinguished debate marked by a great deal of carping.

One target of criticism was the unique administrative arrangement. Shriver's assertion that his proposed bill was a first step in the war on poverty was vehemently denied, with considerable justification. Pointing to existing welfare legislation with an annual cost of billions of dollars, opponents reasoned that it was not necessary to establish a new superagency to combat poverty. They raised the specter that Shriver would be a "poverty czar" who could ride roughshod over established agencies. Aware that several heads of executive agencies were concerned that the antipoverty bill might encroach on their domains, opponents tried unsuccessfully to elicit criticisms from Administration witnesses. The heads of departments replied that jurisdictional prerogatives were inconsequential compared to the larger issue of fighting poverty, and they gave assurances that interdepartmental cooperation was necessary and would be forthcoming.

A second line of attack dealt with states' rights. Fearful that some state governors would sabotage the program, the drafters of the Administration bill had bypassed the states and fashioned direct relationships between the federal government and the localities. Opponents argued that the governors should have a veto power over at least some of the poverty projects launched in their states. A Republican–Southern Democratic coalition succeeded in inserting an amendment authorizing governors to veto community action programs, Job Corps centers, and Neighborhood Youth Corps projects in their states. Although this coalition succeeded on the veto issue, it was unstable as far as the rest of the bill was concerned. In deference to southern supporters of the antipoverty program, their northern allies found it advantageous to ignore the civil rights issue. But when opponents of the bill tried to raise the issue, it was met head on; civil rights had lost its potency as an obstacle to legislation. For example, when Howard W. Smith argued in the Rules Committee for the rejection of the Job Corps because it would be racially integrated, Congressman Phil Landrum of Georgia acknowledged the charge but stated that this was "a matter of law over which neither you nor I can prevail."[36]

Another administrative amendment trimmed the powers of the program administrator in distributing community action funds. The Administration bill imposed no restrictions upon the director in allocating funds among the states. The amendment adopted by Congress established criteria for the distribution of funds.

Substantive Changes

Although much of the congressional discussion concerned the formal structure of the war on poverty, the bill's substantive provi-

sions were not entirely ignored. The Job Corps received closest attention, particularly in the Senate, which had approved similar measures
in 1959 and 1963. Because the members of the Senate Committee on
Labor and Public Welfare were familiar with the issues involved, the
arguments voiced during the Senate floor debate closely followed those
of the earlier years.

The Job Corps proposed by the Administration in 1964 differed
from that proposed in the 1963 bill, however. The former called for
the establishment of residential centers for youths where the enrollees
would receive educational and vocational training; the earlier bill, in
contrast, emphasized conservation work. Aware of the "nature boy"
lobbies represented by the Departments of the Interior and Agriculture and by private conservation organizations, the drafters of the 1964
bill did not preclude the establishment of conservation centers. But
they were intentionally vague on the subject in order to permit maximum flexibility in the administration of the program. It became clear
during the course of the hearings that the pressures of the conservation
lobbies could not be ignored, and the House Committee on Education
and Labor specified two kinds of camps in the bill it reported (H.R.
11377, a revised version of H.R. 10440). Urban centers would stress
vocational training and conservation centers would concentrate on
basic education and conservation work.

The opponents' attack on the Job Corps program focused on the
conservation centers. It was argued that work in a rustic environment
would not give corpsmen from slum areas meaningful preparation for
their world of work. The potentially high cost of maintaining centers
was also emphasized. Senator Winston L. Prouty of Vermont estimated,
on the basis of a 1961 Department of Agriculture figure, that the annual cost of operating a hundred-man rural camp would amount to
$8,263 per boy. These costs were said to be exorbitant, especially in
view of the anticipated ineffectiveness of the camps.[37]

Defenders of the proposal replied that it was better to have
young people doing conservation work than hanging around the
streets. Senator Hubert H. Humphrey, who originally proposed the
Job Corps idea and sponsored the earlier Senate bills, said, "the main
idea is to put these boys to work."[38] In addition, some tangible benefits
would accrue to corpsmen, such as better health, education, and
morale. Senator Humphrey estimated that the cost of the juvenile
delinquency program was $25,000 per boy, considerably more than the
anticipated cost per Job Corpsman. Such arguments prevailed, and an
amendment introduced by Senator Prouty to delete the conservation
camps from the bill was defeated 61 to 33.[39]

It is noteworthy that there was little criticism of urban centers. Sentor Prouty even argued for the elimination of conservation centers and for the allocation of all the Job Corps funds to urban centers. A less rigid position by the Democrats might have attracted Republican support for the Job Corps and still retained the conservation centers. But the Democratic floor leaders refused to yield on the provisions relating to conservation centers. It has been suggested that the Republican attack on the conservation centers was part of a maneuver to defeat the whole Job Corps program. It would seem, however, that with the support of Prouty and other Republicans the Democratic sponsors could have mustered sufficient support for the measure even if some supporters of conservation centers had refused to compromise and had voted against the Job Corps.

The conservation lobbies were even more successful in the House, where an amendment was approved requiring that 40 percent of male Job Corps enrollees be assigned to conservation centers. This amendment was included in the final bill. Another amendment made girls eligible for enrollment in the Job Corps. Congress was also persuaded to add a loyalty oath requirement.

The novel community action concept was poorly understood by Congress, and as a result it stimulated little meaningful debate. Interestingly, the issue of participation by the poor in community action programs was completely ignored. The decision by the drafters of the legislation to omit a listing of the programs and activities that would qualify for assistance under community action proved to be wise. No doubt some members of Congress would have opposed the inclusion of some programs and the deletion of others. Congress thus left the CAP administrators maximum flexibility of operation, with only one exception—adult basic education.

The Administration bill did not contain a provision for adult basic education, and the failure of the Shriver task force to include special provisions for it is understandable. It was anticipated that funds for this activity could be provided from CAP grants. However, because an adult basic education bill had been pending in Congress for several years, the House Education and Labor Committee added a section (Title IIB) authorizing the director to make grants to states to operate adult remedial reading classes and to develop new techniques for improving the quality of instruction.

Another substantive issue dealt with CAP aid to parochial schools, a hotly contested issue which until 1964 proved to be a stumbling block to direct federal aid for primary and secondary schools. The Administration bill specifically prohibited federal poverty aid to private schools. The intent, as Attorney General Robert F. Kennedy and others had pointed out in the hearings, was to exclude parochial schools from the program. This met with strong behind-the-scenes resistance from Representative Hugh L. Carey of New York and others. The bill as finally adopted prohibited general aid to elementary and secondary education in any school, but the House committee report specified that "other programs could be carried on by nonpublic as well as public institutions," thus permitting aid for remedial education but not for "regular" education.[40] This compromise opened the door for passage of the Elementary and Secondary Education Act of 1965.

The most sophisticated economic discussion dealt with loans and grants to low-income rural families and the establishment of corporations authorized to purchase and develop land for resale to poor farmers (Title III). Opponents questioned the wisdom of making special allowances for rural folk and thus discouraging their mobility.[41]

Two important changes were made in Title III of the Administration bill. First, Senator Humphrey, on the Senate floor, proposed to delete a provision allowing direct grants to impoverished farmers. However, he wanted to give the director discretionary authority to release debtors from loan obligations. His amendment was accepted by the Senate, but the House refused to allow loans to be forgiven, though it accepted the rest. Several factors accounted for the deletion of grants from the bill. Some legislators felt that direct grants contradicted the underlying theme of self-help. Also, the logic by which grants would be given to farmers compelled the giving of grants to poor people in cities. Since there was no apparent basis for discrimination against city dwellers, there was no reason to retain rural grants. Finally, some legislators, particularly those from low-income rural districts, feared that farmers who qualified for grants might be enabled to "leap frog" over other marginal farmers who did not qualify.

Second, Senator Frank J. Lausche of Ohio offered an amendment to delete the provision authorizing the establishment of corporations to buy land for resale to poor farmers. This provision was a revival of a New Deal program. Opponents argued that the measure smacked of collectivism and that the idea of cooperatives ran counter to the government's established policy of taking acreage out of production. Both arguments were fallacious. The intent of the legislation was to transfer commercially operated land to subsistence farmers and would therefore not have expanded productive acreage. Nevertheless, the amendment was accepted.[42]

Congress also added a special section to the rural programs that authorized housing, sanitation, education, and day-care assistance for migrants and other seasonal agricultural employees.

Finally, Congress added a provision that exempted the first $85 and half of the additional monthly income earned by the poor under the provisions of the Act (except work experience) from income for purposes of determining basic needs under public assistance programs. This provision was considered desirable, because in most states the earnings of members of families receiving public assistance were deducted from the allowance a family was entitled to receive. Without this provision the incentive for the poor to participate in the antipoverty programs would have been reduced.

One way to appraise the impact of congressional amendments is to compare the funds requested by the Administration with the actual authorization. The Administration called for a total authorization of $962.5 million for the first year of the antipoverty legislation. Congress authorized $15 million less, which reflected the deletion of the farmland redistribution scheme. The final authorization is compared with the Administration request in Table 1–2.

The fact that the antipoverty bill passed through Congress relatively unscathed was not due to a general consensus in favor of the program. When the final vote was taken, Congress was still divided. Had it not been for the sustained pressure by President Johnson, generating wide public support for the legislation particularly among civil rights groups, the bill might have failed. At the very least, it would not have been enacted into law five months and four days after the President sent the antipoverty message to Congress. In the House, the final vote on the bill (August 8, 1964) was 226 to 185. Republicans remained largely opposed to the program, with only 22 of the 167 Republicans voting in favor of it. In the Senate, sentiment for the bill

Table 1–2. OEO Request and Congressional Authorization, Fiscal 1965

	Programs by Title	Congressional Authorization	Administration Request
		(Millions)	
Total		$947.5	$962.5
I	Youth programs	412.5	412.5
II	Community action programs	340.0	315.0
III	Rural assistance	35.0	50.0
IV	Small loans	a	25.0
V	Work experience	150.0	150.0
VI	VISTA and administration	10.0	10.0

a No special funds were authorized; loans were to be made from Small Business Administration funds.
Source: Office of Economic Opportunity.

was stronger. The final vote (July 23, 1964) was 61 in favor to 34 opposed. Ten Republicans joined 51 Democrats in favor, while 22 Republicans, 11 Southern Democrats, and Senator Frank J. Lausche voted against the bill. In both houses, Southern Democrats were equally divided on the bill.

President Johnson signed the Economic Opportunity Act (Public Law 88–452) on August 20, 1964. In signing the bill the President declared: "The measure . . . offers the answer that its title implies— the answer of opportunity. For the purpose of the Economic [Opportunity] Act of 1964 is to offer opportunity, not an opiate."

2.

HOUSEKEEPING

There is nothing more difficult to take in hand,
more perilous to conduct, or more uncertain
in its success, than to take the lead in the
introduction of a new order of things.

Niccolò Machiavelli

New Dimensions

The magnitude and variety of problems implied by the federal government's "unconditional war on poverty" have challenged traditional administrative theories and practices. Except on a limited scale, few people prior to 1964 had considered, let alone attempted, the functional coordination of governmental programs in American communities. The psychological and social characteristics of the poverty-stricken, moreover, demanded a heavy expenditure of manpower and money merely to identify and recruit the clienteles of the poverty programs. Even coordination at the federal level, which would seem a relatively simple task (involving primarily the funding of the efforts), is a story of frustration for those who attempted the job. Clearly, conventional notions of administrative efficiency and structure were not applied to the organization of the antipoverty programs.

Because the problem of poverty permeates many aspects of our national life, the administration of poverty-related programs has stretched the traditional jurisdictions of public institutions. The programs are funded by a number of federal agencies, and are normally administered by state and local agencies, but much of the money Congress appropriated for the first three years' programs under the Economic Opportunity Act was never entered on the ledgers of state and local governments; rather it was spent by nongovernmental entities —a feature of the Act that proved controversial as well as innovative. At the community level, nonprofit organizations worked individually or cooperatively to plan and implement poverty programs, occasionally without an elected officeholder in sight. Not surprisingly, research and demonstration grants were made to educational institutions and a diverse array of other research organizations. And private firms acted as contractors for such tasks as running Job Corps centers. Here again, traditional notions of the lines that divided public and private institutions seemed outmoded.

Levels of Administration

The Federal Level

Although the Office of Economic Opportunity spends only a small portion of the federal antipoverty dollars, it was envisioned in the Economic Opportunity Act as the nerve center of the federal government's antipoverty efforts. OEO is a unique administrative organization. For certain programs—urban Job Corps centers, Community Action, VISTA, and migrant workers—the agency has operating responsibilities. This alone would set OEO apart, for it is actually located in the Executive Office of the President, a status usually reserved for staff or advisory agencies. Other programs under the Economic Opportunity Act, however, are delegated to other federal departments or agencies, including the Departments of Labor (Neighborhood Youth Corps), Agriculture (part of the Job Corps conservation centers and rural loans), Interior (the balance of the conservation centers, except for a few that are operated by states), and Health, Education, and Welfare (adult basic education and work experience), as well as the Small Business Administration (small business loans). Finally, OEO is charged by a vague mandate with the coordination of federal poverty-related programs that are not part of the Economic Opportunity Act.

OEO's operating responsibilities were the result of specific compromises during the legislative history of the Act. The agency's position in the Executive Office, as well as its potential role in coordinating programs not under the Act, were included in the original bill at the insistence of Sargent Shriver, head of the Administration's task force and Director of OEO during its first three and a half years, a period that coincides roughly with the time span covered by this study.

These features are reflected in OEO's organizational structure (Figure 1), which was largely the product of preliminary planning during the summer of 1964. The top levels of the chart reflect staff functions, some traditional and others specifically designed to serve OEO's unique mission. The four assistant directors (third line in chart) are responsible for direct administration of programs charged to OEO. The final level of OEO organization, the seven regional offices, was a later development.

It is apparent from the legislative history of the Economic Opportunity Act that no over-all rational plan dictated either the selection of programs to be included in the Act or their distribution between the new OEO and federal agencies already in the poverty business. The distribution was essentially pragmatic, involving two sets of factors: existing agencies' expectations that they would "get their share" of

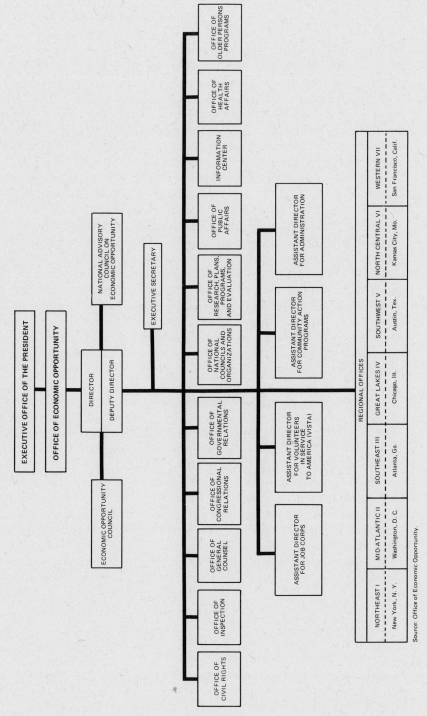

Figure 1. OEO ORGANIZATIONAL CHART, 1968

EXECUTIVE OFFICE OF THE PRESIDENT

OFFICE OF ECONOMIC OPPORTUNITY

ECONOMIC OPPORTUNITY COUNCIL

NATIONAL ADVISORY COUNCIL ON ECONOMIC OPPORTUNITY

DIRECTOR
DEPUTY DIRECTOR

EXECUTIVE SECRETARY

OFFICE OF CIVIL RIGHTS

OFFICE OF INSPECTION

OFFICE OF GENERAL COUNSEL

OFFICE OF CONGRESSIONAL RELATIONS

OFFICE OF GOVERNMENTAL RELATIONS

OFFICE OF NATIONAL COUNCILS AND ORGANIZATIONS

OFFICE OF RESEARCH, PLANS, PROGRAMS, AND EVALUATION

OFFICE OF PUBLIC AFFAIRS

INFORMATION CENTER

OFFICE OF HEALTH AFFAIRS

OFFICE OF OLDER PERSONS PROGRAMS

ASSISTANT DIRECTOR FOR JOB CORPS

ASSISTANT DIRECTOR FOR VOLUNTEERS IN SERVICE TO AMERICA (VISTA)

ASSISTANT DIRECTOR FOR COMMUNITY ACTION PROGRAMS

ASSISTANT DIRECTOR FOR ADMINISTRATION

REGIONAL OFFICES

NORTHEAST I	MID-ATLANTIC II	SOUTHEAST III	GREAT LAKES IV	SOUTHWEST V	NORTH CENTRAL VI	WESTERN VII
New York, N. Y.	Washington, D. C.	Atlanta, Ga.	Chicago, Ill.	Austin, Tex.	Kansas City, Mo.	San Francisco, Calif.

Source: Office of Economic Opportunity.

51

the new program, and the preferences of Shriver and his associates, backed by the President.

The Secretary of Labor received something less than he had hoped for, in view of his department's long-term interest in manpower problems and its responsibilities under the Wagner-Peyser Act (United States Employment Service), the Manpower Development and Training Act, and other legislation. Labor's share was the Neighborhood Youth Corps, administered by the Bureau of Work and Training Programs in the Manpower Administration. Though somewhat less aggressive in bargaining, the Department of Health, Education, and Welfare wound up with three important poverty programs: the Work Experience and Training Program, administered originally by the Welfare Administration and since 1967 by the Social and Rehabilitation Service, and the adult basic education and work-study programs, both administered by the Office of Education and formally transferred to HEW within the first two years of the legislation. Rural antipoverty loans are administered by the Farmers Home Administration in the Department of Agriculture, while financial assistance to small businesses comes from the Small Business Administration's revolving fund. Because the Act places the authority for the administration of all EOA programs with the director of OEO, the delegation of these programs can, in theory, be rescinded by him.

OEO's own operating programs reflect Shriver's interests and his distaste for traditional welfare activities. VISTA, the domestic peace corps, was a natural extension of Shriver's experience with, and enthusiasm for, the Peace Corps. The Job Corps held hopes for spectacular accomplishment (its administrative perils were not anticipated), and Shriver decided to run it himself, overriding the objections of the Labor Department. Finally, the Community Action Program represented the kind of coordinating operation that OEO, as a staff agency, was particularly designed to handle. However, CAP has tended to break down into specific-purpose programs, ranging from birth control to creating jobs for old people. The goal of coordinating programs in aid of the poor remains elusive. Figure 2 shows both the direct and the delegated programs based on the 1967 amendments.

Practically every activity OEO attempted to fund was preempted or already claimed by an established federal agency. Even the neighborhood centers, supposedly a CAP creation, had antecedents in the settlement houses, though these were few. More significantly, newly funded neighborhood centers partially duplicated well-established single-purpose programs, such as employment service offices and health clinics, to mention two of the most frequently available services. The Job Corps was a relatively distinctive program that might be well run

Figure 2. DIRECT AND DELEGATED AUTHORITIES OF ECONOMIC OPPORTUNITY ACT PROGRAMS, 1968

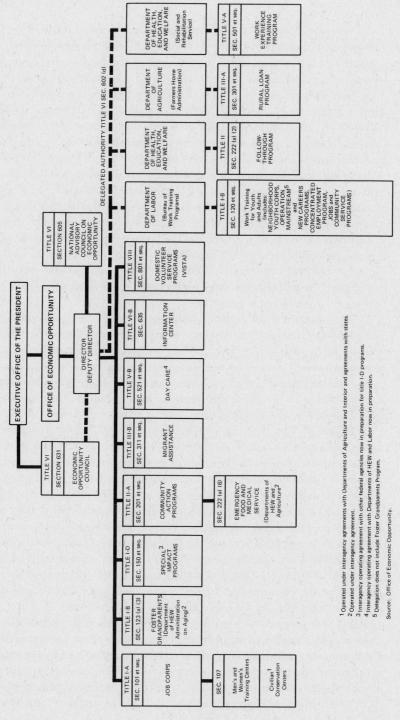

1 Operated under interagency agreements with Departments of Agriculture and Interior and agreements with states.

2 Operated under interagency agreement.

3 Interagency operating agreement with other federal agencies now in preparation for title I-D programs.

4 Interagency operating agreement with Departments of HEW and Labor now in preparation.

5 Delegation does not include Foster Grandparents Program.

Source: Office of Economic Opportunity.

by a new agency with a minimum of duplication of existing activities (previously there were only a few residential facilities—other than "reform" schools and penal institutions—that provided remedial education and training for poor youths). But even here problems of coordination soon appeared. What, for example, was the Job Corps' relation to the Neighborhood Youth Corps? What criteria should be applied in selecting youths for the Job Corps as compared with the Neighborhood Youth Corps, not to mention the various counseling and training programs funded by the Departments of Labor and Health, Education, and Welfare? A coordinated attack on poverty would presumably involve some form of "one-stop" counseling and referral service to evaluate the needs of disadvantaged youths and direct them to appropriate programs. Yet even when a single agency, the U. S. Employment Service, was assigned to recruit enrollees for youth programs, selection remained largely on a haphazard basis, and coordinated referral was rarely achieved. The problem of coordinating poverty-related programs was heightened rather than alleviated by the addition of OEO's new programs.

The problem of coordination may never be "solved," if only because the problem of poverty is likely to continue to demand a variety of institutional arrangements. With the proliferation of related programs, coordination becomes ever more burdensome for officials and clienteles alike; and in many cases the distinctions between programs are, to borrow the words of a bureaucratic memorandum on the subject, "largely artificial and arbitrary."

Different interests, of course, generated different approaches to the problem. The Labor Department, long unhappy at the thought of having other agencies in the manpower field, was more convinced than ever that all work experience and training programs should be placed under its protective care. Labor was especially concerned about the profusion of agencies in its fields and about what it called the "urgent need . . . to rationalize the entire manpower development structure." Quite a different solution for the proliferation of manpower programs was proposed by the National Association for Community Development (NACD) at its December 1965 convention. Composed largely of CAP-financed community action agency officials, NACD urged that, wherever possible, manpower programs be folded into the CAP operations. The community developers specifically recommended that OEO give higher priority to comprehensive manpower programs within the CAP concept, asserting that "it is only through the community action mechanism that such essential resources can be effectively integrated with existing manpower and occupational training programs."[1]

The differing positions of the Labor Department and the CAP

workers were merely indicative of the scramble for advantage among the many interests involved in poverty programming.

In the manpower field, OEO's coordinating efforts at the federal level have been, for the most part, fruitless. The agency initially lost influence over the Neighborhood Youth Corps, and its efforts to reclaim some measure of control were frustrated. With the addition of the Nelson-Scheuer and Kennedy-Javits manpower programs in 1966, and rising congressional criticism, OEO acquiesced to the delegation of these programs to the Labor Department—with the face-saving proviso that funds for these projects would be allocated through local community action agencies. OEO hoped to strengthen the agencies and recoup some influence over NYC by including it as part of the interagency agreement. OEO officials were apprehensive about this agreement (concluded early in 1967), but most thought it was the best way out of a difficult situation. Moreover, the involvement of CAA's gave further promise of coordination at the local level. The 1967 amendments to the Act added legislative force to the arrangements by placing the several EOA manpower programs (exclusive of the Job Corps) under a single authority, to be administered through local CAA's.

A related effort was the Concentrated Employment Program (CEP) for creating jobs and training slum residents in twenty cities and two rural areas. CEP's funds came from MDTA and three EOA programs. In most areas the CAA's were given the prime responsibility for implementing the projects, or at least the grants were funneled through these agencies.

Congress itself stepped in and attempted to force coordination of Work Experience and Training (Title V) projects by requiring HEW to share responsibility with the Labor Department for providing work experience and training to public assistance recipients and other needy persons. This coordination, however, was slow to materialize. With the 1967 legislation, Title V was to be phased out, its functions being largely absorbed by a new work experience and training program for relief recipients that was enacted as part of the 1967 amendments to the Social Security Act.

Early in 1967, OEO and four federal departments involved in administering manpower programs (Labor, HEW, Commerce, and HUD) signed a "treaty" to establish the Cooperative Area Manpower Planning System (CAMPS). The results of one year's experience were not promising, but hope springs eternal.[2]

The problem of coordination was not limited to manpower programs, though the problem was more visible in that area because of the Economic Opportunity Act's stress upon training, work experience, and job creation. Coordination also proved a problem in funding health and education projects. Neighborhood health centers, funded by CAP under a 1966 amendment sponsored by Senator Edward M. Kennedy of Massachusetts, were an attempt to provide comprehensive medical services for some communities by linking the centers with various publicly financed (federal, state, and local) health programs. In the educational sphere, coordination between OEO's Head Start and the Title I programs of the Elementary and Secondary Education Act threatened to become a glaring deficiency. As an early and popular venture of CAP, Head Start underwent a rapid expansion that was accomplished with little intervention from the Office of Education. Later enactment of the Elementary and Secondary Education Act and subsequent efforts to establish the Follow-Through program to supplement Head Start made formal coordination imperative. The two agencies therefore signed an agreement that delegated Follow-Through to the Office of Education even before Congress had authorized the program. The advance planning proved to have been premature when Follow-Through became a victim of "economy" and only one-eighth of the requested funds were allocated for the program during fiscal 1968.

The problem of coordinating poverty-related programs at the federal level is closely tied to the question of which programs OEO should administer itself and which should be "spun off" to other agencies. The original legislative package drew this line rather arbitrarily. Since then, two programs—Work Study (1965) and Adult Basic Education (1966)—have been spun off from the Economic Opportunity Act, and a third program, Upward Bound, is scheduled for spin-off in July 1969. Moreover, OEO's friends and foes alike have from time to time proposed further transfers which they claim would result in a more "logical" or "efficient" operation. That OEO has withstood these attacks upon its programs was confirmed in 1967 when Congress refused to tamper further with the organization's operating responsibilities. In opposing the proposed transfers, OEO claimed that its over-all coordinating functions would be weakened and the antipoverty efforts would suffer by the removal of programs from EOA.

Under the Economic Opportunity Act, OEO's responsibilities for coordination were extended beyond the programs initiated by the Act. The authority given to the director of OEO is broad, but it lacks political muscle. Various sections of the Act provide, as James L. Sundquist phrases it, "statutory basis for OEO's role as Government-wide coordinator of antipoverty efforts."[3] These provisions charge OEO's director with "coordination of antipoverty efforts by all segments of the Federal Government"; establish a Cabinet-level Economic

Opportunity Council chaired by the OEO director; empower the director to obtain data and reports from other agencies; authorize the director to create an information center for all federal antipoverty programs; and require all agencies to give "preference" (within certain limits) to projects that are part of CAA programs.

Implementation of these mandates clearly hinged on the aggressiveness of the OEO officials and the tolerance of program administrators in other agencies. Not surprisingly, therefore, OEO exerted little effort to fulfill its government-wide role, and other agencies, in turn, were not anxious to call attention to the deficiency. For its part, OEO became preoccupied with day-to-day administration of its own programs, devoting attention to non-OEO programs "only as [it] became necessary to the implementation of the programs for which it was responsible."[4] OEO at first sought to meet the problems of coordination by creating an Office of Interagency Relations. Though its primary mission was supervision of delegated programs under the Economic Opportunity Act, the office broadened its functions to embrace all interagency relations as well as OEO's links with local and state governments. The mission of federal-level coordination remained amorphous, and in 1967 the title of the office was changed to Office of Governmental Relations.

The statutory body charged with coordinating functions, the Economic Opportunity Council, has proved ineffective. Because other agencies tended to consider the council a creature of OEO, they did not view it as an ideal forum in which to air problems or resolve differences. Top officials rarely attended EOC meetings, leaving the council in the hands of underlings. OEO's Office of Governmental Relations provided staff assistance for the council, and the director of OEO chaired the meetings, but by all accounts it would be difficult to find any evidence that the council influenced OEO policy. In 1967, Congress approved an OEO-sponsored amendment that gave the council its own staff. By freeing the council from OEO ties, it was hoped that it would attain legitimacy in the eyes of the other participants, but the legislative mandate was not carried out.

If OEO is viewed as a coordinating agency, a "command post for the war on poverty," its record must be viewed with skepticism. However, the task of coordinating federal programs is a mammoth problem, and it pervades many program areas, whether in poverty, health, education, or, for that matter, foreign affairs. In 1967 the Senate Subcommittee on Employment, Manpower, and Poverty noted that a "constant theme" of its field hearings and consultant studies was "the lack of effective coordination among Federal programs."[5] If this is the case, and all the evidence points to this conclusion, then the problem is far too wide and persistent for OEO to resolve on its own, with the weak resources at its command.

Regionalization

OEO approached the matter of regional offices with considerable caution. First, the agency wanted to develop confidence in its procedures; and until such time, final authorization for all projects rested in Washington. Second, additional staff would be required, and toward the end of fiscal 1965 OEO was feeling the effects of a congressionally imposed ceiling on personnel.

Because OEO was in part a coordinating agency, an important question was where the regional offices were to be located. Attempts during the summer of 1965 (made with the active encouragement of the Budget Bureau) to establish common regional boundaries with Labor and HEW could not be resolved because the existing departments and their component bureaus had for a number of years proliferated regional and local offices. The effort ended with the establishment of seven OEO regional offices that parallelled those of the Labor Department's Neighborhood Youth Corps.

By September 1965, grant applications for CAP-funded projects were increasingly handled in the regions, and most of the processing of papers was being done there. This became possible as OEO's guidelines proved workable. Meanwhile, OEO's regional staffs were augmented to prepare for the process of decentralization. Of the three OEO operating agencies, CAP was the first to decentralize, and its operations are presently the most decentralized of OEO's activities. The regionalization of CAP administration occurred with relative ease because procedures were geared to decentralization from the very inception of OEO. On the other hand, OEO's decision to include most CAP grants in its decentralization was especially significant because these programs tended to generate the largest measure of controversy from local officials. Moreover, there were numerous reports of local mismanagement of CAP funds—in Boston, New York, and Mississippi, for example. In light of the potential controversiality of these projects, OEO's willingness to decentralize its review procedure was especially courageous. In addition to review, the regional offices shared in the functions of inspection and civil rights compliance. Here again the delegations were significant in view of the Washington staff's "hard-line" reputation for requiring that projects meet stringent standards.[6]

Other OEO programs were slower to decentralize, and some officials resisted the agency's efforts at regionalization. The Job Corps, for example, was operated on a national basis from the beginning and had decentralized very little. VISTA, too, was operated nationally at its inception and was slow to regionalize. VISTA officials argued that the need to clarify the objectives of their program and the uniqueness of the volunteers' role in the war on poverty made centralized administration desirable, though the nature of the activity, placing volunteers in communities, seemed to argue for decentralization. By late 1967, however, slightly more than half of VISTA's personnel were in the regional offices. These officials were given total responsibility for project development. Headquarters and field staff share responsibility for training VISTA volunteers, recruitment, in-service training, and field support. The migrant workers' program has continued to operate directly out of Washington.

Several types of review were established for regional operations. First, there was a review process in the field similar to that of the headquarters during OEO's first year. Regional offices added personnel (principally lawyers, civil rights specialists, and analysts) to perform these functions. Second, uniform processing systems were established, and personnel exchanges, orientation programs, and field trips by Washington personnel were encouraged to enhance uniformity. Third, OEO headquarters established a grant-review branch within CAP to perform a post-review of CAP grants. A sample of CAP applications is sent to Washington for review as a kind of "quality control."

An early, tangible result of regionalization was the fact that the grant process was shortened considerably, with OEO aiming for an eventual 30- to 60-day cycle between formal application and funding. When backlog problems developed, OEO responded by adding personnel to the regional offices. By mid-1968, regional offices accounted for 49 percent of the 3,100 persons on OEO's permanent payroll. There was little variation in the size of staff among the seven regional offices, which ranged from 184 to 245 (including temporary personnel) at the latest count.

The States

The states occupy an inconspicuous position in the Economic Opportunity Act. As drafted by the Shriver task force and passed by Congress, the Act was clearly designed to give the new OEO maximum flexibility in dealing with state, local, or private organizations. This flexibility was intentional. Many Administration officials who had a hand in drafting the measure foresaw that certain governors, for policy or political reasons, might try to sabotage the objectives of the antipoverty program. (One member of the Shriver task force recalled that whenever the role of the states was discussed, the name of the Alabama governor, George C. Wallace, would be mentioned and the discussion would promptly terminate.) A more fundamental reason for excluding the states was that the community action concept, which many saw as the crux of the new law, implied that the states were not relevant for more than an advisory or supportive role. President Johnson himself appeared to give credence to this notion by speaking repeatedly of local initiative and asserting that the problems of the urban environment "require us to create new concepts of cooperation—a creative federalism—between the National Capital and the leaders of local communities."[7]

It would be a mistake, however, to conclude that the states did not play a role in the EOA programs—even before enactment of the Green amendment in 1967. CAP funds, though allocated directly to communities, are distributed among the states on the basis of (a) the number of public assistance recipients in the states, (b) the average number of unemployed, and (c) the ratio of children in families with an annual income of less than $1,000. OEO may reserve up to 20 percent of the total funds for distribution in accordance with criteria of its own design. In the HEW-administered programs of Title V, the state welfare agency has to approve the project proposal and provide over-all supervision even though the local welfare agency runs the day-to-day operation. In other programs, the states (as well as localities) are eligible to become contractors; for example, six Job Corps conservation centers are operated by state agencies. And where standards for such professional personnel as teachers or social workers are involved, state licensing practices inevitably come into play. The problems of interlevel cooperation are extremely complex, but they have been marked not so much by permanent state-federal fixtures as by the more complicated adjustments required to mesh programs to the many and differing state laws, practices, and personnel.

Technical assistance has provided a particularly hopeful avenue for state participation in the war on poverty. Under the Act, OEO's director is authorized to contract with state agencies for technical assistance to localities in developing community action programs. By the end of 1967, every state had established its own antipoverty headquarters, usually called the state Office of Economic Opportunity. (One state, Indiana, later closed its office.) The federal funds used to create these offices were by no means large, ranging from $5 million in the first year to $6.4 million in 1968. State technical services were especially needed in rural communities, which often lacked the indigenous leadership and expertise to develop CAA's and consequently fell behind the better-organized urban areas in procuring federal funds.

In speaking to the Governors' Conference in mid-1965, Shriver stressed that "too often, it has been the big cities that have been able to get the federal money first—because they can attract the experts—because they know how to put together a staff attached to the mayor—and they know the arts of grantsmanship."[8] After generations of complaints that state governments have favored rural areas at the expense of the cities, one of the larger ironies of the war on poverty has been the rescue operation the states performed for rural areas that were ill prepared to engage in the planning and implementation of federally backed programs.

State technical assistance offices could perform other functions. For example, Shriver called upon the states to encourage research and to stimulate multicounty and metropolitan antipoverty efforts. When a governor appointed a capable person as poverty coordinator and gave him sufficient authority to act, the results were often promising. New Jersey's Governor Richard Hughes devoted particular attention to his poverty program; by appointing Paul Ylvisaker to be Commissioner of Community Affairs and by placing the state OEO in his command, Hughes made sure that the state's poverty programs would receive talented and creative guidance. A result of Ylvisaker's efforts was OEO's observation that New Jersey had obtained a great variety of OEO grants.[9] The New Jersey OEO administered an NYC program, made extensive use of VISTA volunteers in migrant programs, and generally coordinated the development of CAA's in the state. In California, the state coordinator's office stimulated a broad-gauge migrant program that featured day-care and educational programs, overnight camps and sanitary facilities, and the use of transportable housing for migrants at the height of the growing season. Several other states can boast of equally productive contributions to the poverty campaign.[10]

Unfortunately, the gubernatorial veto issue at first threatened to overshadow all other phases of the states' role. The Administration's 1964 draft bill on poverty required gubernatorial consent before VISTA volunteers could be dispatched to that state. In the community action programs, OEO's director was admonished to "facilitate effective participation of the states" and to refer project applications to the state's governor for "comment." Before passing the Act, Congress considerably strengthened the hand of the governors by amending the bill's provisions to include—in addition to the veto for VISTA projects—a governor's veto of Job Corps centers and all contracts with nongovernmental agencies (including community action agencies).

Governors saw the veto as an important weapon, not only for coordinating poverty efforts but for insuring that their own political position would not be jeopardized by policies and "patronage" associated with the programs. It was this latter objective that caused the most bitter disputes between OEO and state officials, provoking a number of threatened vetoes, and actual vetoes on five occasions during the first year of the Act. The most publicized veto came when Governor George Wallace of Alabama turned back OEO funds that had been allocated to a biracial poverty group in Birmingham.[11] Because of the group's racial overtones, Wallace's action was influential in leading Congress to reconsider the whole question.

The Administration's proposed 1965 amendments to the Act failed to mention the governor's veto, but the Wallace incident provoked immediate debate on Capitol Hill. A coalition of Republicans and Southern Democrats in the House insisted on retaining some form of the veto, and in the final version of the amendments the governors were permitted vetoes over Neighborhood Youth Corps, community action, and adult basic education projects. The veto was merely a token power, however, for the OEO director was permitted to reverse the veto if he wished.[12] States' rights forces, while successful in blocking complete deletion of the provision, were never deluded into thinking their victory had been anything but a Pyrrhic one.

Nevertheless, even the diluted veto power gave some governors an opportunity to assume a public stance of fighting "waste and extravagance" by OEO in order to earn political capital. Altogether, ten states used 30 vetoes, or one for every 550 grants made by OEO during its first three years. Governors George and Lurleen Wallace of Alabama and Ronald Reagan of California were the champion vetoers, accounting for three of every five vetoes.[13] Governor Reagan's actions received the greatest public attention. An examination of his veto record indicated, however, that the ten vetoes he exercised during his first year of office accounted for less than one percent of the total funds allocated by OEO to California; and some of the projects he vetoed became effective after the expiration of the thirty-day waiting period. It might be misleading, however, to measure the impact of the veto merely in terms of the magnitude of the funds involved or the percentage of total approved grants. The veto power's propensity to draw attention to questionable or controversial projects may have served to persuade officials to modify their program applications or to prevent OEO approval of certain projects.

The veto question generated considerable publicity and no doubt was symptomatic of very real frustrations on the part of state officials. Nonetheless, though the formal veto has been eliminated for most practical purposes, the states retain a wide variety of potentially significant functions in the war against poverty. What is obvious to date, however, is "the unclear definition of the role of the states" in EOA efforts.[14] Nor is there any consensus on their future role. State officials and their supporters, of course, call for a greater voice in poverty programs, but local officials tend to be suspicious of state involvement. "The State agencies, even when they do not become involved in a local urban program," Detroit Mayor Jerome Cavanagh remarked, ". . . lack either the interest or the sophistication or the understanding of the immediacy of the problem."[15] The ultimate place of the states in the EOA programs will depend, therefore, upon further developments in the system of federal relationships.

The Local Level

The Economic Opportunity Act is innovative in its approach to federal-local relations. The community action concept envisions comprehensive and community-wide planning and implementation of programs aimed at combating poverty. The institutional vehicle at the local level is the umbrella-type "community action agency"—a public or private nonprofit agency designed to pull a locality's existing institutional resources together and to develop its "community action program," a functional agenda for its needs in fighting poverty. Responsibility for the administration of existing programs normally remains with established agencies, and CAP-funded activities may be taken over by the CAA or delegated to other institutions, public or private.

The community action concept is intended to restructure social services in several ways. First, from the standpoint of the federal government, the multipurpose CAP is an alternative to the traditional special-purpose grant-in-aid, and in this respect approaches the concept of the block grant. Only local planning, it is reasoned, can account for unique local needs, which cannot be met by a plethora of federal agencies that sponsor their own specialized grant programs. The means for pulling federal resources together are found in two preference provisions in the Act which direct OEO and every other federal domestic department to assign the highest possible priority to the proposals of CAA's. Understandably the Bureau of the Budget displayed an early interest in CAP as a device for coordinating federal programs and bypassing traditional jurisdictional lines.

Second, the community action concept envisions coordination at the local level inasmuch as CAA's are supposed to be broadly representative of community opinion in matters relating to social welfare. Thus it was with considerable casualness (surprising only in retrospect) that the drafters of the Act specified (Section 202[a][3]) that CAA's be "developed, conducted and administered with the maximum feasible participation of residents of the areas and members of the groups served."

A third aspect of the CAP concept is its functional approach to geographic and political boundaries. Although CAA's frequently parallel existing political boundaries, the concept is open-ended in permitting these boundaries to be crossed for practical purposes in planning or implementing poverty programs. This development is not without significance in view of the proliferation of governmental and political jurisdictions, especially in complex and even multistate urban regions. In addition, contiguous rural counties occasionally coalesced to form a single CAA.

The vast majority of the 1,018 CAA's funded during OEO's first four years proceeded with minimum administrative difficulty. OEO provided the initial funds for developing a program and financing the cost of organizing and hiring staff, and only a few communities refused to accept the "tainted" money. In most of these cases the CAA was simply an administrative framework for the kinds of work community agencies had already been doing; and most of the funds undoubtedly were channeled directly to what OEO called "the local welfare system," that is, schools, welfare agencies, local charities, and so forth.

Most CAA's, moreover, enjoyed at least the tacit support of local government officials. In urban areas, a mayor's task force typically set the process in motion, although a coalition of civil rights, welfare, and related groups sometimes served the same function. Rural areas, lacking the institutional base of their urban counterparts, typically relied on private organization or agricultural extension service agents to organize CAA's. From OEO's point of view, the cooperation of city hall was valuable in providing the needed access to local governmental funds and facilities. Under the Act, a portion of the CAP funding must come from the locality, although this may be contributions "in kind," such as staff time. Originally this local contribution was set at 10 percent, but in 1967 Congress raised the figure to 20 percent and—to the great relief of local poverty officials—killed a proposal that local contributions be in cash. OEO guidelines also specified that CAA's be able to mobilize existing local "service systems," such as schools and welfare agencies.

From the vantage point of city hall, cooperation also had its payoffs. Most local officials preferred to exercise some control over the direction of CAA's, although some found it convenient to pursue a policy of calculated distance, namely, exercising informal direction of the CAA's while appearing to grant independence. Many local officials, nonetheless, soon found the autonomous CAA's a threat to their authority and to their control over local jobs.[16] The U.S. Conference of Mayors, for example, endorsed the original poverty bill with the reservation that CAP funds be channeled through an official agency such as a local human development corporation; the National Association of Counties took a similar position. At one point the bill's House sponsor, Democratic Representative Phil Landrum of Georgia, promised to "draft language" to assure the inclusion of local governments; but the original bill was never altered in this way. For the first three years the community action concept remained free of formal requirements for the involvement of local politicians and officials.

As the CAA's got under way it became apparent that their relationship with local government was occasionally "uneasy and sometimes strained."[17] On the one hand, localities were eager for federal money, and such bodies as the National Municipal League and the U.S. Conference of Mayors gave the war on poverty strong support. On the other hand, many local officials, particularly in large cities and throughout the South, feared that CAA's would organize the poor (and the Negroes) and enable them to upset traditional political power alignments. Thus spokesmen for local governments, such as the Conference of Mayors, continued to insist that the key figure in the selection of a board to plan the city's community action program must be the Mayor, as the chief local elected official.

OEO walked a tightrope on the issue of city hall or county courthouse involvement. The agency's objectives, particularly participation by the poor themselves, could sometimes be achieved only by flying in the face of a community's traditional social prejudices or political arrangements. Thus one agency directive called for the rejection of CAA's "set up in a manner calculated to ensure domination by a single individual or organization." Political pressures, however, proved too powerful to prevent incursions upon the autonomy of CAA's. By March 1966, OEO was informing its regional offices that city or county elected officials could veto all or any portion of a CAA proposal. The OEO directive stated:

> There may be occasion where no community action agency may be better than one with the veto power resting in a prejudiced local government.

> Our policy is to accept a veto where this will produce community action. This policy does not mean that we must accept a veto where the effect will be to prevent community action.[18]

Though militants were inclined to view this move as a sellout, OEO officials defended it as a response to political realities. When asked about the action, Bernard L. Boutin, then deputy director of the agency, explained that "concurrence" of local officials was sought in certain communities "where it is the best part of prudence in order to get a program going."[19]

In 1967 Congress curtailed the autonomy the Economic Opportunity Act had originally conferred on the CAA's. With Adam Clayton Powell removed as chairman of the House Education and Labor Committee, House Democrats were free to explore means of saving the embattled poverty program by making it more palatable to hostile politicians. The vehicle was the so-called Green amendment (its original sponsor was Representative Edith Green of Oregon), which redefined the CAA concept. This amendment, voted by the House and accepted somewhat reluctantly by the Senate, required that CAA's be designated by state or local governments. The CAA itself might be an agency of the state or local government, or a nonprofit (public or private) agency designated by them. In the event that a state or local government failed to create or designate a CAA, or failed to submit or support a satisfactory CAA, the OEO director was authorized to select a nonprofit organization as the CAA. Whatever the character of the CAA, it was required to have a governing board not exceeding 51 members and divided equally among three groups: public officials, democratically selected representatives of the poverty areas, and representatives of business, labor, civic, and charitable groups (Sections 210 and 211 of the 1967 Act).

The Green provision was attacked as the "bosses and boll weevil amendment" because it neutralized opposition to OEO among southern and big-city Democrats, and it became a major factor in the 1967 extension of EOA. Clearly, the amendment does violence to the original CAA concept. Yet at least two things may be said in behalf of the change. First, in the long run, it is probably desirable for CAA's to draw closer to local governments. Second, the CAA role as lobbyist for social change, while undoubtedly impaired, is nonetheless not precluded under the newer arrangement.

OEO's interpretation of the Green amendment and the guidelines for its implementation[20] drew attacks from diverse groups, including the U.S. Conference of Mayors, the National Association of Counties, the Citizens' Crusade Against Poverty, and many others. Even Mrs. Green was reported to have expressed dissatisfaction with OEO's guidelines, charging that the agency had misinterpreted the spirit of her amendment and watered down the responsibility of elected officials for administering CAA's. She claimed that OEO was conducting "business as usual."[21] OEO spokesmen, recognizing "the wealth of problems" inherent in the Green amendment, anticipated "small wars among political jurisdictions. . . . The big issue will be which politicians grab control."[22]

The Green amendment may have been a tempest in a teapot. While it helped save OEO during the critical 1967 debate on the extension of the legislation, later developments seemed to indicate that the presumed irreconcilable friction between city halls or courthouses and CAA's existed more in flamboyant newspaper stories than in the communities. Within eight months after the Green amendment became law, 792 of the 1,018 affected state, county, or city governments took action on designating local antipoverty agencies, and 96.7 percent elected to continue the existing CAA's without change.

Staff Support

Because of its publicized claims to the position of command post for the nation's scattered poverty programs, OEO is likely to be judged ultimately not only upon its performance of operating functions but also upon its performance of supporting, or staff, functions: coordination, planning, evaluation, research, and generating interest in poverty problems. In the realm of coordination, OEO has responded by creating two unique administrative organs: the Office of Governmental Relations, which has already been alluded to, and the Office of National Councils and Organizations, which is designed to handle the agency's relations with the "outside world." The latter will bear examination later in a different context. OEO has also developed some fresh approaches to the problems of research and evaluation that merit consideration at this point.

Planning and Research

OEO's Office of Research, Plans, Programs, and Evaluation (RPPE) is charged with the long-range responsibilities implied by its title. Joseph A. Kershaw, the Williams College provost who first headed this office, described it as "a RAND Corporation in the poverty program . . . a facility to study the long-range problems of poverty in a basic, as opposed to an operational, sense." This ambitious job description was in keeping with the "cost effectiveness" concept, first introduced on a large scale in the Department of Defense and later spread throughout the federal establishment. The research staff under Kershaw, and later under Robert A. Levine, took the leadership among federal agencies in applying systems analysis techniques to welfare efforts. Drawing on the vast supply of pertinent statistics, the RPPE staff classified and quantified the various subuniverses of the poverty population, analyzed the applicability of existing welfare programs to these groups, and prepared complementary and alternative plans for combating poverty.

Regrettably, the findings of RPPE remain largely in the files of the "Poverty House" (as OEO's headquarters is known), though some have been transmitted to the Bureau of the Budget. Since the work was part of the regular five-year planning cycle in which government agencies engaged, it was withheld from the public under the cloak of "executive privilege." During the course of the 1967 hearings on the Economic Opportunity Act, Senator Joseph S. Clark, chairman of the Senate Subcommitte on Employment, Manpower, and Poverty, tried unsuccessfully to obtain the products of OEO's planning. The following exchange took place:

> Senator Clark. . . . I think there must be something definitive in this record which would show any overall plan or any overall strategy as to how you would hope by 1976 to win this war against poverty. . . . This phobia with executive secrecy is doing the poverty program no good on the Hill. . . . We on this subcommittee are entitled to know as a matter of right what your overall plan and strategy is for winning the war on poverty. . . .
> Mr. Shriver. Mr. Chairman, if we give something to the Bureau of the Budget, that is no longer our document. It is their document, not ours.
> Senator Clark. Let's be candid about that. You keep carbon copies.
> Mr. Shriver. Yes, but that is not our document. When I send you a letter, when you receive it, it's your property. There is a copy of our letter, and I don't release it.
> Senator Clark. Would that that were the general rule in politics. [Laughter.]
> Mr. Shriver. That is the general rule at OEO.[23]

Public information about significant RPPE work is limited to a few sketchy newspaper reports—the result of leaks, either inadvertent or contrived. Neither Congress nor the public, therefore, may ever have an opportunity to assess OEO's proposed programs from the vantage point of OEO's own research findings. The Freedom of Information Act of 1966 was of little help since RPPE claimed that its work was not covered by the legislation.

Although RPPE's basic function was planning strategies to combat poverty, it became involved in more mundane matters. The office underwent three distinct phases of emphasis during its first four years of operation. During OEO's first few months, RPPE activities were largely confined to developing the agency's budget for fiscal 1966. In doing so, it filled a vacuum produced by OEO's lack of regular staff for budgeting. This activity also reflected the interest of the acting director, Leon Gilgoff, who had served as associate budget director for the U.S. Air Force before joining OEO. When Kershaw took over in June 1965, he emphasized long-range planning and divorced RPPE from operational responsibilities. In these early stages of OEO, RPPE took seriously the mandate of planning a "total war on poverty," assuming that there would be steeply increasing resources for waging the war. Despite the escalation of the other war in Vietnam, Kershaw continued to develop his plans; and as late as the summer of 1966 Shriver anticipated that poverty could be eliminated by 1976, the 200th anniversary of the Declaration of Independence. His prediction was based upon RPPE estimates that the job could be done "merely" by doubling the total federal outlay for antipoverty efforts. By the time Kershaw left, fourteen months after he assumed office, it had become clear that the domestic war would have to be delayed. Instead of expanding antipoverty programs, OEO was fighting for its very life in 1967. In this atmosphere there was no need to refine its grandiose planning, and RPPE shifted its concern to operational research and planning for the immediate programs within its narrow budgetary constraints. The grand designs of 1965 and 1966 were kept in the files, awaiting more propitious times. Regrettably, RPPE placed little emphasis upon its mandate to evaluate ongoing EOA programs, and its work in this area never advanced beyond the design of studies or self-serving assessments.

In addition to in-house research, RPPE's mission included basic research into the dimensions of poverty and existing programs to combat it. Under an early contract, a research institute prepared a catalog of existing federal poverty programs. RPPE also helped design evaluations of the programs and projects initiated under the Economic Opportunity Act. For example, several universities were given funds to evaluate in depth CAA programs in their immediate vicinities. Possibly the most significant project undertaken by RPPE was funding an Institute for Poverty Research at the University of Wisconsin to undertake "fundamental and applied research into poverty." In this case, RPPE played a "seeding" function by financing the institute during its formative years, with the university accepting responsibility for continuing the effort after OEO support expired.

Another significant RPPE-funded project, which reflected the widespread interest in income maintenance schemes, provided for a field study to investigate the impact of graduated work-incentive payments upon the lives of the poor. The $4 million demonstration project provided a three-year study of a sample of 1,000 urban families, including some who would receive income support, and a control group to whom payments would not be made. The project, Robert A. Levine anticipated, would shed light upon the feasibility of "providing income support for those normally excluded from welfare, . . . the working poor."[24] The experiment was conducted in six New Jersey cities by a private research firm.

Information Center

As originally conceived, RPPE's mission included development of OEO's operational statistics and the broader task of compiling data on the distribution of all federal antipoverty programs and expenditures. In the fall of 1965, these functions were separated from RPPE and placed in a new Information Center. In the rhetoric of OEO, this center was described as "the national center room for the war on poverty." A number of factors contributed to its creation. Gilgoff, who was *de facto* director of RPPE before Kershaw assumed office and who had gained the status of a major adviser to Shriver, was awarded responsibility for a separate office. Kershaw, who preferred to concentrate on long-range planning, welcomed the opportunity to divest himself of day-to-day operational responsibilities. There was also a substantive rationalization for the separation of the two offices: it was felt that operating agencies might be reluctant to have operational data in the hands of RPPE, whose function was to review and evaluate their programs. However, because RPPE had access to reports filed with the Information Center, there was little substance to this justification for establishing a separate information office.

A major achievement of the Information Center was development of the Federal Information Exchange System, which included catalogs of federal antipoverty programs, community profiles, and federal expenditures by county and by type of classification, particularly concentrating on poverty programs. Such a need might appropriately have been met by the Bureau of the Budget, but that agency took no steps to perform the function. As head of the Information Center, Gilgoff stressed development of this information as part of OEO's interest in over-all federal antipoverty efforts. Though he set up the system for the development of these data, he died before the project was completed.

The Information Center was less successful in the more immediate task of gathering, collating, and disseminating current information about EOA programs. In part this was due to its overambitious plans for developing a complete "systems approach to EOA efforts." The center might have succeeded had it settled for traditional statistical data relating to the characteristics of the persons served by the several programs, allocation and distribution of project funding, follow-up on program participants, and related questions. Some officials wanted data that would provide longitudinal measures for the effectiveness of EOA programs. When Head Start was initiated, for example, there were some who advocated a follow-up on Head Start participants to permit measurement of the impact of the program. Since more than half a million children were enrolled during the first summer of the program, it was quite evident that the task was beyond the capacity of the center's limited resources. Several months elapsed before OEO gave up on this effort, but meanwhile precious time and resources were wasted.

Lack of effective communication and cooperation from OEO operating agencies and the administrators of delegate programs was an equally serious obstacle to the development of operational data. Not surprisingly, program administrators insisted upon maintaining their own operational statistics and were not cooperative in feeding the necessary data to the Information Center's computers. The Job Corps developed its own statistics independently. CAP experienced a different set of problems. Most of the newly organized CAA's placed low priority on the collection of data and failed to report on program operations, except to the extent required by law in accounting for their expenditures. In addition, a major portion of CAA funds was assigned to delegate agencies, many of which were neither accustomed nor inclined to submit operational reports to the CAA's. Head Start projects, which were administered mostly by local school systems, offered an excellent illustration.

The work experience and training administrators in HEW's Welfare Administration faced yet another set of obstacles. Accustomed to making grants to states and delegating the responsibility for the administration of programs to state officials, they were not very successful in getting projects or persuading the welfare agencies to cooperate in regular and complete reporting of their activities. The Neighborhood Youth Corps did not develop a satisfactory reporting system during its first four years and therefore had little data to feed to the Information Center. Friction developed early between the Neighborhood Youth Corps and the Information Center, each agency maintaining that the other was responsible for developing the data. By the summer of 1967, NYC had set up its own information system which was independent of the Information Center.

Underlying all the difficulties was a failure to develop, much less agree upon, program goals that were prerequisites to the development of the planning, programming, and budgeting systems concept. In the absence of clearly set goals, technicians found it difficult to design measurements of program achievements.

Office of Inspection

The seemingly thankless task of checking complaints and halting incipient scandals is handled by OEO's Office of Inspection. Such an office appeared to be worthwhile political insurance with programs as fraught with potential controversy as those handled by OEO, and this reasoning undoubtedly led Shriver to borrow the concept he had originally developed in the Peace Corps. William F. Haddad, who as first head of this division had the military title of Inspector General, described his activities as an "early warning system." Because Haddad and his staff of investigators had authority to investigate any EOA project at any time, other OEO officials soon labeled it the "fink shop."

Of the various complaints that pour into OEO offices, many are baseless, a few are not. In either case, investigation is needed to determine the facts. First, an examination must be made to ascertain whether there are any grounds for the complaint. If preliminary checking indicates that field study would be advisable, an investigator, perhaps a former news reporter or an investigative lawyer, may be sent to the scene.[25] In view of the nature of this function, it is hardly surprising that many OEO operating officials grew to resent such "snooping." Since Haddad reported directly to Shriver, other administrators often were unaware of his forays until they actually took place. As a former OEO official lamented, "I had operating responsibilities, but Haddad had the power to stir up everyone." Partly as the result of opposition both outside and inside OEO, Haddad left his job in late 1965. The title Inspector General was dropped, and Edgar May, a Pulitzer Prize-winning newspaperman and author of a popular book on poverty,[26] was appointed to the job.

Under May's leadership the Office of Inspection began to function as a confidential reporting service for OEO officials. "This office should neither be seen nor heard, except by the people responsible for the programs," May explained. "I see this not as a spy operation, but as a continuing service to the operating officials." Aware of the earlier criticism, May was careful to check with OEO operating officials and regional directors before initiating investigations. In addition, his findings were reported to the OEO director only after they had been submitted to the responsible official. In part as a result of this change of style, the Office of Inspection had an increasing number of requests for studies from officials within OEO.

No doubt the Office of Inspection was a fortunate addition to OEO. Much has been said about the "scandal-prone" character of OEO programs, and indeed there are many reasons why the antipoverty programs should be expected to receive controversial press treatment. In this perspective, the really impressive fact about OEO programs was how *few* damaging scandals actually resulted.[27]

The Search for Personnel

The recruitment of competent personnel is a crucial task for any agency, and especially for one that is starting its work *de novo*. Unlike many new agencies, OEO had no organizational base in the federal government except for the hastily created Shriver task force. In the summer and fall of 1964, therefore, the recruitment problem was a challenge and a peril for OEO: if a capable, enthusiastic, and creative staff could be put together, it might be able to shape the new agency's mission unencumbered by notions left over from previous organizations. Without a staff of such quality, however, the new agency could flounder badly, no matter how promising its mission might be.

A new agency needs several distinct types of personnel to operate effectively. Most important, it must have administrators who are capable of taking an expansive view of the agency's mission while maintaining its political relations with the White House, Capitol Hill, and other federal agencies. Second, it must have technical specialists who are familiar with the policy problems with which the agency is concerned and who are able to supply information and insights in implementing these policies. Third, every agency has need of "old government hands"—people who are at home in the bureaucratic environment of Washington and familiar with the traditional relationships between the executive and legislative branches and among the federal bureaus and agencies. Finally, and not least important, capable clerical and supportive personnel must be found, a considerable task even for established agencies.

This personnel problem was formidable enough, but OEO faced an unfavorable manpower situation as well. The paradoxical task of launching an antipoverty effort in a time of booming economy meant that potential poverty warriors were in short supply. A tight market prevailed, especially for skilled professional and clerical workers. Moreover, the "poverty profession," if it could be called that, was not an established calling in 1964. Since no one had ever attempted a coordinated attack on poverty, it was not clear exactly what skills would be necessary or where they could be found. The conventional professions—social work especially, but also sociology, economics, public administration, and political science—were obviously relevant, but personnel in these fields were already in short supply. And since many OEO planners apparently believed that professionals in these fields had already failed in dealing with poverty, it was not a settled opinion whether these professions had anything to offer the new enterprise.

As with many of its administrative policies, OEO's approach to personnel, at least at the top level, was highly colored by the views of Shriver, its first director. His experience, both in and out of government, had provided him with two distinctive and related beliefs about personnel: a faith in the "inspired amateur" and a consequent acceptance of frequent rotation among high-level personnel.

Shriver himself was something of an amateur in government. Before he arrived in Washington in 1961 to organize the Peace Corps, Shriver had had broad experience in the fields of business and education. In planning the Peace Corps, he utilized a barnstorming task force composed of educators, businessmen, labor leaders, churchmen, and others. Shriver, who often recalled that most experts in foreign affairs were distrustful of the Peace Corps idea, noted: "The world is better off because the amateurs, those who had faith and trust in mankind, did not listen to the experts, who had lost both."[28] The Peace Corps experience demonstrated to Shriver that intelligent and concerned amateurs could succeed where experts had failed—by demonstrating their interest, getting close to the people with whom they were dealing, and applying common sense.

Shriver took an identical approach to OEO. Of course, he could not delude himself with the assumption that no one had ever fought poverty before, any more than he could have believed that no one had tried foreign aid prior to the Peace Corps. But his enthusiasm sometimes gave this impression. Again and again during his first year as OEO's director, Shriver stressed the revolutionary characteristics of the war on poverty. Radical changes in structures and techniques, he repeated, would be required to succeed in this "new enterprise." A variety of experts and skilled technicians must bring their insights to bear on the problem, but no group or profession had a monopoly of information. Such talk of a "new personnel" was not calculated to please social workers who felt that they had been fighting poverty for many years, and the theme was repeated in too many speeches to be dismissed as anything less than a deep-seated disdain for the so-called professionals. To be sure, it was not long before Shriver had to concede that he could not combat poverty without the professionals, but his basic faith in the creativity, combined skills, and simple humanity of the "inspired amateur" was not diminished.

The extremely fluid group known as the "Shriver task force" did not go out of business once the Administration's draft bill was completed in March 1964. It continued to work throughout the spring and summer, attempting to plan the structure and procedures to be used by OEO once the agency was created. The group also helped to sell the bill on Capitol Hill and was able to provide House and Senate committees with technical advice. Many in this group remained with OEO.

Businessmen, as a special species of "inspired amateurs," were especially attractive to Shriver. His affinity for businessmen seemed to be a composite of several considerations. For example, he seemed to believe that a high salary was a rough indicator of a man's worth. If men on whom the business world had conferred a high price could be induced to join OEO at a considerable financial sacrifice, this fact might convince skeptics of the "soundness" of the antipoverty efforts. Thus Shriver often appeared to recruit with an eye to the press release that could be issued on the man's appointment. Persons from other professions, where pay scales were not as high, were in his viewpoint less attractive since their tour of government duty would not represent as great a financial sacrifice.

Measured by these standards, many of the men brought in by Shriver were impressive "catches." In some cases, however, men were induced to leave their jobs and join OEO when there were no specific functions for them to perform. A former Shriver associate told of the plight of one such man, a successful businessman lured to Washington by the prospect of fighting poverty at Shriver's side. When the businessman showed up at OEO, a subordinate official had to call Shriver to ascertain what job the man was to perform. "Oh, I don't know," Shriver replied. "Why don't you set up a series of interviews so he can go around and see people?" According to several OEO officials, this was not an isolated incident.

If personnel were to be recruited broadly from the ranks of private life, it followed that they had to be accepted for short-term assignments. There were several reasons for this. First, if they were successful in their professions, it was unlikely that they would be willing to endure the financial sacrifice of government service for an extended period of time. Second, their employers were often eager to get them back. Finally, if not settled in careers, they tended to be restless and eager to shift to a new venture once the initial excitement of the poverty war had worn off.

Shriver, however, seemed to consider such turnover a positive blessing. In his view, turnover—within limits—was beneficial to an organization. The possible dangers of discontinuity in policy were more than outweighed by the constant infusion of new ideas. Thus a really good man could enter the agency, make his contribution, and depart, leaving the agency better for it.

Whatever benefits could be claimed for its high turnover, OEO paid heavily to obtain such personnel. Turnover was most functional during the period of the Shriver task force and during the first few months of OEO's existence. There were no precedents, and the need was for fresh ideas and creative planning. But as soon as the agency turned to implementing its programs, the inspired amateur often proved inept. OEO's coordinating functions, for example, demanded personnel who could promise a degree of continuity. Familiarity with governmental procedures, as well as time to master intricate problems and establish rapport with counterparts in other agencies, were qualities badly needed by the OEO staff and were not always forthcoming. Also, continuity was desirable in OEO's relations with clienteles in the field, especially the local CAA's. Officers of local CAA's sometimes complained that they had started to negotiate with a particular OEO official in developing a project idea but by the time the project was submitted for funding, the official was no longer on the scene. Particularly as the agency grew and developed its own precedents, new employees, no matter how bright and capable, required months to learn the ropes. Often they left the agency just as they began to be most useful to it, a phenomenon that may have contributed to their own education but at some cost to OEO.

Lack of continuity was particularly damaging in the post of deputy director, the official responsible for OEO's internal administration. Indeed, the position did not acquire continuity until the appointment of Bertrand M. Harding, an able federal administrator who came to OEO in June 1966 and later succeeded Shriver as head of the agency. A variety of other factors may also have been responsible for the rapid turnover of deputies and the periods of vacancy in their office, but the point is that an essential continuity was lacking in a critical position.

In one important instance an early political decision deprived OEO of a man who was reputed to be a highly talented administrator. Adam Yarmolinsky, who was on loan from the Office of the Secretary of Defense, had served as operating head of the Shriver task force and was slated to be named OEO's deputy director. Yarmolinsky was anathema to many southern Congressmen, for as special assistant to Defense Secretary Robert McNamara he had helped to draw up a 1963 directive aimed at halting off-base discrimination against Negro servicemen stationed in the South. The Administration felt it needed southern votes for passage of the Act, and a number of powerful southerners pressed Shriver to sacrifice Yarmolinsky. So Shriver gave the word, enabling floor manager Phil Landrum to announce on the floor of the House: "I have been told on the highest authority that not only will he not be appointed, but that he will not be considered if he is recommended for a place in this agency."[29] It seemed a necessary concession at the moment, but it left a vacancy in the OEO hierarchy that was not filled until seven months after the Act was signed. In April 1965, Jack Conway, the highly respected director of the AFL–CIO's Industrial Union Department, was chosen for the job that Yarmolinsky would have held. In the intervening months, the vacancy in this key position may have been responsible for some of OEO's operating difficulties.

The delay in appointing a deputy director was especially damaging because, during OEO's first year and a half, Shriver retained his earlier job as director of the Peace Corps. Shriver, who maintained offices (linked by a "hot line" phone) in both agencies, attempted to shuttle between them and allocate his time between the two operations. Although in this initial period Shriver was popular on Capitol Hill, there was recurrent congressional criticism of the dual arrangement. Senator Winston Prouty of Vermont, for example, complained that "the poverty army is led by a part-time general."[30] Shriver's response to the criticism was that the decision lay with the President. "Both positions are Presidential appointments," he told one reporter. "It's his responsibility to decide whether the jobs are being done."[31] Finally, in early 1966, the President appointed a new director of the Peace Corps to succeed Shriver.

OEO's top leadership was drawn from a variety of sources. Many were experienced federal bureaucrats; others came from business, education, state and municipal government, journalism, social work, and the labor movement. The sources of OEO's "supergrade" personnel (the top three grades of the federal civil service) and executive appointments—as of November 1967—are shown in Table 2–1. As can be seen, a solid majority of OEO's leaders had been recruited from the federal government, either from other executive agencies or from the legislative branch. There is reason to believe, however, that these figures somewhat overstate OEO's reliance upon nonfederal personnel during its first three years. By the time these figures were compiled, many of OEO's original officers had returned to private life and been replaced from the ranks of governmental personnel. As the agency matured, it probably tended to recruit more of its top personnel from within the federal establishment. Among these personnel, too, a change in OEO's practices apparently occurred during the three-year period. To replace the original wave of "outsiders," OEO at first turned to proven administrators from other federal agencies; later the agency tended to promote from within its own ranks.

Table 2–1. Source of OEO Top Officials, November 1967

Total	51
Federal government	31
Business	9[a]
Local or state government	6[a]
Education	4
Other	2

[a] One individual appears in both these categories.
Source: Office of Economic Opportunity.

As would be expected, turnover was high during OEO's first four years; its separation rates during this period never dipped below 50 percent, and for two of these years they hovered around 60 percent. It is true that these percentages tend to exaggerate the turnover of OEO personnel: they include all employees and terminations for all reasons. They also reflect OEO's extensive use of part-time and full-time consultants during most of the period. (As of June 30, 1965, its temporary staff constituted 9 percent of the total.) Nonetheless, the figures give some indication of the instability of OEO's personnel.

In OEO's highest positions, turnover was particularly high. Of the twenty-four top posts in OEO, all but three had experienced turnover by mid-1968, and some jobs had had three or four incumbents. Of the three positions that had not turned over, two were created long after the agency itself. Thus only Donald M. Baker, the general counsel, had been in his post from the inception of OEO. Nor do these figures give the full story, for in many instances jobs were vacant for extended periods of time or were in the hands of acting directors.

OEO's rate of turnover occasioned considerable comment. Frequent newspaper articles, no doubt based on fragmentary or exaggerated impressions, pointed to the number of staff vacancies and implied that OEO was on the brink of disaster.

OEO's personnel problems were compounded by legislative and administrative ceilings on personnel. By the summer of 1965, OEO was becoming cramped by the ceiling because of the growing staff demands of Job Corps conservation centers and the planned strengthening of OEO's regional offices. OEO had to live with the ceilings upon its personnel, exclusive of the Job Corps conservation center workers. These levels were set by the basic legislation (for fiscal 1965)[32] and then by Budget Bureau directives (for subsequent fiscal years). Table 2-2 presents the actual "on board" staffing for each year as of June 30. The figures demonstrate OEO's tendency to rely heavily, until fiscal 1968, upon temporary personnel, including consultants and part-time personnel. Although the personnel ceiling for the initial year

Table 2-2. OEO Staffing Levels, Fiscal 1965–68

Fiscal Year (June 30)	Total	Permanent	Temporary
1965	1,259	1,150	109
1966	2,908	2,093	815
1967	3,015	2,565	450
1968	3,216	3,106	110

Source: Office of Economic Opportunity.

of OEO's operations was not constraining, subsequent ceilings soon became so as OEO expanded its operation for implementing its various programs. To circumvent the personnel ceiling as it related to both quality and pay level, OEO resorted to contracting some of its functions. Work performed under contract was not subject to ceiling restrictions. According to the textbooks Congress may dispose, but bureaucrats frequently have the last word.

One final aspect of the personnel question needs to be mentioned. Critics of the poverty program regularly charged that OEO was hiring too many high-priced personnel. In 1965 Republicans on the Senate Labor and Public Welfare Committee, for example, pointed out that one of every 18 OEO employees was of "supergrade" status, a figure that compared favorably with most other federal agencies.[33] By mid-1968, however, this ratio had declined to one in every 54. On other occasions critics produced figures or lists purporting to show the high salaries paid the poverty warriors.[34] Finally, it was charged that the salary schedules of CAA's were unduly high, often considerably above those of local or state officials who performed similar functions. In 1966 Congress reacted to the "getting-rich-by-fighting-poverty" charges by limiting federal contributions to local community employees to a maximum $15,000 a year. Local funds had to be used to pay salaries above that amount and could not be counted as part of the 10 percent local contribution. This amendment was one of Congressman Powell's contributions to the war on poverty.

Without defending each and every personnel decision made by OEO, it must be observed that this was not one of the more provocative charges made against the agency. It is true that OEO had no shortage of supergrades on its payroll and that CAA salaries were often generous (though hardly extravagant), but several features of OEO's personnel needs must be reiterated. First, a ready labor force of poverty warriors simply did not exist at the time OEO was setting up shop. Second, the skills most relevant to the war on poverty were already in short supply. Finally, it would be misleading to compare OEO's proportion of high-grade personnel with that of other agencies. As a coordinative and administrative agency, OEO would be expected to have a larger proportion of high-level personnel than an agency— the Post Office or Defense Department, for example—that includes large numbers of relatively low-paid operatives.

The tight labor market for such personnel as the antipoverty programs demanded also accounts for some imbalances at the local level, though it is relevant to note that salaries for local and state personnel involved in the poverty program (in community action agencies, for example) are set in the first instance by the localities themselves and not by OEO. And if there are imbalances in comparison to local and state civil service rates, this does not necessarily mean that the poverty program's salaries are out of line. It is quite likely, in fact, that the program would be utterly unable to obtain qualified personnel if it were tied to local civil service rates.[35]

OEO and the Several Establishments

Few agencies have as wide and varied contacts with public and private interests as the Office of Economic Opportunity. In addition to dealing with agencies at all levels of government, OEO engages many private or quasi-private interests, lobbies, and professional and civic organizations. These multiple relationships, which emanate from the agency's programs and from the Economic Opportunity Act itself, have been alluded to previously. It remains, however, to detail the institutional devices OEO has developed to maintain these relationships.

Church-State Relations

Those who drafted the Economic Opportunity Act foresaw the difficulties of defining the role of sectarian institutions; in fact this was one of the most thoroughly discussed issues during congressional consideration of the war on poverty. For the Shriver task force, the basic policy constraint was the Kennedy Administration's position on church-state relations, embodied in a 1961 memorandum from the general counsel of the Department of Health, Education, and Welfare and growing out of the long-standing controversies over federal aid to education. The memorandum held that *general* aid to sectarian institutions was unconstitutional because, as with elementary and secondary schools, it would be impossible to separate sectarian and nonsectarian activities. Federal programs should therefore be administered by public agencies but they must be open to students from parochial schools.

Working in cooperation with HEW officials who were knowledgeable about the school issue, the Shriver task force's drafting team adopted this "shared time" concept for Title II of the Administration's bill. After intensive negotiations, Congressmen and Shriver's staff reached an acceptable compromise that provided for "special remedial noncurricular" programs which could be administered either by public or private schools.[36] Fortunately, as it turned out (a task force charged with defining "special remedial non-curricular aid" soon became hopelessly bogged down), this provision was deleted in the final version of the Act. The final wording in Title II was entirely open-ended about the recipients of aid, merely requiring that "no grant or contract . . .

may provide for general aid to elementary or secondary education in any school or school system" (Section 205[b]).

The church-state issue was somewhat more easily dealt with when, as in the work-study programs of Title I, institutions of higher education were involved. Under the Senate amendment that found its way into the final version of the Act,[37] there was no prohibition against grants to sectarian colleges and universities. However, student work projects under the program could not involve the "construction, operation, or maintenance of so much of any facility as is used or is to be used for sectarian instruction or as a place for religious worship."[38]

OEO's officials soon evolved a complicated set of guidelines for controlling church participation. Their caution, however, did not prevent several outside groups, including the New York Civil Liberties Union and the American Jewish Congress, from questioning whether the restrictions were sufficient or whether they were being effectively administered. A single lawsuit, challenging the constitutionality of church participation in Head Start projects in Kansas City, Missouri, was filed but later withdrawn.[39]

In general, the churches have had a growing, and largely happy, relationship with the antipoverty program; criticism of the type just mentioned has been exceedingly rare. And for their part, the churches have increasingly broadened their sense of mission in such social issues as poverty (not to mention civil rights). Church-related groups have been active participants in such programs as Head Start, Neighborhood Youth Corps, and Title III migrant labor programs. Antipoverty programs have been granted extensive and sympathetic coverage by many religious publications. In early 1966, leaders from the Protestant, Catholic, and Jewish faiths formed the Interreligious Committee Against Poverty. "Our opposition to involuntary and unnecessary poverty," the group announced, "is deeply rooted in theological convictions which are shared by our three religious communities."[40] This group was able to provide liaison among religious social action organizations and between these organizations and OEO. Many of the religious leaders associated with these bodies were also found on the rolls of such organizations as the Citizens' Crusade Against Poverty.

The Welfare Professionals

At first, Shriver and some of his associates conceived OEO as independent of the "welfare professionals" who had traditionally dealt with the needy and the unskilled—educators, training specialists, and social workers. OEO spokesmen charged that the traditional welfare programs had stagnated in the hands of the professional associations and state agencies that controlled them. Moreover, these groups were accused of having "captured" the welfare bureaus in the Department of Health, Education, and Welfare. Consistent with this attitude toward the professionals, the poverty warriors at first seemed to want to strike out on their own. Their independence was stressed repeatedly in speeches that called for new blood in the administration of welfare services.[41]

Realistically, this kind of hostility could not continue. Whether OEO liked it or not, the existing organizational and personnel resources were firmly in the hands of the so-called professionals. Of necessity, OEO found that many of its dollars were going to the same interests that had been administering the more traditional programs. Who, for example, was to implement Head Start or in-school Neighborhood Youth Corps? In most cases the only available resources lay in the hands of the local school boards, and it was they who contracted with CAA's to do the job. As in its relationships with local governments, OEO inevitably found that it could not live without the professionals.

OEO soon created an unofficial work group to facilitate liaison with the welfare professionals. The official peace overture, however, came in December 1965 in a speech by Shriver to 2,000 social workers at the biennial conference of the American Public Welfare Association in Chicago. Declaring that OEO had "new weapons" against poverty, Shriver said: "We want you to use them. We want your help."[42] Terming himself only a "recruit" in the antipoverty field who was making his appeal "humbly," Shriver sought to placate the social workers by calling for higher salaries and more welfare spending generally.

OEO's change of direction was largely a matter of attitude and rhetoric. In reality, it had dealt with the welfare professionals from the very beginning, but as one OEO official expressed it, the agency's "early actions were sometimes combative." Feeling that these traditional groups had failed the poor, OEO officials apparently believed they could teach these groups to do the job properly. The same officials would subsequently argue that the later "soft-line" policy represented no fundamental change of thinking. What had been done earlier, they maintained, had been done merely to stimulate the social-work fraternity into greater awareness of the problems of poverty and to reveal the limitations of earlier approaches. Whether OEO succeeded in this intended role is certainly open to question. What is beyond question, however, is that OEO unnecessarily antagonized the welfare profession, and it soon realized that the cooperation of this group was essential to OEO.

Business and Labor Groups

One of the most intriguing aspects of OEO has surely been its acceptance by a significant portion of the business community. The long-standing coolness of businessmen toward federal welfare programs did not necessarily apply to the EOA programs; on the contrary, many have been eager to respond to Shriver's appeals and to enlist in the effort.[43] As David K. Carlisle of Litton Industries, an active and early contractor in the program, explained it: "We got into the poverty war for two reasons. One was the opportunity to serve the community. The other, the business opportunity."[44]

To be sure, businessmen had always donated their time and money to charitable endeavors, but businessmen in the 1960's were interested in social problems as never before.[45] Frederick R. Kappel, board chairman of American Telephone and Telegraph Company, reminded businessmen that the "social responsibilities of business are increasing." The civil rights movement and the anguish of summer riots in major cities were pointed reminders that poverty and discrimination had contributed to the racial crisis, and businessmen drew the obvious conclusion that they must grapple with these problems if civil disorder and riots were not to shake the very foundations of the society. Participation in antipoverty programs, creation of special job and training programs, and membership in the Urban Coalition (formed in 1967) were manifestations of business concern over the social issues of race and poverty.

Hard economic facts also argued for business participation in the poverty program at the inception of OEO. Before the Vietnam war escalation in the summer of 1965, many businessmen were concerned about actual or anticipated reductions in federal defense and space program spending. The problem of adjusting from "guns to butter" weighed especially heavily upon the large defense contractors who had extensive resources tied up in government contracting activities and who could not easily adjust these to a consumer market. One solution would be to diversify some manufacturing to services, the growth industries of the future; and among the service industries, education and training offered the most promising opportunities. Such a shift would not be as far-fetched as it may have sounded because management believed that many of the "systems" concepts developed in the production of hardware could also be applied to human resources. Contracts from OEO for specialized educational tasks, let on a cost-plus-fixed-fee basis, would offer a risk-free opportunity for business to "get in on the ground floor," experiment with new techniques, and develop the expertise needed to exploit this market.[46] The secondary motivations for business involvement no doubt included the desire to make a useful contribution to society and the realization that business must respond if its own long-term needs for skilled manpower were to be met.

The Job Corps offered a particularly useful vehicle for this business involvement. It was John Rubel, vice president of Litton Industries, who first suggested to Shriver that private industries might run the Job Corps training centers. As a direct result, Title I was written to authorize OEO's director to contract with "any federal, state, or local agency or *private organization* for the establishment and operation of rural or urban Job Corps centers" (Section 103[a]) (italics added). The largest share of funds for urban Job Corps centers went to private industries. Contracts were awarded to such firms as the Burroughs Corporation, General Electric, Ford-Philco Corporation, International Telephone and Telegraph, International Business Machines, Litton Industries, and Packard-Bell Electronics Corporation. Many other firms received or applied for contracts.

The business-government partnership may well turn out to be profitable for all concerned. To be sure, the profits cannot be measured in monetary terms. "Most of the companies aren't in this just for money," Milton Fogelman, OEO's contract negotiator, explained. "This is not a staggeringly profitable business," agreed Robert Chasen, president of Federal Electric Corporation, an IT&T subsidiary which had the contract for the Kilmer Job Corps Center. But to have the federal government underwrite a firm's experimentation in a promising field (and on a cost-plus-fixed-fee basis) is an attractive proposition.

Not quite all of OEO's activities were enthusiastically received by the business community. The traditional business opposition to welfare programs continued to express itself from time to time. Other complaints were more specific. Some businessmen, for example, complained that CAA's were sponsoring consumer education programs that adversely affected local retail merchants. In some cases, it was charged, "consumer advisors" directed consumers into or away from specific stores, propagated their own judgments as to what constituted "deceptive" packaging, and instigated such "massive mobilization" of the poor as boycotts or buyers' strikes.[47] It is entirely possible that local poverty workers sometimes attempted to give consumer advice when in fact they possessed little information beyond personal prejudices against local businesses. On the other hand, the impoverished have long been the victims not only of their own ignorance of buying practices but also of the manipulations of irresponsible businessmen. The poor desperately need guidance, and complaints about the type of advice they have thus far received only emphasize how little attention our consumer-oriented society has actually given to consumption practices.

The labor movement, as one of its publications declared, "has been enlisted in the war on poverty from the day the first union was organized."[48] Organized labor, an early supporter of the Economic Opportunity Act, has continued to give strong political support to OEO. In February 1967 the AFL–CIO executive council termed the Act "a vital part of the over-all effort to break the poverty cycle" and repudiated "attacks . . . aimed at crippling or destroying the entire program."[49] In early 1965, AFL–CIO President George Meany named Miles C. Stanley, the West Virginia AFL–CIO president, as a special aide to coordinate labor's participation in antipoverty programs. And Walter Reuther's United Auto Workers gave consistently strong support to the programs—including, in 1965, a $1 million grant to create the public organization called the Citizens' Crusade Against Poverty (CCAP).

At the local level, labor unions are frequent participants in CAA programs. In fact, CAP guidelines stress the point that local union officers, along with representatives of other interests, should be consulted in drawing up the community action plan. In some cases unions have become contractors for antipoverty programs. An engineers' union in Tennessee launched a Job Corps training program, for example, and a number of central labor councils have participated in NYC programs.[50] To serve as a link between organized labor and OEO, there is the National Labor Advisory Council, which was described by its OEO staff man as "a channel of communication that has provided some program results."

Labor's support has not been unequivocal, however. Some unions feared that jobs for nonunion workers might come at the expense of union members, a fear that was sustained by the demands of some CAA's that the poor be hired to rehabilitate slum areas. Nor were all unions equally active participants in local antipoverty programs. Shriver candidly told a national labor convention in December 1965 that "despite the leadership and the vision demonstrated by our own leaders, there has been a dragging of the feet at the local level." Reuther has been even more pointed and has laid some of the blame on the AFL–CIO leadership. In 1966 he charged that the AFL–CIO policy on social welfare and antipoverty questions demonstrated "insufficient commitment" and "a sense of complacency and adherence to the *status quo*."[51]

OEO and the Civil Rights Movement

Although the majority of poor people in the United States are white, the battle against poverty has become an adjunct to the battle for Negro equality. The ties are no less strong because those who drafted the Economic Opportunity Act of 1964 were unaware that they were drafting a civil rights law. In a thousand different ways, black citizens have become the special objects and beneficiaries of anti-poverty programs. While not confined to Negroes, economic deprivation is especially prevalent among this segment of our population, and is related to educational inequalities, job discrimination, and social and political injustices. Moreover, the first phase of the modern civil rights struggle, the fight for political and social rights, gave the Negro (especially in urban areas) an organizational base which was lacking among whites who were poor. For these and other reasons, Negroes received greater benefits from the antipoverty programs than their proportion in the poor population would have indicated. Indeed, it was possible to view the early OEO as a potential institutional base for the second phase of the civil rights movement—the achievement of more effective economic participation in our society.

In reality, however, OEO found itself caught between the civil rights militants and the white "establishment." At first, the views of civil rights militants were effectively represented by militants within the OEO organization. As time went on it became apparent that OEO would have to settle for something short of the militants' objectives; and within a year or so, many militants left OEO. The antipoverty programs came under increasing criticism from civil rights activists. Thus civil rights tensions were intimately tied to the political tensions OEO was experiencing with city halls and the social welfare establishment. As an NAACP official expressed the problem in mid-1965: "We must rescue the anti-poverty program from the social work profession and from the politicians who want merely a sterile and ineffective program that will mean little or nothing for the Negro community."[52] Such sentiments were shared by many militant activists, white and black, inside OEO and out. Nonetheless, most Negro organizations continued to play an active role in antipoverty programs. The National Urban League, for example, worked to recruit Job Corps enrollees, operated some NYC projects, and served as a delegate agency for CAA projects.

In local communities the ferment of the civil rights movement sometimes generated problems for OEO's relations with other outside interests. For instance, a minor controversy arose when it was discovered that a multimillion-dollar HARYOU-Act program was subsidizing a theater project known as the Black Arts Theatre, which was using some of the funds to stage antiwhite plays by Negro dramatist LeRoi Jones. The plays were offensive to many citizens, and Shriver himself referred to them as "vicious racism." But even such a controversial activity may have had some redeeming value. As OEO deputy director of public affairs James Kelleher remarked, "We'd rather see these kids fussing on the stage than on the streets."[53]

A similar flurry of criticism arose in the summer of 1967 when it was discovered that one of the items proposed in the summer package of a delegate agency of the Nashville, Tennessee, CAA called for a "liberation school."[54] In this case OEO ordered withdrawal of the funds that were to have been allocated for this part of the proposal.

Potentially more explosive was the National Center for Community Action Education, Inc., a group that was created to combine private and foundation funds with federal grants for a major assault on illiteracy. James Farmer, national director of the Congress of Racial Equality (CORE), resigned his position late in 1965 to take over the new organization. Farmer's presence suggested that the group would be concerned not only with adult basic education—its ostensible objective—but with political mobilization of the poor. The National Center, endorsed by every major civil rights group, soon applied for a grant of $860,000 from OEO to launch a pilot adult education program. OEO project reviewers and outside experts agreed that the program, which would have trained poor persons to teach others, was an "unconventional but promising venture."[55]

Farmer's program was never funded, however, because political pressures developed against it. A number of congressmen reportedly feared the political implications of a mass literacy drive, and they were no doubt backed up by local politicians. The crucial opponent of the program, however, was Adam Clayton Powell, then chairman of the House Education and Labor Committee. Though Powell never explained his position (a restraint unusual for Powell), OEO acquiesced to the pressures and killed the proposal in mid-1966, explaining only that "this proposal just hasn't made it up to this point."[56] The explanation lacked candor, however, for the proposal—submitted in August 1965—had apparently passed all OEO's reviewers and was so close to funding in late 1965 that news was leaked on its funding. Farmer, who had resigned his CORE job on the assumption that funding was imminent, charged OEO with "a colossal betrayal."[57] Although OEO officially denied that political pressures had killed the project, some officials informally confirmed the fact.

In other ways, and inevitably, OEO became involved in the ferment of the civil rights movement. In most cases OEO had the courage of its convictions in insisting that Negroes be included in its programs. The controversies over "maximum feasible participation," for example, often had racial overtones. Here OEO tended to be flexible without losing sight of its direction, which was full participation by black citizens in policy evolution and implementation.

OEO has taken to civil rights instinctively, but it is hard to say whether it fully recognizes the centrality of civil rights in its task. OEO may ultimately be evaluated more for its role in the political mobilization of disadvantaged citizens than for the number of dollars it puts into their pocketbooks. Civil rights groups have provided direction and purpose for OEO's tasks, and in many cases they have supplied the bulk of the skilled leadership. Whether OEO will be successful in meeting the demands of Negro groups is open to question and depends on a variety of factors, not the least of which are the resources available to the agency and the future role of local governments. And whether the poverty program can at the same time mobilize the non-Negroes among the poor depends on the insight and perspective of both the OEO and the Negro action groups.

The Care and Cultivation of Clienteles

From the inception of the antipoverty programs it was clearly understood that one of their major objectives was to mobilize private as well as public welfare activities. This goal emerged from the legislative history, from the wording of the Act itself, and from President Johnson's various messages on poverty. Thus OEO has paid particular attention to its "external affairs," and such activity is not entirely unique within the federal government. Many agencies employ advisory councils or committees that are composed of representatives of the groups served by the agencies' programs.

The bulk of OEO's formal relationships with nongovernmental organizations was handled by its Office of National Councils and Organizations (ONCO), headed during the first three years by Hyman Bookbinder. (Because of a recently popular television program, Bookbinder quickly earned the title, "The Man From ONCO.") Not an operating office, ONCO provided such service functions as information, liaison, and coordination with private groups. In addition, Bookbinder, a vigorous and accomplished speaker, served as one of OEO's most active spokesmen, spreading the OEO gospel with inimitable fervor and replying to countless criticisms of the agency. When Bookbinder left OEO, ONCO was merged with the Office of Governmental Relations.

The merged Office of Governmental Relations and National

Councils (OGRNC) also serves as secretariat for most of the advisory councils established by OEO. The first of these, the National Advisory Council on Economic Opportunity, is composed of nongovernmental individuals appointed by the President. For two years ONCO coordinated the group's activities, but a 1966 amendment made the group independent of OEO. The new chairman of the group (Shriver had served in this capacity until 1966) was Morris I. Liebman, a Chicago lawyer. The revamped council, all but three of whose members were new to the group, consisted of the usual sprinkling of lawyers, doctors, clergymen, politicians, and labor representatives, including (one each) a Negro, an Indian, an economist, and a woman. The council had a strong southern flavor, and the President authorized a small staff of investigators for it, presumably to help the council monitor OEO's activities. Thus far, the group has received minimal publicity and has given OEO no cause for worry. The only publication of the council during its first two years of existence was a review of the Community Action Program, which might just as well have been released by OEO's public relations office.[58]

In addition, OEO's director is empowered to create such advisory groups as he deems necessary (Section 602[c]) and by mid-1968 OEO had created five such groups. The first, chronologically, were the Business and Labor Advisory Councils, both served by OGRNC. A Public Officials Advisory Council, composed of 26 local government representatives, was created in the fall of 1965 as part of OEO's efforts to improve its contacts with local and state officials. Originally linked with ONCO, this group was later transferred to OEO's Office of Governmental Relations. In early 1966 a 28-member Community Representative Advisory Council was created. The title was a euphemism for "council of the poor" since the membership was composed of what one OEO official termed "articulate, independent, local CAA people who are also recognized as representatives of the poor." Two-thirds of the members were themselves poor, and about the same proportion were Negro. Frankly experimental, this group represented an effort by OEO to obtain direct responses from the representatives of the poor.[59] Though the group's role was to act strictly as a sounding board for OEO policies, officials conceded that it originated many thoughtful critiques. The establishment of a national council representing the poor received much public attention, but little was heard from the group during the following years. Finally, late in 1967, a Women's Advisory Council was created. The latter two groups are served by OGRNC.

OGRNC also deals, formally or otherwise, with many other groups, including local government representatives, church groups, and welfare organizations. Many established interest groups, ranging from the AFL–CIO and the National Council of Churches to the U.S. Chamber of Commerce and the American Bankers' Association, have created special committees or task forces on poverty. It is OGRNC's function to provide liaison between OEO and these private-sector organizations.

Financial Troubles

Of all OEO travails, those associated with funding were the most serious impediment to efficient and smooth operations. That there was not enough money to wage "an unconditional war on poverty" needs no repetition, but the way Congress handled the annual OEO appropriations warrants particular emphasis. The antipoverty warriors were treated in the manner to which the poor, whom they represented, have always been accustomed. The annual handout was given grudgingly, with many strings attached, and after delaying as long as possible. Even within the usual constraints of annual budgeting, Congress seemed to do its utmost to prevent orderly planning and administration of EOA efforts.

Congress must undertake two separate steps before a federal agency can receive spending money. The first step is authorization of an activity or program, and the second step is appropriation of funds to implement the enabling legislation. The first step also involves the authorization of funds, but this need not be specific; the enabling legislation need authorize only "whatever appropriations are deemed necessary" to carry out the particular piece of legislation. In the case of the Economic Opportunity Act, Congress in each of the first three years determined to limit the authorization of expenditures to one year, requiring an annual review of the enabling legislation before funds could be appropriated. In 1967, Congress authorized expenditures of funds for two years.

During each of the first three years of OEO, Congress delayed not only the appropriations of the agency but also the enabling legislation. Almost half of fiscal year 1968 had passed before Congress approved the EOA enabling legislation and appropriations. Since a federal agency is prohibited from spending unappropriated funds after the beginning of each fiscal year (starting July 1), Congress normally passes a "continuing resolution" permitting each agency whose appropriations have not been approved to continue operations at the same level of expenditure as the previous year. In the case of long-established agencies with continuing and stable programs, such delays may not be too damaging. This, however, did not apply to the EOA, whose programs changed from year to year. These alterations required that OEO juggle its fund allocations, retrenching ongoing efforts and expanding new ones, to adjust to the ever changing mandates of Congress, which normally did not provide adequate funds to meet the requirements of new programs.

OEO sometimes compounded its own difficulties. For example, in response to pressures to expand assistance to rural areas, it funded 135 CAA's during fiscal 1967, giving them initial grants for program development. "What that really means," Shriver explained to a Senate Appropriations Subcommittee while pleading for additional funds, "[is that] we gave them enough money to get set up to go into business. . . . We have to have more money to finance their operations."[60] OEO can hardly be faulted for generating pressure to get additional funds, but the point is that effective planning was precluded. Commenting on this problem, Paul Ylvisaker, a veteran antipoverty warrior and one of the most sophisticated men in the business, said:

> Even more important than the amounts of money to be made available, is the more secure commitment of funds over a longer period of time, and I would like to emphasize this: No industry I know of would venture the development of a new product on a sudden-death basis and with uncertain financing. Yet this is what the poverty program has had to do—attempting fundamental reforms and incredibly complex innovations on short-term budgets subject to change without notice.[61]

OEO had precious little money to fight its war. Fiscally, 1964 was a propitious time for launching the Economic Opportunity Act; the economy was expanding (which it continued to do during the following four years), and the efficient federal revenue system assured the government that it would get its share of the growing national product. The preoccupation of economists in those days was the comforting one (considering later developments) that federal tax collections would create a fiscal drag that would slow economic growth. Two major alternatives were available: to cut taxes or to expand federal expenditures. Policy shapers found the first alternative more to their liking, and tax cuts were adopted in 1964 and again in the following year. The future expansion of expenditures was not excluded, however, and antipoverty planners hoped to get a good share of the "automatic" increases in federal revenue.

When the antipoverty effort was launched in 1964 with only modest resources, it was assumed that the programs would be rapidly expanded and new ones added as the situation required. The funds were there but they never materialized. And, initially at least, it was not because the nation had to make a choice between "guns and butter"—the escalation of the war in Vietnam was still in the future. When the President presented his budget in 1965 for the following year, he requested $1.5 billion for OEO. Superficially this appeared to support a commitment to wage the domestic war, since Congress had appropriated about half that amount for the initial year of OEO. The apparent increase was misleading, however, since the $800 million appropriated for fiscal 1965 was considered by OEO officials and other supporters of the antipoverty effort to be adequate only for launching, certainly not for fighting, the "war." It is known that before the budgetary request of $1.5 billion for fiscal 1966 was made public, several of Shriver's closest advisers urged him to demand more funds for OEO and to offer his resignation if the demands were not approved. Of course the President had other welfare items on his agenda—Medicare and federal aid to education, to mention the most significant bills. But the confrontation between the President and Shriver apparently never took place, and by the time the next budget was presented to Congress the nation was facing two wars. The war on poverty was not escalated but continued at an even pace; the increases were adequate to cover the average boosts in wages and salaries, but little was left for expansion.

While Congress is usually blamed for blocking the expansion of EOA programs, the President must also share responsibility. The best opportunity to expand EOA programs existed in 1965, but the President did not take advantage of it. It is generally conceded that the 89th Congress (1965–66) was the most liberal in more than a generation; in 1965 Congress authorized more funds for OEO than the President requested but appropriated the full amount the President recommended. In the next two years Congress trimmed the amount the President recommended. Even OEO finally despaired of expanding its programs. In the fall of 1965, when the agency submitted its budget for the following year (beginning July 1, 1966), OEO asked for $3.4 billion but the Administration cut this by nearly one-half and requested only $1.75 billion of Congress.[62] One year later, OEO lowered its sights and requested $900 million less than it had asked for fiscal 1967, but indicated that it would settle for a "low option" of $1.85 billion, almost as much as Congress appropriated.[63]

Had EOA programs been given the opportunity to expand in 1965, it is unlikely that Congress would have cut the existing projects during the subsequent two years. It is easier to prevent expansion of programs than to retrench on-going efforts. Reduction of the OEO budget would have meant loss of jobs in communities and elimination of services, and few congressmen would take such a step lightly. The President's annual recommended budget, the authorization, and the actual appropriations to OEO during its first four years are presented in Table 2–3.

While appropriations rose only slightly, Congress persisted in adding to OEO's responsibilities and earmarking specific amounts for the new activities. Because appropriations did not provide sufficient additional funds to cover the new activities, OEO was forced to reallocate funds among the EOA programs. This annual robbing-Peter-to-pay-Paul exercise further delayed the allocation of funds to specific programs. OEO's difficulties were compounded by the fact that (1) the annual appropriation was made in a lump sum, and (2) the agency was not free to distribute the funds because of constraints imposed in the authorizing legislation, which, beginning with fiscal 1966, specified the amounts to be allocated to each program. However, the authorized funds exceeded the actual appropriations each year. To distribute the available funds among the several claimants, protracted negotiations were required. These were complicated by the fact that the administration of some programs was delegated to agencies outside OEO. By the time a program administrator knew the exact amount that would be allocated to his activity, half of the fiscal year, or more, had passed. As a result, there was an annual scramble at the end of the fiscal year to obligate available funds lest they expire at the end of the year. In 1966 and 1967 almost 40 percent of the total annual appropriation was obligated during the last two months of the year; and in 1967 more than a fourth of the total appropriation was obligated during the final month of the fiscal year. Despite the annual eleventh-hour rush, program administrators did lose part of their funds. During the first two years, OEO lost a total of $100 million, nearly 4 percent of the appropriated funds. In the third year the unobligated funds diminished to a trickle and amounted to 0.4 percent of total appropriations; in the fourth year this rose to 1.7 percent.

Table 2–3. OEO Budget: Presidential Request and Congressional Authorization and Appropriation, Fiscal 1965–68

Fiscal Year	President's Request (Millions)	Authorization (Millions)	Appropriation (Millions)
1965	$ 947.5	$ 947.5	$ 800.0[a]
1966	1,500.0	1,785.0	1,500.0
1967	1,750.0	1,750.0	1,687.5
1968	2,060.0	1,980.0	1,773.0

[a] This covered only part of the fiscal year because the appropriation was voted after the first quarter of the year had elapsed.

Source: Office of Economic Opportunity.

There may be a considerable wait from the time funds are obligated until they are expended; it takes time to spend money. Only two-thirds of the nearly $4 billion that Congress appropriated during the first three years of the program was expended by the end of that period. As the various programs developed and attracted clienteles, the demand expanded. Not only did total expenditures rise each year in absolute terms, but the proportion of expenditures to available funds also continued to mount. During the fourth year of OEO, expenditures actually exceeded the appropriations for that year, drawing from the unexpended funds accumulated during the preceding years. It was thought that this factor would bring greater pressures upon Congress to increase OEO's appropriations as more people participated in the programs.

During the first three years there was wide variation in the extent to which OEO programs managed to expend their available funds, with CAP the most laggard spender, accounting for three-fifths of OEO's total unexpended funds. The Job Corps had a slow start, but during the fourth year, along with the migrant and work experience programs, it lived beyond its current means and used up previously unexpended funds, and some that were transferred from other programs as well (Table 2–4). By the end of fiscal 1968, OEO had expended 94 percent of its four-year allocation.

Public and Congressional Relations

Since the appointment of the Shriver task force in early 1964, the nation's war on poverty has remained in the public eye. Writing in 1966, two knowledgeable journalists observed that "the war on poverty has ranked second only to the related area of civil rights as a continuing domestic news story."[64] Fifteen or twenty Washington newsmen include OEO in their regular "beat" and countless local reporters write about the antipoverty programs from time to time. Although such attention is not always desirable, it has signaled the elevation of poverty to the status of a major public issue for the first time since the New Deal. Few federal agencies have been more exposed to the mass media than OEO.

OEO began its work in a flurry of favorable publicity. President Johnson's "unconditional war on poverty" caught the fancy of the press and public, and the selection of Shriver as "the field general" of the war added luster to the effort. Shriver was able to deliver the poverty message effectively. OEO has been expertly organized to capitalize on its relationship with the communications media. Its information pro-

Table 2–4. OEO Allocations, Obligations, Expenditures by Program, Fiscal 1965–68[a]

Program	EOA Title	Allocations (Millions)	Obligations (Millions)	Expenditures	
				(Millions)	Allocated Funds
Total		$5,705.0	$5,634.1	$5,385.9	94.4%
Job Corps	IA	989.0	993.3	1,018.8	103.0
NYC	IB	957.8	935.8	889.5	92.8
Comprehensive employment and special impact	IB	384.6	391.4	318.7	82.8
CAP	II	2,561.2	2,535.2	2,464.7	96.2
Rural loans	IIIA	101.7	95.6	99.8	98.1
Migrants	IIIB	99.0	98.5	101.3	102.3
Work experience and training	V	369.0	362.1	381.0	103.2
VISTA	VIII	75.2	74.5	70.6	93.8
Administration	VI	47.5	44.0	41.5	87.3
Adult literacy[b]	IIB	40.0	37.3	—	—
Work-study[b]	IC	56.0	55.8	—	—
Transfers[c]		24.0	10.6	—	—

[a] These data are at best estimates and may not agree with those in succeeding chapters. OEO program offices use different bases for compilation of their statistics. Expenditures during the four years may exceed allocations because OEO is authorized to transfer up to 10 percent of total funds from one program to another.

[b] Transferred to Health, Education, and Welfare.

[c] Transfers include $10 million to the U.S. Public Health Service for medical draft rejectees' programs and $10 million to vocational education under special congressional instructions.

Source: Office of Economic Opportunity.

95

gram was specifically authorized in the Economic Opportunity Act, which empowers OEO's director to distribute "data and information, in such form as he shall deem appropriate, to public agencies, private organizations and the general public."[65] "The agency has taken this injunction to heart. During most of the period its Office of Public Affairs was headed by Herbert J. Kramer, who had formerly been in charge of public relations and advertising for a large insurance company. "We're organized in a sense like an in-house advertising agency," Kramer stated. "It's patterned after my own experience in a 72-man operation in a multi-product organization."[66] He explained that his office (about 50 persons) follow both "vertical" and "horizontal" tables of organization. Vertically, staff members specialize in major OEO programs which lack their own public information staffs; horizontally, staff members specialize in various media techniques.

In addition to the usual public relations activities, OEO's Office of Public Affairs became involved in more esoteric ventures. A comic book on the Job Corps was commissioned from cartoonist Al Capp and half a million copies were printed (but never distributed). VISTA training films (not shown to the general public) won Academy Award nominations in 1967 and 1968. Some of OEO's publicity gambits have raised eyebrows—for example, when OEO persuaded a network television rock 'n' roll personality to appeal to disadvantaged teenagers to participate in OEO programs. Though the idea was innovative and sensible, a storm of editorial and congressional criticism ensued, presumably because these representatives of middle-class values could not see the connection between disadvantaged youth and rock 'n' roll.

The very success of OEO's early publicity was unfortunate, if only because the agency could not hope to live up to the fanfare. Lacking reliable data or experience, OEO officials sometimes created projections of success which they later conceded were "visionary" or "unrealistic." Even after the successful conclusion of the first summer's Head Start program, there were no hard figures to lend substance to OEO's press claims. In this vacuum, OEO officials succumbed to the "numbers game," making unrealistic promises and projections. The agency's first congressional presentation, for example, contained figures which were, in the words of one official, "generated out of whole cloth."

Even after OEO's programs had begun to generate real accomplishments and frustrations, public reporting by the agency still left much to be desired. First, there was a credibility gap in some of the statistics. Expenditures per enrollee in the Job Corps, for example, were the subject of conflicting reports, and there were several revisions of the figures. Second, public statements by OEO officials often used imprecise words to describe the scope or impact of their programs.

Third, OEO naturally sought to interpret its statistics in the most favorable light. OEO's propensity to exaggerate success claims is legendary and needs no repetition here.

In a larger sense, OEO's public information activities—aided and abetted, it must be stressed, by the news media—had the effect of raising expectations that could never be fulfilled. An example is Shriver's exhortation to Congress to eliminate poverty by the 200th anniversary of the Declaration of Independence. Few would quarrel with such a goal, but Shriver neglected to tell Congress that achievement of this goal would require additional expenditures of at least $20 billion annually in aid of the poor. It is hard to see what benefit such pronouncements served as long as they were not accompanied by an indication of their costs, their prospects for implementation, and their realistic chances of success. Indeed, unfulfilled promises of this sort have given added ammunition to foes of the poverty programs. And more important, they have created cruel disappointment among those who hoped to benefit from them.

With difficulty OEO has outgrown its youthful enthusiasm. The agency's expansive handling of the press was perhaps to be expected, given the high-minded enthusiasm of the poverty efforts, the journalistic background of a number of OEO officials, and the style of OEO's director. In 1966, however, Kramer's office began to counteract the earlier press agentry and exercise more caution. First, the big circuslike press conferences were abandoned. Second, the elaborate ceremonies for signing each contract were eliminated. All press releases on local grants and programs are now handled by OEO's regional offices. Third, few new programs have been launched since the early days, which has decreased the opportunities for making extravagant claims. Finally, OEO initiated a policy of making evaluation reports available to outsiders.

The softening of OEO's early "hard sell" has not deterred the critics who charge that OEO spends an inordinate amount of resources on public information.[67] On the other hand, these same critics are in part responsible for OEO's constant need for cultivation of its public image. For example, the appendix of the *Congressional Record* is full of stories of OEO's shortcomings, major and minor, inserted by hostile congressmen. Moreover, it must be recognized that antipoverty programs are by nature scandal-prone. There are two reasons for this. First, the participants in poverty programs are not solid, middle-class citizens; they are "high-risk" persons who are unemployed, uneducated, bitter, and perhaps with prison records. If they get into trouble while enrolled in an OEO program their transgressions are easy targets for hostile politicians or journalists of the "man-bites-dog" approach to news reporting. Second, many of those in charge of local OEO programs were well meaning but inexperienced. For example, a worker in Texas decided to purchase old gunsights to use as microscopes for a training project and in the resultant "scandal" it was falsely implied that he was buying guns with which to arm Negro trainees.

OEO's original philosophy was that criticism should be answered swiftly. "We owe this to the poor," Kramer explained. "We've got to come back fast." While early rebuttal might serve to quash the charges, there were at least two disadvantages to this strategy. First, carefully documented responses to charges often require much time to prepare. Second, OEO's apparent sensitivity to criticism may have given its critics' charges more attention than they deserved.

OEO began to show greater restraint as time wore on, particularly after Bertrand M. Harding became deputy director and later head of the agency. OEO officials maintained by 1968 that they must have documentation before they released rebuttals. As one of them remarked: "The simple wise crack response went out long ago." Before this, in defending itself OEO had sometimes gone far beyond a clarification of factual matters. Direct attacks upon critics were sometimes indulged in, as when OEO press releases referred to a statement of Representative William H. Ayres (ranking Republican on the House Education and Labor Committee) as "typical misrepresentation for political purposes" and to House Minority Leader Gerald Ford as "the only Ford that acts like an Edsel when he'd like to be a Mustang."[68]

Perhaps the most extreme use of this technique occurred in mid-1966, when OEO decided to take on the Republican National Committee. The object of OEO's ire was a Republican report which had urged drastic revisions of the antipoverty efforts, including the spin-off of several key programs to other federal and local agencies. These reforms, the report explained, were based on "the Republican approach to *assist* the poor and disadvantaged in their climb up the economic and social ladder; not to *drag* them up forcibly by a green rope of dollar bills."[69] OEO lost no time in replying. Its press release, dated the very same day as the GOP press release, was nothing more than a string of superficial rebuttals of the Republican arguments. Particularly unwise were such partisan remarks as the following:

[OEO] welcomes responsible review of the antipoverty program but it resents the hit-and-run guerilla warfare of Republican poverty memos and party pronouncements. . . . Those hurt most by Republican cynicism and ill-founded criticism of the War on Poverty are the poor themselves. The Republican party will conveniently forget them when election day is over.[70]

If anything, OEO's response served to give the Republican charges more readership than is usually accorded the pronouncements of national party committees. And it gave Republicans further cause for resentment against OEO. A few days later House Minority Leader Ford, charging that the agency had concentrated on publicity while neglecting the poor, demanded an end to "the use of public funds for a partisan attack upon the Republican party by a government agency."[71]

This incident was perhaps OEO's most controversial foray into the political use of the press release, but it was by no means unique. One can sympathize with the natural frustration of dedicated public officials under attack, but greater tactical restraint in such cases would certainly have been advisable. As it was, Republican spokesmen continued their attacks upon the OEO publicity mills.

During the House hearings on OEO the following year, Charles Goodell (later appointed Senator from New York) referred to some articles in which Shriver was quoted as having accused Republicans of being throat slitters and doing professional hatchet jobs. Chiding Shriver, he went on to say, "Glib terms like 'throat slitting,' 'professional hatchet job' . . . don't advance the cause of good legislation at all."[72]

OEO's Public Affairs Office has perhaps the most demanding public information assignment in Washington. Poverty programs are newsworthy, but they are vulnerable to unfavorable publicity. Not only political opponents of the program but well-meaning reporters whose concept of significant news extends no further than scandal hunting are untiring in their search for flaws in the implementation of antipoverty programs. And because of the inherent design of the programs and the character of their clienteles, OEO is often the victim of a bad press. A mature response to this problem would probably acknowledge it as unavoidable and try to help the media put their stories in proper perspective. But the "mature" response is not easy, either psychologically or politically, for it presupposes a "mature" public that is willing to accept "scandals" as the inevitable price of achieving difficult objectives.

A corollary of OEO's media exposure, and a partial cause of it, is the political exposure of the antipoverty efforts. The first fact that bears emphasis is the relatively low level of political participation by the disadvantaged people in the United States. Other things being equal, poor people are less likely to vote, to take part in other political activities, or even to have much information about politics. If the poor do not participate, they are not a promising object of the politicians' attentions.[73]

Therefore, at the outset at least, OEO's clientele had only limited political resources with which to defend their claims. One segment of this clientele, the civil rights movement, did possess impressive organization and influence, and indeed was able to link OEO's objectives to those of Negro citizens. But the civil rights movement of the late 1960's was suffering dwindling support from the white majority—a trend which intensified the problems faced by the federal programs associated with the movement. As long as OEO insisted on full participation of Negroes in its programs, it fell prey to resentment from southern politicians and their representatives in Congress. In turn, southern delegations in Congress wield disproportionate influence because of their high seniority and command of key committee posts.

Programs aimed at alleviating poverty are likely to produce increased political participation by the poor. Such participation creates pressures on established political leaders and may even generate hostility toward poverty programs. Articulate and activist representatives of the poor are bound to clash with merchants, landlords, welfare officials, and politicians. In many communities, northern as well as southern, OEO's clienteles threatened to grow into "anti-establishment" political groups. Local political leaders transmitted their concerns to their congressmen, who, especially within the Democratic party, were sensitive to challenges to the party's big-city base of power. Thus the war on poverty's skirmishes with the political establishment were in some measure a gauge of its success in fulfilling its mission.

OEO found itself pulled in opposite directions. On one hand, increasingly militant reformers were demanding a radical shake-up of existing political and social service practices. On the other hand, established political groups were alternately responsive and hostile. The more members of disadvantaged groups were brought to the threshold of political participation, the greater the potential impact upon established leaders. To the extent that OEO insisted on "maximum feasible participation" or racial integration in its programs, it encountered hostility from City Hall and Congress. To the extent that it yielded to political realities and compromised, it faced rejection by the militants. OEO found itself in an unenviable position in the middle of a thousand different battlegrounds.

In addition, OEO could count on the opposition of many traditionally conservative groups that viewed with horror any genuine war on poverty. Conservative opposition was not alleviated by the fact that some of OEO's supporters, including Congressman Adam Clayton Powell, preferred to label the antipoverty programs as partisan Democratic efforts. Some Republicans were genuinely interested in supporting a bipartisan antipoverty effort, but their support was usually spurned by Democratic congressional leaders. Resenting the exclusions, these Republicans repaid in kind by attacking OEO.

Other factors conspired to endanger OEO's support on Capitol Hill. The Education and Labor Committee, charged with the responsibility for antipoverty legislation in the House, has in recent years been a divided and highly partisan committee that lacks strong leadership. Its chairman in the 88th and the 89th Congress was Adam Clayton Powell, whose espousal of antipoverty legislation was not calculated to win new friends for the programs. Moreover, Powell's support was inconsistent; at times he attacked OEO bitterly, appearing to be more interested in preserving his Harlem leadership than in advancing OEO's interest. OEO's congressional liaison team also ran into difficulties. During OEO's first four years, four men held the post of director of congressional relations. This office took upon itself the virtually impossible task of handling all congressional inquiries, in addition to essential lobbying on Capitol Hill. The resultant bottleneck led to complaints from senators and representatives that their inquiries were being ignored.

From OEO's point of view, the cultivation of good will on Capitol Hill demanded an excessive amount of the agency's time and energies. In addition to responding to many requests for information, OEO's congressional liaison staff, not to mention other officials, devoted an inordinate amount of time to lobbying or testifying. Beyond the annual appropriations process that most federal agencies must face, OEO had to gain renewed authorization of the basic legislation each year until 1967. In the process, Congress managed to void some of the original flexibility given OEO by the Act, and it curtailed the agency's freedom to allocate funds among the various programs, especially in connection with CAP. It can only be concluded that Congress did not help OEO to plan ahead or to operate at maximum efficiency.

Congressional review and scrutiny of OEO's work during the first four years were, moreover, dominated by narrow political motivations that revealed little understanding of program contents and direction. However, the 1967 hearing and floor debates displayed increased sophistication on the part of many legislators; and the investigation mounted that year by Senator Joseph S. Clark's Subcommittee on Employment, Manpower, and Poverty was a careful and competent review of the programs. The subcommittee's efforts were directed by Howard W. Hallman.

OEO's political problems were endemic and pervasive. Perhaps the most useful way to explain OEO's political context is to describe, in some detail, the circumstances surrounding the 1967 renewal of the Economic Opportunity Act. Many political forces converged on OEO that year, and there was even doubt that the agency would be permitted to continue. The result was a controversial compromise that assured the extension of the Economic Opportunity Act for a period of two years.[74] The vote of 247 to 149 was the greatest show of strength for the Act since its passage in 1964. Sixty-four Republicans—two of every five—strayed from their usual party position to join 183 Democrats (including 38 southerners) to vote in favor of the Act. The final vote on EOA appropriations was even more lopsided, 308 to 78.

The outcome was a surprise to most observers, for OEO was in serious political trouble. Because of their pessimism over the outcome, House Democratic leaders had postponed final action until the closing days of the session. Two months before the House vote, Representative Sam Gibbons, the floor leader of the 1966 EOA debate, is reported to have stated: "I have checked. The outcome is really dismal . . . there will be better than 230 negative votes on any antipoverty bill we write."[75] On two earlier occasions, a majority of House members had expressed displeasure with OEO. In October, in an unusual step, they voted to exclude OEO employees from the general salary increase to be granted government employees. Later in the month they refused to pass a "continuing resolution" authorizing OEO operating funds at the previous year's level. For a short period between October 23 and November 9, OEO had no money and was forced to discontinue its expiring projects.

There was no simple explanation for the change that took place in the House during the two months following Congressman Gibbons' count. Indeed, several forces that were eventually to influence fourscore congressmen to vote for extending EOA were already in operation when Gibbons surveyed the mood of Congress. The House's petulent action in denying the 3,000 OEO employees their salary increase generated sympathy for the agency both in and out of Congress. The failure of Congress to pass the continuing resolution had a more decisive effect, for it was soon felt in a number of communities. As projects were terminated and local jobs lost, congressmen began to hear from their constituents. Because a number of popular Head Start projects were imperiled, congressional inaction provided a ready-made issue for attracting sympathy for the antipoverty effort and a basis for attacking the "reckless irresponsibility" of Congress. An OEO count found no fewer than 450 newspaper editorials during October and November that favored the continuation of EOA. These events closely followed the much-publicized defeat of the "rat bill," under which many congressmen were still smarting. During the debate on this bill its opponents had displayed a sick humor in arguing against it that was widely denounced by the news media. Later the House of Representatives reversed itself and took a position against rodents, but it was too late to save itself from public criticism.

The Republicans had tactical reasons for opposing the continuing resolution and for excluding OEO employees from the federal wage increase. They hoped to convince OEO supporters that there was not enough support in the House for extending the EOA and that its passage would require acceptance of Republican amendments. These signals were overlooked by the news media, however, and the message the public received was merely that the Republicans and some of their Democratic colleagues were against the antipoverty legislation. Though the "overkill" of OEO backfired, proponents of the agency still had to break the Republican–southern Democrat coalition which had been working effectively in the 90th Congress. Economy in social legislation was the watchword, and a majority in the House still opposed the Administration's antipoverty bill with its proposed $2.06 billion authorization. Since too many members had publicly opposed it, an alternative to the Administration bill was needed.

The alternative was an amendment supplied by Representative Edith Green, an advocate of the antipoverty efforts but a persistent critic of OEO. Mrs. Green sought to limit Shriver's authority to permit private nonprofit organizations to operate as community action agencies, thus providing northern Democrats a selling point with their southern colleagues. They claimed that the amendment would put the antipoverty legislation in the hands of local elected officials. The amendment apparently satisfied southern Democrats, for many sided with their northern colleagues rather than cooperate with the opposition.

To sustain the impression that the Green amendment meant a radical change in the administration and direction of community action programs, OEO spokesmen were persuaded to denounce the amendment as signaling the death knell of community action agencies. Although some OEO officials strongly opposed the amendment and needed no persuasion, others privately supported the amendment and shed crocodile tears about the supposed demise of CAP. The tactics proved effective in solidifying congressional support for the amendment. Southerners who had formerly denounced community action efforts as the work of "power-grasping bureaucrats from Washington" could now vote for the new program.[76]

Given this face-saving device, many southerners were receptive to the appeals of Congressman Carl D. Perkins, the new chairman of the House Education and Labor Committee. Having obtained the Green amendment, Perkins told his southern colleagues that they could hardly let him down and defeat the antipoverty program, leaving him open to the charge that he could not do as well for the poor as his predecessor, Adam Clayton Powell. According to a South Carolina congressman: "I never heard his name mentioned but I know that a lot of southerners were thinking unconsciously of Powell. . . . We didn't want to pull the rug out from under Carl."[77]

The mobilization of businessmen, mayors, and other city officials to lobby for OEO also helped make it respectable to vote for the extension of the Economic Opportunity Act. OEO officials also lobbied intensively for the legislation, but it is not known how persuasive they were.

With this rare display of Democratic unity, the Republicans were unable to split the Democratic ranks with an attractive alternative. Most Republicans agreed that they could not afford the blame for killing the Act, even if they could get the votes to achieve this end. And many opposed its outright defeat, hoping to amend it more to their liking. The major Republican spokesmen on the issue, Charles E. Goodell of New York and Albert H. Quie of Minnesota, did not seek a coalition with the southern Democrats. They concentrated their efforts on getting approval of substantive amendments so as to transform the program along the lines proposed in their Opportunity Crusade. Quie explained later: "I was caught . . . between two different views—those in the Administration who simply wanted to continue the present program . . . and those of us who wanted to greatly strengthen the antipoverty program."[78] Goodell went out of his way to antagonize southern Democrats by charging that the Green provision was the "bosses and boll weevil amendment."

Whatever the substantive merits of the Opportunity Crusade, Goodell and Quie had little that was politically attractive to offer the Democrats. Their proposal would have transferred several EOA programs, including Head Start, to the Office of Education. This agency was headed by Harold Howe II, who was anathema to the southerners because he had tried to enforce the antisegregation provisions of the Elementary and Secondary Education Act and other education legislation. Northern Democrats who might have found attractive provisions in the Opportunity Crusade were not about to do business with Republicans if they could get a majority to pass an Administration bill, and they did not consider the Green amendment too high a price to pay. Many northern Democrats who were closely associated with Democratic city machines saw nothing wrong in a "bosses" amendment, even if "boll weevils" were also involved.

The Republicans found themselves not only a minority but a divided one at that. A few favored the Administration bill, and two Republicans on the House Education and Labor Committee deserted their party to vote with the majority in reporting the committee bill. A larger group, which included most of the Republican leaders in the House, cared little about the substantive amendments offered by their colleagues in the Opportunity Crusade but were preoccupied with cutting antipoverty funds. Had the Republicans closed ranks, they might have been able to attract enough Democratic votes to pass some of their amendments. Aside from their numerous defeats, the House Republican leadership scored a victory by cutting funds in the anti-poverty legislation. By deserting Quie and Goodell and siding with economy-minded southerners, the Republican leaders were able to cut the authorization from the $2.06 billion proposed by the Administration to $1.6 billion. The final appropriation approved by Congress was $1.773 billion, only slightly less than the amount Shriver had indicated as the bare minimum if OEO were to operate for the balance of the year without cutting major projects.[79]

Part II

Community Action Programs

3.

CONCEPTS AND OPERATIONS

Who shall speak for the people?
who has the answers?
who knows what to say?
where is the sure interpreter?

Carl Sandburg

A Strategy to Fight Poverty

The Community Action Program is a catch-all for projects to aid the poor. Practically any effort aimed at reducing poverty may be funded through it, provided the poor or their spokesmen participate in planning and execution, and provided racial discrimination is barred. Approved projects have included preschool and remedial education, employment and job training, birth control, consumer education, legal aid to challenge existing welfare institutions, new systems of delivering health services to the poor, recreation, and neighborhood centers aimed at providing "one-stop" services. The list is not exhaustive but indicates the broad scope of CAP activities.

Given this range, it is clear that CAP is not a "program" but a strategy for combating poverty. The designers of the Economic Opportunity Act evidently appreciated the wide horizons possible for CAP. In submitting the bill to Congress on March 16, 1964, President Johnson stated that the Community Action Program

> ... asks men and women throughout the country to prepare long-range plans for the attack on poverty in their own local communities.
>
> These plans will be local plans striking at the many unfilled needs which underlie poverty in each community, not just one or two. Their components and emphasis will differ as needs differ.
>
> These plans will be local plans calling upon all the resources available to the community—Federal and State, local and private, human and material.

Yet the rhetoric was not accompanied by practical designs for the implementation of the program. The architects of the legislation, it seemed, had only a vague idea of the over-all function of CAP, beyond perhaps a general conviction that planning was needed for a concerted attack upon poverty. There is no evidence that the presidential task force which planned the "war on poverty," or anyone else in the Ad-

109

ministration for that matter, had thought through the implications of CAP or attempted to chart its future course. Later critics of the program (including some of the original architects) who claim to have foreseen CAP'S difficulties, rely too heavily on the wisdom of hindsight; indeed, no one in 1964 could have foreseen such developments as the transformation of the civil rights movement, the advocacy by many of black power, the riots in scores of American cities, and the political and social reactions of many whites to Negro demands.

The section of the Act defining the Community Action Program was passed by Congress virtually as it was drafted by the Administration, and reads:

(a) The term "community action program" means a program—
  (1) which mobilizes and utilizes resources, public or private, or any . . . geographical area . . . in an attack on poverty;
  (2) which provides services, assistance, and other activities . . . to give promise of progress toward elimination of poverty or a cause or causes of poverty. . . .
  (3) which is developed, conducted, and administered with the maximum feasible participation of residents of the areas and members of the groups served; and
  (4) which is conducted, administered, or coordinated by a public or private nonprofit agency (other than a political party), or a combination thereof.

Such a far-reaching provision would normally stimulate detailed and protracted debate in Congress. The provision was certainly unique. It meant, among other things, that federal funds could be given to "any . . . geographic area," ignoring established political boundaries and elected public officials. Administration officials testifying in behalf of the Economic Opportunity Act failed to cast light on the provision, with the exception of Robert F. Kennedy, then Attorney General, who declared: "It must be a total effort to bring about broad community change. And this cannot be done by the Federal Government. We can only help by stimulating local action. It must be done by local people and local agencies working closely together."[1]

In retrospect it is not surprising that Kennedy was the only federal official to attempt an explanation of the CAP concept. As chairman of the Cabinet Committee on Juvenile Delinquency, he was exposed to the nascent community action efforts funded by the federal government.[2] Apparently, other Administration spokesmen were quite innocent of CAP's meaning and had not been briefed by their departmental representatives on the task force that planned the legislation. Included among these latter were some who later claimed to have predicted the future course of CAP.

While Administration spokesmen were silent, a number of legislators and mayors did see the implications of the provision. Representative Roman C. Pucinski of Illinois indicated concern about ". . . a tendency on the part of the Government in Washington to deal directly with organizations in local communities, bypassing the local governments."[3] Kennedy tried to allay Pucinski's misgivings by noting that it was occasionally necessary to bypass state and local governments that were not equipped to do the job envisioned by CAP. He argued that ". . . there certainly should be an opening to deal with local agencies, private and public, who could get together and come up with a plan or an organization which could handle a particular function."[4] Instead of being comforted, Pucinski retorted: "That is what scares me . . . a tendency to bypass . . . elected officials . . . to set up . . . so-called nonprofit private organizations which have become somewhat notorious as empire builders. . . ."[5]

The mayors were naturally apprehensive of the provision that established grants to communities, bypassing local elected officials. They were enthusiastic about the CAP concept but unanimously opposed to bypassing city hall. New York's Mayor Robert F. Wagner said that he felt "very strongly that the sovereign government of each locality in which . . . a community action program is proposed, should have the power of approval over the makeup of the planning group, the structure of the planning group, and over the plan."[6] Mayor Richard J. Daley of Chicago reacted similarly: "We think very strongly that any program of this kind, in order to succeed, must be administered by the duly constituted elected officials of the areas with the cooperation of the private agencies."[7] And William F. Walsh of Syracuse, the only Republican mayor to testify on the merits of the Economic Opportunity Act, declared that "If we could not have direct control of the program, we did not want it."[8]

Opponents of the legislation, particularly the Republican minority on the House Committee on Education and Labor, tried unsuccessfully to exploit the reservations raised by supporters. President Johnson pressed for immediate passage of the Economic Opportunity Act and a majority in Congress supported him. Outright opponents had no chance to halt the Act's passage and could muster little support from the doubters. Few cared to be accused of lacking enthusiasm to fight poverty, and it appeared in 1964 that anyone who opposed the Economic Opportunity Act was against helping the poor.

In retrospect, it would seem that the prompt legislative "processing" of the Act—only five months elapsed from the time the President proposed the bill until Congress enacted the legislation—argues against passing major legislation in haste. While the compassion generated in 1964 to wage a "total war on poverty" was commendable, *wisdom of hindsight* indicates that more careful consideration of the legislation might have avoided some of the pitfalls encountered by OEO in administering the law.

Representation and Structure of CAA's

Once the Economic Opportunity Act became law, the greatest controversy centered around the meaning of "maximum feasible participation" in implementing the Community Action Program. Despite later claims by kibitzers inside and outside of government, including some celebrated Great Society dropouts, nobody knew in 1964 the meaning of these three words. Certainly there was no consensus within OEO as to how to interpret the provision. The director of the Community Action Program, Theodore M. Berry, is reported to have said that "There is a positive legislative history of the phrase and its related intentions"; while Hyman Bookbinder, a key man in drafting the legislation and an assistant director of OEO, assured an inquirer that "There is no explicit legislative history covering this particular phrase."[9] The failure to agree on the meaning or philosophy of "maximum feasible participation" might not have been so significant if OEO officials and their local clients had been able to agree on the design of organizations that would act as recipients of CAP funds. This was not in the cards during the first few years of OEO.

The Economic Opportunity Act is unabashedly class legislation, designating a special group in the population as eligible to receive the benefits of the law. There is, of course, nothing new in class legislation; our laws are replete with provisions that benefit one group or another. Normally these groups banded into organizations to assure that the rights or special privileges granted them by the laws were preserved. The novelty of the EOA lay in the fact that the poor were not represented by trade or other conventional organizations. Welfare agencies, public or private, could hardly claim to represent the poor, though they could and did insist that they did a great deal *for* the poor, if not *with* them.

Selection of representatives of the poor was complicated by the civil rights movement. Increasingly, Negroes and other minority groups insisted that only "brothers" of the same color or ethnic origin could properly represent the poor in their communities. In addition, the Act provided a new organizational structure through which to funnel antipoverty money. The programs, money, and jobs were attractive and competed favorably with the familiar welfare and philanthropic agencies in luring mercenaries for the war on poverty.

OEO had to establish a mechanism to enable communities to select representatives to the policy and governing bodies of community action agencies. In most communities, elected officials, welfare officials, and individuals associated with the various social "causes" got together and established community action agencies. In most cases, city hall and court house officials preferred to keep the antipoverty agency separate from the local governments, and frequently the geographic jurisdiction of the antipoverty agency differed from established political jurisdictions, encompassing either a part of an area, or two or more such areas, to form a community action agency.

Who Represents the Poor?

A major task faced by OEO was determining who would govern CAA's and administer their programs. OEO sought maximum feasible flexibility in determining representation on CAA's, allowing communities to work out their own arrangements. This did not, of course, satisfy the various contending groups. Some city halls and court houses wanted complete control over "their" CAA's, while militant advocates of "maximum feasible participation" sought also to gain control. OEO was caught between the factions: "We have no intention," stated OEO's director, "of letting any one group, even the poor themselves, run the programs. That's not *Community* action."[10]

OEO's difficulties were further compounded by the initial failure of the law to specify eligibility criteria for representatives of the poor on CAA boards, except for the stipulation that they reside in the areas served. Thus, affluent citizens who happened to live in a "target area" could represent the poor. The law could therefore be observed without having a single low-income person on the CAA board. This was exactly the case in the early days of the Atlanta CAA, where the only person who could claim to be a representative of the poor within the vague criteria of the provision was Martin Luther King, Sr., a minister living in the poverty area. On the other hand, in some communities the poor themselves served on, and in a few isolated cases even controlled, the governing boards of community action agencies.

Given the wide diversity of community practices and a desire to allow communities maximum freedom to determine the organization of their antipoverty agencies, OEO was at a loss to spell out guidelines regulating the selection and composition of CAA boards. Detailed guidelines would have brought charges that Washington was trying to dictate matters properly left to the communities; failure to set guidelines left OEO open to charges of practicing "welfare colonialism" and capitulating to city halls and court houses.

One obvious solution was to let the people in the communities determine their representation via the ballot box, but experience showed that this was not an effective means of securing citizen participation in the poverty program. One of the reasons new institutions were necessary to fight poverty was that the poor had little political power and that elected officials were not responsive to their needs. It turned out that most poor people were no more interested in voting for their representatives on CAA boards than in selecting their local governmental representatives. During OEO's first year about a dozen cities held elections for membership on CAA boards, neighborhood planning councils, or both. The turnout for these elections was meager, and the whole concept of election had a dubious impact. Even the sober assertion by one OEO official that elections were "a mixed bag of results" seemed too optimistic. Voter participation ranged from a low of 1 percent to a high of less than 5 percent of those eligible. A committee of the American Arbitration Association, which analyzed CAA elections during the first 18 months of OEO, concluded that the lack of participation stemmed from absence of issues or constituencies, from the fact that there were few contestants with charisma to inspire a large turnout, and from general skepticism of the poor that the new program would be more successful than previous efforts had been.[11] Early in 1966, agency spokesmen were ready to declare that the experiment of financing CAA elections had been a failure; and in testifying before a congressional committee, Sargent Shriver volunteered that he did not believe that OEO had received its money's worth in these elections.[12]

Diversity of Accommodation

As an alternative to direct elections, OEO could have influenced participation of the poor by the type of programs and agencies it funded. As long as CAP funds went to local boards controlled by the "Establishment," it was reasonable to assume that the programs would differ little from those of older welfare agencies. As an alternative, activists within and without OEO urged CAP funding of projects specifically aimed to encourage political education and involvement of the poor. Frequently these organizations were headed by political activists and militants who wanted to use CAA's to attack the bastions of city hall. Possibly the most publicized and controversial CAP grant in this category was the funding of the Syracuse Community Development Association, which used the funds to set up neighborhood groups to help register new voters in slum areas. The Republican mayor of Syracuse considered this an exercise in helping Democrats rather than democracy. By the end of 1955 the Syracuse Community Development Association grant was terminated, and the organization was advised to seek new funds through the Crusade For Opportunity, the local CAA.[13]

The termination of the Syracuse grant, and the disclosure early in

1966 that OEO had made private arrangements with the mayors of some fifteen cities to clear all CAP grants in their jurisidictions through city hall, opened OEO to charges of having succumbed to the Establishment. Militants viewed the OEO action as confirmation of their view that the government was not to be trusted with the war on poverty, and Saul Alinsky charged OEO with having a "zoo-keeper mentality."

A more objective appraisal would have indicated that most city halls were not fighting the poor and in many cases were receptive to involving the poor in antipoverty efforts, though not necessarily in policy determination. The vast majority of CAA's has enjoyed at least the tacit acceptance of local officials. These officials were not insensitive to the new political forces at work; and while involvement of the poor was not "maximum," at least it was considerably more than had been previously attempted. In 1966 the U.S. Conference of Mayors urged local officials to allow the poor "some actual *sharing* of planning and decision-making power."[14]

Within two years of the Economic Opportunity Act's passage, a *Christian Science Monitor* survey of 40 major cities across the country found that "poor people . . . have gained a foothold in running many local antipoverty programs."[15] The 40 cities surveyed used a variety of approaches in securing participation of the poor, usually without external pressure. However, on occasion results would not have been achieved without OEO's delaying or threatening to cut off funds until the cities complied with the proposed standard that one-third of CAA boards be composed of the poor or their representatives. The picture was not all success, however, and many representatives of the poor were not themselves poor. The mayor of Nashville, Tennessee, argued that "You can't have unqualified people running good programs." In other cities, the survey found that "Uncle Toms" were placed on CAA boards to "represent" the poor. Indeed, in some neighborhood elections, only nonpoor were selected to represent the poor, the idea apparently being that people who had shown they could help themselves would be best able to help the poor.[16]

In 1966 Congress formalized OEO's practice and required that public officials, private groups, and representatives of the poor each constitute one-third of the CAA boards. Whatever the shortcomings of OEO's practices, there is no denying the fact that in many cases CAA's gave the poor unprecedented opportunity to plan and participate in programs. And while it cannot be claimed that participation by the poor automatically improved the quantity or quality of services offered to them and to their neighbors, it undoubtedly made these services more satisfying. There is ample evidence that doing things for people is not an effective way of helping them. A regard for basic democratic concepts also dictates that people have a say in society's efforts on their behalf.

The Establishment nonetheless played a major role in CAP. Contrary to the usual OEO claims, even most CAP-funded national programs originated not with OEO or the CAA's but with traditional welfare and educational agencies, public and private. Many of the people associated with these traditional welfare programs were active participants in CAA's, either as members of governing boards or as staff members; some of them even initiated CAA's. In most communities mayors, county supervisors, and other members of the "power structure" reached accommodation with the representatives of local organizations, often through the addition of several minority representatives to the governing board of the CAA and other advisory groups and the hiring of minority members in responsible administrative and executive positions. There has been a continuing trend in CAA's of upgrading Negro and other minority staff members. A major achievement of CAA's was that they offered young Negroes and representatives of other minority groups the opportunity to develop administrative and executive capabilities.

Conceptualizing Diversity

While OEO attempted to define the operations of CAP by disseminating guidelines, the proper balance between representatives of the poor and control by the Establishment has been a matter of case-by-case resolution. An authoritative study by Howard W. Hallman, director of the 1967 study by the Senate Subcommittee on Employment, Manpower, and Poverty, found wide diversity in the administration, the services delivered, and the role played by the clients of the program among different CAA's. The subcommittee studied in detail 35 of the more than 1,000 CAA's. But the consultants to the subcommittee, many of whom had intimate and detailed knowledge of the communities studied, could not arrive at any "clear and comparable findings on the theoretical underpinnings of the programs studied."[17] Hallman despaired of finding common trends in the agencies' attacks on the complex problems of poverty, though he found that invariably the CAA's provided useful new services to the poor.

The diversity of the agencies did not prevent other observers from finding definite trends in the development of CAA's during the first four years. According to Daniel P. Moynihan, militant CAA's could not survive under OEO and were invariably taken over by the established institutions or ended up in bitter conflict with them. The evidence supplied to prove this "trend" is based only upon the history of the community action agency in Syracuse and on two in New York

City during the first two years of OEO, and there is room to question Moynihan's interpretation of the facts in these two cities.[18]

Whatever the patterns of community accommodations with CAA's, there are those who hold that successful community action must be independent of political control by the Establishment.[19] According to this view, only CAA's that are in direct conflict with elected officials can succeed, because an effective CAA must be controlled by the indigenous indigent who are sufficiently indignant to challenge the Establishment. While Kenneth Clark would not necessarily hold to this extreme view, he did attack CAP for having failed to place the antipoverty program under the control of indigenous representatives. Since Clark is among the most sympathetic critics of CAP, his exchange with Senator Joseph S. Clark of Pennsylvania before the latter's Senate subcommittee is worth quoting. After an attack on some urban as well as rural CAA's, the following exchange took place:

> Senator Clark. Let us say democracy does not work, period.

> Dr. Clark. I do not know whether I am willing to go that far, but to the extent that Government-funded, publicly supported antipoverty programs can do nothing but deal with surface conditions of the poor, and that when these funds are being used, or seemingly as if they are going to be used for any serious political confrontation, the inevitable consequence is that the resolution of this kind of confrontation is in the direction of the people who control the public funds, who are political officials, and who see the threat as a threat to the basis of their power.[20]

Carried to its logical conclusion, this argument would suggest that a goal of the CAA is to put power in the hands of the poor rather than to deliver needed services to them. The assumption is that once the poor obtain power, they will be in a position to demand delivery of services. It appears to be rather fuzzy thinking to assume that such power will be of long-term value without the education and training necessary to exercise it.

Other commentators placed less weight on the political role of CAA's. Joseph A. Kershaw, OEO's first assistant director for Research, Plans, Programs, and Evaluation, questioned the assertion that an effective community action program should concentrate on changing political conditions at a cost of ignoring delivery of services. While he indicated that political change was needed in some communities before CAA's could operate effectively, Kershaw thought that "innovation, organization, and delivery of services" was a more important ingredient of effective community action.[21]

Along the same line, S. M. Miller suggested that maximum feasible participation could be implemented in many ways. Among the concept's many connotations, he said, were creating jobs for the poor;

providing services which reduce apathy and alienation; involving the poor in policy formulation; and the ultimate transfer of power to the poor.[22]

Whatever interpretation of maximum feasible participation is used, effective community action demands that the poor be organized to express themselves. Such expression tends to focus on specific grievances against established institutions such as school systems, welfare agencies, and other institutions serving the "political power structure." As long as such protests concentrate on specific problems and present realistic and curable grievances, community action is a viable tool to correct social ills. Most community action has centered upon correcting minor but real grievances of the poor. News headlines are made, however, when community groups attack general social problems without offering viable solutions.

Community action agencies would do well to take a look at the American labor movement and learn from its experience. The unions' success in protecting the rights of their members and establishing a system of industrial jurisprudence has been a result of the labor movement's ability to focus on specific, immediate grievances. Recognizing the need to respect "management prerogatives," they concentrated on processing grievances and protecting members' rights without trying to reform the whole fabric of society at once. However, by improving the rights and status of the members, they also succeeded in changing fundamentally the quality of American life. In the long run, the results may have been more radical than if the transformation had been forced by drastic and sudden action.

By emulating the "reformist" exercise of power by American unions, CAA's could establish viable organizations which would improve the quantity and quality of services offered to the poor and in so doing give the poor greater political power. Like the labor unions more than three decades ago, CAA's could utilize the machinery established for improving services to the community to forge new political coalitions. The parallel cannot be carried too far, however. Unions soon established clear-cut jurisdictions and economic independence, while CAA's will have to remain dependent upon outside support to carry out their activities.

Community action programs have a deeper implication than merely that of improving welfare services, but often when CAA's concentrate on broad social and political issues they tend to deemphasize the more immediate services needed by the poor. If the experience of the labor movement is at all relevant to the antipoverty program, it is worth noting that those unions which stressed the "big picture" largely dissipated their energies and resources without visibly improving the immediate economic condition of their members.

OEO and Congress Know Best

The CAP concept of community planning, coordination of efforts, and mobilization of resources requires local capability and sophistication as well as commitment. Effective community planning—whether for economic development, fighting poverty, or area rehabilitation—cannot be directed from Washington. The federal government may supply economic resources and even some technical assistance, but the initiative for planning, coordination, and mobilization of resources must originate in the community. No matter how good the plan, it is of little value unless implemented, and it is difficult for community residents to develop the commitment needed for effective implementation if plans are entirely designed and funded by Washington. Federal requirements that communities engage in economic planning have been a dismal failure.

Those in the President's Council of Economic Advisors and in the Bureau of the Budget who helped draft the Economic Opportunity Act had learned the futility of planning by ukase from the experience of the Area Redevelopment Administration and other federal efforts. The ARA required each participating community to submit an Overall Economic Development Plan as a condition of receiving aid. Nearly a thousand communities—cities, counties, Indian reservations, and other political jurisdictions—complied with this requirement. In most cases, the plans were drawn not to mobilize community resources but to meet the superficial federal requirements.

The EOA's architects realized that if the federal government wished to induce communities to initiate concerted antipoverty efforts, the federal government would have to offer meaningful carrots—cash as well as technical assistance. Accordingly, they viewed their initial proposal for a community action program as a series of demonstration projects, expecting that the federal dollars would be a significant addition to expenditures in the ten to twenty selected localities. More than scarcity of funds impelled this thinking. The planners knew that few communities would be able to mount a sophisticated and coordinated attack on poverty with the limited technical resources available.

Needless to say, the sharp restriction on the number of communities to be involved in the effort did not jibe with the image of a "total war on poverty." As soon as the planning of the antipoverty effort was transferred in February 1964 from the Council of Economic Advisors and the Bureau of the Budget to the special presidential task force headed by Sargent Shriver, the demonstration-project notion was dropped, and the legislation imposed no restrictions on the number of participating communities. Every community with poor people was entitled to a CAA; every community that evidenced any interest, and some that did not, received federal funds to create a CAA.

A Thousand CAA's

Though many local leaders claimed that poverty was not a significant problem in their areas, remarkably few communities refused federal support of CAA's. As long as one local dollar—which could be supplied in kind and not necessarily in cash—could beget nine federal dollars, communities were eager to receive the federal grants, even if some of the citizenry considered the funds tainted. Only a few communities refused to make the token contributions necessary to receive funds. Bakersfield, California, and Baltimore County, Maryland, drew a great deal of attention when the citizenry rejected a bid to participate in the program. Rejection did not foreclose participation, because private resources satisfied the 10 percent local share requirement, and OEO could ignore the results of the referenda.[23]

With almost every community eligible for CAP dollars, distribution of funds on the basis of poverty population was virtually impossible. Table 3-1 shows the discrepancies of CAP dollars per poor person for the ten leading recipient cities. Disproportionate funding was equally apparent among states. For example, Illinois received $39.4 million in CAP funds in fiscal 1967, while Alabama, with almost the same number of poor people, received only $17.5 million; New Jersey and Wisconsin, despite similar poverty populations, were granted $26.4 million and $8.9 million, respectively. Moreover, there was strong evidence of "rural discrimination." For the nation as a whole, CAP grants over the first four years averaged roughly $97 per poor person. The comparable figure in the ten cities that received the

Table 3-1.   The Ten Largest Recipients of CAP Funds, Fiscal 1965-68

City	Number of Poor in 1965 (Thousands)	Total CAP Grants (Millions)	Average Per Poor Person
New York	1,239	$115.1	$93
Chicago	383	80.3	210
Los Angeles	371	77.2	208
Philadelphia	359	35.6	99
Detroit	243	41.2	170
St. Louis	158	23.6	149
Washington, D.C.	152	37.8	249
Boston	112	20.8	185
Atlanta	89	19.1	214
Pittsburgh	76	21.0	276

Source: Community Action Program, Office of Economic Opportunity.

largest grants was almost three times the national average, ranging from a low of $93 for New York City to three times as much for Pittsburgh.

The only explanation for the distribution of CAP funds is that areas with the most effective organization and sophistication in the art of grantsmanship received the largest proportion of funds. "Rural discrimination" was closely related to the absence of effective local organization in sparsely populated rural areas. Thus, with about 40 percent of the nation's poor residing in them, rural areas received about 30 percent of CAP funds (Table 3–2). In 1967 Congress required that an assistant OEO director be appointed for rural programs and that CAP appoint separate urban and rural assistant directors. However, Congress rejected an amendment which would have required specific allocation of CAP funds for rural and urban CAA's.

Since there are poor people in virtually every community in the United States, most of them anxious or at least willing to establish their own CAA's and partake of the federal antipoverty dollars, any restraint upon the number of CAA's had to come from OEO. The agency's top officials were divided on how broadly CAP funds should be scattered. OEO's top planner, Joseph A. Kershaw, argued that even if increased appropriations materialized, the total CAP effort would still be more effective if its resources were applied only to areas where poverty was concentrated. Underlying the argument for focusing CAP efforts on "heavy impact" areas was the belief that small grants would be frittered away and would require disproportionately large salary expenditures, while concentration would enable economies of size as well as major new programs. Other officials argued that the initial funding of CAA's would generate community demand for additional federal antipoverty dollars, which would in turn escalate the "war on poverty." Sargent Shriver was among the proponents of this view, and needless to say, it was the one that prevailed. Eighteen months after

Table 3–2. Proportion of CAP Funds Allocated to Rural Areas, Fiscal 1966–68

Program	Percent		
	Fiscal 1966	Fiscal 1967	Fiscal 1968
Community Action Programs	27	29	30
Head Start	38	38	37
Demonstration projects and technical assistance	27	31	33
Upward Bound	25	25	26
Legal Services	20	19	20
Local initiative	20	20	23
Health centers	0	14	18

Source: Office of Economic Opportunity.

the Community Action Program was inaugurated over 1,000 CAA's had been funded. But the hopes of those who favored proliferation of CAA's did not materialize, because after the second year CAP appropriations increased only moderately. As a result, the activities of hundreds of CAA's were confined to hiring a small staff, followed up by grants for Head Start and one or two small additional components.

There was a wide scope in the types of programs funded by CAP. By mid-1968, total CAP obligations amounted to nearly $3 billion, including 15 percent non-federal contributions which were largely "in kind." Costs of the Head Start program and neighborhood centers accounted for two of every three dollars obligated by CAP. Table 3–3 presents annual breakdowns of total grants by purpose and shows the non-federal contributions to the program.

National Programs

The decision to fund more than a thousand CAA's and many different types of programs placed great strain on the basic objective of relying upon community efforts to initiate and develop community action projects. And the Washington warriors were at a loss to quantify the programs on which the funds were expended. It would have been extravagant to anticipate that a thousand CAA's would or could come up with useful planning designs or innovative approaches to poverty, or that a small inexperienced staff in Washington (later in the regional offices) would be in a position to identify the more promising proposals and establish priorities among applications.

At the same time the President, the director of OEO, and many others had made exaggerated promises and claims for the program's achievements. Under this pressure to produce results the agency grew increasingly impatient with waiting for innovative approaches from communities. Once new CAA's were coaxed into existence, there was a considerable time lag before they came up with applications for actual projects. To speed up activity, OEO decided to develop prepackaged national programs among which communities could shop for something that suited their needs. Recognizing that these national priority programs did violence to the concept of local planning, OEO planners rationalized by saying that localities could still suggest alternative approaches to community action. In reality, however, the communities quickly recognized that Congress and OEO were "pushing" certain items and that applications for these programs were likely to receive more expeditious treatment from the agency than projects dreamed up locally. Another rationalization was that federally packaged programs would give CAA's a start and help them gain sufficient experience in running projects to design their own. Yet many CAA's

Table 3–3. Distribution of CAP Obligations, Fiscal 1965–68 (Amounts in Millions)

	Amounts					Percents				
	Total	1965	1966	1967	1968	Total	1965	1966	1967	1968
TOTAL FEDERAL	$2535.4	$236.5	$627.9	$804.2	$866.8	100.0	100.0	100.0	100.0	100.0
Local Initiative Programs	988.6	115.2	274.6	275.5	323.3	39.0	48.7	43.7	34.2	37.3
CAA development, administration, planning, and evaluation	193.4	18.7	41.0	58.2	75.5	7.6	7.9	6.5	7.2	8.7
Neighborhood service systems	333.2	24.3	77.0	99.5	132.4	13.1	10.3	12.3	12.4	15.3
Manpower	88.7	13.0	33.0	20.0	22.7	3.5	5.5	5.3	2.5	2.6
Education	100.5	18.1	39.0	21.9	21.5	4.0	7.6	6.2	2.7	2.5
Housing	14.4	c	3.0	3.0	8.4	.6	—	.5	.4	1.0
Health	65.2	5.0	19.0	22.6	18.6	2.6	2.1	3.0	2.8	2.1
Social services and economic development	182.6	36.1	58.6	47.7	40.2	7.2	15.3	9.3	5.9	4.6
Consumer action and financial assistance	10.6	c	4.0	2.6	4.0	.4	—	.6	.3	.5
National Emphasis Programs	1259.1	96.4	248.5	453.4	460.8	49.7	40.8	39.6	56.4	53.2
Head Start	965.6	96.4	198.8	349.2	321.2	38.0	40.8	31.7	43.4	37.1
Head Start Follow-Through	14.6	—	—	—	14.6	.6	—	—	—	1.7
Upward Bound	84.7	a	24.9	28.2	31.6	3.3	—	4.0	3.5	3.6
Comprehensive health services	84.0	—	a	50.8	33.2	3.3	—	—	6.3	3.8
Family planning	9.0	—	b	b	9.0	.4	—	—	—	1.0
Emergency food and medical services	12.8	b	b	b	12.8	.5	—	—	—	1.5
Senior opportunity services	2.5	b	b	b	2.5	.1	—	—	—	.3
Legal services	85.9	a	24.8	25.2	35.9	3.4	—	3.9	3.1	4.1
Support Programs	287.7	24.9	104.8	75.3	82.7	11.3	10.5	16.7	9.4	9.5
Training	33.5	—	9.0	12.3	12.2	1.3	—	1.4	1.5	1.4
Technical assistance	41.3	5.3	9.6	12.5	13.9	1.6	2.2	1.5	1.6	1.6
Research, pilot programs, evaluation	157.2	16.6	72.3	34.0	34.3	6.2	7.0	11.5	4.2	3.9
Program administration	55.7	3.0	13.9	16.5	22.3	2.2	1.3	2.2	2.1	2.6
TOTAL NON-FEDERAL	448.8	18.1	78.3	148.8	203.6	—	—	—	—	—

[a] Included in Research and Pilot programs.
[b] Included in Local Initiative.
[c] Included in General Social Services.

Note: Data in this table do not always coincide with information presented elsewhere in this study, since various components of OEO occasionally list different statistics on the distribution of their funds.

Source: Office of Economic Opportunity.

never advanced beyond the stage of operating national priority programs; and even if they did so, there was little CAP money left for locally initiated projects after the allocations to national programs.

Much of the attractiveness of national priority programs lay in their acceptability to selected and frequently influential groups within the communities, and in their national and local visibility. Many indigenously sponsored projects generated controversy and attacks on OEO. For example, what appeared to be a harmless cultural project sponsored by the HARYOU-Act in Harlem turned out to be a racist theater group. In contrast, prepackaged programs were "safe" and served to give the CAA's respectability, and they were quantifiable and therefore easier to "sell." Head Start projects were especially favored because few people could object to giving poor children preschool education, medical attention, and hot meals. The immense popularity of Head Start, the first national program, stimulated OEO to advance others.

Taking its cue from OEO, Congress began in 1966 to make mandatory certain programs, which became known as national emphasis programs as compared with local initiative programs. During OEO's first fiscal year, all CAP programs except Head Start were discretionary and presumably initiated locally. But by fiscal 1968 more than six of every ten CAP dollars were allocated to the national emphasis programs and other nationally directed efforts (Table 3–3). This left OEO officials far less flexibility in approving local initiative projects. Since the total funds available for community action programs remained relatively stable during 1967 and 1968, approval of a new locally initiated program often required the termination of an on-going project, a difficult decision to make under the best of circumstances.

OEO's detractors in the radical camp saw the increasing allocation of CAP funds to national emphasis programs as *prima facie* evidence that OEO was losing its innovative mission and becoming another Washington bureaucracy. Two major factors, which became increasingly prominent, underlay this criticism. First, there were the demands by vociferous, and growing, sections of the Negro community for an increasing measure of self-determination in community life and for greater control over the institutions that affected their lives. The second major objection to national emphasis programs stemmed from a general disillusionment with welfare programs, a pervasive feeling that "big government" had failed, and a desire for decentralized governmental activity. The premise was that the decentralization of program planning and direction encouraged greater flexibility and responsiveness to people's needs. Advocates of decentralization assumed that there would be greater and more meaningful participation by the poor in localized decision-making, and that this would result in increased initiative, effort, and assumption of responsibility.

Though there is much to be said for the decentralization of social welfare programs, it appears that the critics of national emphasis programs frequently overstated their case. The romantic notion that localized decision-making is more responsive to the "public interest" is not always borne out. Historically, "grass roots democracy" has often permitted the most vicious disregard of local minorities. Moreover, centralization is necessary to effect quick large-scale transfers of resources from one use to another. Finally, given the shortage of trained personnel to administer community action programs, centralization may be the most efficient way of utilizing limited resources. Thus, there is no reason why the CAA's should not learn from each other's mistakes and achievements, and there is no need for each community to reinvent the wheel. While there is great diversity among communities, the poor share common needs. National emphasis programs attempted to allocate funds within OEO's limited resources to support programs for which there was broad consensus.

Without defending OEO's guidelines regulating the administration of national emphasis programs, the allegation that they robbed local communities of initiative has been greatly exaggerated. In too many cases the attacks seemed to be a substitute and an excuse for avoiding the hard work needed to implement programs at the local level. It is easier to extol the virtues of grass roots democracy and self-determination and to attack power-grasping and meddling Washington bureaucrats than it is to organize community efforts. Some vociferous opponents of CAP national emphasis programs also found that attacking the "sprawling and proliferating Great Society programs" was a sure way to catch headlines, or at least some attention, in the press. Attention on such a scale was seldom granted to those who administered antipoverty programs, devoted careful analysis to the operations of CAA's, and performed painstaking evaluations of the programs.

In fact, national emphasis programs did not rob communities of autonomy or of involvement in their planning or operation. For as S. M. Miller pointed out, "maximum feasible participation" may be expressed in many forms. Moreover, the OEO guidelines were not so detailed as to preclude local initiative; rather, they provided a framework on which local community leaders, and the poor, could build with considerable freedom. The situation was analogous to that of people living in similar houses on the same block. Each family can express its individuality and personal tastes by the color of paint it selects for the house, the planting and care of shrubbery, and the interior decoration.

By initiating projects and providing the basis for further programs, national emphasis programs may have stimulated community
participation as well as the development of neighborhood leadership.
The impression created by opponents of the programs that the efforts
originated exclusively in the heads of OEO bureaucrats in Washington
is not an accurate one. After all, most of the national emphasis programs developed from experiments and demonstrations in the communities. Local planners and project administrators frequently played
important roles in designing the basic concepts, and guidelines were
built up from these early experiences.

Research and Demonstration

Originally CAP offered a unique opportunity for social experimentation, as the Act provided that 15 percent of CAP funds could be
allocated for research and demonstration projects. Sanford Kravitz, the
CAP official responsible for the research and demonstration program
during the first two years of OEO, used the $67 million allocated to it
in fiscal 1965 and 1966 to develop visible national demonstration
projects. Instead of limiting its demonstration programs to a few
communities, CAP funded projects in a number of areas, allowing
OEO to gather the experiences and reactions of different communities
to similar efforts. Upward Bound, neighborhood health centers, and, in
fact, most of the national emphasis programs developed from demonstration projects.

Not all of the projects undertaken by CAP's research and demonstration program were winners, and the experimental nature of the
program invited criticism. R and D had its opponents within OEO's
regional offices, because grants were made directly by the national
office to the community, bypassing the regional office. Lack of funds
made it rare that a successful demonstration could be duplicated.
Similarly, CAA's frequently opposed R and D because many of the
projects operated independently. Possibly the most controversial
projects R and D financed were those ineligible for funding under
other CAP rules and those that bypassed state and local governments
that refused to cooperate in certain antipoverty efforts. CAP research
and demonstration projects could be funded without any local participation and could be administered by any nonprofit private organization. The funding of controversial projects led Congress to clip the
wings of R and D by cutting the maximum amount of CAP funds
that could be allocated to it from 15 to 5 percent and by requiring
advance approval of R and D projects by the appropriate CAA or local
government.

As operated by CAP, the research and demonstration program remained somewhat independent of the rest of OEO. This created a basic policy question—whether R and D should continue to operate without specific restraints, or whether it would be appropriate to spell out guidelines for its operations and make its grants subject to approval by a review board. These questions were never formally resolved, but as OEO became more stable and bureaucratic, internal controls were imposed upon the research and demonstration officials. The congressional restriction of R and D funds to 5 percent of total CAP appropriations further hampered experimentation. A large proportion of the $40 million obligated by the R and D office in fiscal 1967 and of the $35 million in the following year went to support on-going projects, leaving little opportunity to explore new areas.

Considering the wide support of community self-determination corporations, the most significant R and D efforts during fiscal 1967 and 1968 may have been the pilot community economic self-help projects. Among these were the Harlem Commonwealth Corporation, Crawfordsville Enterprises, and other early prototypes of community development corporations. It is ironic that the severest critics of these CAP activities are also among the most ardent supporters of community self-determination efforts, and that Washington bureaucrats encouraged and funded prototypes of community development corporations.

Local Initiative Programs

About 40 percent of the $2.5 billion obligated by CAP during its initial four fiscal years was allocated to CAA-initiated programs. These became known as "versatile" funds because the CAA's could use them for any of the broad purposes allowed under the legislation. A breakdown in the types of projects for which these funds were used is presented in Table 3–3.

No doubt the billion dollars bought a great many services and helped a great many people, but the total assistance defies evaluation since it was distributed in thousands of cities, towns, and hamlets. The projects supported by these funds ranged from cultural uplift—taking poor children to a museum or giving them a music lesson—to providing housing for Indians living on remote reservations or remedial education to migrants.

These local and often fragmented programs elude over-all description and can best be studied on a case-by-case basis. And though anecdotes are no substitute for evaluation, isolated incidents help to provide some insight into the impact of the local programs. There are numerous ways in which the locally initiated projects helped the poor. The case of a woman with nine young children in Pittsburgh is illus-

trative. While the community action programs did not produce fundamental changes in the status of the family, they offered numerous
minor forms of assistance. According to the story, "Poverty workers
have helped here with some second-hand furniture, a good deal of
expert advice, a few dollars when money was badly needed—but her
income hasn't improved, nor [is] it likely to [be]." The children were
also helped, though the impact cannot be measured: "They've gone
places and done things they might never have without the poverty
program. They've attended special schools to upgrade their educational
skills, they've romped in the countryside away from the city slums,
been taught to see possibilities for self-expression in painting or sculp-
ting or sawing away at a violin."[24] Whether the poor receive maximum
help from each public dollar spent is a question impossible to answer.
While the program did not pull the Pittsburgh family out of poverty,
it made life a little more bearable.

An internal CAP memorandum, asserting that experience showed
that local initiative programs helped the poor in scores of communities
could support the claim only by offering a number of anecdotes. The
memo concluded: "We have invested over $1 billion in local initiative
Community Action to date. Based on what we know . . . this program
should be able to match its achievements against the results . . . of any
other comparable social investments."[25] To support this claim, CAP
collected forty-four CAA success stories. Unwilling to rest the case of
CAA local initiative efforts on faith alone, OEO attempted to quantify
the impact of CAA operations. Although there are still no hard data
to rely on, OEO concluded that many CAA's had played a role in
significantly changing at least one of the following local institutions:
public and private welfare agencies, public employment services, and
school systems.

The institution most closely identified with the CAA's was the
neighborhood service center. As defined by OEO, neighborhood centers
serve a definite target area, offering clients a variety of services or
referring them to other facilities. In line with the CAP doctrine, neighborhood centers must reach out into the neighborhood and involve
the poor in their activities, both as employees and as policy makers.

Like community action agencies, the neighborhood centers differ
in structure, clientele, services, and perception of functions. The
centers' physical aspects range from small store fronts to large structures; their annual budgets range from a few thousand to more than a
million dollars. Because OEO has left the design and operations of
the centers to the CAA's, little information is available about their
activities. There were neighborhood center programs in some 870
communities in 1968, but CAP officials could not indicate the actual
number of centers in operation. The funds spent by the centers can
only be guessed at.

A major goal of OEO was to make the centers a focal point for ministering to the needs of the poor, coordinating and consolidating services, and lending sympathy. Various CAP activities, including other national emphasis programs, were frequently housed in neighborhood centers. According to OEO's statistics, $132 million of 1968 CAP funds, 15 percent of the total, was allocated to neighborhood centers. In addition, many legal service offices, Head Start classes, and birth control clinics operated out of neighborhood centers, though funds for these activities came from different CAP accounts. On the other hand, neighborhood centers sometimes spent their own funds on service components provided elsewhere.

Late in 1966 OEO made an effort to obtain statistics on the 400 centers that were supposedly in operation at that time. The data contained many flaws and were never released, but the survey suggested that the resources allocated to the centers were about equally divided between administration (which included the hiring of the poor) and services, most prominent of which were employment and manpower operations. This emphasis was confirmed by another OEO-sponsored study of neighborhood centers in 20 communities, which revealed that the most widely represented of all the programs were employment counseling and job placement, found in 85 percent of the centers. Welfare services, health and education (adult basic, tutoring, nurseries) were next in popularity.[26]

Basic to the operation of the centers was the employment of poor people from the area. Again, OEO collected no systematic data on the number of poor employed by the CAA's or by the centers. However, approximate figures gathered from the grant funding data system showed that in fiscal 1968 about 68,500 nonprofessionals were employed on a year-round basis, with an additional 75,000 taken on during the summer. The former group was divided among the neighborhood centers, full year Head Start, and CAA central staffs. All we know about the pay of these people is that they received at least the minimum wage. Generally the poor were hired as neighborhood workers to provide outreach and referral services and to interest the neighborhood residents in the center and the community. These workers were the backbone of community organization, which was the emphasis of most neighborhood center programs. The OEO-commissioned study attempted to investigate the role of the nonprofessional employee. The nine-agency survey found that three of every four were females and that the same proportion were employed only part time. The explanation given was that the CAA's tried to stretch their limited dollars to involve as many community residents as possible.

In addition to supplying services and employing the poor, an essential function of the centers was to organize the poor to help themselves. The two OEO-sponsored studies on community centers reached different conclusions on this point. The Kirschner study, cited earlier, concluded that with a few exceptions the centers had not attempted to organize the poor and had failed to alter the political structure of their communities. Kirschner concluded that it was "extremely rare to find both aggressive community action and well-executed service programs within the same center."[27]

The other study, by the consulting firm of Daniel Yankelovitch, stressed the conflict between "welfare professionals," who favored investing CAP dollars in "solid services and job training," and civil rights leaders, who urged the centers to engage in organizing the poor. This study concluded that OEO could have the best of both worlds, providing both service programs and community organization.[28]

Since neighborhood centers were the epitome of federally supported decentralized programs, other agencies attempted to get into the act by sponsoring them. Not that OEO could claim to have invented the neighborhood centers; settlement houses have existed since the turn of the century, and single-purpose neighborhood organizations have been sponsored by welfare organizations, employment offices, and others. The Department of Health, Education, and Welfare favored itself as the administrator of the neighborhood center program. HEW's concept of neighborhood centers differed from OEO's only in regard to jurisdiction. While OEO urged that CAA's be the sole developers, coordinators, and funders of neighborhood centers, HEW wanted to designate welfare, employment services, school systems, housing projects, as well as CAA's or other agencies as sponsors. The Department of Labor endorsed the one-stop center concept of OEO and HEW, but insisted that its manpower programs be a significant part of the program. The last entry into the field was the Department of Housing and Urban Development. OEO, for its part, saw the other federal agencies as providers of certain specialized services in neighborhood centers. The only agency truly in a position to coordinate all services and reach the poor, according to OEO, was OEO itself.

Given the ever increasing emphasis on decentralization and on delivering services to the poor, the role and importance of neighborhood centers should grow. Exactly what the future holds for them is difficult to foresee, in part because there is so little information with which to measure their record of effectiveness and popularity. However, insofar as community activities aimed at self-determination and resident participation receive increased support, the neighborhood centers are likely to play a central role.

A New Approach to Welfare?

Though the Community Action Program is barely four years old (most CAA's have been in operation for an even shorter period), many people have already reached conclusions about these efforts. The present review rejects a summary judgment on the effectiveness of a thousand CAA's. Not only is there a paucity of data about their operations, particularly their "versatile" activities, but there is no accepted index by which to measure the success or failure of this social experiment. Even if better data were available on the costs and budgets of specific operations, over-all assessments would still be illusive. How is one to measure the impact of the CAA's upon the operations of welfare agencies, or the effect of hiring Negroes for administrative and executive positions upon life in the ghettos? There is not even agreement on the desirability of CAP's basic tenet calling for the involvement of the poor in the planning and operation of CAA undertakings.

In an era in which participatory democracy has become the demand of many sectors of the population, it is not at all surprising that OEO's modest efforts at involving the poor in the CAA's have brought more condemnation than praise. Spokesmen for civil rights and other groups have demanded even greater local control—not only over CAA affairs but over all community institutions—and have not been satisfied with the changes that CAP tried to make in the welfare system. At the same time, even these modest efforts have produced tensions with established public and private institutions.

An objective evaluation of the CAA's, and particularly of the role of the poor in these programs, should compare the CAP-funded agencies with traditional welfare organizations rather than with some ideal model. On that score, CAP must certainly be judged an innovative agency which gave the poor their first social and political role. Few would disagree with the basic CAP premise of the need for a new federal approach to welfare. Many CAA's have made faltering steps toward revising the method of delivering aid to the poor. The effort should be nourished, even if progress thus far has been uneven and falls short of the hopes advanced by the antipoverty warriors that CAP would eliminate the need for a welfare system by eradicating poverty.

Given the number and diversity of CAA's, and the dearth of information about their operations, no meaningful summary judgment can be made about their effectiveness. The national emphasis programs, however, offer somewhat better documentation, permitting some over-all summary of their operations and a tentative judgment on their effectiveness. The rest of our discussion of CAP is therefore devoted to these programs: Head Start, Upward Bound, Neighborhood Health Centers, Family Planning, Legal Services, and VISTA.

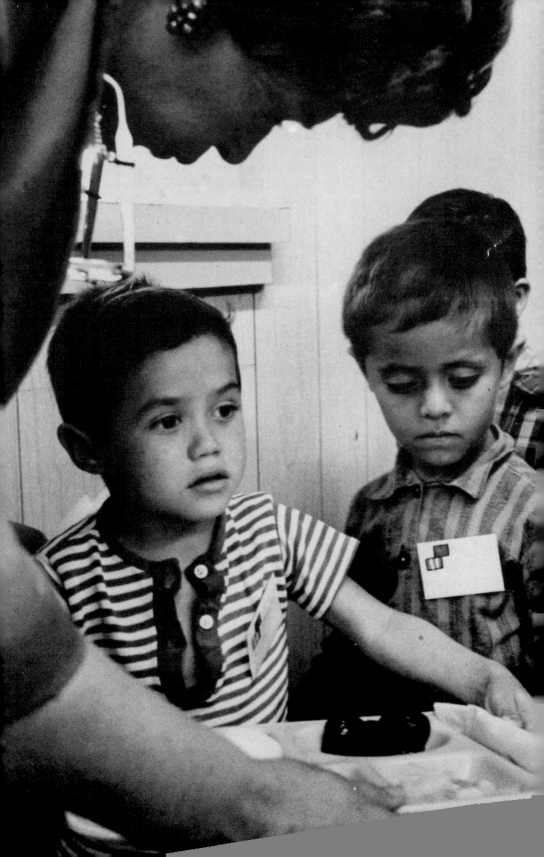

4.

IT IS NEVER TOO EARLY
TO FIGHT POVERTY

Train up a child in the way he should go:
and when he is old, he will not depart from it.

Proverbs 22:6

"Prep School" for Poor Kids

Without a doubt, Head Start is the most popular component in the antipoverty Community Action Program. Focusing on early physical and educational development, the program is designed to prepare impoverished preschool children for primary school experience. Head Start was sold to the American public as an expanded kindergarten program for the poor, with health and nutrition components. The child-oriented and educationally conscious public has not seriously questioned the need or value of such efforts.

Public preschool education as a concept is the product of natural, historical evolution. The battle for free primary and secondary public education was fought and won in the late nineteenth century. With public education for six- to eighteen-year-olds a solid achievement, attention in recent years has shifted to other categories of students. A recent thrust of the public education movement has been directed at the older age groups and has manifested itself in the growth of higher education in colleges and universities and an increasing federal commitment to such education. Almost a quarter of the costs of higher education are now financed with federal funds.

A second thrust in recent years has been the result of an increasing realization of the need for publicly supported preschool efforts. The preschool movement received a great stimulus during World War II, when daytime care for preschool children of working mothers became a necessity. Thirty-four states now provide support for kindergartens. However, these and other facilities for younger children are still unavailable in many areas of the country: only three of every ten preschoolers attended nursery school or kindergarten in 1966, and very few of the three- and four-year-olds attended any school at all (Table 4–1). Participation in these programs is related in part to income level; therefore, children of minority groups have very limited oppor-

*Table 4–1. Children Aged 3 to 5 Enrolled in Kindergarten or Nursery School,
October 1966*

Age Group	Population	Number Enrolled in School[a] (Thousands)	Percent Enrolled in School[a]
3- to 5-year-olds	12,486	3,674	29.4
White	10,514	3,142	29.9
Nonwhite	1,970	532	27.0
3-year-olds	4,087	248	6.1
White	3,431	193	5.6
Nonwhite	655	54	8.2
4-year-olds	4,155	785	18.9
White	3,499	659	18.8
Nonwhite	656	126	19.2
5-year-olds	4,244	2,642	62.2
White	3,584	2,290	63.9
Nonwhite	659	352	53.4

[a] Excluded from this table are the following enrollment figures: (a) 505,000 5-year-olds in elementary schools (above the kindergarten level), (b) 127,000 6-year-olds in kindergarten, and (c) 2,000 6-year-olds in nursery school.
Note: Totals may not add because of rounding.
Source: Office of Education, U.S. Department of Health, Education, and Welfare, *Nursery-Kindergarten Enrollment of Children under Six,* October 1966.

tunities for attending preschool programs (Table 4–2). Fifty-three percent of the five-year-old nonwhites in the nation are enrolled in a kindergarten or nursery school, compared to 64 percent for the white population.

The lack of preschool educational experience affects the disadvantaged child more adversely than a middle-class child. In recent years it has become increasingly clear that many impoverished children experience serious difficulties throughout their school years because

*Table 4–2. Percent of Children in Kindergarten or Nursery School by Family Income
Level, October 1966[a]*

Age Group	Annual Family Income			
	Under $3,000	$3,000–$4,999	$5,000–$7,499	$7,500 and Over
3-year-olds	5.4	3.5	3.9	8.8
4-year-olds	13.2	11.1	15.1	29.1
5-year-olds	40.1	49.6	66.5	72.2

[a] Footnote a, Table 4–1.
Source: Same as Table 4–1.

they lacked intellectual stimulation and emotional adjustment in their early family life.[1] For these children, preschool programs might compensate for background deficiencies and bring them closer to the achievement level of their middle-class peers. This reasoning seems to have particular relevance to the war on poverty. By extending free public education to the poor during a formative period of growth— ages three to six—the advocates of the Head Start program hoped to give children a better chance to succeed in school. The program was thus conceived as a "prep school" for poor kids.

Magnitude of Program and Needs

The Economic Opportunity Act of 1964 did not specifically address itself to the educational problems of poor children. In fact, a leading educator, Dr. Urie Bronfenbrenner, argued during the congressional hearings that the Act placed too much emphasis on sixteen- to twenty-two-year-olds. A program for preschoolers, he said, could accomplish much more with the same funds. If the "legislation [is] to strike at poverty at its source," he testified, "this means striking at poverty where it hits first and most damagingly—in early childhood."[2] But Congress deferred the educational component of the war on poverty until passage of the Elementary and Secondary Education Act of 1965. Advocates of a preschool program for poor children persisted in the cause and found Shriver sympathetic to the idea. Even though the Economic Opportunity Act emphasized an exit from poverty through training and work, it was never too early to start building the bridges leading from poverty. Deprived of cultural advantages at home, the poor child is disadvantaged when he enters school, and falls ever further behind as he moves through the elementary grades. The failure of the school system to help many poor children is well documented.

The fact that CAP made no explicit provision for aiding poor children did not preclude allocation of funds for this purpose. Indeed, Congress had initially given OEO administrators maximum flexibility in allocating CAP funds. Communities were expected to initiate and design their own projects, whose funding would be provided by the federal government. But no more than a handful of communities were in a position to take this sort of initiative in 1964. Except for a few communities, mostly large metropolitan areas, which had had experience in the earlier prototypes of community action—the Ford-funded "gray areas" projects or the federally sponsored juvenile delinquency programs—most areas were slow to organize community action agencies and to file acceptable applications. During its initial months, OEO faced the dual task of determining the components that would go into CAP and actually committing the $240 million Congress allocated to the program. Fearing that inaction might be interpreted as an absence of need, OEO felt it was necessary to commit the available funds before its next budgetary authorization request was presented to Congress. Packaged programs were desperately needed.

Sympathetic with the views expressed by Bronfenbrenner, the House Committee on Education and Labor considered a Republican amendment that would earmark Community Action Program funds for a preschool program. The amendment was withdrawn when it received bipartisan support and assurances that OEO would support such a program. The idea also received enthusiastic support from a panel of medical and educational experts appointed by Sargent Shriver "to consider the kinds of programs which might be most effective in increasing achievement and opportunities for the children of the poor."[3] The decision to fund a preschool program named Head Start under the antipoverty program was announced in President Johnson's education message on January 12, 1965. Even then some advisers counseled delay, noting that a large-scale summer preschool program would require considerable planning. Shriver rejected the cautious approach, and the Head Start program was officially announced on February 19, 1965, at a White House tea party. The quick public acceptance of the program went beyond the fondest expectations of its most ardent advocates. "It stands," one observer commented, "as a rare example of the speed with which a Government program can be organized—given money, adroit press-agentry, and co-operation by volunteer groups."[4]

The program was to be largely experimental, and few knew what to expect. The need for a Head Start program seemed obvious, but how would communities around the nation respond? OEO intended to commit only $17 million for the summer of 1965, enabling 100,000 children to participate. Although more CAP funds were available, OEO did not anticipate a greater demand. Shriver followed up the program's announcement with personal letters to 35,000 school administrators, welfare officials, mayors, and other community officials. Within a few weeks localities were besieging OEO headquarters with an unforeseen volume of requests. OEO officials in Washington were suddenly faced with the decision of whether to reject many applications or to support a program many times larger than the one originally conceived. OEO decided to meet the demand, and Head Start grew like Topsy. Program costs, which rose to $103 million for the summer of 1965, provided places for 560,000 children, as well as some staff training. This expansion easily swallowed uncommitted CAP funds, which were more than two-fifths of the total CAP budget. OEO rapidly expanded Head Start's skeletal national staff, and many temporary hands were recruited to help with the increased workload.

Aside from its intrinsic value in the education of the poor, Head Start presented several attractive features that motivated OEO to launch the large crash program in the summer of 1965. Perhaps the most important factor—inasmuch as most CAP funds were uncommitted in the spring of 1965—was OEO's search for innovative and attractive programs to catch the public eye and help the agency secure greater appropriations for fiscal 1966. Head Start was tailor-made for the situation: it used large amounts of funds quickly and was capable of gaining wide support. Moreover, Head Start was a prepackaged project that could be adopted immediately by newly formed community action agencies struggling to design appropriate and acceptable programs for their communities. Where no CAA existed, other public and nonprofit private agencies could use the funds. School boards were interested in preschool programs and were eligible as recipients; and they possessed the expertise and administrative capacity to deploy the funds during fiscal 1965.

Head Start also had the potential for forming the core of a community action program in areas that had failed to set up CAA's. Often the established political powers were neither concerned nor sufficiently skilled to set up CAA's, and OEO thus conceived that Head Start might be part of a "building block" approach to a CAA. Because Head Start required the establishment of advisory boards by the fall of 1965, it was hoped that these boards would serve as nuclei for CAA's, around which other CAP projects could be added. In communities that were hostile to the idea of a CAA, Head Start was the brightest hope that one would be created.

Underlying all the other factors that induced OEO to fund Head Start on such a large scale for the summer of 1965 was the program's enormous popularity. No doubt the secret of Head Start's success was that it directed attention to preschool poor children, who readily aroused the public's sympathy. Whatever its source, the unexpected and overwhelming response contrasted sharply with the apathy or antagonism with which many other OEO programs were greeted. OEO needed no public relations experts to discern that Head Start was a hit, and it continued to be the antipoverty program's most popular effort. In contrast to other poverty programs, which were plagued by charges of waste and inefficiency, Head Start was widely acclaimed. The major criticism of it was directed at delays in grants and inadequacy of funds.

Viewed at first as a temporary summer effort, it was not until late summer of 1965 that Head Start was expanded into a year-round program and achieved permanent status. On August 31, 1965, President Johnson, anxious to bolster the poverty program, made this announcement.

During its first four years of operation, Head Start was by far the largest single component of CAP. Its $978 million allocation accounted for almost two-fifths of the total CAP budget during the period (Table 4–3). Despite its relatively large expenditures, however, the demand for projects exceeded the available funds. By 1968 Head Start was funding 1,300 summer projects and 1,100 full-year projects. Sharing the general public's enthusiasm for the program, Congress displayed unusual generosity. For fiscal 1967, for example, Congress allocated $42 million more to Head Start than the Administration had requested.

Head Start's popularity was not universal, however. Paradoxically, opposition to expansion of the program came most often from the most ardent supporters of community action programs, including CAP officials at the national and local level. Their resistance stemmed from a conviction that Head Start (and other prepackaged projects) contributed little to the community action concept, delivering only limited funds while diverting attention from the more important task. In many communities, moreover, Head Start became an adjunct to the school system, thus reducing the resources available to CAA's for encouraging their communities to mount a coordinated attack on poverty. Finally, Head Start was a national program, and some CAP personnel feared that it and other "national emphasis" programs would destroy local initiative, ignoring the fact that innovative local proposals were scarce.

The summer efforts have remained about the size established during the first summer, and the major program expansion has involved full-year projects. The median length of the full-year program is nine months. Projects average five hours a day, but 28 percent of the full-year programs run seven hours or more, reflecting the fact that many of these projects double as day-care centers for the children of working parents.

Full-year programs tend to serve younger children than the summer projects do. The launching of parent-child projects for families that have at least one child below three years of age, and the funding of nursery, and even pre-nursery, projects reflects the belief of Head Start's officials that programs should be made available to children at the earliest possible age. Also, in some communities where kindergarten facilities are universally available, Head Start has been able to fund nursery projects. As Table 4–4 shows, the majority of children enrolled in full-year Head Start projects were less than five years old; many of these no doubt enter kindergarten upon completion of the

Table 4-3. Head Start Allocations and Enrollment, Fiscal 1965-68 (Amounts in Millions)

Fiscal Year	Total	Summer Programs		Full-Year Programs		Training	Evaluation and Research
		Children	Dollars	Children	Dollars		
1965	$103	560,000	$84	20,000	$8	$11	
1966	198	573,000	99[b]	160,000	81	16	$2
1967	352	466,000	117.5[c]	215,000	212	16	6
1968	330[a]	473,000	101.5[d]	218,000	239[e]	21	6

[a] $325 million original appropriation; $5 million subsequently added.
[b] An additional $14 million was obligated in fiscal 1967 to supplement the 1966 summer programs in nine large cities. This amount includes $2 million for follow-up activities for children in 1966 summer programs.
[c] Includes $14 million obligated in fiscal 1967 to supplement summer 1966 programs and $1 million for NYC aides in 1967 summer programs.
[d] Includes $10.8 million in funds carried over from fiscal year 1967.
[e] Includes $36 million in funds carried over from fiscal year 1967 and $5 million for parent-child centers.

Source: Community Action Program, Office of Economic Opportunity.

Table 4–4. Age Distribution of Head Start Participants, 1965–67

Age Group	Summer 1965	Full Year 1965–66	Summer 1966	Full Year 1966–67	Summer 1967
Total	100.0%	100.0%	100.0%	100.0%	100.0%
Below 4 years	.7	10.9	2.3	13.4	1.7
4 to 5 years	14.0	47.9	18.2	44.1	19.8
5 to 6 years	44.2	31.6	44.5	34.3	45.0
6 years and over	41.0	9.6	35.0	5.1	30.6

Source: Community Action Program, Office of Economic Opportunity.

Head Start experience. The objective, however, has been to provide year-round Head Start facilities during the year before the child's entry into public schools. Some have questioned this policy and have urged that Head Start concentrate its funds in areas where public schools do not offer kindergarten. The most effective way to distribute limited resources may be questioned, but the need to give poor children a head start as early as possible is acknowledged.

Head Start has been able to serve only a portion of the children in the poverty category. To reach all impoverished children between the ages of three and six, facilities would have to be provided for more than 2 million children—more than three times the number who attended Head Start programs during fiscal 1967 (Table 4–5). OEO officials estimate that the initial annual cost of establishing a full-year Head Start effort for all eligible children would amount to $6.5 billion, more than the total OEO budget during its first four years.[5] Lack of sufficient funds is therefore the major barrier to expansion of Head Start. Inadequate facilities and a shortage of teachers are other constraints upon expansion. More than $3.6 billion would be needed to construct, renovate, and equip adequate facilities to provide full-year Head Start for the 2.2 million impoverished children who need such a program.

Table 4–5. Head Start Universe, 1966

Category	3-Year-Olds	4-Year-Olds	5-Year-Olds
Total poor children	1,000,000	1,000,000	1,000,000
Poor in other programs (excluding Title I preschools)	—	34,000	467,000
Total universe for Head Start	1,000,000	966,000	533,000
Universe the program may reach (80%)	800,000	773,000	427,000
Net Head Start universe (including 10% nonpoor)	880,000	850,000	470,000

Source: Community Action Program, Office of Economic Opportunity.

Program Components and Operation

Head Start differs from the usual nursery school or kindergarten. The latter presumably enrich the preschool experience of children and allow mothers respite from their offspring. As envisioned by educators, the nursery school function is to "influence only the child's emotional and social development—not his mental growth. . . . Deliberate teaching of mathematical or language skills is frowned upon in these schools."[6] In contrast, the objectives of Head Start are much broader (though the social-emotional element is still very strong) and stress the educational development of the preschool child.

Because the average child from a poor home is intellectually "retarded" by the time he enters Head Start, the brief summer program is presumably designed to offer a "cram" course to prepare him for school. Although this would appear to be the formal rationale for the summer program as presented by the OEO, some spokesmen for Head Start have refrained from making such broad claims. Rather, they indicate that it is basically a diagnostic program. That is, Head Start is concerned with improving the nutrition and health of the children in the hope of increasing their readiness for school. In more affluent homes, these aspects of a child's development are normally assumed by the family as a matter of course.

Finally, as a component of the Community Action Program, Head Start provides a further avenue for involving the poor in the planning and administration of projects.

Child Development

The children with whom the program deals come from deprived backgrounds and broken homes (Table 4–6). More than a fourth came from families that were on welfare or whose father was absent from home. Given the deprivation of these children, the program planners felt that only a "comprehensive program" would be adequate, preferring the name "child development centers" to emphasize the broad scope of the program's concern.

Because the program concentrates on meeting the individual needs of each child, it demands a high teacher-student ratio. One professional teacher for every 15 children is considered optimal, although the actual median has been one to 16. Head Start also favors a ratio of one adult (including volunteers) to every five children.

In line with other community action operations, Head Start has emphasized the employment of subprofessionals and volunteers to relieve the workload of the teacher and to provide additional attention

Table 4–6.   Family Profile of Head Start Children, 1965-67

Characteristics	1965–66 Full-Year Program	1966 Summer Program	1966–67 Full-Year Program	1967 Summer Program
Past Medical Treatment				
No visit to doctor in past 2 years	14%	15%	7%	14%
No visit to dentist in past 2 years	41	43	31	37
Their Families				
Father not living with child	26	21	30	23
Parent or guardian with 8 grades or less education				
Father	39	43	40	44
Mother	28	31	29	29
Parent or guardian presently employed				
Father	85	85	82	86
Mother	26	25	30	26
On Welfare	24	20	27	21
Their Homes				
No running water inside	9	17	14	15
Telephone not available	34	32	34	32

Source: Bureau of the Census, U.S. Department of Commerce.

to the child. Each teacher is expected to have one paid subprofessional and one volunteer assistant. Over 50,000 subprofessionals and nearly twice that number of volunteers have worked on Head Start projects during each of the summer efforts. About 30,000 subprofessionals and 39,000 volunteers participated in the full-year projects during fiscal 1968.

Many of the subprofessional workers and volunteers have been parents (primarily mothers) of children participating in the program. Parental involvement is a major goal of the Head Start effort because it is recognized that a child's needs cannot usually be met without parental cooperation and even changes in the home environment. Bringing parents into the day-to-day operation of the centers has proved an effective way to enlighten parents on child-rearing practices and to increase their interest in the schooling of their children. According to Bureau of the Census surveys of the 1965 and 1966 summer programs, and the full-year 1965–66 programs, the Head Start professional staff observed that the parents themselves benefited from the children's preschool experience—they were more involved in community activities and the child's education.[7]

Parents of Head Start children frequently suffer from physical, psychological, or educational handicaps. OEO has estimated that a third of Head Start parents need adult literacy training. Some centers

Table 4–7.   Characteristics of Subprofessionals, 1967[a]

Characteristics	Summer Program	Full-Year Program
Age		
Under 21 years	52%	16%
22–33 years	24	37
34–45 years	17	32
46–57 years	6	13
58 years and over	1	2
Sex		
Male	7	4
Female	93	96
Ethnic Group		
White	54	31
Negro	33	45
Spanish-American	6	12
American Indian	6	8
Other	1	2
School Years Completed		
8 years or less	13	15
9–10 years	16	15
11–12 years	41	51
1 or more years of college	30	19
University-sponsored Training		
8 weeks	3	9
6 days	33	14
Worker Status at Center		
Paid	82	83
Volunteer	16	12
Annual Family Income		
Under $1,500	13	12
$1,500–$2,999	19	25
$3,000–$4,999	25	29
$5,000–$7,999	18	17
$8,000 and over	13	9

[a] Categories do not necessarily add up to 100 percent because of incomplete reporting.

Source: Bureau of the Census, U.S. Department of Commerce.

provide special education courses in homemaking and literacy, and, when called upon, refer parents to other community action or welfare services.

Perhaps the most conspicuous difference between Head Start and traditional kindergarten programs is the attempt by the former to provide health care. In both rural and urban areas, poverty-stricken parents often lack the knowledge or resources to provide their children with adequate medical attention. To meet this need, Head Start projects were required to plan for identifying and attempting to correct or alleviate the children's medical or dental problems.

Medical examinations of Head Start children revealed that many poor children were in serious need of medical help. In Los Angeles, for example, more than 60 percent of the Head Start participants in the 1966 summer program needed medical, dental, or psychological services.[8] Although Head Start has been successful in diagnosing the medical problems of the children, it has experienced great difficulty in providing adequate treatment after examination. There was very little follow-up medical assistance for the 1965 summer program. Improvements were sought in subsequent programs, but according to Dr. Frederick North, senior pediatrician for Head Start, treatment was "rather like the care of the poor child—fragmented, discontinuous and often not too well recorded."[9] Dr. North blamed the inadequacy of treatment in part to "institutional and bureaucratic inertia, especially in large cities." He charged that in some cases public health departments that were responsible for Head Start diagnostic examinations refused to allow their doctors to treat even the minor defects they discovered, thus creating the need for cumbersome and often unsuccessful referral systems. Data from the 1966 summer health program indicate that the medical needs of the children were very great, and that almost 40 percent required dental care. More than half the disorders discovered, according to OEO figures, received some form of treatment.[10]

Health services in the child development centers highlight the problem of coordinating federal and local resources. Funds are available for Head Start–designed health services from a multitude of federal, state, and local sources. Indeed, the diversity of fund sources poses a serious challenge to local Head Start officials. The national office recommends that plans and budgets for examination, treatment, and preventive services be prepared only after extensive consultation with physicians, dentists, and public health officials. Head Start funds are to be used only to fill gaps in a community's health programs. Knowing all the sources that may be tapped, much less integrating them in a medical program, has proved an enormous task. To improve the health services offered Head Start children, OEO has contracted with the American Academy of Pediatrics to select 300 physician consultants to help plan and evaluate project health programs.[11]

Head Start also attempts to provide a mental health program for the children. Many children of illiterate and unemployed parents suffer from special psychological problems that require treatment if they are to progress through school, and national guidelines specify that Head Start centers provide psychologists and social workers to help disturbed children. In actuality, however, such services have not been forthcoming. Census Bureau surveys of the summer and full-year programs revealed that professional, subprofessional, and volunteer workers believed the psychological and psychiatric services were among the least adequate features of Head Start programs. Budgetary limitation and shortage of qualified personnel are the major obstacles.

The Head Start centers also offer one and often two meals and snacks per day to the children, many of whom do not have proper diets at home. Head Start centers are also expected to educate parents concerning proper nutritional requirements.

Head Start was thus conceived as a multifaceted program to meet the needs of the impoverished child. Understandably, it has excited the imagination of many communities throughout the country. At the same time, the program has been very expensive; the full-year program more than doubled the normal cost per child in kindergarten programs (Table 4-8).

In line with the customary Great Society numbers game, President Johnson announced in 1967 that he contemplated increasing the number of children enrolled in summer Head Start while at the same time reducing OEO's budget for the program. It was eventually decided that total enrollment for the summer of 1968 would remain at the same level as the previous year.

Faced with the task of imposing economies in line with a reduced funding level, the southeast regional office imposed standards for controlling the funding of Head Start projects, thus limiting the discretion of individual reviewers. Savings were obtained by setting maximums for personnel, salaries, fringe benefits, and other costs. The plan was designed to avoid losses in program quality, to eliminate nonessential spending, and to evoke more meaningful contributions from communities in facilities, personnel, medical treatment, and other services. Other regional offices adapted the southeast region's plan, removing the "padding" found in earlier Head Start projects. OEO claimed that the reduced costs per child did not involve sacrifices in the quality of Head Start projects during the summer of 1968.

Community Role

As a component of the community action program, Head Start has objectives that extend beyond providing for the children. These added goals have occasionally produced politically explosive issues, such as the controversy over parent participation on Head Start advisory committees. Each Head Start project was required to have an advisory committee, in order to involve the parents and the local community

Table 4–8. *Head Start Costs per Child by Program Component, 1965–67*

| Service | Summer | | | Year-Round | | | | |
| | | | | Part-Day | | Full-Day | | |
	1965	1966	1967	1965–66	1966–67	1965–66	1966–67	
Total program cost per child	$150	$192	$200	$900	$1,050	$1,260	$1,380	
Cost/child/month	75	96	100	90	105	105	115	
Percent Distribution	100.0	100.0	100.0	100.0	100.0	100.0	100.0	
Parent and family (recruitment, social services, parent involvement)	1.7	6.3	6.3	4.6	5.9	5.3	5.4	
Health (medical, dental, psychological)	6.0	18.2	18.2	4.6	6.3	3.3	4.0	
Nutrition	8.0	13.5	13.5	12.7	13.7	13.8	14.0	
Daily activities (personnel, equipment, child transportation)	77.3	54.2	54.2	70.4	66.9	69.6	68.6	
Research, evaluation and training	2.0	4.7	4.7	3.4	3.2	4.0	4.0	
Administration	5.0	3.1	3.1	3.4	4.0	4.0	4.0	

Source: Community Action Program, Office of Economic Opportunity.

in the administration of the Head Start program. Half of the committee members were to be parents of the children; the other members would be representatives of community groups and professional organizations, and teachers and school administrators. It was hoped that through participation parents would develop greater concern for the education of their children. Moreover, it was thought that their involvement in the planning and administration of Head Start projects would give parents the experience and self-confidence to pressure local school boards to undertake increased efforts to educate the poor.

These advisory committees were officially assigned broad responsibilities, including concurrence in the selection of the Head Start director and review of Head Start applications. Many school boards running Head Start projects did not take kindly to such "outside" interference with their traditional authority. In the Washington, D.C., suburban area, for example, school superintendents from Maryland and Virginia joined in objecting to Head Start criteria which gave the advisory committee power to reject the school board's choice and pick its own staff director.[12] The superintendents charged that this was contrary to Maryland and Virginia laws which gave them exclusive power to hire school personnel. In the face of this opposition, the OEO's mid-Atlantic CAP director "clarified" the role of the advisory committee, stressing that it was a consultative body whose views must be sought on the selection of the Head Start director.[13] Head Start officials are apparently leaving the power struggles to the local level. However, they continue to press for advisory committee involvement and urge that it be consulted in the selection of project directors, even though the official appointment is left to the agency that has been selected to run the program. Head Start officials have also stressed the need for involving low-income parents, though their entreaties have usually been ignored by the school officials who run the projects.

Inasmuch as Head Start programs could be administered by private nonprofit and public agencies (including civil rights organizations) as well as by school boards, the projects could serve to challenge backward school systems that cling to traditional educational methods. In some areas, in fact, the availability of other agencies has forced reluctant school boards to sponsor projects.

Although Head Start has been relatively free of the political controversy that has plagued community action agencies generally, the case of the Child Development Group of Mississippi (CDGM) was a conspicuous exception. In conducting Head Start centers for more than 6,000 children in 28 counties, CDGM won two OEO grants (in summer 1965 and February 1966) and unusual praise, as well as criticism, from OEO officials and outside observers. But the group's association with civil rights activism proved irritating to local politicians, including the state's congressional delegation. Also, there were reports, within and outside OEO, of fiscal mismanagement, property misuse, payroll padding, and nepotism. Thus in September 1966, OEO suddenly announced that it was withdrawing support in favor of a newly formed biracial group, Mississippi Action for Progress (MAP), which had the governor's backing. The primary reason for OEO's action was the charge of fiscal mismanagement. But vocal outside pressure from civil rights groups and other liberals resulted two months later in OEO's renewal, in essence, of the CDGM grant (with reduced funds) through Mary Holmes Junior College.

Caught between two extreme positions, OEO's shifts did not enable it to escape unscathed from this incident. Civil rights advocates were embittered by what they saw as an attempt to remove their power by a compromise with the segregationists, and the latter continued to resent OEO's financing a project associated with Negro activists.[14]

Training and Research

As with any education program, an appraisal of Head Start must begin with the quality of the teachers and other personnel associated with the programs. The studies that have been undertaken have indicated that the quality of the Head Start program and the caliber of the teaching personnel are vitally important factors that affect the gains of the children. Teachers for full-year programs are, where possible, given eight-week child development and education programs in qualified colleges and universities. Some subprofessional aides also participate in these courses. Summer teachers, teachers' aides, and occasional volunteers are given a week of orientation.

The training program has apparently been inadequate. Only 2,700 of the 18,000 teachers for the full-year 1966–67 program participated in the eight-week orientation course that was held in the summer of 1966. About 32,000 persons participated in the summer 1966 week-long orientation session, although 46,000 teachers, 57,000 nonprofessionals, and 93,000 volunteers were involved in Head Start that summer. It may also be questioned whether the week-long summer orientation courses are long enough to impart the necessary level of training.

Most of the training for Head Start staff workers is presumably accomplished by in-service training programs. However, Bureau of the Census surveys of the summer and full-year Head Start staff have revealed that many staff members receive no training at all, despite the fact that more than a third have had no prior experience with preschoolers, and almost a half had never before worked with poor children.

Costs, facilities, and trained personnel are the major constraints upon expanding the training program. Reports on the 1967 summer training (week-long orientation courses for summer personnel) state that 38,000 people were trained at a cost of $6.2 million, or $163 per trainee. To provide a similar course for the entire summer teaching staff, including volunteers, would require a program almost five times as large.

Head Start has devoted considerable funds to research and evaluation. Two million dollars was spent in fiscal 1966 and more than $6 million in fiscal 1967 and in fiscal 1968. The budget has been distributed about equally among independent research projects; research, demonstration, and development projects; and thirteen evaluation and research centers located at various universities that specialize in child development studies. In addition to conducting independent research, the centers are assigned a major responsibility for collecting data on the operation of various Head Start centers in their region and for evaluating the over-all success of the program. More than a million dollars was devoted to this effort in fiscal 1967, the objective being to pinpoint the factors that make Head Start programs successful.

The research, demonstration, and development projects consist of a dozen experimental Head Start programs in which new techniques of training are developed, curricula enriched, and controlled research projects undertaken. Although these demonstration projects are expensive to administer, Head Start officials justify the extra costs on the basis that the projects provide an opportunity to test hypotheses and use control groups—conditions impossible to obtain in regular Head Start projects run by school systems or CAA's.

The research effort is directed at testing a number of hypotheses and at discovering the factors that determine the success of Head Start programs. The effect on the child of the teaching quality and the nature of the school has been measured. Research was then directed to whether the child's development is related to family involvement in the Head Start program; tentative results support a relationship. Much of the research is inconclusive, however, because measuring and testing the factors associated with the complex educational and psychological development of preschoolers is exceedingly difficult. And there is little to build upon, because our educational system has neglected the evaluation of motives, values, goals, and attitudes related to school achievement. Thus a great deal of research is devoted exclusively to developing better instruments of measurement.

Although the Head Start effort cannot as yet claim any major breakthroughs, it is one of the most comprehensive federal research designs ever undertaken in a single area of educational development, and it has attracted outstanding authorities in the field. Because of the experimental nature of the effort, Head Start officials have emphasized that satisfactory answers to some of the pressing questions cannot be expected for several years. Moreover, Head Start research has detractors, who claim that the agency supports disjointed projects and that the research lacks a central design.

Administration of the Program

The Head Start program is administered through OEO's seven regional offices; the grantee at the local level is the community action agency for the locality. Where no CAA has been formed or where special conditions prevail, a public or nonprofit organization may administer a project as the grantee, provided the agency organizes a policy board that includes representatives of the poor before it submits an application. In the summer of 1965 a number of projects were administered by public and nonprofit organizations as the direct grantees. By 1967, most participating localities had formed functioning CAA's, and the number of other grantees had dwindled. About nine of every ten grantees of full-year Head Start projects are community action agencies.

The CAA, as the direct grantee, may delegate the operation of Head Start programs to public or nonprofit agencies, including religious organizations, but the public school systems have played a large role in administering the program (Table 4–9). In the 1966 summer program, 67 percent of the agencies administering the program were school systems (the direct grantee in most cases being the local CAA). Fifty-five percent of the children who participated in Head Start that summer were in school-administered programs. In the full-year Head Start projects, the school systems play a smaller role, and the CAA's

Table 4–9.   Delegate Agency Affiliations[a]

Delegate Agency	Full-Year 1965–66	Summer 1966	Full-Year 1966–67	Summer 1967
School	35%	67%	31%	66%
Church	10	10	3	5
Private nonprofit	26	14	30	15
CAA's (actually running the program)	29	9	37	14

[a] A delegate agency is a grantee that actually administers a Head Start program, or an organization that has contracted with a direct grantee. Most of the schools, churches, and private nonprofit agencies administering the program were delegate agencies of the local CAA's.

Sources: Community Action Program, Office of Economic Opportunity, and Bureau of the Census estimates.

themselves, with the help of private nonprofit institutions, run a majority of the projects.

The distribution of delegate agencies differs greatly among the various states. In the southeast region (Alabama, Florida, Georgia, Mississippi, South Carolina, and Tennessee), 24 percent of the agencies administering the full-year 1965–66 programs were public schools, compared with the national figure of 35 percent. In the deep south fifty-two percent of the delegate agencies for full-year programs are community action agencies. Difficulties in complying with civil rights criteria account for the diminished role of the schools in this region.

The eligibility of religious institutions to be recipients of Head Start funds has been a unique feature of the program. Although religious institutions are not eligible for direct federal grants under the Elementary and Secondary Education Act of 1965, Head Start has supported projects sponsored by church groups with the understanding that the funds would not be used for religious instruction, proselytizing, or worship. Admission to such church-sponsored projects cannot be based on religious affiliation or attendance in a church-related school. In addition, the facilities used for Head Start classes must be devoid of sectarian or religious symbols.[15]

National Head Start guidelines regulate the proportion of the nonpoor that can participate. The rationale for participation of the nonpoor was that children from more advantaged families would enrich the classroom activities, thus providing better programs for the poor children. During the summer of 1965, 15 percent of the children in a Head Start project could come from families that exceeded the standard poverty criteria. The figure was later decreased to 10 percent in response to public and congressional criticism. However, Head Start continues to permit a number of more advantaged children to participate in projects if the cost of these additional children is met by other than federal funds or the required local contribution. Although there were a number of reports that the percentage of children from above the poverty line exceeded the national guidelines (one congressman reported that his son had been invited to join a Head Start program), the requirement was by and large met. The median family income of the children was $3,400 and the median family size was six, which was well within the national poverty income criteria.

Some communities, on the other hand, have criticized the exclusion of middle-class children, charging that the program was guilty of "economic discrimination."[16] The Educational Policy Commission of the National Education Association advocated expansion of Head Start programs to four- and five-year-olds who fall in the "large middle group—between the well-to-do and the disadvantaged."[17] The commission was understandably concerned that more than half of the nation's four- and five-year-olds are not enrolled in any school; but Head Start maintains an ambivalent position on enrolling nonpoor children. For political reasons Head Start officials prefer to limit enrollment to the poor in order to avoid charges that the program serves children from affluent homes. In addition, broadening the enrollment base creates policing problems—checking to see that local and state funds cover the costs of enrolling children who are ineligible on the basis of income criteria. On substantive grounds, however, Head Start spokesmen acknowledge the advantages of including in the program children from more affluent homes, as long as the extra costs are covered by non–Head Start funds.

Fund Allocation

Head Start projects are part of CAP appropriations, a fact that has led to wide controversy. Opponents of the Community Action Program no doubt have resented the bolstering of CAP appropriations with the popularity of Head Start; and friends of Head Start feel that it has been damaged by its inclusion in CAP requests.

The allocation of Head Start funds among the states and counties is based on the same criteria that govern the distribution of other CAP funds.[18] In January 1966, OEO itself added the requirement that no CAA could spend more than one-third of its funds on Head Start projects. This limitation was prompted by concern among CAP advocates that the CAA's would concentrate disproportionately on the popular Head Start program. This restriction triggered widespread opposition, and it soon became apparent that CAA's as well as Head Start programs would be damaged.[19] The issue became a moot point when Congress earmarked more than a third of the total CAP authorization for Head Start.

Local School Boards, Title I, and Head Start

The administrative relationship between the public school systems and Head Start has been one of the most controversial aspects of the program. Public schools that administer Head Start projects operate, by and large, as "delegate agencies" responsible to the local CAA. Each CAA submits its application to the regional office and is held responsible for obtaining public school compliance with regional and national Head Start standards. National and regional headquarters have urged the CAA's to keep a watchful eye on public school-administered Head Start projects in order to ensure quality programs and to persuade the school systems to devote more effort to the poor in the primary grades. Too frequently, however, the CAA's act as little more than a funnel for school board requests. Some school boards deal directly with the OEO regional representative on financial matters, without going through the CAA. The CAA's and school-administered Head Start programs often operate autonomously. Many school boards continue to show no special concern for the poor and are jealous of Head Start's interference in educational matters.

The administrative arrangement favored by OEO contrasts sharply with the structure of traditional federal-state programs in education and welfare. The Elementary and Secondary Education Act of 1965, for example, provides for the allocation and distribution of federal money to state education authorities according to congressional guidelines, with little federal monitoring. State education authorities, which distribute the funds to the local school boards, are the only agencies in a position to exert control over the use of the money. The federal role is strictly circumscribed. Head Start, in contrast, follows no rigid allocation formula, bypasses state education authorities, and assigns local CAA's the role of federal watchdog over Head Start funds.

The controversy over the administration of Head Start is heightened by the availability, under Title I of the Elementary and Secondary Education Act (ESEA), of funds for preschool programs that might be devoted to the same efforts as Head Start. In fiscal 1966, more than 100,000 children participated in prekindergarten programs under Title I assistance, and 380,000 children attended kindergartens financed in whole or in part under Title I.[20] The provision of funds for similar purposes from two different federal sources through different administrative channels has increased the pressure for a unified program.

Head Start officials have resisted proposals to merge the two programs in the Office of Education; more than narrow bureaucratic interests are involved. Head Start's monitoring of projects to assure that grantees follow national goals, albeit not always successful, would be precluded by the Elementary and Secondary Education Act structure, in which the Office of Education serves primarily as a funnel for allocating federal funds to state educational authorities. Moreover, Head Start is the most popular CAP component, and in many areas the only justification for the existence of the local CAA. Removal of Head Start would unquestionably damage, if not kill, some of the community action agencies.

The more sanguine Head Start advocates have also hoped that the program could give federal authorities and local CAA's more leverage in persuading local school boards to devote more effort in the primary grades to the education of the poor. Channeling Head Start funds through state educational authorities would completely shield school boards from federal and CAA pressures for change.

Another advantage of the present Head Start administrative structure, as seen by OEO officials, is that Head Start projects can be operated by non-public-school agencies. As Table 4–9 indicates, a large number of projects are administered by agencies other than school boards. This makes it possible to establish Head Start in areas where school boards are unable or reluctant to embark on the venture, and it may also increase the pressure that can be brought to bear on local school boards to establish Head Start projects. Restricting grants to state education authorities and local school boards would destroy this leverage. And where local authorities are willing to undertake such projects, the federal influence is often necessary to induce them to run the programs on other than traditional kindergarten lines. If Head Start were administered by the Office of Education under a Title I structure, state and local authorities would be free to run their own kind of program.

The experience of Title I operations to date supports OEO's argument. The Council on the Education of Disadvantaged Children, an advisory group of distinguished educators established under the Elementary and Secondary Education Act of 1965, reported to President Johnson that most summer programs under Title I were "piecemeal, fragmented efforts at remediation or vaguely directed enrichment."[21] The content of Title I preschool programs is left almost entirely to local school boards, many of which seem to place little value in parent participation or medical, dental, and nutritional services for participants. Rarely did the council find a "strategically planned, comprehensive program for change." Many Head Start projects may fall short of such a high standard, but at least federal pressures operate in that direction.

Critics of OEO respond that transfer of Head Start to the Office of Education would be desirable in eliminating unnecessary duplication and returning educational matters to local and state school authorities. The federal "interference" that accompanies Head Start funds is rarely welcomed and usually resented by the educational establishment. Many congressmen, finding the arguments of school administrators persuasive, have favored the transfer of Head Start to the Office of Education. However, an amendment to that effect, introduced during consideration of the extension of EOA in 1967, was defeated—not because the majority liked OEO more than the Office of Education, but because southern segregationists objected to transferring Head Start to an agency headed by Harold Howe II, who at that time was more unacceptable to them than Sargent Shriver. As one southern congressman put it, somewhat inelegantly: "The best thing . . . to do is to keep all the trash in one pile, do not scatter it."[22]

Efforts to transfer Head Start to the Office of Education were revived during the succeeding year, and the Senate approved an amendment to that effect. But the strong opposition of Carl Perkins, chairman of the House Education and Labor Committee, to the transfer prevailed and Congress postponed consideration of it until 1969, when the future of the Economic Opportunity Act was to be studied.[23]

Coordination

The availability of funds for preschool programs from both OEO and the Office of Education has prompted demands for coordinated efforts at the local and national level. Although Title I funds can be used to supplement Head Start projects, in most cases the two programs have operated independently. The cooperation between the Office of Education and OEO to prevent school systems from violating civil rights standards is an exception. Also, the two national offices have agreed to open Head Start summer-session orientation programs to personnel who participate in ESEA programs.[24]

Despite such efforts at coordination, OEO and OE do not integrate their major policy determinations; each agency goes its separate way. OEO, for example, asked the Office of Education to earmark its Title I funds for Follow-Through programs for former Head Start participants in the primary grades. The Office of Education refused to do this and reduced the Title I preference provision drafted by OEO to a hortatory message. In part, the lack of coordination between the two agencies reflects the fact that the Office of Education makes no major policy decisions. Under Title I, decisions on how money is spent are left to local school systems and state education authorities. Hence the coordination of preschool programs that Head Start officials might have preferred could not be made with the Office of Education because major decisions on the use of Title I funds are made elsewhere. The difficulty of coordinating Title I and Head Start funding is illustrative of the relationships between other CAP-funded projects and older grant-in-aid programs that distribute funds through state agencies.

Local coordination between school boards and CAA's on Title I and Head Start funds is also weak. A formal checkpoint procedure, which is prescribed, forms the basis of cooperation. In the case of Head Start, the applying agency must certify in its application that it has consulted the local school board about obtaining Title I funds. And under Title I, the Office of Education must require local boards of education to consult with the CAA's in the formulation of their plans and programs. However, these procedures for coordination are usually little more than paper arrangements.

Information on the use of Title I money in Head Start projects is scarce. The national offices of Head Start and the Office of Education have no data on the utilization af funds, and only impressions can be gathered from disparate sources. In Washington, D.C., the 1966 summer program used Head Start funds for five-year-olds and Title I funds for younger preschoolers. In Dade County (Miami), Florida, Title I funds were used to provide facilities for Head Start programs, with Head Start financing the operating costs. Los Angeles combined three sources of funds for its Head Start program, using $4 million from Head Start, $2.6 million from California's Compensatory Education Act, and $100,00 from ESEA. In New York City, the board of education paid teachers' salaries for a program that involved 28,000 Head Start children, while OEO provided the health, social services, and food components.[25]

Racial Segregation

The large number of Head Start programs in the South, combined with OEO's insistence on racially integrated efforts, has been a continuing source of conflict. For Head Start officials, segregated programs pose a severe dilemma: violations of civil rights guidelines warrant a termination of federal funds, yet such action may result in denying the poorest children a preschool program.

Three methods have frequently been used to evade the civil rights requirement.[26] First, local officers may refrain from using white schools, even where there are substantial numbers of eligible white children. Second, virtually all-Negro staffs may be selected. And third, recruitment efforts for Negro and white children may differ (Negro families are actively solicited whereas white families get only a general notice). The nature of these violations indicates that such communities run their Head Start programs primarily for Negro children.

Southern Head Start projects, though not exclusively serving Negro children, have indeed concentrated on them. Although there are twice as many poor white families in the South as poor nonwhite families, Negro children have constituted the majority of Head Start participants in the South. The South has not been alone in mounting racially imbalanced Head Start programs: nationally, Negro preschoolers have participated in the program in greater proportion than their percentage of the poverty population (Table 4–10). Nonwhite children have accounted for about two of every five Head Start enrollees, although they constitute a third of the poor children in the nation.

Some communities have utilized the availability of funds for preschools under Title I to avoid integrated programs, a tactic in which Title I money is used to finance all-white projects while Negroes are provided Head Start facilities. Another favorite technique of segre-

Table 4–10. Estimated Percentage of First-Grade Students Participating in Project
Head Start, 1965–66

Area	Negro	White
Metropolitan		
Total	13.8	2.0
Northeast	14.2	1.9
Midwest	2.7	1.3
South	25.1	7.4
Southwest	19.3	1.2
West	1.9	.5
Nonmetropolitan		
Total	32.6	7.0
North and West	35.8	4.1
South	35.2	12.0
Southwest	12.8	4.8

Source: James S. Coleman et al., Equality of Educational Opportunity. Office of Education, U.S. Department of Health, Education, and Welfare (Washington: U.S. Government Printing Office, 1966), p. 492.

gated southern communities was to allow parents and children "freedom of choice" between two or more centers.[27] Negro families gravitated toward Negro centers while white children attended all-white centers. Subsequently, OEO has forbidden "freedom of choice" and has required children to attend the Head Start center in their geographical district.[28] Although this action prevents segregation in mixed housing communities, it does nothing to assist integration where the housing pattern is itself segregated.

Although segregation is most flagrant in the South, it is a national malady. More than one-third of all Head Start projects visited during the summer of 1966 by the Head Start inspection staff lacked an integrated program. The administrators were not necessarily guilty of civil rights violations; often the projects only reflected the racially segregated nature of the communities.

Though OEO could cut off funding to projects where civil rights were violated, it has used this authority sparingly. Faced with the choice between a segregated preschool program and no preschool program at all, Head Start officials have usually limited themselves to threats, and stopped short of actual project termination. OEO announced that of the 2,400 Head Start projects during the summer of 1965, about 60 communities ultimately were denied funding for failing to meet OEO's nondiscrimination requirements. In the summer of 1968, three summer Head Start programs were refused funds for civil rights violations. In all cases the communities were offered an opportunity to defend their action in public hearings. Later, however, there were several more serious problems, but OEO policy at that time was to make every attempt to iron them out before taking drastic action. Only where there is complete refusal to compromise or cooperate are funds refused.

An Assessment

The Head Start program has sustained its original popularity, managing to avoid the disenchantment that has beset other poverty projects. But popularity does not necessarily connote program effectiveness, and despite congressional and public support, many basic questions regarding Head Start's value, scope, and direction remain unanswered. For example, should the limited resources be concentrated upon summer programs preparing poor children for school entry, and maximizing the number of participants? Or should the funds be devoted to year-round facilities? Would cost effectiveness be maximized by restricting participation to even fewer children who would be provided with preschool facilities at age three or even earlier? And, if we assume a determination to concentrate resources on a limited number of children, should the resources be restricted to preschool facilities or should they be devoted to enriching the primary grade education of poor children? Finally, what are the merits of expending funds on services—health, nutrition, and family stability—compared with concentrating on classroom education?

Head Start research efforts have not yet produced conclusive answers to these basic questions. For that matter, it is not even clear whether the resources devoted to the child development program produce lasting improvement in the poverty child's school performance. This issue is fundamental to an assessment of Head Start because tentative findings suggest that a two- or three-month summer program for preschoolers may yield only temporary benefits. The children's needs are simply too overwhelming to be met by a summer program.

During its early phases, Head Start was able to capitalize on research that indicated significant educational advancements. Dr. Leon Eisenberg of The Johns Hopkins University found improvements of 8 to 10 points in the IQs of 480 children who took part in Baltimore's 1965 Head Start project.[29] These findings were supported by additional studies during the following year. Follow-up studies of the 1965 summer program participants indicated, however, that benefits of the Head Start program soon faded. A widely publicized study by Max Wolff and Annie Stein of Yeshiva University among kindergartens in four public New York City elementary schools showed that, six months after the Head Start program ended, participants scored no higher on achievement tests than nonparticipants from similar socioeconomic backgrounds.[30] A later study by the Office of Education also indicated that, several months after completion of the 1965 summer program, discernible gains could be detected only among participants from the most disadvantaged backgrounds—especially among rural Negroes of the South.[31] For most Head Start children, achievement level gains were not appreciably different from those of non–Head Start children. The inconclusive results of this study are best summarized in a study by Harold W. Watts and David L. Horner of the Institute for Research on Poverty at the University of Wisconsin. They concluded in their study of Head Start's impact on the subsequent educational progress of school children: "A balanced summary statement would perhaps indicate that a respectable gain was found by the analysis but that the evidence was too weak to disprove the contentions of doubters or enthusiasts."[32]

Most studies of the effect of Head Start have focused on the cognitive achievements of participants. Because Head Start aspires to broader goals, however, consideration must also be given to other factors in appraising the total impact of the program. Most significant, perhaps, is the fact that Head Start children are frequently observed to be more motivated and responsive than their non–Head Start peers. More than 90 percent of a sample of Head Start parents and workers testified that the children gained self-confidence and developed new interests, according to the Census Bureau survey. The Wolff and Stein study, as well as the Office of Education survey, also indicated that Head Start participants showed much more noticeable gains in educational motivation than in achievement levels several months after the 1965 summer program.

The rapid "fade out" effect in achievement levels, together with the realization that a short summer course is often inadequate to meet the comprehensive needs of the preschool children, has provided the major impetus for the creation of full-year Head Start programs. These projects, with a median length of nine months, are expected to have greater impact on the achievement levels of disadvantaged children. The study conducted by the Office of Education showed that first grade children from almost all socioeconomic backgrounds who attended kindergarten had significantly higher achievement levels than comparable first graders who had not attended kindergarten. The Head Start program, which is generally conceded to be of higher quality than kindergarten, might be anticipated to produce even better results. But the benefits of the longer Head Start program may not be sustained unless the primary school programs the children enter are similarly enriched.

In terms of their impact on the children, then, full-year Head Start projects would seem preferable to the shorter summer programs.

Although a summer's exposure is beneficial in some respects, it is not long enough to leave an indelible effect, and its benefits (at least in terms of achievement levels) soon fade. If these facts are accepted, why has OEO not been quicker to shift its resources to the full-year concept? The answer is as much political as programmatic. Because they are much more expensive, full year programs cannot serve nearly as many children as the summer programs, given the current levels of spending. The Administration has shown a distinct penchant for the "numbers racket," and the huge numbers of children who have passed through summer Head Start projects unquestionably provide impressive publicity. In this case, however, it has probably amounted to a sacrifice of quality for quantity—a result no doubt regretted by Head Start officials themselves. Aside from these political considerations, it is also more difficult to mount full-year projects than programs for the summer, when school facilities are unutilized and regular teachers are available.

Head Start's inability to turn impoverished preschoolers into middle-class high achievers should not be surprising. A realistic evaluation of Head Start must begin with a realistic appraisal of its objectives. Prominent educators and social observers like Martin Deutsch and S. M. Miller have warned that it would be naïve to expect the children to emerge from the program transformed.[33] The "fade out" effect that researchers have observed, then, only confirms what Head Start officials early realized:

> The initial gains are not likely to hold up in the absence of a continuity in educational experience. Pre-school education, then, to be meaningful, must be followed by appropriate educational experiences of good quality in the subsequent years.[34]

In view of these considerations, it is unfortunate that OEO attempted to sell Head Start as an educational panacea. While preschool programs unquestionably have an important place in the total school strategy, it would be a mistake to give the public the notion that preschool is the central focus of such a strategy.[35] And although the politics of the moment dictated emphasis on a popular program, claims that the program was capable of giving the children a "head start" must be considered part of OEO's penchant for rhetoric. Regrettably, one by-product of OEO's sloganeering has been skepticism when the program proved incapable of achieving the lofty goals established by OEO spokesmen.

A more realistic role for Head Start—as acknowledged by educators as well as Head Start planners—is as a preschool program in the context of a strategy for change in the primary schools offering poor children an enriched and more comprehensive education. On this count, Head Start has made a contribution.

Another significant innovation, initiated on a large scale by Head Start and now being adopted by educational systems throughout the country, is the use of subprofessional aides to provide individual attention to students, to relieve teachers of routine tasks, and to provide employment to the poor.[36] In fiscal 1966, Title I money was used to employ 73,000 teachers' aides and 44,000 other subprofessionals, equaling more than one-quarter of all new staff positions created by Title I funds.[37] It should be noted, however, that the maximum potential of many subprofessionals has not been utilized; they are often assigned routine duties as lunchroom monitors or keepers of simple records. Rarely have they been allowed to contribute to the educational process, as Head Start planners would have liked.

Head Start's broad approach to services for children is another concept that has been widely and profitably copied. The Council on the Education of Disadvantaged Children reports that the provision of breakfasts and lunches, basic medical care and eyeglasses, shoes and overcoats—the most elemental bodily requisites for learning—is one of the most rapidly spreading practices under Title I. Only a few years ago one major southern city refused to provide free lunches to poor children on the ground that food had no relation to the child's education. Today the lunches are provided.

There is also increasing concern among local educational authorities to improve teachers' attitudes toward poor children and to increase the flexibility of the curriculum. Although these changes cannot be attributed entirely to Head Start, appropriate credit must be given to its emphasis on innovative techniques dealing with each child as a developing individual. Several colleges and universities have established new departments or programs in early childhood education. One-third of the states have commissioned studies on establishing certification standards for early childhood teaching, and Iowa, Vermont, and Oklahoma established such certification early in 1967. This preoccupation with certification is a well-established trait of educators, but Head Start may at least claim credit for generating the added interest in preschool education. Head Start programs have increased demands for state support of public kindergartens. Virginia has established free public kindergartens, using Head Start money to finance the costs allocated to special services for poor children, and several other states are now considering legislation for statewide kindergartens.

One of the most controversial concepts in the Head Start package has been the involvement of parents in an advisory capacity. School boards and educators have been ambivalent, if not antagonistic, to the prospect of integrating this practice into the regular school program. Head Start has succeeded, however, in raising the issue of parent involvement in some communities. In April 1967 in Washington, D.C., for example, the superintendent of schools proposed the establishment of parent advisory councils that would have a major voice in determining the policies of each neighborhood school.[38]

The Head Start preschool program has also stimulated inquiry and research into the educational needs of two- and three-year-olds. A project sponsored by the National Institutes of Health found that after a year of tutoring for an hour a day, the average IQ of a group of 30 slum children was substantially raised while the average IQ of a control group of untutored poor children actually dropped.[39] The psychologist in charge of the project has concluded that slum children will make more educational progress if they are properly stimulated by words when they are learning to talk.

Findings of this nature prompted a White House task force on early childhood to recommend to the President that treatment centers be established for very young children and their parents. Thus on February 8, 1967, in his message to Congress on America's children and youth, the President directed OEO to begin "a pilot program of child and parent centers through its community action program in areas of acute poverty." The centers would attempt a broad range of care and education for children under the age of three—and for their parents—such as health and welfare services, counseling for parents on prenatal and infant care, home management, and providing the child with necessary emotional and educational reinforcement.

Although 100 centers were called for by the task force, budgetary constraints forced reduction and delay. By June 30, 1967, 36 planning grants of $10,000 had been awarded, a majority of which were operational in the fall of 1968.[40]

Potential Catalyst

Whether Head Start is a successful strategy for change ultimately depends on the evolution of the American public school system. More than a change of heart is necessary, for substantial funds must be forthcoming. Commissioner Harold Howe of the Office of Education has estimated that an annual expenditure of $1,200 per child would be a useful benchmark in estimating the cost of providing adequate education for poor children in the primary grades.[41] This is more than twice the amount currently spent per pupil for primary education. Indeed, the financial commitment necessary to make Head Start's goal of quality education for the poor a reality may lie beyond realistic expectations for the immediate years ahead.

The federal government will undoubtedly be the major source of the financial support necessary to provide educational programs adequate to meet the needs of poor children. In December 1967, Congress approved President Johnson's request for a Follow-Through program to extend Head Start services for Head Start and Title I (Elementary and Secondary Education Act) preschool graduates into the first year of regular school. Under an agreement between HEW and OEO, the program is delegated to the Office of Education, and funds are allocated directly to local public educational agencies.[42] However, Follow-Through guidelines reflect the OEO approach in setting program requirements by giving local school boards less discretion in the use of the money than they enjoy with Title I funds. Indeed, OEO has urged Congress that Follow-Through "be operated by local education agencies, with a view to changing their approach to primary grade education of disadvantaged children."[43]

The Follow-Through grant of $15 million (the President requested $120 million) provided 40 programs that served 4,000 children during the 1967–68 academic year, and 80 programs that served another 12,000 during 1968–69. Projects are directed to improving language skills and analytical abilities and to providing medical and dental attention and other noncurricular assistance. Special training programs are provided for teachers and other personnel who deal with Follow-Through children. Parents participate in activities aimed at increasing their ability to help their children, and they assist in planning and executing the program. Thus the program package for Follow-Through includes essentially the same components as Head Start. Half of the Follow-Through participants will be Head Start graduates.

The sharply reduced allocation of funds to Follow-Through has largely limited the program to experimentation. The magnitude of the task confronting the American educational system has long been recognized, and competition for scarce educational resources is not new. From its very beginnings Head Start has been a demonstration project to mobilize the resources and thinking of educators and administrators to the needs of poor children. By this standard, Head Start has been successful in dramatizing the educational needs of the poor and in selling to the nation a program package whose components provide guidelines for dealing with the impoverished child's needs. Head Start has challenged local school boards which lacked the understanding, concern, or commitment for the education of the poor. Its impact must ultimately be judged by the changes it induces in the American educational system.

5.

FIGHTING POVERTY
WITH A SHEEPSKIN

**The foundation of every state
is the education of its youth.**

Diogenes

The Development of an Idea

The Economic Opportunity Act emphasizes the needs of young people. A substantial proportion of its budget is to be used for teenagers, with most of the programs setting such modest horizons as encouraging youths to stay in high school or providing school dropouts with elementary training and work experience. However, as the antipoverty warriors strove to raise their sights they sought to provide institutional arrangements that would enable youths with potential to gain entry to higher education. OEO named this ambitious effort Upward Bound.

The origins of Upward Bound can be traced to an ad hoc committee of the American Council on Education, established prior to the passage of the Economic Opportunity Act and concerned with "expanding opportunities in higher education for disadvantaged youth." In October 1963, a subgroup of this committee formed an organization to design curricula and teaching materials for experimental precollege programs to be launched at Negro colleges in the summer of 1964.[1]

Several colleges and universities—including Brandeis, Dartmouth, Princeton, and Yale—were meanwhile attacking the same problem by setting up special educational programs that would motivate and prepare poverty-area high school students for college. Aided by grants from the Rockefeller, Carnegie, and other foundations, these programs concentrated on the basic skills needed for a college education, especially reading and mathematics.

In the academic year that followed the inauguration of the Economic Opportunity Act, a number of schools submitted proposals to OEO for similar programs, and OEO funded 17 pilot projects. These projects, which underscored the feasibility of a major program for disadvantaged and "undermotivated" teenagers, were utilized by CAP in formulating a program to help prepare low-income high school students for a college education. Though conceding the desirability of

165

such a program, some thought it would be better handled by the Office of Education, and the Higher Education Act of 1965 authorized establishment of a program akin to Upward Bound.

The modest effort mounted in the summer of 1965 to help 2,000 youths was announced with OEO's usual fanfare as a "war on talent waste."[2] No doubt influenced by the public's support of Head Start, OEO sought to identify the new Upward Bound program as a "Head Start for teenagers." Top OEO officialdom thought enough of Upward Bound to include it as one of the "national emphasis" efforts. Upward Bound received statutory recognition when it was incorporated into the Economic Opportunity Act amendments of 1967 (Section 222 of Title II). As expressed in the legislation, the goal of Upward Bound was to "generate skills and motivation necessary for success in education beyond high school among young people from low-income backgrounds and inadequate secondary school preparation."

Needs and Resources

Because of Upward Bound's broad aims and vague eligibility criteria, a precise estimate of the number that could be helped by the program is not available. Many youths from poor homes reach college on their own, but few would claim that a college education is a function of ability only. Forty percent of all children who enter high school enroll in college, but OEO has estimated that only 8 percent of poor children do so. OEO also estimates that more than 500,000 high school students could benefit annually from Upward Bound or similar programs.[3] These figures do not indicate how many "underachievers" Upward Bound could reach, but it is assumed that a substantial portion of the total fall into this category. The President's Commission on Civil Disorders suggested that Upward Bound could benefit 600,000 such students.[4]

As with practically all OEO-sponsored programs, Upward Bound's available resources fell far short of the need (Table 5-1). Remedial education is expensive: the annual cost of maintaining a student in Upward Bound is about twice the average public high school expendi-

Table 5–1.   Upward Bound Funds and Enrollment, Fiscal 1965–68

Year	Funds	Number of Projects	Number of Students
1965	$2,500,000	17	2,061
1966	25,044,000	216	20,337
1967	28,161,000	249	23,000
1968	30,100,000	295	26,200

Source: Community Action Program, Office of Economic Opportunity.

ture per student. The $30 million that OEO invested in Upward Bound during fiscal 1968, for example, was enough to enroll 26,000 students in the program—or about one of every twenty who could have benefited by it (if the estimates of OEO and the President's Commission on Civil Disorders are anywhere near the mark).

Although the cost per student varies from project to project, OEO estimates for planning purposes that the annual cost per enrollee is about $1,250, ranging from $800 to $2,100. Because most Upward Bound students enroll in their second or third year of high school (37 and 47 percent respectively), they usually participate in the program for two to three years. The actual cost of preparing a student for college through Upward Bound therefore ranges from about $2,400 to $3,600, depending upon one's length of time in the program.

To provide maximum individual attention to enrollees, Upward Bound favors small classes and encourages utilization of the tutorial system. During 1968 the program employed one teacher for every eleven students. Teachers' salaries have amounted to 45 percent of the yearly budget, with summer residential facilities and stipends accounting for another 30 percent. Other budget items include medical and dental care, travel (including field trips), instructional materials, and administrative costs that amount to 5 percent of the total budget.

Because need by far outruns the available funds, one point of controversy has been the relatively costly residential facilities for students who live within commuting distance of the colleges they attend. Having initiated the dormitory component as an integral part of the program, administrators proceeded on the assumption that enrollees had to be separated from their home environment during the summer. Some consultants, engaged by Upward Bound to appraise the project's performance, questioned the value of dormitory life in motivating students. Upward Bound officials have reiterated their "gut feeling" that residential programs are essential, but they have not produced hard data to support their position.

Another possible way of reducing per capita costs would be to increase the number of students for each instructor. But again, educational authorities do not have a party line on the desirability of small classes or on the impact of a higher student-to-teacher ratio on student learning. Aside from these possible savings—elimination of room and board for summer students and an increased teacher-student ratio—there appears to be little fat in the Upward Bound program.

Administrative Design and Operations

OEO established a unique administrative arrangement for Upward Bound, in violation of its cardinal maxim that, whenever feasible, funds should be channeled through community action agencies. For all practical purposes, OEO in October 1965 turned over administration of Upward Bound to a private nonprofit organization, an offshoot of a committee of the American Council for Education established in 1963. In April 1967, a group of individuals associated with the organization formed Educational Associates, Inc., and on July 1, 1967, this single-purpose agency was awarded the Upward Bound contract on a cost-plus-fixed-fee basis. The contract was renewed a year later.

Spokesmen for Upward Bound have defended its separation from community action programs on the grounds that this move was necessary to sell the program to colleges and universities. Upward Bound officials have argued that contracting out administration of the program relieved them from adherence to bureaucratic regulations and permitted maximum flexibility in dealing with educational institutions. Obviously, the same argument could be applied to comprehensive neighborhood health centers which involve hospitals and other medical organizations; to legal services projects, which deal with local bar associations; or to Head Start projects, which are normally operated by school systems. Carried to its logical conclusion, the Upward Bound argument could justify the contracting out of most, if not all, CAP operations.

There is a simpler and more persuasive explanation for OEO's departure from its normal administrative stance: it seems that the first administrator of Upward Bound believed that it was a good idea to separate the program from the CAA's and his views prevailed. Once the initial contract was let, inertia prevailed, and OEO apparently did not question the issue until it was raised by members of Congress who felt that Upward Bound belonged in the Office of Education. Because Upward Bound was not an integral part of the community action program, OEO officials could hardly defend keeping it as part of CAP. Moreover, the Office of Education already administered a small program $4 million in 1968–69), Talent Search. Set up in 1965 under the Higher Education Act, Talent Search is an information and counseling program designed to "identify, motivate and encourage youngsters to go to college."[5] In October 1968 Congress decided to transfer Upward Bound to the Office of Education, effective July 1969, and thus combine it with Talent Search.[6]

Under the terms of OEO's contract, Educational Associates, Inc. was assigned the responsibility for screening and selecting applicants, making funding recommendations, providing technical assistance to applicants, preparing guidelines, assembling operational data, and evaluating projects. CAP retained the final authority to approve projects and to determine "policy." Since OEO's total Upward Bound personnel consisted of a director and three staff members, it seems quite clear that for all practical purposes Upward Bound was run by EAI.

There is nothing novel about a federal government agency's contracting out part of its activities. One can only conjecture whether OEO got its money's worth or whether Upward Bound could have been operated more efficiently in some other fashion. The concern here is not with the administrative cost, which was not excessive in comparison with other OEO programs; the issue is whether the program was operated to serve the neediest in the best way. The record is clear, however, that Upward Bound bypassed community action agencies. Only 6 percent of all Upward Bound projects in fiscal 1968 were funded through CAA's, and the selection of students was left to the project administrators in the grantee colleges and universities. According to Upward Bound, the higher educational institutions are urged to "involve" CAA's in the projects and to include representatives of local CAA's on public advisory committees to assist in planning the programs. Since professors do not have a reputation for accepting advice from outside sources, one can wonder whether the project administrators paid attention to the exhortations of Upward Bound. Most Upward Bound grants were awarded directly to accredited two- or four-year colleges and universities. Once they obtained the funds, the grantees had considerable autonomy in administering the program—though they were required to form a public advisory committee composed of CAA members, local groups, parents, and other residents of the area from which the students were drawn.[7] Neither Upward Bound nor EAI, however, could supply any data about the role of the CAA's in planning or implementing Upward Bound projects. For many projects, the contracting universities discharged their obligation to establish advisory committees by merely preparing lists of nominal members.

The guidelines instruct academic institutions that operate projects to recruit Upward Bound enrollees through community action agencies, neighborhood and community groups, high school personnel, and other local agencies or individuals. A study of the 1967 enrollees found that over three-quarters of the students were told about the program by high school personnel or friends and were recommended by them.[8] The same study found that one-half of Upward Bound enrollees were Negro, indicating that the projects reach minority groups (Table 5-2). Little is known, however, about the enrollees' prior interest in, or plans for, attending college. In selecting students, colleges probably do what comes naturally to them and pick the best available students, presumably from poor homes, who are interested in the program because they are already motivated to attend college.

Table 5–2. Characteristics of Upward Bound Enrollees and High School Students, 1967

Characteristics	Upward Bound	High School
Age		
Under 16 years	15%	34%
16 years	35	31
17 years	34	27
18 years	13	5
Over 18 years	3	3
Sex		
Male	49	51
Female	51	49
Ethnic Composition		
Negro	51	13
White	33	84
Spanish-American	8	2
American Indian	5	0.3
Other	3	0.6
Type of Community		
Urban	74	67
Rural	26	33
Size of Family		
Less than 6	46	70
6 to 8	34	25
9 or more	19	5
Family Composition		
Both parents	48	81
Mother only	31	8
Father only	2	2
Other	19	9
Education of Parents		
High school graduates		
Mother	27	33
Father	19	22
Median Family Income (1966)	$3,341	$7,518

Source: David E. Hunt and Robert H. Hardt, *National Profile of 1967 Upward Bound Students* (Syracuse University, Youth Development Center, October 31, 1967), p. 7. High school estimates are based on Census Bureau data.

Program Components

The Upward Bound program consists of a six- to eight-week residential summer session on a college campus, with a follow-up session during the academic year to provide academic support and motivate the enrollees to pursue higher education. The summer course of study and extracurricular activities are designed by each sponsoring institution. While allowing wide variation among projects, the guidelines establish a general pattern to be adhered to. In addition to an academic curriculum, programs are to provide athletics, social recreation, and exposure to a variety of "cultural enrichment" activities. These might include visits to theaters, exhibits, and museums. For planning purposes, Upward Bound allocated an annual expenditure of $70 per student for field trips.

The teaching staff is composed of college and high school teachers (supposedly at least one third), and art, speech, or other specialists as is deemed fit. Instructors and other staff members, who are chosen by the project director, are to be selected for their interest in students from poor homes and for their ability to relate to them in and out of the classroom. Classes frequently consist of small discussion groups. Some project directors prefer a program with a high degree of casualness and flexibility, with the students setting the pace. Others, such as Yale's Upward Bound director, believe in a rigorous academic atmosphere: "We've got a short time to instill in these youngsters a love of learning. It's too easy to be impressed by what you think you are doing for them and to offer them what amounts to one pleasant summer."[9] Similarly, Thomas Billings, the national director of Upward Bound, stresses the importance of finding novel ways to display the basic tools with which to build the knowledge necessary for college.[10]

Most of the students enter the program after the tenth or eleventh grade and thus have the opportunity to attend two summer sessions and at least one full academic year follow-up program. Many colleges have at least one teacher who spends part of his time, and perhaps weekends, with the students, who are generally brought from their homes or schools to the campus. In many urban areas the students travel to the college at least once a week for tutoring sessions, guidance, or outings with teachers. This is more difficult in rural areas, where students may find it expensive or difficult to visit the campus. Some experiments are being conducted in sending a tutor-counselor to the rural areas; others use local high school teachers to provide extra tutoring and guidance.

Each college is expected to form an Upward Bound academic policy group from its faculty, regular students, and Upward Bound staff. This group serves as the policymaking body for the program. According to OEO's instructions, it should (for some unexplained reason) "be broadly representative of the academic institution's own competencies."[11]

College Admissions and Student Retention

In view of Upward Bound's goal—to prepare enrollees to gain admission to college and to remain until graduation—it would appear that the program has been remarkably successful. OEO has claimed that of the nearly 5,000 who participated in the program during 1967 and who graduated from Upward Bound, nearly 80 percent entered college. A follow-up study found that nine out of every ten were still enrolled in college during the spring of 1968. Similarly, eight of every ten Upward Bound participants who graduated from high school in 1966 were in college two years later. The record of former Upward Bound enrollees was about the same as that of other students who entered college in 1966.[12]

More careful scrutiny of the record of former enrollees neither supports nor refutes OEO's success claims. Not only has EAI failed thus far to gather reliable follow-up data on former enrollees, the available information about students who are admitted to the program leaves much to be desired. A sample survey, conducted for Upward Bound, showed that the grade distribution of enrollees conformed closely to the grades of other students in their high schools. However, since the majority of Upward Bound students come from poor and nonwhite homes, the chances are that they attended poorer high schools, where average achievement scores (as measured by American College Testing Service) are appreciably below the norm.[13]

The retention of Upward Bound students in colleges should not be surprising, even if the results of the sample studies released by OEO are accurate. Many colleges that operate Upward Bound programs pledge to accept a certain number of students, provided that they satisfactorily complete the summer program. OEO states that 46 percent of all Upward Bound students attend the host institutions. But while the "prestige" colleges do accept Upward Bounders, it is often a token gesture of admitting one or two students. Thus many students enroll in community or junior colleges, teachers' colleges, or similar institutions that maintain relatively low admission barriers and do not impose excessively rigorous standards. About 80 percent of the black Upward Bound students enrolled in Negro colleges.

The high college admission and survival rate of Upward Bound students may be due to careful screening, which lessens the risk of accepting poorly motivated or underachieving students. A random selection of EAI consultants' reports shows that at least some projects seek students who are already getting good grades and are likely to go to college even without benefit of Upward Bound. Several consultants of midwestern and western college projects (a majority in the sample) criticized the projects for failing to recruit high-risk students.

Based on the available fragmentary data, it would appear that Upward Bound improves the chances of participants to enter college and motivates some students to continue their education. In addition, some colleges have lowered their admission standards to accept Upward Bound students.

Financial Assistance

One obstacle to college attendance that is encountered by Upward Bound graduates is securing financial help. EAI has estimated the average yearly financial need of an Upward Bound student to be $1,800. Of the nearly 5,000 Upward Bound students who entered college in the fall of 1967, three of every four received financial assistance to complete the year of schooling. Based on the 1968 level of operations, OEO has estimated that approximately 10,000 Upward Bound students would enter colleges during the year. A crucial problem is securing financial assistance to support them. Aside from the numerous private and state scholarships that are available to poor students, the federal government operated three major programs in 1968 to help college students.

1. The college work-study program, administered by the U.S. Office of Education through grants to colleges, is designed to supplement other types of scholarships, grants, and loans. The student may work up to fifteen hours per week at the federal minimum wage ($1.60) or more, depending on the college's wage scale and the duties performed. Recipients of this program and most of the other assistance programs must be full-time students in good academic standing. In fiscal 1967, approximately 370,000 students received help from this program.

2. Educational opportunity grants (USOE) of $200 to $800 per year are available to students who show both financial need and promise. In fiscal 1967, about 134,000 awards, averaging $430, were made to students. These grants must be matched in equal amounts by financial aid from the student's college.

3. National Defense Education Act loans are made to students who attend classes on at least a half-time basis, to a maximum $1,000 per year. These loans are repayable at 3 percent interest within ten years of leaving college. About 400,000 students received such loans in fiscal 1967.[14]

Despite the considerable expansion of federal assistance to college students during the past decade, the available programs were inadequate to provide for an expanded college enrollment of students from poor homes. Upward Bound students have to compete with many others for the available resources. The work-study program, originally enacted as part of the Economic Opportunity Act, no longer restricts its clientele to youths from impoverished homes; it serves middle-class

students as well. The loan program, according to the EAI, is not suitable for students from slums who "have grown up in a world where
loans represent merely another kind of exploitation, and the store-front
loan shark is the only lender they know."[15]

EAI has not revealed the basis for this claim, which has the earmark of "instant sociology" rather than documented fact. Whatever
the merits of the claim, EAI has argued that additional financial
assistance must be provided to former Upward Bound students if they
are to complete their college education. Several private corporations
have assumed the responsibility of supporting Upward Bound students
in college. More of this support is being encouraged by OEO, and
efforts are being directed toward establishing a national Upward
Bound foundation, supported from private sources, to provide assistance to students for at least one or two years.

An Assessment

Because of the fragmentary data available on the operation, only
an impressionistic judgment can be made about the Upward Bound
program.[16] The best available study, undertaken by the Syracuse University Youth Development Center, covered a 10 percent sample of
1966 Upward Bound enrollees and concluded that participation in the
program increased motivation to attend college and successfully complete a degree course. The findings were qualified by this statement:

> Whether or not these increases in academically relevant areas will
> be sustained and transformed into increases in academic accom-
> plishment remains to be seen, but they give considerable encour-
> agement in terms of the effects produced by a relatively short
> program.[17]

The original plans to limit Upward Bound to summer sessions were
discarded when it was found that the six- to eight-week program was
inadequate. The full-year follow-up program was established to expand
and extend the impact by providing for weekly sessions of counseling
and tutoring.

Despite the tenuous contact between Upward Bound and other
CAP activities, OEO has maintained (as it has with other programs)
that Upward Bound will influence the participating institutions to
adopt admission standards more "relevant" to disadvantaged youth
and to develop new curricula and teaching methods.[18] But it is not
clear how the enrollment of some 26,000 students on a part-time basis
during the year will affect the course of higher education in the United
States. OEO has made similar claims about the impact of Upward

Bound upon high school education. The agency hopes that participating high school teachers, as well as the students, will persuade their schools to pay greater attention to the needs of poor students. In practice, the role of secondary schools is limited to recommending enrollees; few high school officials had any chance to shape or direct the projects. It is difficult to visualize Upward Bound as having an effect upon the attitude of more than a few secondary school educators.

Speculation about Upward Bound's impact on the course of education in the United States may be irrelevant, for it can hardly be expected that a $30 million program will have any discernible impact upon a multibillion-dollar "industry." The effort makes sense if the mandate specified by Congress is implemented, if participants in the program are properly screened, and if only those children who cannot make it to college on their own are selected for participation. Upward Bound proclaims the need of providing a remedial program for students who possess intellectual capacity but nevertheless have failed in school. A simple explanation of the costs of Upward Bound shows that such a remedial effort is far more expensive than providing the right kind of education within the school system in the first instance. As much as any other OEO program, Upward Bound reflects a change in societal attitudes in offering youths a chance to acquire a college education. They are not being handed the better life, but they are offered some tools with which to make it.

6.

THE POOR AND THE LAW

Thou shalt not ration Justice.

Judge Learned Hand

Legal Assistance

The poor and the law are constant companions. Landlord-tenant problems, wage garnishments for unpaid debts, and excessive credit terms on consumer purchases beset the low-income population. The poor most frequently encounter the police and juvenile authorities, and many are dependent on welfare legislation and administrative decisions for their very subsistence. Nevertheless, the myth persists that the law is oblivious to income. Anatole France put it best when he extolled the law that "in its majestic equality, forbids all men to sleep under bridges, to beg in the streets, and to steal bread—the rich as well as the poor."

Organized legal aid societies have traditionally been the major vehicle for providing legal services to the poor. The legal aid movement began before the turn of the century. Its central idea was to supply legal advice and representation for the poor through a community law office manned by lawyers who were employed by the organization, or by volunteers. In the early twenties, the organized bar responded to Reginald Heber Smith's classic, *Justice and the Poor*, and began to take a more active interest in the problem.[1] Yet the growth of the legal aid movement has been stunted, and the needs of the poor have far exceeded the resources devoted to the effort.

Private Legal Aid

The National Legal Aid and Defender Association, a private organization, reported that in 1966 there were 252 legal aid offices affiliated with the organization and giving assistance in civil matters. In addition, 125 voluntary committees of state and local legal associations offered varying degrees of legal assistance to the poor in civil matters. Nearly 200 local public defender organizations also were affiliated with the national organization to supply legal assistance in criminal cases.[2]

The quality of the service offered to the poor is indicated by the case load and resources of the organizations affiliated with the NLADA. During 1965 these local organizations claimed to have given assistance to 426,000 indigents on civil matters at a total cost of $5.4 million, or

$17 per case (not counting the volunteer help offered by some lawyers).
A survey of 78 offices affiliated with NLADA revealed that the average
annual case load per full-time attorney ranged from 541 (in 22 offices)
to 1,792 (in 27 offices).[3] In New York City, in contrast, half the private
practitioners handle no more than 50 cases a year, and only 2 percent
of the private lawyers handled more than 500 cases a year.[4] The average
annual salary for attorneys in NLADA-affiliated offices was about
$7,500, well below the level for government, business, or private
practice. Some authorities estimated that only about 10 percent of the
indigents needing legal aid were being served by the existing legal aid
organizations.[5]

The president of NLADA concluded in the association's 1964
report: "Too often troubled people find that legal aid does not really
exist in their communities or that it is fenced off from them by too
stringent eligibility rules, anachronistic policy on the type of cases
handled, lack of publicity, insufficient staff personnel or unconscion-
able delay in services. Too often . . . there is but an illusion of service—
an attractive facade."[6] Legal aid, dependent on the charitable contributions of the community, was unable to fulfill the pressing needs of the
poor for legal assistance and representation. Studies by the American
Bar Foundation, and the experience of OEO's Legal Services program,
indicate that it would require an estimated $300 to $500 million to
provide adequate legal representation to all poor people who have
civil legal problems that merit the attention of a lawyer.[7]

OEO's Legal Services

When the Office of Economic Opportunity was established, only
minimal legal services were available to the poor. The need to expand
and improve these services was fully documented and needed no new
briefs. OEO determined to launch a Legal Services program as part
of its Community Action Program. The concept of the neighborhood
legal office is identical to the idea that had for decades motivated legal
aid societies. The Legal Services program has, however, adopted a
number of additional objectives that legal aid societies, either because
of lack of funds or limited scope, had previously shunned.

The origin of the Legal Services program can be traced to a number of converging developments. Primary credit must certainly be
given to the struggling legal aid societies which provided the background and structure on which to build a program. Decisions of the
Supreme Court in the past decade in the area of criminal procedure,
highlighted by *Gideon* v. *Wainwright*, have emphasized the role of
lawyers in safeguarding the interests of indigent defendants.[8] Thus the
legal profession's responsibility to the poor could not be ignored in
the antipoverty program. Nascent community action agencies estab-

lished prior to 1964, for example in New Haven, included provisions for lawyers.[9]

The blueprint for the Legal Services program was provided by Edgar S. and Jean C. Cahn in a widely circulated article.[10] The Cahns, who were later employed by OEO to plan the program, argued that the poor must participate in helping themselves and that neighborhood law firms could contribute to this objective. Effective advocacy of the needs of the poor was a *sine qua non* for instilling a sense of dignity and responsibility. The Cahns outlined the several objectives of the neighborhood legal firms, all of which were adopted as objectives of OEO's Legal Services program: traditional legal assistance in establishing or asserting clearly defined rights; legal analysis and representation directed toward reform where the law is vague, uncertain, or destructively complex; legal representation where the law appears to be contrary to the interests of the slum community; and legal representation in contexts that appear to be nonlegal.

Though OEO endorsed the concepts of the Cahns and continued to voice their approach, the Legal Services program fell far short of these objectives. The vast resources needed to realize the ambitious plans envisioned by the Cahns were not available. Nonetheless, within one year after OEO was established, the budget of Legal Services was nearly double that of the legal aid societies affiliated with the NLADA ($20 million as compared with $11.7 million). During fiscal 1967, OEO boosted the funds allocated to Legal Services projects by another $5 million and planned to almost double that amount during the subsequent year, Congress willing. Limited funds forced OEO to lower the sights of the program, and only $36 million was allocated to the effort during fiscal 1968. By the end of 1967, however, the Legal Services program was funding 250 projects, providing legal assistance in 48 states, employing nearly 2,000 lawyers in 800 neighborhood law offices, and devoting another 49 projects to research, training, and technical assistance.

Relations with the Legal Establishment

Initially, OEO was confronted with a major policy decision: Should legal aid societies, where they existed, administer the Legal Services projects or should new agencies be established? The dilemma was not peculiar to this program; it was shared by practically all OEO efforts—the choice was between strengthening existing organizations and establishing new institutions. The National Legal Aid and Defenders Association naturally took the position that the creation of separate duplicating agencies to offer legal services would be more costly and less effective than the use of existing facilities under the

Economic Opportunity Act.[11] More objective observers within the legal profession, however, suggested that deficiencies of the existing legal aid organizations would prevent them from accomplishing the broad objectives of the program.[12] Legal aid was accused of "settled bureaucratization" and "welfare colonialism"—favorite phrases among OEO advocates—whereby the business community and the bar provided services to a passive poor. Critics also charged that legal aid traditionally followed the practice of providing a centralized legal office that was inaccessible to many of the poor. Some considered that existing legal aid was derelict in excluding those who were unable to pay a fee; others found fault with the policy of many legal aid organizations in refusing to take divorce and bankruptcy cases, let alone cases involving challenges to government agencies.

A compromise was finally reached on the role of the legal aid societies. OEO delegated the choice of whether an existing legal aid society would run a CAP-funded Legal Services project to local CAA's.[13] The decision of which organization would administer the program thus depended on the local CAA, the initiative of the legal aid society, and the position of the local bar association.

Nearly 40 percent of the 250 Legal Services projects funded by OEO were administered by existing legal aid societies. In order to qualify for federal funds, legal aid societies were required to change their structure, decentralize their offices, and expand the scope of their services.[14] In line with the standing practice of OEO's community action programs, the governing boards of the agency administering the legal services projects were required to contain representatives of the area to be served. Problems also arose in the spring of 1965, when tentative guidelines for the Legal Services program directed that projects adopt law reform as a major goal. Despite reported pressure from the NLADA, which asserted that many legal aid societies could not in good faith undertake such a goal, OEO refused to compromise on this issue. It would seem, however, that some of the pre-OEO legal aid societies accepted Legal Services program funds without changing the scope of their activities.

The cooperation of the organized bar has been vitally important to the Legal Services program. The American Bar Association's endorsement (in February 1965) of the CAP's legal services component was constantly reiterated as the charge of "socialization of the bar" began to be heard. In the summer of 1965 Sargent Shriver, a lawyer himself, reassured the American Bar Association that OEO was not "trying to take paying customers away from private practitioners" or to "subvert lawyers' canons of ethics dealing with solicitation of business or the use of non-lawyer intermediaries in the provision of legal services." Nor, he said, was OEO trying to turn legal aid into a political patronage system.[15]

As Shriver indicated in his ABA address, more than lofty principles were involved. This became clear in the initial position taken by the American Trial Lawyers' Association (ATLA), an organization of tort lawyers (one OEO spokesman referred to ATLA as a group of ambulance chasers). Initially, the ATLA withheld its approval. Disowning any concern (perish the thought) over "questions of economics or pocketbook," the ATLA explained that its opposition was directed "to certain questions of principle that are involved in this matter." The issue was "the independence of the American Bar."[16] But spokesmen for ATLA were quick to add that the association's objections would be overcome if OEO would permit qualified clients to select an attorney and then pay his bill, rather than hire full-time neighborhood lawyers. Finally recognizing that its position of opposing free legal services to the poor was not tenable, ATLA decided to support the Legal Services program.

Support by the national bar organizations has not been without cost. In exchange for this support, OEO has been forced to play down some of the broader conceptions of the program. Although the original guidelines emphasizing institutional change through group organization and efforts at law reform were retained, and although the local agencies administering the programs were formally required to undertake such tasks to receive funds, there is no evidence that the legal aid societies have lived up to the promises they made. Louis Powell, Jr., a former president of the ABA, indicated the extent of the compromise OEO had made to achieve national support: "So long as this program stays within the broad framework of [the] legal aid concept," he reminded OEO, "there should be very few serious problems."[17]

The support of the national bar associations has not necessarily insured the cooperation of state and local bar associations, which are autonomous organizations. Initially, bar associations in Florida, North Carolina, and Tennessee officially opposed the operation of the neighborhood legal services program—though the North Carolina and Tennessee groups later reversed their position, and Florida withdrew its opposition without taking formal action. New Haven Legal Assistance, Inc., was confronted with an official attitude of hostility by the New Haven County Bar Association. The hostility in New Haven was primarily the result of poor tactical maneuvering on the part of the legal services agency. Rather than seek cooperation from the local bar at the outset, the New Haven legal services officials reasoned that support should be sought only after the program was in operation.

This tactic backfired and the local bar opposed the program.[18] This experience was unique, however; most local bar associations have cooperated with the local legal services projects, and virtually all legal services projects have bar association representatives on their boards.

The fears of the local bar associations, not to mention those of individual attorneys, have been numerous. Some lawyers earn a livelihood by handling the legal problems of the poor and lower-middle-class clients and thus fear the competition. OEO has assured them, however, that clients who are able to pay a fee, and fee-earning cases, will be referred to private attorneys. Though the Legal Services program has not adopted national eligibility standards based on the income of clients, each project has imposed such criteria—ranging from $2,000 annual income to $5,200 for a family of four, with an average income of $3,600 or roughly 10 percent above the OEO poverty criteria. The legal profession also maintains certain rules and practices that are designed to maintain its standards and to exclude nonlawyers from legal practice. The American Bar Association promulgates "canons of professional ethics" which all state bar associations have adopted. These canons prohibit advertising and soliciting (Canon 27), stirring up litigation (Canon 28), procuring legal business through intermediaries (Canon 35), and any practice that impairs the confidentiality of the attorney-client relationship (Canon 37).

The Neighborhood Legal Services program has raised fundamental questions concerning the appropriateness of these canons. For example, a rigid interpretation of Canon 37 would prevent Legal Services from sharing information with other neighborhood services.[19] Moreover, the ethical concepts have provided ammunition for local opposition. The courts themselves have the responsibility for regulating the practice of the law (lawyers are the agents of the court) and on several occasions have been asked to rule on the compatibility of legal services projects with the administration of justice and the accepted canons. While the program was upheld in most cases, it was denied a charter in New York City (with leave to file a new application) on the grounds that the proposed program violated some rules of legal ethics.[20] The New York court objected to lay control over the program and was concerned about the absence of safeguards which would prevent neighborhood legal offices from becoming involved in political and lobbying activities. On reconsideration, the New York court apparently determined that the presence of the poor on the board of legal services projects would not subvert the ends of justice, though it restricted the number of neighborhood offices to a maximum of twelve.

Although many lawyers have opposed the operations of the Legal Services program, they are not necessarily oblivious to the needs of the poor, and many have come up with alternative suggestions. Some have favored the British legal aid system, under which the poor receive services from regular private attorneys who are reimbursed by the government.[21] Such a program—named Judicare—would direct business to local attorneys, ensure bar association control, minimize federal interference, and do away with neighborhood legal offices.

The Legal Services program experimented with Judicare and funded such projects in rural northern Wisconsin and Montana, Alameda County, California, and New Haven, Connecticut. From these experiments, program officials have failed to develop enthusiasm for the idea. Testifying before a congressional committee, Earl Johnson, director of the Legal Services program, listed these objections to Judicare: (1) It negates the concept of a "coordinated attack on the legal problems facing the poor. . . . Full-term lawyers can provide the necessary concerted and thoughtful analysis to challenge the basic legal problems of the poor on a consistent basis." (2) The costs of Judicare are nearly three times higher than those under the neighborhood law office approach—$139 per case compared with $48. (3) Judicare involves governmental investigation of fees charged and services rendered, a control that the Legal Services program does not have.[22]

Advocates of Judicare deny its alleged high costs and charge that OEO's calculations exaggerated them. The director of the northern Wisconsin Judicare project claimed that the cost per case amounted to about half the amount indicated by OEO, though this was still higher than under neighborhood offices.[23] The expansion of the constitutional rights of indigent criminal defendants has posed a serious problem for the Legal Services' limited resources. In *Gideon* v. *Wainwright* the Supreme Court ruled that all criminal defendants in felony cases have a right to the assistance of council; and in *Miranda* v. *Arizona*[24] it established the right to the assistance of counsel during police interrogation. The Supreme Court opened up yet another area in *In re Gault* v. *Arizona*, ruling that juvenile courts must provide youths with counsel, even though these courts are formally considered civil proceedings.[25]

The Legal Services program has taken the position that federal funds should not be used to fulfill the requirements the Constitution imposes on the states in criminal cases.[26] The Neighborhood Legal Services offices are designed primarily for civil cases, and assistance in criminal cases is permitted only where the state fails to meet its constitutional duty or where the indigent accused asks for a lawyer that the state need not provide (for example, in misdemeanor cases, or in felony cases prior to arraignment). This policy, which has precluded federal funding of many defender agencies, was subject to sharp criticism by National Public Defenders officials.[27]

Program Operations

The Legal Services program has added several resources to aid the poor in their encounters with the law, but the combined efforts of the older legal aid societies and OEO-supported legal services projects still fall short of the need. The program has therefore been subject to pressures to accept cases beyond the available facilities. Despite exhortations by Legal Services spokesmen about legal reforms, day-to-day demands for services have received priority in most legal services projects, and the caseloads of the legal aid societies and legal services projects reveal a similar pattern.

During fiscal 1968 legal services projects accepted 282,000 cases. The breakdown of these cases is presented in Table 6–1 and parallels the operations reported by the National Legal Aid and Defender Association, though exact comparisons are not possible since not all categories used by the two organizations are uniform. "Family problems"—divorce, annulment, nonsupport, and custody of children—accounted for 45 percent of NLADA's cases and 40 percent of the Legal Services program case load. The other categories are not comparable but appear to be similar for both organizations. The services offered by both also show similarity. The large numbers of clients served, as reported by the two organizations, is misleading: a majority of the clients receive only consultation, or are referred to other agencies.

Table 6–1. Case Load of Legal Services Programs, Fiscal 1968

Type of Case	Number (Thousands)	Percent
Total	282	100.0
Consumer and Employment	*48*	*17.1*
Sales contracts	(16)	(5.7)
Garnishment and attachment	(7)	(2.9)
Bankruptcy	(7)	(2.9)
Administrative	*21*	*7.5*
State and local welfare	(7)	(2.9)
Social security, Workmen's compensation and Unemployment insurance	(7)	(2.9)
Housing	24	8.5
Family	*112*	*39.8*
Divorce, annulment and separation	(61)	(21.7)
Nonsupport	(17)	(6.0)
Paternity	(4)	(1.4)
Criminal	37	13.1
Juvenile	16	5.7
Torts	5	1.7
Other	(19)	6.6

Note: Because of omissions, details do not add to totals.
Source: Community Action Program, Office of Economic Opportunity.

The high percentage of family problems handled by legal services projects, especially divorce and anullment, has been a subject of wide criticism. Critics seemed surprised to discover that in a society where one out of every four marriages ends in divorce, marital life among the poor is not all bliss. Some were hostile to the idea of using poverty funds for such "frivolous" activities. The Legal Services program has taken the position that the poor are entitled to the same rights as the rich and that the same scope of legal services should be offered them.[28] Though the sentiment is commendable, it begs the issue of determining priorities. Given the fact that the funds available to the programs were barely adequate to cover a tenth of the total needs, the declaration that the rich and the poor should be treated alike remains hortatory. Nonetheless, the American Bar Association and the National Advisory Committee of the Legal Services Program, composed of several bar representatives, have supported these pronouncements of the Legal Services program officials.

The salaries paid to the lawyers in the neighborhood law offices have averaged $9,500 per year. Project director salaries have ranged from $10,000 to $20,000 per year, and averaged $14,300.[29] These salaries have been sufficient to attract promising young lawyers to the program because they are comparable to those paid in private practice. It is estimated that more than half the lawyers serving on local legal services projects are in their twenties. The salaries are not sufficient, however, to attract older and more experienced lawyers.

Over half the 850 neighborhood law offices operated by some 250 legal services projects have been located within neighborhood centers set up by community action agencies. This has increased the potential for cooperation between lawyers and other social service personnel. Occasionally social workers have been added to the staffs of the legal services projects, but usually a system of mutual referral has been established. Although the value and need for cooperation has been widely recognized, friction between legal and social workers has emerged in several areas, prompted in part by the role of lawyers in challenging the decisions of other public agencies.

Although representatives of the poor accounted for a third of the members serving on the boards of legal services projects, their participation has not been great. A study conducted by two Harvard Law School students, who visited 19 cities and interviewed 75 persons associated with legal services projects, revealed that representatives of the poor often did not show enthusiasm for the projects and failed to attend meetings. And those who attended the meetings were reluctant to initiate proposals or to participate actively.[30] The study also disclosed that participation by the poor in community education campaigns was often disappointing. The students noted that a lecture in

Detroit—publicized by 1,800 handbills, 50 posters, and radio spot announcements—attracted no audience. The authors concluded that other means of participation by the poor were more fruitful, especially employment in the programs—as receptionists, clerical workers, and investigators. As in other community action projects, OEO has pushed for employment of the poor in these capacities, and many projects are hiring the poor as investigative aides. Again, as in other CAA activities, a serious problem has been the lack of training facilities to develop this subprofessional talent.

New Trends and Dimensions?

By and large, the Legal Services program has operated much as the traditional legal aid organizations do. The additional objectives of the newer program—legal reform, education, representing organizations of the poor—have not been ignored, but the overwhelming press of cases has forced the legal services attorneys, who often handle 50 or 100 new cases each month, to spend their entire time on routine: going to court, making phone calls, interviewing witnesses, attempting to reach settlements. The average new case load per attorney was about 500 cases in 1967, and increased to 800 in the subsequent year when an anticipated rise in funds did not materialize.

While the number of cases is indicative of the vast number of persons who seek and need legal aid, of much more significance are the types of cases undertaken by legal services. On this score the "administrative" cases, constituting only 7 percent of the total case load, may in the long run prove more significant than all the other cases undertaken. A single administrative case may affect the rights of thousands. These cases, involving challenge of governmental agencies, are also the most controversial. The idea that lawyers who are paid with federal funds will challenge the government has appeared inappropriate to many observers. Even a federal judge is reported to have noted, in dismissing a case against the District of Columbia Welfare Agency: "Here are lawyers being paid by the government to sue another government department."[31] The learned judge obviously missed a basic point. If the poor are to secure justice, they must get outside help, and the Economic Opportunity Act was passed by Congress to provide just such help. Similarly, when California Rural Legal Assistance, a major project funded by the legal services program, filed suit against the implementation of restrictions imposed by the state Medi-Cal (California Medicaid) plan and prevented the state from implementing the restrictions, objections were raised against the federal government's funding a project that attempted to prevent the state from "saving" the taxpayers money.[32] Certainly, implementation of these restrictions would deny opportunity to the poor. The issue was not whether California's Medicaid program was too liberal but whether the governor acted illegally under the existing law and would indirectly deny the rights of indigent claimants. It is due process for a company to appeal a decision of a governmental regulatory agency. But some view as inherently subversive an attempt on behalf of the poor to obtain legal recourse by suing a welfare agency that denies them the right to relief.[33]

The possible impact of legal aid in keeping a government agency honest is best illustrated in another CRLA case in which suit was brought against the United States Department of Labor for excessive liberality in admitting Mexican labor into the country to work in harvesting tomatoes. Undeniably, property rights were involved for the CRLA clients, whose wages and income might be affected by the additional labor. Instead of fighting the case in courts, the Labor Department settled out of court, agreeing to do a more careful screening job in the future. A congressman from California considered the incident "groveling submission" by a federal agency, but Senator Edward Kennedy considered the results achieved by CRLA as "legal services at its best."[34] And Professor Howard B. Miller of the University of Southern California School of Law commented on CRLA as follows: "It has given the rural Mexican-American community and the rural poor generally the hope that the highest ideals of American justice may be available to them as well as their wealthy neighbors."[35]

The indirect impact of the Legal Services program should not be minimized. Professor Allison Dunham has argued that the availability of lawyers, even on the scale that OEO provides, should make businessmen wary of using high-handed practices. Administrative agencies, too, may treat their clients in less arbitrary fashion and not view welfare recipients as passive wards of the state.[36]

Giving first priority to the handling of cases, however, has severe limitations. Much of the time is consumed in menial tasks—keeping up with the dockets, waiting in courtrooms, processing forms through judges and clerks. An inordinate amount of time must be spent on the intake process—simply talking with great numbers of people who cannot be helped by a lawyer. Forty percent of the cases that came to the legal services offices during fiscal 1967 received only advice and 15 percent were ineligible for services. Many times there is simply nothing that can be done—no fraud, no overreaching—just wretched poor judgment on the part of the individual.

Moreover, the legal structure of the community within which the poor and their advocates must operate exploits the weaknesses of the disadvantaged. The new OEO lawyers often can do no more than the old legal aid attorneys could to help the poor in many landlord-and-tenant problems and consumer and criminal cases. Where actual questions of law are involved, the poor may simply be stuck. As one legal aid lawyer told the *New York Times:* "We have no law on our side; all we have is *chutzpah* [gall]."[37] Despite all the rhetoric, Finley Peter Dunne's observation about equality of justice appears to hold today: "Don't I think a poor man has a chanst in court? Iv coorse he has. He has the same chanst there he has outside. He has a splendid poor man's chanst."

The Legal Services program's national officials have recognized the lack of balance in the program and urged a reorientation of goals. Earl Johnson, addressing the Conference on Law and Poverty sponsored by the Harvard Law School in March 1967, set the primary goal of legal services as law reform.[38] This would be achieved through significant test cases in the judicial and administrative areas and through proposals to legislatures. Law reform is the best method, he declared, of providing assistance to the poor on a broad scale with limited resources. However, the director's emphasis on legal reform did not necessarily mean that the Legal Services program would adopt this as its primary objective. Local programs are often dominated by traditional legal aid societies and bar associations, and conservative lawyers are not anxious to adopt the ideas of the few crusaders. Moreover, the tremendous case load continues to burden the program.

Legal services attorneys have already achieved several victories in the area of law reform, and there is a potential for meaningful change in many areas of consumer, housing, and administrative law. Like many other antipoverty programs, Legal Services has been spurred by the civil rights movement and societal recognition of the many-faceted needs of the poor. The funds provided by legal services programs have been bolstered by private grants. For example, the Ford Foundation has expended $35 million in recent years to improve legal services, stressing the legal needs of criminally accused poor people. A million-dollar grant to the National Office for the Rights of Indigents "helped test cases involving basic legal precedence that may affect low-income people."[39]

Law schools have also responded to the new climate, seeking "justice for all" with an assist by the Legal Services program. During fiscal 1967, OEO pumped more than $2 million into law schools for research, changes in curricula, and various projects dealing with the poor. Forty law schools instituted courses on law and poverty (three or four of these courses were funded by OEO) attended by some 2,000 students during the 1965–67 academic years. The Wayne State University Law School received an OEO grant to develop and operate pilot programs in legal education at several Detroit area high schools, thus advancing the role of the law school as a community educator.

Law schools have been oriented for many decades toward the interests of the business community; now, however, new dimensions are being added to the traditional law school program. Instead of offering courses exclusively on the rights of landlords, the rights of tenants are also recognized. This movement in legal education provides the impetus for much potential change in the American legal system. The law schools are the centers of legal thinking in the United States, as well as training schools that influence each new generation of attorneys.

Obviously, the dream of Edgar and Jean Cahn that the Legal Services program would instill dignity and self-respect in the poor has not been fulfilled.[40] They maintain that the deficiencies in the program can be traced to the nature of the legal system itself, that serious problems are experienced by the middle class as well as the poor. Legal remedies are too expensive and time-consuming to pursue, legal rules are too technical and complex for mass understanding, and the supply of persons capable of giving legal advice is curtailed by unnecessary protectionist guild restrictions. Although still committed to the concept of neighborhood legal services with as broad a scope as originally envisioned, the Cahns propose a series of bold innovations to make the "justice industry" more responsive to the poor. They suggest that nonprofessionals can fulfill many of the functions performed in the "neighborhood court system."

Too often legal services projects have fallen into the same trap as the traditional legal aid societies. The attorneys believe they are dispensing charity to the undeserving rather than serving clients with a right to representation. And too often legal services attorneys have discovered that the legal problems of the poor are inextricably intertwined with social and economic ills.

Still, the Legal Services program must be credited with expanding legal services to the poor on a scale never before possible. Where the program has been effective, business and government officials may tread more warily when dealing with the poor community. And the program has highlighted the particular legal problems and needs of the poor, bringing the legal profession and its law schools to a level of recognition that offers a potential for future change in the legal system.

Some of these changes are already in the judicial "pipeline." A case pending before the Supreme Court that challenges welfare residence laws, held unconstitutional by four lower courts, may annually qualify some 100,000 indigent persons who now are denied public assistance because they fail to meet residence requirements. Other cases instituted by legal services attorneys, testing the constitutionality of man-in-the-house rules and similar questionable public assistance practices, still pending in the lower courts, may result in significant modifications of our welfare system, the Supreme Court willing. Related cases dealing with tenants' rights, garnishment, and consumer credit will further protect the poor, if the challenges are upheld by the courts.

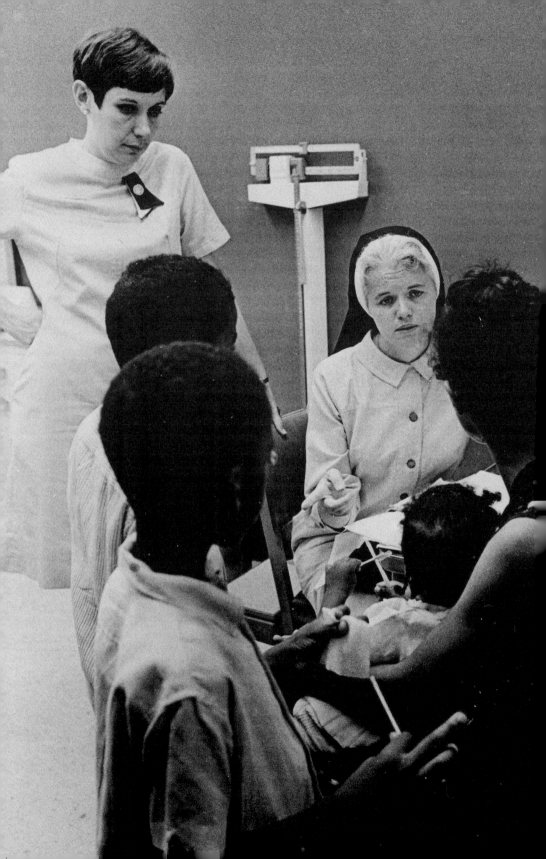

7.

HEALING THE POOR
IN THEIR BACK YARD

**Behold, I will bring . . . health and cure,
and I will cure them, and will reveal
unto them the abundance of peace and truth.**

Jeremiah 33:6

OEO's Medical Program

It was inevitable that the programs initiated under the Economic Opportunity Act would become involved in the health business. The linkage between poverty and poor health has long been recognized, and most of the major EOA programs included a health component. Entry into training and employment programs normally included at least a diagnostic medical check-up, and frequently remedial treatment was needed to help the poor bridge the gap from poverty to gainful employment. Altogether, expenditures on health activities accounted for about 5 percent of the total OEO budget during its first four years, and 11 percent of CAP funds.

Although medical care as a supportive service for EOA programs was taken for granted, the extent to which the Community Action Program should fund health programs became an immediate issue. OEO's policymakers could not agree whether CAP's limited resources should be allocated to health programs rather than to housing, education, or other competing needs of the poor. The case for allocating funds to health programs was weakened by the already enormous expenditures for health care of the poor. In 1964, federal, state, and local governments were already spending nearly $8 billion for health and medical services, and legislation on the drawing board would double these annual outlays within three years. An estimated $9.7 billion, over half of total health expenditures in 1968, supported programs benefiting poor and low-income persons. On a per capita basis, medical expenditures for the poor equaled the average annual U.S. expenditure of $200 per person for the entire population.

Despite these massive public expenditures, the deficit in health care of the poor was startling, whether measured in terms of life expectancy, infant mortality rate, or incidence of visits to physicians or dentists.[1] In view of these high governmental expenditures, what ac-

191

counts for the deficiencies in health care? No doubt some of the funds are wasted by inept administration; and, as in other areas, the poor pay more, particularly when the government foots the bill. More importantly, three additional factors help explain the deficiencies.

1. The poor, on the average, need more medical attention, since aged persons are disproportionately represented among the poor, and since physical and mental handicaps are associated with poverty.

2. The poor are offered little preventive medical attention. Moreover, the health care that is available encourages them to ignore correctable health problems or defects until they become major problems.

3. The delivery of existing health services to the poor is inefficient, and community health services are fragmented, disorganized, and often inaccessible. Shortages of medical and allied manpower have added to the difficulties of establishing adequate health services in neighborhoods where economic incentives are limited.

When community action agencies began to submit their plans, a number of them included health components as part of the total package. Most of the funds were for fragmented or specialized services: visual screening, immunization clinics, prenatal care courses, or supplements to existing clinics. Innovative projects were hard to come by, and Head Start accounted for more than half of the funds that were spent in the first two years. In fiscal 1967 neighborhood health centers became the major OEO health program (Table 7–1).

Compared with other government contributions to medical services for the poor, the CAP outlay for health and medical services was no more than the proverbial drop in the bucket. Local CAA's could develop neither the planning capability, staffing, nor institutional base for medical care. Obviously, if CAP was to come to grips with these

Table 7–1. *Estimated OEO Allocations for Health, Fiscal 1965–68 (Millions)*

Programs	1965	1966	1967	1968
Total	$18.8	$59.0	$117.7	$99.5
Neighborhood health centers	2.0	7.8	50.8	33.2
Family planning	.4	2.4	4.6	8.3
Other research and demonstration projects	1.8	1.0	1.7	1.8
Narcotics programs	—	—	9.4	—
Other community programs	3.4	8.8	7.0	9.5
Head Start health programs	10.3	31.7	31.6	32.9
Job Corps health programs	.5	6.9	11.7	12.8
VISTA health programs	.5	.5	.9	1.0

Note: Details do not necessarily add to totals because of rounding.
Source: Community Action Program, Office of Economic Opportunity.

problems with the money available to it, it could fund only demonstration projects. The challenge to OEO was to develop innovative comprehensive health service programs.

The argument for emphasizing comprehensive health services rather than individual and isolated health components was not subscribed to by all concerned at the outset, and the concept remains a matter of controversy to the present time. The great expense and complexity of setting up any sort of comprehensive program were considered important obstacles, as was the anticipated difficulty in enlisting the substantial number of trained professionals that would be required. Simpler programs, which focused on specific health problems such as faulty hearing and vision, or narrow parts of the health care spectrum, such as screening and diagnosis, were seen by many as more practical and feasible. Officials of the U.S. Public Health Service were among those who recommended that if OEO became involved in the health field, it should merely support programs that would fill specific loopholes in existing community services.

On the other hand, the argument was made that while the gaps were substantial, health care for the poor was already so fragmented and disorganized that the addition of a few more unrelated projects would not be particularly helpful. According to this argument, the health needs of the poor would not and could not be adequately met without major changes in the health care system. OEO was the first federal agency to have the flexibility, as well as the mandate, to undertake programs that could have significant influence in changing the health care delivery system.

A Comprehensive Health Care Program

The proposal for developing a health program was made to CAP by professionals rather than by community agencies. Early in 1965, Professors H. Jack Geiger and Count D. Gibson, Jr., of Tufts University's College of Medicine, approached OEO with a plan for comprehensive neighborhood health centers that would be designed specifically to serve the multiple needs of the poor. Their plan was inspired by comprehensive health clinics that were operating in several developing nations. Geiger and Gibson had first presented their idea to the Public Health Service but were referred to the antipoverty agency. Their original proposal, to establish a model center in the Columbia Point public housing development in Boston (which had about 6,000 residents), was expanded to include the operation of two centers—one in Boston and the other in a rural southern area, which turned out to be Mound Bayou, Mississippi. The centers were designed to provide the full range of out-patient services to everyone who lived in the target areas. Particularly appealing to CAP officials was the proposal that the centers use indigenous community residents to perform many functions, and include them in making decisions concerning operation of the centers. In line with OEO goals, Geiger hoped that the neighborhood health centers would stimulate broader social action and institutional changes in other areas.[2] CAP funded the proposed project in June 1965.

The Denver antipoverty board, meanwhile, was having problems assembling a package of proposals. Although some of its members insisted on their own pet projects to the exclusion of others, they all favored inclusion of a health component. With cooperation from the Denver Health Department and guidance from OEO, the Denver community group developed a comprehensive neighborhood health center proposal. CAP funded its application two months after the approval of the Tufts project, and five additional centers during the balance of the fiscal year.

Out of the negotiations over funding these centers, CAP developed a four-point model for comprehensive neighborhood health centers: (1) a full range of ambulatory health services; (2) close liaison with other community services, which implied referrals and exchanges of services; (3) close working relationships with a hospital, preferably one with a medical school affiliation; and (4) participation of the indigenous population in descision-making that affected the center and, whenever feasible, their employment in subprofessional and other positions.[3]

The comprehensive health centers gained a devoted and valuable ally in Senator Edward Kennedy of Massachusetts. Concerned over the health deficiencies and needs of children enrolled in Head Start projects and of adults in training programs, Kennedy first explored the possibility of adding various health services provisions to each of these programs. After extensive discussion, Kennedy concluded that the simple addition of new funds for the purchase of services would not effectively meet the need and that a profound change in the organization of health services for the poor was needed. He was impressed with the potential of the embryonic neighborhood health center program, which he thought might be able to accomplish this. Cognizant that myriad other demands would be competing for the meager resources, in 1966 he proposed a neighborhood health center program with earmarked funds. Fifty-one million dollars was allocated to the program, a sixfold increase over the previous year, but during the following year the amount allocated to one-stop neighborhood health centers declined to $33 million.

The reduced allocation did not, however, reflect a decline in the popularity of the program. During fiscal 1968 CAP funded six additional health centers while most other CAP programs remained at their previous levels or were reduced. The launching of new health centers during fiscal 1968 with reduced funds was made possible by the fact that the operations of most projects that were funded in fiscal 1967 were delayed and consequently did not require refunding during 1968. The Senate Appropriations Subcommittee indicated its enthusiasm for comprehensive health centers by insisting that the $90 million requested for them not be affected despite a recommendation that total OEO appropriations for 1969 be reduced to $1,873 million, or $337 million below the Administration's request.[4]

Earmarking the funds induced some communities which had previously proposed fragmented health programs to apply for comprehensive projects. Thirty-two centers were in operation by August 1968, and an additional 16 were funded and in various stages of planning. Three of every four projects were located in urban areas. The 12 rural centers included a project on an Indian reservation in Minnesota; another rural center served an area in California where migratory labor is concentrated. The projects were designed to serve 1 million people, assuming they are funded to reach full operating capacity. At the 1968 funding level, neighborhood health centers would provide medical services to about one of every 25 people eligible to receive assistance, including some who qualify as medically indigent even though their income exceeds OEO's poverty criteria.

As with most CAP activities, applications for neighborhood health centers exceeded the available resources; moreover, OEO's criteria were too general to indicate priorities for funding the proposed centers.[5] A number of factors presumably were used to determine whether a community "deserved" to receive support for a center: the extent to which the community had received CAP funds for other purposes; the availability of health and medical services to the indigent of the community; the degree of community support (or pressure), including cooperation from pertinent state and local organizations; and the innovative elements of the proposal. It is not clear what weight these considerations actually carried in the approval of projects, for CAP developed no indices of need for health services, and even with the best intentions, subjective judgments had to enter into the final selection. It appears that "first-come first-served" was a controlling criterion, and the committing of available resources on this basis made more refined standards superfluous. Inasmuch as additional funds were not forthcoming, once CAP had committted itself to a project it was difficult to terminate funding in favor of another proposal, even if the latter seemed more desirable.

A "Typical" Center

Wherever feasible, the neighborhood health centers took over available facilities and used the new funds to expand their services. In the majority of cases, however, facilities were inadequate or altogether lacking, which required the establishment of a new center by renovating an existing building or constructing a new one. The intent was to use indigenous labor for this work, but the practices of the building trades made this hard to achieve. OEO also tried to encourage the use of local contractors and labor, but for obvious political reasons it failed to include utilization of local labor in the official guidelines. The Watts center was built by local contractors who employed low-income residents to put up the structural modules. Although neighborhood people were employed in the construction and renovation of other projects as well, it may be significant that Watts had a riot prior to the approval of its neighborhood health center; in other cities local labor was not so "lucky," and construction or renovation was done by outsiders.

Professional staff were recruited from diverse sources, including returning Peace Corps personnel and recent medical or dental school graduates. Though salaries were competitive with those of other publicly supported institutions, they were too low to attract already established and more experienced personnel, particularly full-time physicians and dentists. Program standards called for one physician for every 1,500 people served and one dentist for every 2,500 people. In addition, centers employed medical technicians, social workers, and other technical personnel. To complement the trained personnel, neighborhood aides were hired for subprofessional roles. These low-income workers were to be trained either in the centers or in existing training programs in hospitals, local health departments, or federally supported programs. On-the-job training at the neighborhood health centers attempted not only to fill the needs of the facility but also to increase the future employability of the trainees in the competitive labor market.[6] It is hoped that the centers will provide the setting in which a variety of health roles can be restructured to enable the training of persons with a limited formal education to perform functions previously performed by persons with much more training and education. The extent to which these goals are being achieved is not known because CAP has not yet collected hard data on the operation of the centers. OEO's Health Service Office estimated that about a thousand local residents were employed in the summer of 1968 by the centers then in operation, citing this as evidence that the training goals of the program were being achieved. However, OEO could not supply information on the occupational distribution or the wage or salary rates of the neighborhood employees. Given the general shortage of personnel in medical occupations, trainees should have little difficulty in finding jobs in other institutions, provided they receive meaningful training.

As in other CAP programs, indigenous residents served on the policymaking bodies of the health centers and were included in decisions on staffing, hours of operation, development of community support, organization of school health screening clinics, and other non-technical problems.

Eligibility Criteria and Funding

Initially, all residents of a poor neighborhood were eligible to receive health center services. This standard was criticized by practicing physicians in the neighborhoods and by others who argued that benefits ought to be limited to the poor. In countering these criticisms, OEO spokesmen pointed out that the broad eligibility criterion was being applied in areas where 80 percent of the population qualified under the official poverty indices.[7] OEO did not identify the data it had utilized to determine the income level of all the residents in a designated area. Certainly the 1960 census data were obsolete by the time the centers were established. Moreover, many Negro and other minority-group families were forced to reside in slum areas even when they had an income that would have enabled them to move out. To overcome criticisms that the OEO-funded health centers were serving the nonpoor, Congress in 1967 limited eligibility to low-income families. Accordingly, the 1968 guidelines specified that the standards of "closely related programs" would control eligibility, in effect making the clientele of neighborhood centers consistent with Medicaid standards, which vary from state to state, or with OEO poverty standards, whichever is higher.

OEO grants for operating centers have varied considerably, depending upon location, population served, facilities needed, and the supportive services offered. Thus the size of grants has ranged from about $300,000 to $3.5 million. Little data is available on the actual utilization of funds, but OEO's Health Affairs Office has estimated that the grants, exclusive of construction and renovation costs, were expended as follows:

	Percent
Medical care	60
Dental care	10
Social services, training, community organization	10
Evaluation	5
Administration	15

To conserve its limited funds, CAP arranged with FHA to assist applicants for neighborhood health centers to secure, whenever feasible, loan guarantees for the renovation or construction of facilities.

In 1967 OEO's Office of Health Affairs assumed (for planning purposes) that the annual cost of care would amount to $125 per person, excluding reimbursement or contributions from other government programs. The actual costs ranged from about $85 per person in Denver, with its target population of 20,000, to double that amount in Boston's Columbia Point. Costs varied with the range of services offered by the centers, the relatively high cost at Columbia Point being attributable to the "highly innovative" approaches and to the small number served. Based on these data, it is estimated that comprehensive medical services for the 22 million poor in the United States would cost about $2.7 billion. If the services could be extended to all the medically indigent, the cost would rise by 30 to 40 percent. However, since OEO's neighborhood health centers are suitable primarily in areas where poor people are concentrated, Dr. Ruth Covell and her associates in HEW have estimated that only about a third of the poor could be served by comprehensive health centers at a total annual cost of $1.3 billion—assuming that adequate personnel and facilities could be secured. Over-all public outlays for health services would not necessarily increase by that amount because comprehensive health centers would absorb part of the current expenditures. The savings would be achieved by reducing the duration of hospitalization and by preventive measures that would decrease the need for costly hospitalization. Also, a network of comprehensive health centers would supplant some of the existing health facilities and services.[8]

Further insights concerning the true costs of delivering health and medical services to the poor may come from a special project OEO is funding in Portland, Oregon, where prepaid medical services are being purchased from the Kaiser Health Plan for 1,200 poor families (selected from four neighborhoods by the local community action agencies). The Kaiser organization, under a grant from the Public Health Service, is attempting to compare utilization and the expenses incurred by the

OEO-supported group with the experience of its regular participants. On the assumption that the poor will need more health services because of previous neglect, the Kaiser Health Plan initially charged OEO about 30 percent above its normal rates for OEO's participants. This rate will be adjusted on the basis of actual utilization, and the experiment should help fix the true costs of providing comprehensive health and medical services for the poor.[9]

Coordination of Funding and Services

Granted the soundness of the neighborhood health center approach, OEO could hardly have been expected to bring about major changes in the delivery of health services to the poor; and the agency's officials recognized that OEO could not compete with the billions of dollars available for that purpose to the Department of Health, Education, and Welfare. OEO hoped rather to serve as a catalytic agent in bringing about changes in the health care delivery system and in pooling the funds received from scattered sources. Thus it has used its resuorces to fund a few demonstration projects. To avoid duplication and to maximize the impact of the demonstrations, OEO entered into an "agreement" with HEW. The role of the centers was spelled out in a joint statement by the two agencies:

> OEO is undertaking the program . . . to make possible the pulling together of disparate sources of funds and services into a coherent whole, by (1) providing the needed 'seed money' and (2) by paying directly for services which cannot be supported by other sources or services to poor persons who may not be eligible under other programs.[10]

Since HEW grants were normally designed to serve a target area larger than the neighborhood health centers funded by OEO, the larger programs were encouraged to contract with the neighborhood center to provide services offered by the grantee, to assign personnel and/or equipment to the neighborhood center, or to provide specialized services to the neighborhood health center population (for example, mental health clinics).

Neighborhood health center clients are often eligible for medical assistance from Medicaid and federally supported public assistance programs; and when a center offers medical services, it is entitled to reimbursement. Since public funds are used in either case, it might appear that there would be no point in the health centers' collecting these fees. But if the centers are to exploit their innovative features and prove the claim that they deliver a "bigger bang for the buck," then a case can be made for the vigorous collection of "debts" from other programs. However, the necessary arrangements have often been difficult to conclude, and considerably less money has come into the centers from other sources than had been anticipated. If it is assumed that the centers will remain part of CAP and not be transferred to HEW, OEO may intensify its attempts to collect reimbursable outlays in order to maximize the funds available for the operation of comprehensive health centers and to demonstrate its claims about the superiority of the centers in delivering health services to the poor.

The Denver Health Center provides an illustration of the coordination envisioned. Before OEO initiated the neighborhood health center program, the Denver Health Department was planning, together with the Children's Bureau of HEW, to establish a children's center in a poverty neighborhood. OEO proposed to cooperate with the Children's Bureau so that the Denver Health Department could establish a neighborhood health center that would serve the entire family. Instead of one center, two centers were established under one roof, with OEO providing funds for the adult services and the Children's Bureau supporting the pediatric services. Additional funds were provided by the Public Health Service to operate activities within its domain.[11]

Generally, however, agreement on cooperation and coordination at high levels does not necessarily extend to the administration of the program. The agreement reached by HEW and OEO has not permeated the lower levels of their own agencies, let alone the state and local officials responsible for the administration of health programs. The HEW official who distributes federal health funds on the basis of formulas prescribed by Congress may find it difficult to adjust his funding practices to the special needs of a neighborhood health center. Similarly, even a well-intentioned state official may find that allocating federal resources to neighborhood centers that serve a select few in a predetermined area does not fit in with his over-all program for the distribution of funds in the state. Local health officials may also find it difficult to adjust their programs for aiding the poor to a restricted project that has regulations and rules that are different from those to which they have been accustomed. The difficulties are not insurmountable, but change requires time, and the health service bureaucrats, like most other humans, do not take kindly to change.

Relations with the Medical Establishment

Either the American Medical Association has mellowed or the fight has been taken out of it by the series of defeats that culminated in the congressional approval of Medicare. The AMA had cried wolf too frequently and too shrilly to raise again the specter of "socialized medicine" when OEO proposed the establishment of neighborhood health centers. Also, the AMA had in the past been tolerant of legislation on behalf of the poor who could not pay "standard" fees. Although its president, Dr. Charles Hudson, formally endorsed the concept on behalf of AMA the day after OEO published its initial guidelines, the AMA's position on neighborhood health centers can best be described as schizophrenic. Dr. Hudson's views were reinforced in June 1966 by an official of AMA's Division of Socio-Economic Activities, who commented that "this is something that the AMA looks to with great warmth, to which the AMA is pledging full cooperation, and for which we think there is a very good future."[12] But Dr. Milford O. Rouse, Hudson's successor as AMA president, "viewed with alarm" the establishment of neighborhood health centers, and upon taking office warned the assembled physicians that "we are faced with the concept of health care as a right rather than a privilege." He failed to explain why physicians should not welcome a positive attitude on the part of the American public toward medical services. The AMA's House of Delegates gave OEO an unsolicited warning to stop meddling in health affairs and to leave medical services for the poor under the auspices of Title XIX (Medicaid) of the Social Security Act. Some 18 months later, in December 1967, the AMA held its first conference on health care for the poor. One of the discussion groups at this conference rejected the House of Delegates' position and voted unanimously that health care should be regarded as a human right rather than a privilege. With regard to neighborhood health centers, the conferees acknowledged that local hospitals are frequently "unable to adapt themselves to pockets of poverty," and stated that slum residents should be given opportunities to help plan neighborhood health centers.[13] Other medical groups—the Medical Committee on Human Rights, the Physicians' Forum, the American Dental Association, the National Dental Association, and the National Medical Association (the latter two composed mostly of Negro physicians and dentists)—have been consistent supporters of the neighborhood health center concept.

At the local level, OEO's health centers have had remarkably little opposition, and OEO has been careful to court the cooperation of local medical groups. According to a CAP memorandum:

> Interested professional associations *must* be consulted, and every effort must be made to establish a close working relationship with professional health personnel who are or will be serving the target neighborhood.[14]

Aside from their concern for the health of indigents, local medical and dental associations were led to cooperate with the health program as

a matter of simple economics: far from robbing doctors and dentists of
their bread and butter, the centers promised to free them of unpaying
patients. Where funds were already available for indigent health
care, OEO was careful to advise the health centers that patients eligible
to receive care under Title XIX "are free to obtain any of these services where they see fit."[15] Physicians and dentists could find little to
complain about in the administration of the neighborhood health
centers. Two of every three grants for health centers were made to
community action agencies, which in all but two cases delegated their
administration to the local medical institutions (Table 7–2). These
institutions—hospitals, medical schools, city health departments—had
formerly provided out-patient and clinic services to the poor and
continued to do so under the neighborhood health centers. Thus
medical personnel were apt to regard the new centers as a modification
in the delivery of charitable services rather than as a threat to existing
medical institutions.

Pharmacists, however, presented a problem, since the health centers normally included a pharmacy which competed with private drug-
stores in the neighborhoods. Again, OEO instructed the neighborhood
center officials to inform Title XIX patients of their right to fill pre-
scriptions at the local pharmacies, but the immediate accessibility of
clinic dispensaries makes this a continuing issue. There are, however,
signs that pharmacists and OEO are seeking a rapprochement. According to a spokesman for the registered pharmacists, "The profession's best interest will be served by pharmacists getting active in these
community antipoverty programs which are going to roll on, with or
without us."[16] But spokesmen for the National Association of Retail

Table 7–2. *Grantees and Administering Agencies of Neighborhood Health Centers,
July 1968*

	Grantees	Administering Agencies
Total	48	49[a]
Community action agencies	32	2
Hospitals	4	13
Medical schools	3	10
Health departments	0	7
Medical societies	1	2
Group practice	1	3
New Health Corporation	1	8
Other nonprofit agencies	6	4

[a] Includes one instance of joint administration.
Source: Community Action Program, Office of Economic Opportunity.

Druggists prefer that the health centers be transferred to HEW, anticipating that under HEW the centers would abandon the operation of pharmacies. The druggists apparently feared that the neighborhood health centers would be successful and that this would lead to the establishment of more such facilities.[17]

Administration of Health Centers

The variety of OEO health programs has demanded some in-house coordination, and the day-to-day administration of neighborhood health centers and of narcotic and birth control programs falls within the scope of the CAP Office of Health Affairs. Over-all coordination, program planning, and evaluation (such as it is) are provided by OEO's Office of Health Affairs, which was established in April 1967. It was envisioned (or dreamed) that in addition to planning and coordinating programs under EOA, the Office of Health Affairs would be responsible for coordinating the entire federal health effort for the poor. This mission was an extension of OEO's statutory authorization to coordinate all federal antipoverty programs, but the ambitious effort is of too recent origin to be appraised. However, because of its limited personnel and funds, it is not likely that the Office of Health Affairs can successfully coordinate the diverse multibillion-dollar efforts of the federal government for health and medical services to the poor. It is more likely that HEW will absorb the health centers than tolerate coordination by OEO.

In 1967, Senator Edward Kennedy introduced an EOA amendment to further expand OEO's health programs. The new amendment authorizes financial assistance to public agencies, private organizations, and individuals for programs or projects designed to develop knowledge and enhance skills in providing health services to the poor. More specifically, it was designed to help the poor enter the health science professions and to improve existing training facilities, with special emphasis on preparing them to serve the poor.[18] This amendment grew out of a successful OEO health demonstration project that was proposed in 1966 by a group of health science students at the University of Southern California. The students, members of the Student Health Organization (SHO), sought to combine their formal training with community service to alleviate some of the critical health manpower shortages in poor communities. The OEO-funded projects, sponsored by the USC School of Medicine and the Student Medical Conference of Los Angeles, enrolled 90 students of medicine, dentistry, nursing, dental hygiene, social work, and other health professions, from 40 institutions in 11 states, to work in poverty areas throughout California. Each student was assigned to a team consisting of regular professional personnel concerned with the health problems of the indigenous population, and community workers who received the same stipends as the students. The teams helped provide a variety of services, from health education to diagnostic screening. The program was expanded to three projects in the summer of 1967 and to eight projects the following summer, with funding from a variety of sources. The SHO projects generated grants from the Public Health Service to study patterns of delivery of health care to the poor and to investigate curriculum changes that would encourage further work by students in these fields.

These demonstration projects strongly suggested the desirability of expending additional resources for such efforts, and the Kennedy amendment attempted to exploit the lessons that had been learned. However, the appropriations that followed the 1967 amendments were barely adequate to continue EOA programs at the level of the preceding year. And if OEO decided to implement the Kennedy amendment, it would have to reduce its support for other efforts.

Is There a Future for the Centers?

In mid-1968 the neighborhood centers were of too recent origin and limited scope to permit evaluation: only 32 centers were actually in operation and the oldest had been in existence for only about two years. It will be some time before definitive judgments can be made about the centers' impact in improving the quality and accessibility of medical services to the poor. Nor is there sufficient evidence that the neighborhood health centers are attractive to professionals, or that they can provide the setting for training the poor to perform subprofessional functions to meet continued manpower shortages. More crucial to the future of the centers is whether separate health care centers for the poor—compounded in many instances by racial or ethnic segregation—can remain viable institutions. And it is not at all clear whether these centers will be more successful than earlier efforts in involving clients in planning and administration and in training indigenous populations to assume subprofessional roles. In these aspects, the health centers share the difficulties and problems of other CAP efforts.

Nonetheless, the concept of one-stop health centers for the poor has already won many adherents. A recent presidential commission on health manpower and its utilization addressed itself to the problem of quality and delivery of medical services to the poor. While concluding that "no clear-cut solution for care of the disadvantaged in our country has been developed," the commission singled out the neighborhood health centers as promising and urged that "such experimentation be markedly expanded."[19] The American Public Health Association and the U.S. Public Health Service have also gone on record in favor of the comprehensive health service approach; and the PHS has pledged that it will "encourage and promote the concept of comprehensive health services through the use of its own resources and its own consultation and assistance activities." The Surgeon General has assigned "high priority for funding of those programs aimed primarily at improvement of the health status of the indigent" and has urged his field staff, in its work with state health planning agencies, to emphasize the need for delivering comprehensive health services to the poor.[20] The emphasis by the Surgeon General on the needs of the poor is a departure from the traditional approach and activities of his agency.

Such examples of support were duplicated many times, but the testimonials have not resulted in any significant funding priority for the program. Although more neighborhood health centers will probably be added to the program, this will not be done at the rate initially envisioned. The ability to recoup current expenditures from Title XIX or from other government sources will be a telling factor. OEO's health officials have estimated that more than half of the current expenditures of neighborhood health centers might be reimbursed from other governmental programs. Therefore, if the claims of neighborhood health service proponents prove correct, even the present allocation of public funds to provide medical services to the poor could result in improving the quality and quantity of health services, as these funds are increasingly spent within the framework of a more effective organization and delivery system.

8.

FIGHTING POVERTY WITH A PILL

There are people whose only legacy to their children
is the same one of poverty and deprivation that they
received from their own parents.

Mollie Orshansky

The Case for Birth Control

The close relationship between large families, unwanted children, and poverty has been long recognized. Medical technology has made it possible to reduce the number of unwanted children and thus alleviate poverty. From its inception, OEO has recognized that birth control may be the most cost-effective tool for fighting poverty. And crucial though it is, the economic argument is not the sole justification for birth control, for smaller families contribute to the health and well-being of each member.

Public opinion surveys have repeatedly revealed widespread acceptance of family planning and support for dissemination of information about it. The desire to limit family size is almost universal, cutting across social, geographic, economic, and racial lines. According to one study, farm wives wanted 3.5 children as against 3.3 for all wives, and nonwhite wives wanted 2.9 compared to 3.3 for white wives. Contrary to popular myths, lower-income couples want smaller families than higher-income couples, and nonwhites want smaller families than whites. Families whose incomes were below $3,000 wanted 2.5 children while those with incomes above $8,000 wanted 3.1.[1]

But as happens too frequently, the aspirations of the poor are unrealized, and one of the most common traits of poverty is "excess fertility," or having more children than desired. Based on an examination of the available data, a study prepared for the Senate Committee on Labor and Public Welfare concluded that many poor children are unwanted and that their birth was due either to the parents' ignorance or to the unavailability of birth control information and devices.[2] In 1960, 17 percent of the white and 31 percent of the nonwhite couples interviewed said they had not wanted more children before the last conception had occurred. Lack of education is surely a deterrent to family planning. Of those families in which the wife had no more than a grade school education, 32 percent of white couples and 43 percent of the nonwhites had unwanted children.[3] Mollie Orshansky, in her well-known examination of poverty statistics, concluded that "the larger the family, the greater the poverty hazards for children. . . . The poverty rate for all families with 5 or 6 children is three and a half times as high as for families with 1 or 2 children."[4] The percentage of poor families by number of children is presented in Table 8–1.

Excess fertility not only pulls many families below the poverty threshold, it compounds the difficulties faced by such families. For example, large low-income families face serious housing problems. A presidential commission has estimated that in the 61 largest U.S. cities there is a large-family housing shortage affecting more than half a million families with 2.5 million children.[5]

According to 1967 estimates, of the approximately 5 million medically indigent females of childbearing age who needed subsidized family planning services, only about 700,000 were actually receiving them. At an average annual cost of $30 per person, the total cost of supplying the potential clientele with birth control information and devices would amount to about $150 million. Wilbur J. Cohen, former Secretary of Health, Education, and Welfare, has estimated that if low-income women had the same access to information and devices as the nonpoor, the number of children born to the low-income women in 1966 would have been reduced by some 450,000 births. Cohen assumed this was the number of unwanted children among the poor.[6] Whether the expenditure of $150 million for birth control would have eliminated all unwanted births among the poor cannot be ascertained. If, however, the expenditure could have prevented only a third of the total estimated unwanted children, or 150,000 births, the cost would have been $1,000 per child. This amount is roughly equivalent to the support payment for a child on relief for two years. President Johnson claimed that "$5 invested in population control is worth $100 invested in economic development." Planned Parenthood–World Population, the leading private organization in the field of

Table 8–1. Risk of Poverty by Size of Family, 1966

Number of Children	Percent of Families Who Are Poor
1	9.3
2	10.2
3	12.8
4	18.6
5	27.7
6 or more	42.1

Source: Mollie Orshansky, "The Shape of Poverty in 1966," Social Security Bulletin (March 1968), Table 4.

birth control, collected more than a score of statements by the President that repeated the theme that "all families have access to information and services that will allow freedom to choose the number and spacing of their children within the dictates of individual conscience."[7]

OEO's Approach to Birth Control

Joseph A. Kershaw, OEO's first assistant director for research and planning, stated: "We looked into the family planning with some care and were amazed to discover that here is probably the single most cost-effective antipoverty measure."[8] But OEO was slow to catch up with the changing attitudes toward birth control and allocated only $16.5 million, or 0.6 percent of the total CAP budget, to family planning projects during the agency's first four years. During its first two years it did not encourage applications for birth control projects, spending only 0.2 percent of the CAP budget for that function. (A wag suggests that OEO did not support birth control because instant success could not be claimed.) When external as well as local pressures began to mount, OEO created a headquarters family planning office and increased its funds for the program to $4.5 million in fiscal 1967 and $10 million the succeeding year.

Restrictive Regulations

OEO's timid approach to birth control is reflected not only in the skimpiness of the allocated funds but also in the regulations it imposed on grantees.[9] Contrary to the usual OEO tactic of trying to secure the maximum feasible visibility for all its activities, OEO prohibited grantees from using program funds "to announce or promote through mass media the availability of the family planning program funded by this grant." This approach was so out of character that a columnist who is sympathetic to OEO suggested that "whispers, presumably, are permissible."[10]

Initially, OEO tried to impose additional restrictions upon the use of family planning funds. OEO insisted that its funds be used only to aid married women and it prohibited the issuance of contraceptive devices to unmarried women and to married women who did not live with their husbands. Because many OEO officials were not in sympathy with the regulation, it was enforced rather quixotically. Local antipoverty units were reportedly encouraged by some OEO officials to circumvent the instructions by juggling their bookkeeping entries to show that nonfederal money was being used to supply materials to unmarried women while federal funds were used only for the married.[11] This rigid restriction drew considerable public criticism, and in February 1966 the United Planning Organization of Washington, D.C., rejected a $79,000 family planning grant because of its board's opposition to the proviso. Finally Congress stepped in and spelled out a policy that recognized the facts of life and made all poor individuals eligible to receive birth control information and supplies.[12]

Administration and Operation

Instead of funding existing family planning organizations directly, OEO chose to funnel all of its family planning funds through community action agencies. The CAA's could operate the projects themselves or delegate them to appropriate local agencies; and Planned Parenthood–World Population contributed its expertise and enthusiastic cooperation. In fiscal 1968 the organization's affiliates received two of every five projects delegated by the CAA's, while an almost equal number was administered directly by the CAA's. The balance of the family planning grants was made to health organizations (Table 8–2).

Planned Parenthood–World Population affiliates were the first and most frequent seekers of family planning funds, and because in many communities they were the only groups able or willing to mount family planning programs, CAA's often delegated the programs to them. They tended to use the money to open new clinics in poverty neighborhoods rather than expand existing facilities, a practice that was in line with OEO's policy of bringing services to the poor and encouraging them to participate in the projects. In contrast, public health departments typically used OEO funds to expand their services in existing clinics by simply increasing the number and variety of people served.

Table 8–2. OEO Family Planning Program Grantees and Delegate Agencies, Fiscal 1968

Agency	Number	Percent
Total	159	100
Planned Parenthood–World Population	63	40
Health departments	25	16
Hospitals	2	1
Other	8	5
CAA[a]	61	38

[a] No delegate-agency arrangement.
Source: Office of Economic Opportunity.

Where no new facilities were established, it seemed feasible to utilize fully equipped mobile vans to bring birth control information and devices to poverty neighborhoods, but this idea was never implemented on a large scale. Alternatively, the CAA's that did not delegate the programs often simply paid physicians for services they rendered in their own offices, or made loose agreements with heatlh department personnel. OEO gathered little information on how the non-delegated programs were operated.

On the whole, there appears to have been little cooperation among the local agencies concerned with family planning programs. Each operating agency established its own methods of procedure and operation without coordinating its activities with those of the other family planning facilities. An exception is the Los Angeles Regional Family Planning Council, funded by OEO in 1968 as a means of establishing a single, coordinated program.[13] Another coordination effort was the comprehensive health center program, also funded by OEO. At the end of 1968, 48 centers had been funded, and all of the 32 centers in actual operation had family planning programs.

As with other OEO activities, the availability of facilities is no guarantee of use; the poor must be reached and "sold" on the use of family planning facilities. One study estimated that only 15 to 25 percent of the poor would take advantage of centrally located clinics but that percentage would double when clinics were established in a poverty neighborhood. The estimated effect of various services and the location of clinics upon the utilization by the poor is represented in Table 8–3.

Program Operations

Little capital investment is required to operate a family planning clinic. A storefront can do nicely if it is divided into three rooms: one

Table 8–3. *Estimated Response to Birth Control Programs by Program Type*

Program	Target-Population Response
Initial central clinics	15–25%
Neighborhood clinics	35–50
Home visiting, transportation, etc.	20–30
Counseling and supportive measures	10–15

Source: Frederick S. Jaffe and Steven Polgar, "Family Planning and Public Policy: Is the 'Culture of Poverty' the New Cop-Out?" *Journal of Marriage and the Family* (May 1968), p. 229.

for examination and the other two for interviews and waiting. The equipment cost is minimal; most of the cost is for personnel—a part-time doctor and nurse for the hours that the facility is open. In addition, the clinic must have a clerk to maintain medical and social histories of the patients and keep records of the supplies. OEO family planning clinics also attempted to assign indigenous aides to each clinic for purposes of "outreach."

According to Planned Parenthood–World Population, the annual cost of the program should range from $30 to $40 per patient, but the per capita cost for OEO to date has been much higher, in some areas more than $70. OEO insists that this was because one-half to two-thirds of the programs funded each year were new and did not become fully operational for several months, thereby raising the initial per capita cost. Nevertheless, OEO's experience is too skimpy to permit firm annual cost estimates. In addition, the cost per patient varied according to the number and quality of educational, counseling, and outreach services, the number of visits required of the clients, and the contraceptive method chosen. OEO estimated that two of every three women choose the pills, which are supplied to them without cost (the bulk cost to the clinics was $7 to $10 per patient per year). According to Planned Parenthood estimates, OEO-supported clinics could have provided family planning services for about 300,000 women at the 1968 funding level. The actual number was between 150,000 and 200,000, or about one of every 25 to 30 women needing the service.[14] Other government agencies also fund birth control programs, but no reliable data are available on the number of persons served by them.

Because of the controversy that has surrounded birth control, other federal agencies were even more reluctant than OEO to maintain records on the extent of their support for family planning. Again, Congress took the lead with the 1967 Social Security Act amendments, which provided that from fiscal 1969 no less than 6 percent of total maternal and child health expenditures were to be earmarked for family planning services. At the current rate of authorizations, the funds allocated to family planning would amount to $21 million by fiscal 1973. In October 1968, Congress directed that $18.5 million of the funds appropriated for the Children's Bureau's maternal and child health programs be allocated to family planning grants. If these plans are carried out, this will triple federal contributions to family planning under the maternal and child welfare programs, assuming that states and communities take full advantage of the contribution of three federal dollars for every one of theirs. Although the 1967 legislation also required that states develop plans to make family planning service available in all parts of their jurisdiction, it was problematic whether the states would comply and contribute their share for developing effective birth control programs for public assistance recipients and others.

An Appraisal

To conclude that the birth control program is justified because the benefits exceed its costs is, of course, to tell only part of the story. The effectiveness of birth control should be measured not in terms of public assistance savings or similar cost-benefit analyses but on the basis of whether it improves the quality of human life and reduces poverty. Economic measurements are not sufficient. As noted, there is considerable evidence that birth control is an effective means of reducing potential poverty and that, given the opportunity, poor people want to plan the size of their families and avail themselves of family planning information and birth control devices.

Reluctant to enter the field of birth control, OEO was forced into funding family planning projects by changing public opinion; and it was forced by Congress to adopt realistic measures and guidelines for its projects. Only when Congress indicated strong support of family planning did OEO expend funds for this purpose. To emphasize congressional support of family planning, the 1967 amendments to the Economic Opportunity Act raised family planning to the status of a national emphasis program and specifically directed OEO to allocate additional funds for birth control projects.

While OEO has moved cautiously to support family planning projects, it has directed a major proportion of the funds to the activities of Planned Parenthood–World Population organization. This agency used the funds effectively to expand birth control services in poverty areas. In comparison, birth control activities funded by HEW have remained incidental to such programs as maternal and child health care. A separate OEO birth control program continues to be necessary because HEW has been even slower than OEO in adopting family planning efforts.

9.

THE GREAT SOCIETY'S DOMESTIC VOLUNTEERS

If you want to raise a man from mud and filth, do not think
it is enough to keep standing on top and reaching a helping
hand down to him. You must go all the way down yourself,
down into mud and filth. Then take hold of him with strong
hands and pull him and yourself out into the light as others.

Shelomo of Karlin

Origins and Mission

Rediscovery of the wheel has been an earmark of the Great Society's antipoverty effort, and invariably, OEO officials have claimed
novelty for their programs. Their insistence on the uniqueness of
OEO efforts vis-à-vis age-old programs was especially true of the organized volunteer activities sponsored by OEO. Volunteer service programs have long been part of American society, as comfortably situ-
ated citizens have found outlets for "doing good" through volunteer
work in men's service clubs, Junior League programs, Scouting, the
Red Cross, the Salvation Army, the American Rescue Workers, church
missions, and settlement houses. According to one estimate, some 4
million volunteers participate in United Givers' fund raising and
planning activities.[1] Dedicated volunteers have always come forth in
great numbers, and whatever their means or motivation, their goal has
been essentially the same—to help society fulfill its responsibilities by
supplementing institutional efforts with personal involvement and
services.

Volunteers have traditionally been associated with some federally
sponsored programs—on behalf of servicemen and veterans, for example—but the concept of a volunteer service corps under federal
sponsorship emerged with the establishment of the Peace Corps in
1961. With the proclaimed success of the Peace Corps (it has never
undergone a hard-nosed evaluation), legislation was introduced in
Congress calling for the creation of a 5,000-man "domestic Peace
Corps." Proponents of the measure, which passed the Senate by a narrow vote in August 1963, argued that trained and dedicated volunteers
were needed no less at home than abroad to supplement "development
efforts," and that a National Service Corps would enable thousands of
willing young men and women to serve their country in a special way

at home. Opponents argued that such a corps would duplicate private welfare efforts and lead to a huge new federal agency with vast expenditures. Privately, some members of Congress were inclined to view such a corps as federal shock troops for "disrupting social order"; they especially feared its involvement in civil rights activities in the South.

As the Economic Opportunity Act of 1964 evolved, a more precise mission was seen for a volunteer corps: it could become the vehicle for citizen participation in the national effort to combat poverty. Serving as a national clearinghouse for volunteers, it could develop full-time skilled manpower where shortages were most acute. In addition, it was hoped that volunteers would be encouraged to enter careers of service to the needy at the end of their "tour of duty." To allay persisting congressional doubts, volunteers would be sent only at the request of a state or local agency or nonprofit organization and would work under the direction of the sponsoring organization. In addition, the governor would be given veto power over the use of volunteers in his state. Volunteers in Service to America (VISTA), the domestic Peace Corps, was incorporated into Title VI of the Economic Opportunity Act of 1964. Two years later the status of VISTA was raised when an entire title of the EOA was devoted to the agency.

Program Administration in Operation

Six months after the passage of the 1964 Act, VISTA began operations. The other agencies established by the Act had planned their futures with staffs borrowed from other governmental departments, but Glenn Ferguson, a former Peace Corps official who became VISTA's first administrator, appropriately launched his agency with the help of unpaid volunteers.[2]

Recruitment and Selection

VISTA shared with other EOA efforts a propensity for the numbers game. Foreseeing the dangers of haste, the congressional committees responsible for the legislation warned against sacrificing "the quality of the volunteers, volunteer training, or the care with which requests for volunteers are analyzed and selected in order to increase the number of enrolled volunteers by the end of the first fiscal year. . . . Quality of personnel will be of greater importance than quantity."[3] This admonition did not discourage Sargent Shriver from predicting shortly after the Act was passed that 2,000 volunteers—to be drawn from a pool of 25,000 applicants—would be in the field or in training

by June 30, 1965. As with most of its early predictions, OEO's delivery fell far short of its promise.

Because VISTA, at least during its initial period, lacked the iden-
tity and the romantic appeal of the Peace Corps, it was not able to fire
the imagination of young college graduates. Thus for the first three
years VISTA experienced difficulties in attracting personnel and
filling its quotas. With intensified civil strife and greater emphasis on
domestic poverty, however, interest in VISTA increased. "It is becoming increasingly difficult for college students to concentrate on
youth in Malawi," a VISTA official explained, "when they know
children are starving in Mississippi, or to focus on Latin American
problems when Puerto Ricans and Mexican Americans are rejected by
racists in our own land."⁴ In short, many volunteers decided that
charity should begin at home. Instead of taking the two-year grand
tour with the Peace Corps, volunteers applied to VISTA, which by mid-
1968 was meeting, even exceeding, its quota of volunteers.⁵

As with the Peace Corps, college students were the primary source
of volunteers. Yet VISTA felt a need to attract a cross section of the
population, and it thus carried on recruitment at four levels: (1) at
colleges, in competition with the Peace Corps; (2) in communities,
often in tandem with college drives, using local communications
media; (3) among specific target groups—retired teachers, senior citizens, and so on—reached by direct mailings and appeals at organization meetings; and (4) within poverty communities, sometimes pirating
volunteers already at work. In 1968, VISTA's goal was to recruit 15
percent of its workers from the ranks of the poor. The private sector
has provided assistance as well: a New York agency donates time and
talent to preparing VISTA ads, and the communications media donate
time and space to present them.

A VISTA candidate fills out a detailed application form and lists
ten personal references, seven of whom are selected by the Washington
office to receive a reference form. The references and the applicant's
statement are evaluated along with medical and legal information, and
each applicant receives a rating on a one-to-seven scale. Those who
score 1 to 3 are rejected; 4 is satisfactory; 5 and 6 are excellent; and 7
is superior. The average score in 1967 was 5.2, up from 4.5 the year
before, suggesting that the caliber of volunteers was improving.

Training

Once selected, the volunteer enters a six-week training program.
The first two weeks are spent in orientation, and four weeks are de-

voted to on-the-job training in the area where he will work. Until mid-1967 most training was conducted in the classroom by universities. More recently, training has been assigned to business organizations, social agencies, action groups, and hospitals. The diversity of projects to which VISTA volunteers were assigned made it apparent that a uniform training curriculum was often not relevant to the field service that followed. Organizing a credit union, for example, would be pertinent for a few trainees in every six-week training cycle but could be a waste of time for the group as a whole.

The initial sessions concentrate on general orientation. Volunteers learn about life styles of the poor, resources available for help, and community organization, hopefully gaining skills in tutoring and counseling as well as empathy for and identification with the community. The extent to which the volunteers master these subjects must be left to conjecture, but the subjects are covered in the training curricula. After completing the two-week orientation, the volunteer moves into a field situation for on-site training. This system, permitting a flow of information on expectations, job performance, and support between the trainee, the sponsor, and the VISTA training center, presumably assures that the training is directly relevant to actual problems in the field. This aspect of the training also helps VISTA sponsors, who often are not sure exactly what to expect of volunteers. Besides this new training format and the belated decentralization of the VISTA staff, there is now more direct coordination between VISTA, the training center, the volunteer, and a project's sponsor. In addition to the in-service training provided by the sponsor, the volunteer receives six days of in-service training by the training contractor.

Associates and Local Volunteers

In the summer of 1966 VISTA initiated a program to use college students full time during their summer vacations. Known as VISTA Associates, the students undergo more limited training and are used to supplement the efforts of regular volunteers. About 500 students served in 1966, close to 2,000 in 1967, and 1,600 in the summer of 1968. VISTA funds support most of the volunteers, but contributions from other federal agencies or local and state organizations cover about a fourth of the total costs.

The Citizens' Volunteer Corps, composed of private citizens who donate time to help implement VISTA activities in their own communities, was initiated in 1967. By the end of fiscal 1968 VISTA claimed that 40,000 citizen corpsmen were working with regular volunteers. It is hoped that volunteers can be recruited for full-time VISTA work from the ranks of Citizen Corpsmen at considerable savings in recruitment, selection, and training.[6]

Program Content

Some 5,000 full-year volunteers were working in June 1968 on 447 projects located in every state but Mississippi; 3,200 were assigned to these various projects and the rest were in training. Requests from nearly 2,000 private groups and agencies for an additional 23,000 volunteers had been logged in the Washington office. With plans that call for only a moderate increase in volunteer strength, the demand obviously outweighs the supply; therefore the criteria determining the selection of projects are of special interest. These criteria are: (1) the activities must appear likely to produce improvement in the lives of the poor; (2) the volunteers must come into direct contact with the poor; (3) the sponsoring organization must be able to provide supervision; (4) the project must be located in an area of greatest need, according to the poverty indices; and (5) volunteers must be invited to serve in the area, and the projects must have the approval of the governor. Among projects that meet these admittedly broad criteria, final approval may depend upon chance or whim.

VISTA has assigned about 85 percent of its volunteers to community action agencies or CAP-funded programs; the remainder work with the mentally ill or retarded or with the Job Corps or other EOA programs. Volunteers were about equally allocated between urban community action agencies, including delegate organizations, and rural projects, including Indian reservations and migrants (Table 9–1).

Table 9–1.   Distribution of VISTA Field Assignments, June 1968

Agency	Projects		Volunteers	
	Number	Percent	Number	Percent
Total	447	100.0	3,204[a]	100.0
Urban CAA or delegate	184	41.2	1,662	51.9
Rural CAA or delegate	148	33.1	1,004	31.3
Indian reservation	50	11.2	224	7.0
Job Corps	34	7.6	73	2.3
Migrant camps	22	4.9	131	4.1
Mental health	9	2.0	110	3.4

[a] Excludes 1,828 in training.
Source: VISTA, Office of Economic Opportunity.

Volunteers' Characteristics and Performance

The assignments of VISTA volunteers are as diverse as the agencies and programs that sponsor them. CAA's and their delegate agencies may assign the volunteers to tasks that range from referral services, health screening, Head Start recruitment, and recreation programs to the development of training programs or support for tenant unions and rent strikes.

Most volunteers do not have special skills or preparation for their assignments; they are about equally divided between the sexes; and they are typically between the ages of 20 and 24 and possess some college training (Table 9–2). Although no records are kept of race or previous income, VISTA officials estimate that perhaps 10 percent of the volunteers are from the ranks of the poor.[7] Three of every four volunteers serve for one year or less. Upon leaving the program, roughly half return to school; one in every four enters a "helping profession"—teaching, social work, health services—or other EOA-funded programs; 17 percent enter military service; and 10 percent retire.

In most cases the volunteer's effectiveness hinges not so much on the merits of his project as on the rapport he is able to establish with the community. Volunteers not only work with the poor, they live among them—in mountain hollows, remote Eskimo villages, or urban ghettos. This "experiment in living" is not always successful. VISTA volunteers in a New England village were attacked by angry townspeople who saw them as another example of government frivolity with tax dollars. The mountain people of Kentucky often don't take kindly to "feds" (or any strangers for that matter), and unmarried females

Table 9–2. Distribution of VISTA Volunteers by Age, Sex, and Education,
            June 1968

Age	
18 to 19 years	7%
20 to 24 years	53
25 to 49 years	24
50 years and over	16
Sex	
Male	51
Female	49
Education	
College graduate	36
Some college	44
Technical school	4
High school or less	16

Source: VISTA, Office of Economic Opportunity.

above the age of eighteen are especially suspect. The slum, with its peculiar social organization, is also a difficult experience for those who are new to the ways of the ghetto.

A common problem for volunteers is "overidentification" with their clientele, which causes them to become overzealous "advocates of the alienated" (to use VISTA terminology) and suspect in the eyes of the rest of the community. Possibly the skill most needed for VISTA volunteers to function effectively is the ability to walk the tightrope of identifying with *their* community's problems while not alienating other community groups.

On Indian reservations and in the hollows of Appalachia, VISTA volunteers have launched literacy programs, started libraries and recreational programs for youth, and organized preschool and self-help housing projects. In Eskimo villages that can be reached only by bush plane, volunteers have brought the only technical skills and contact with the outside world that many of these Americans have ever known. Volunteers have even brought refrigeration to Eskimo fishermen, helping them keep their catch fresh until it can be flown to market. In the cities, they have developed youth "outreach" and recreation programs, narcotics addiction control programs, and bail bond projects. In Job Corps centers, the volunteers counsel, work on remedial programs, and organize recreational activities. In mental health projects, VISTA workers have set up classes and activities in mental hospitals to help prepare patients for the world outside. VISTA volunteers have supplemented the regular staffs in schools and workshops for the mentally retarded and have developed recreational and tutorial programs.

Volunteers are also engaged in more controversial activities, such as the formation of tenant unions, cooperative buying programs, and welfare-rights committees. In the Kentucky mountains, they are praised (or blamed) for whipping up local support for campaigns to stop strip mining and to place privately owned coal reserves under local public ownership. Several volunteers in Newark, N.J., assigned by their sponsor, the mayor's office, to routine jobs as aides and general helpers in county hospitals, released a report on the substandard treatment and other unfavorable conditions encountered by charity patients. Other volunteers in Newark organized slum tenants to press city hall for improvement in inspection and prosecution of housing code violations. They were asked to transfer, and when they refused, were dismissed.

As with other antipoverty programs, the Establishment has "viewed with alarm" the various controversial VISTA activities—voter registration drives, peace marches, and other activities with "political" overtones. Even friends of VISTA have questioned whether tax dollars should be used to "import outsiders" to support activities opposed by the majority in a community. Of course the line between legitimate VISTA goals and unacceptable militant action is not at all clear. OEO is not helpful in this regard since it fails to spell out VISTA's goals, beyond stating that the agency has a twofold mission: "(1) to help people and communities out of poverty; and (2) to strive for significant social change which will remedy the conditions which cause poverty."

OEO was reluctant to spell out the "proper" behavior of VISTA volunteers; stringent rules would have discouraged many potential and dedicated applicants, the types VISTA needs. Thus OEO, characteristically, decided to play it by ear and approved applications on a project-by-project basis, hoping thereby to reduce or scatter the attacks on the program. Also, VISTA can shift part of the responsibility for the actions of excessively zealous volunteers to the local sponsors who requested the project or the state governor who approved it.

VISTA does have guidelines to govern the political and protest activities of its volunteers; and a 1966 EOA amendment places workers under the provisions of the Hatch Act, which prohibits partisan political activity. The guidelines state that volunteers are not to assume positions of political leadership or to become "prominently identified with any political party or candidate." As for protest activities, the volunteers are instructed to subordinate "personal views on specific issues to the primary goal of helping build a community able and determined to arrive at its own decisions and to assert its own influence." The guidelines continue: "while engaged in carrying out his duties, the Volunteer may participate in lawful and nonpolitical demonstrations and protest activities."[8]

Presumably, a volunteer is free to demonstrate against the war in Vietnam or in favor of increased welfare payments or to participate in organizing tenant strikes so long as this activity is "subordinate" to "helping build a community able . . . to arrive at its own decisions." A spokesman for VISTA indicates that the agency chooses to view such activities as "pointing out options and alternatives, or educating the community" on a public issue so that it is capable of making unbiased decisions. Those on the other side of an issue consider such involvement as agitation rather than education.

Funding

During its first four years of operation, VISTA obligated a total of $75 million. Starting modestly with $3 million in fiscal 1965, VISTA's obligations rose to $16 million in 1966 and $26 million in 1967. For

fiscal 1968 VISTA was allocated $30 million, which provided an esti-
mated 4,150 man-years of service during the year (Table 9–3).

The average annual cost per volunteer, $8,300 in 1966, has been
reduced to $6,850. Economies of size accounted for the decline in the
total costs of monitoring volunteers, while direct costs remained about
the same. Increases in medical insurance and transportation allowances were absorbed by savings in training by cutting overhead on
contracts and reducing part-time staffs. The annual direct cost of supporting a volunteer, $3,300 in 1968, was modest by any standard. There
is no fat in the volunteer's allowance; he receives an annual stipend of
$600 and an additional $2,428 for food, lodging, and other living expenses. The balance of direct expenditures covers transportation, medical care, and social security taxes. The major indirect costs (as indicated in Table 9–3) include training, program administration, and
recruitment.

Is VISTA Paying Off?

A meaningful appraisal of VISTA is elusive. Even a detached
observer must be all in favor of "do gooders" and volunteers who
dedicate a year or more of their lives in aid of the poor, which may
explain VISTA's favorable press and the abundance of human-interest
stories about volunteers, in turn creating a favorable image of the
agency. But heartrending anecdotes are no substitute for objective
evaluation, and the computer has not yet been built that—in the best
rational manner—can classify and evaluate the diverse individual activities of several thousand volunteers. One might speculate that at an
average annual cost of $6,850 per full-time volunteer, the taxpayer is
getting a good buy for his dollar. But three of every four volunteers
are under 25 and unskilled, and only about one in four reenlists for a

Table 9–3. *VISTA Obligations by Major Components, Fiscal 1967 and 1968 (Millions)*

	1967 (Actual)	1968 (Estimated)
	Millions	
Total	$26.2	$30.0
Recruitment, selection, and community relations	1.5	1.5
Training	4.8	3.7
Volunteer support	11.2	14.5
VISTA associates	2.0	1.5
Research and demonstration	.7	1.8
Program administration	6.0	7.0

Source: VISTA, Office of Economic Opportunity.

second tour of duty. Thus there is reason to question the bargain. Any attempt to evaluate VISTA must therefore take into account "dedication," "involvement," and similar unmeasurable qualities.

OEO offers little help. One illustration of the agency's "analysis" appeared as part of its fiscal 1969 budget justification. Asserting that the benefits of a VISTA project exceeded costs by 443 percent (benefits $438,046 and costs $80,708), with almost 90 percent of the benefits in the form of wages of clients who were placed by volunteers, the analysis apparently assumed that these clients would have had no income in the absence of VISTA.[9] Aside from such "quantification" of benefits, VISTA has neither defined its mission beyond the generalities listed in its enabling legislation nor has it spelled out the strategies the volunteers should use as warriors in the fight against poverty. Though OEO claims that requests for volunteers by some 2,000 public and private agencies attest to the success of VISTA, the requests prove only that the demand for free labor exceeds the supply.

In urban areas there is a real question as to whether VISTA has a legitimate role other than as a manpower subsidy to local agencies. Many volunteers seem to perform tasks that could be performed by trained nonprofessionals from the ranks of the poor, and by placing VISTA volunteers in assignments that require simple skills, a local agency may be evading its responsibility for recruiting and training the poor to fill such positions. For functions that require training and skills, it is questionable whether VISTA volunteers are doing more to instill hope or plant ideas than other personnel who work for the same sponsor, and whether in urban areas they are contributing a technical skill that is not otherwise available.

Rural areas that lack social services, technical skills, and efficient communication with the "outside world" would seem to provide the most fertile ground for VISTA efforts. VISTA would be well advised to concentrate its resources on efforts where the supply of essential services to the poor is limited and cannot be mobilized. Indian reservations and migrant camps offer especially promising work assignments; and a 5,000-man volunteer corps might well have a discernible impact on their conditions of poverty. It is otherwise difficult to conceive of VISTA as affecting the course of poverty in the nation, though it offers an opportunity for widened horizons to some middle-class youths who can claim they also have served in the war on poverty.

Part III

Rural Programs

10.

RURAL LOANS: SELF-IMPROVEMENT OR INCOME MAINTENANCE?

Greater is he who lends than he who gives, and
greater still is he who lends, and with the loan,
helps the poor man to help himself.

Shabbat

The Dilemma of Rural Programs

The machinery OEO uses to fund projects varies from program to program, and a major problem faced by OEO in funding rural projects has been the lack of delegate agencies that are capable of administering OEO's programs. Sparseness of population in rural areas has compounded the problem of designing delivery systems for providing services to the rural poor.

Aside from knotty administrative problems, there was substantive debate over the types of programs most suitable for helping the rural poor. This does not mean that there was consensus on urban programs, but for rural areas it was undecided whether the poor should be helped to adjust on their home grounds or encouraged to migrate to urban areas where economic opportunity may be more abundant. The issue, according to a symposium on rural poverty, was "flight or fight."[1] Of course, this phraseology ignored a number of alternative strategies that might alleviate rural poverty; nonetheless, the basic alternatives were to move the jobless to areas where gainful employment was available or to bring new employment opportunities to job-starved areas. The federal government, which had avoided choosing between the two, frequently adopted contradictory policies; for example, government appeals to industry to move to rural areas were counteracted by an agricultural policy that paid landowners for not tilling their soil, thus further depleting the number of rural jobs. Though the over-all thrust of federal policy had been to subsidize jobs in areas of labor surplus, it had also funded small experimental programs to aid migration, mostly from rural areas to smaller urban centers.

OEO policymakers have reflected this governmental ambivalence in the funding of rural EOA programs. OEO's research and planning staff urged the agency to concentrate on training the rural poor so that they could find employment in urban areas and to provide assistance to them while they were settling in their new environment. For immobile persons, OEO's planners hoped to provide income maintenance, which was to be achieved at some future date because OEO's resources were certainly inadequate to offer immediate relief. In effect, OEO's research staff rejected reliance on economic development as a means of aiding the rural poor.[2]

Not surprisingly, operators of OEO programs in rural areas wanted to serve their clients in the home environment rather than encourage them to migrate. This meant helping needy rural residents improve their farming operation or financing a small, non-farm business, as long as there was a "reasonable possibility" of permanently increasing the incomes of those receiving help. Another form of rural assistance was subsidization of "sweat equity" housing: helping the poor acquire housing while performing the actual construction (under skilled technical supervision), thus obtaining better housing more cheaply and learning building skills at the same time. Adult and youth remedial education classes were available for migrant and seasonal farm workers, and some prevocational and vocational training, either on a part-time or a full-time basis (the latter with income maintenance stipends).

Related programs subsidized jobs in rural areas through the Nelson amendment, originally passed in 1965 and expanded in 1966. OEO has also funded special programs on Indian reservations to deal with the problems besetting the original Americans, who are also among the poorest U.S. citizens—three of every four American Indians who live on reservations live in poverty as defined by OEO.

Most major OEO programs operate in urban and in rural areas. Job Corps centers may be located near cities or in the countryside, and sometimes in very isolated areas; community action agencies are, of course, located throughout the country; and VISTA volunteers may be assigned to various OEO activities. However, the balance of Part III will focus on three programs that are exclusively rural in nature: the rural loan program, aid to migrant and seasonal farm labor, and assistance to Indians residing on reservations.

Legislative Background and Scope

After four years it still is not clear whether the Economic Opportunity or Rural Loan program (Title IIIA) is an income maintenance program or an effort to help the rural poor achieve "self-improvement." In the original Administration proposal, the program was designed as a mixture of grants and loans. The Senate approved a provision granting program administrators the authority to release debtors from loan obligations secured under Title IIIA, but the House balked at this, so Title IIIA provided only for loans.

Those who were satisfied with the final version believed that the program would help the rural poor (both farmers and non-farmers) improve their economic position either by initiating profitable enterprises or by expanding their self-employment efforts. On the other hand, those who saw out-migration as the ultimate solution to rural poverty supported the loan program as a temporary substitute for outright grants that could mitigate the plight of the "boxed-in" poor. These critics did not view the program as self-sustaining but rather as disguised grants for the most disadvantaged and least mobile of the poor. Taking literally the biblical admonition that "sufficient unto the day is the evil thereof," they left the problem of repaying the loans to some future date.

Farm loan programs (for the operation or ownership of farms) had existed in the Department of Agriculture since the New Deal. Operating loans aimed at increasing the productivity of farm operations; the maximum credit under the program was $35,000, though the average loan was only one-fifth of this figure. Borrowers were given the privilege of obtaining additional loans before they repaid the full amount of the initial loans. Farm ownership loans could be made to a maximum of $60,000, but they averaged one-third of that amount. Both types of loans were subsidized and carried a 5 percent interest rate.

Under the law, rich and poor farmers alike were eligible to borrow from the Farmers Home Administration, the USDA agency that administered the loan programs. The large maximum size of the loans indicates that affluent farmers could benefit disproportionately from the program, although FHA officials claim that about 50 percent of the borrowers were marginal farmers who operate "less than adequate" farms. Even so, two of every three rural poor were non-farmers and therefore not eligible to receive loans from the FHA. New legislation enacted in 1968 extended the scope of traditional FHA programs to non-farm-purpose loans for farmers.

The Economic Opportunity loan program sought to fill the gaps left by existing loan programs and to augment assistance to poor farmers. Title IIIA of the Economic Opportunity Act authorized loans to any low-income rural family that was unable to get a loan elsewhere and had a "reasonable possibility of effecting a permanent increase" in its income through these loans. Thus the clientele embraced non-farm rural persons, farmers who sought money for nonagricultural enterprises, and cooperatives composed predominantly of low income families, as well as farmers seeking loans to operate and improve their farms.

Debate on Title IIIA centered not on the definition of the clientele but rather on the program's formal structure and substantive provisions. The original Administration proposal had provided for outright grants of up to $1,500 to accompany loans of up to $2,500. This feature was opposed by some representatives of urban areas who saw this as discrimination against the urban poor, as well as by advocates of rural aid who thought that direct grants contradicted the underlying theme of self-help. Senator Hubert H. Humphrey of Minnesota, speaking for those who were dubious of the permanent usefulness of small loans to the rural poor, attempted to compromise with these opponents. His amendment would have deleted the provision for direct grants and substituted a provision to release loan recipients from repayment obligations if the funded enterprises failed or if indebtedness exceeded the debtor's "reasonable payment ability." Given the low income of the target population, almost any indebtedness might be interpreted as exceeding the "reasonable payment ability" of the debtor. However, Humphrey's amendment was rejected along with the Administration's grant proposal. Title IIIA thus provided only a loan program.

Program officials were given latitude in administering the terms and conditions of the loans. The requirement that Title IIIA loans be restricted to those not qualified to obtain such funds from other federal programs left a wide degree of flexibility. Since farmers were eligible to receive FHA credit, a strict interpretation could have limited Economic Opportunity loans to the very poorest farmers, who would not be considered for traditional FHA loans. The Treasury has set the interest rate on rural loans at $4\frac{1}{8}$ percent, whereas the rate on older FHA loans is 5 percent.

Debate over the size of loans, between the proponents of a strict loan program and those advocating a more "flexible" repayment policy, was resolved when individual loans were initially limited to an aggregate level of $2,500. This limit was based on the supposition that poor families would be unable to repay larger loans. The 1966 amendments to the Economic Opportunity Act raised the limit to $3,500 and provided that the initial loans could be followed by secondary loans as long as the total outstanding debt did not exceed $3,500. Advocates of a strict loan program interpreted this as a means of testing enterprises with initial loans and extending secondary (subsequent) loans only where profitability had been proved. But it also opened the possibility of disguised subsidization—the extension of secondary loans to cover repayments. Although officials of both FHA and OEO are quick to assert that disguised subsidization is not permissible under administrative policies, it can be manipulated within the legislative framework.

Needs and Resources

According to FHA estimates, about 900,000 rural poor people, equally divided between marginal farmers and other rural poor, were eligible to receive Economic Opportunity loans. About the same number, not necessarily distinct from those above, were estimated to be eligible for cooperative loans.[3] According to these estimates, about one of every nineteen eligible families, or some 48,000, received individual loans during the first four years of the program. Less than one-third of that number were members of cooperatives who received rural opportunity loans.

The geographical distribution of the Economic Opportunity loans generally followed the distribution of rural poverty. Loans were heavily concentrated in the southeastern states and Puerto Rico. In order of magnitude, the six largest recipients of individual loans during the first four years were Puerto Rico, Mississippi, Kentucky, Texas, North Carolina, and Arkansas; the six largest recipients of cooperative loans were Mississippi, North Carolina, Louisiana, Minnesota, Arkansas, and Tennessee.

The Farmers Home Administration attempted to concentrate the meager resources allocated through Economic Opportunity loans into areas of greatest poverty. At first no attempt was made to allocate rural loan funds by states. In August 1968, however, FHA announced that it would restrict loans, except in cases of unusual hardship, to the 1,230 poorest counties—a move that still left four of every ten counties eligible to receive loans. A review of earlier loans disclosed that prior to the announcement of the new policy the bulk of the earlier loans had been made in these counties as well.

Because of the propensity of government programs to spread their resources thin, distributing the loans over 1,230 counties may have been politically unavoidable. FHA did not consider OEO poverty criteria as controlling, and about one of every four borrowers was not within the government's poverty classification. Spokesmen for FHA claim that in making loans to marginal farmers or other rural poor it is more equitable to consider applications case by case than to utilize an arbitrary cut-off point. It may be that, far from being a rationalization of "creaming," this approach is a means of maximizing limited resources to help those who can be assisted by the loans.

Data on the characteristics of borrowers suggest the following

portrait of the program's clientele. First, the program favored those
who were least mobile. Nearly two of every three borrowers were over
forty years of age, and four out of ten were over fifty. Eleven percent
were receiving public assistance when they obtained the loan. Regrettably, no information is available concerning the proportion who
left public assistance on receipt of the loan. The average borrower had
completed seven years of schooling, and seven of every ten had only an
elementary school education or less (Table 10–1). The bulk of the
loans seems to have reached families—not necessarily the poorest—
whose mobility was restricted by age and lack of skill or education.
No one can say whether the program would have been more "successful" or relevant if FHA had limited the loans to those who were designated as poor by the accepted government statistical definition. Implicit in the loan program is the assumption that successful applicants
would have at least some resources for operating a farm or a business,
which almost automatically excludes those who are completely destitute or have very little potential for success in running an enterprise.
It was difficult, therefore, to fault FHA for "creaming" the applicants.

Table 10–1.   Recipients of Economic Opportunity Loans[a]

	Sex		
Male	95%	Female	5%
	Race		
White	66	Negro	29
Other	5		
	Age		
Less than 30 years	21	40 to 49 years	23
31 to 39 years	17	50 years and over	39
	Education (Average Grade Completed: 7th)		
0–4 years	21	8 years	24
5–7 years	24	High school and over	32
	Family Size (Average Size: 4)		
1–4	53	8 and over	17
5–7	30		
	Primary Occupation		
Farmer	41	Craftsman or operative	17
Farm laborer	6	Other	15
Laborer (non-farm)	19	Unemployed	3
	Public Assistance		
Recipients	11	Average amount	$1,249
	Average Family Income in Year before Loan (by Loan Type)		
All	$2,082	Non-farm (to farmers)	$2,199
Farm	$1,891	Non-farm (to non-farmers)	$2,366

[a] For about 2,900 borrowers between December 15, 1966 and April 15, 1967.
Note: Details may not add to 100 percent because of rounding.
Source: Derived from OEO and FHA data.

Another criticism of the rural loan program is that it has been racially discriminatory.[4] Although Negroes constitute about one-fifth of the rural poor and accounted for 29 percent of all individual loan recipients, closer examination of program statistics indicates that white and Negro borrowers were indeed treated differently. During the first half of fiscal 1968, agricultural loans to Negroes averaged $1,755 and loans to others averaged $2,050. A similar differential existed for non-farm loans, which averaged $2,187 for whites and $1,779 for Negroes. The differential is not *a priori* evidence of discrimination. The size of the loan is based on the chance of success, and if Negroes are more disadvantaged they have less chance of success and thus receive smaller loans. But the circularity of this reasoning is not very satisfying, especially when one reflects upon the correlation between larger loans and the probability of success of the funded enterprises.

The administrative organization of the rural loan program has also been open to charges of discrimination. Three-member FHA county committees determine the eligibility of loan applicants, and until recently Negroes were not proportionately represented on these committees. In 1961 none of the approximately 7,000 local committeemen was Negro, and by January 1, 1966, there were only 374 Negroes. Today, in counties where 20 percent or more of the farmers are Negro, the state FHA director must appoint at least one Negro to each committee, and more than 300 Negroes are now on county committees in the South alone.[5] With three members on every committee, however, even in counties where Negroes have a representative, their influence may be minimal. No figures are available on the distribution of loan rejections by race, but informal estimates show that approximately one of every two applications is rejected or withdrawn, and the possibility of abuse is large.

Administration and Funding

Administration of the rural loan program has been delegated to the Farmers Home Administration of the Department of Agriculture; and the Office of Economic Opportunity establishes general administrative guidelines and provides funds for a staff of about 250. Apart from a small group in Washington, this staff is distributed among the 1,600 county FHA offices and is indistinguishable from regular FHA county workers who administer a wide variety of FHA loan programs as well as Title IIIA loans. At the same time, many county officials who are funded by FHA contribute staff time to Economic Opportunity loans.

It is estimated that FHA provides as much "free" staff time as is funded by OEO.

Considerable autonomy was given FHA local offices in disposing of applications. Once a local office had made its decision, no approval was necessary by the district office, except for cooperative loans in excess of $15,000 (though samples of loan dockets were reviewed for monitoring purposes). FHA felt no need to allocate funds or review local office decisions because its staff had long experience in handling loans; in fact, during the first three years of the program available funds exceeded loan approvals. Failure to utilize all the funds was due to the lack of eligible borrowers who could meet FHA loan criteria. It would appear that as long as FHA conducted business as usual and applied the same criteria to Economic Opportunity loans that it had previously used for other programs, the number of eligible borrowers was greatly restricted. There was also the problem of outreach, the lack of which further restricted the number of eligible applicants. As in other antipoverty programs, the potential clientele had to be advised of the availability and terms of the program. For example, a marginal Negro farmer with little chance of receiving a traditional FHA loan would have to be advised and counseled about Economic Opportunity loans. There was, therefore, an element of truth in the contention that the failure to utilize all the available funds was due to lack of staff, for the new program clearly demanded more intensive management supervision and counseling than was required for the traditional FHA loans. As OEO explained to the Bureau of the Budget in November 1966: "The factors impeding the growth and total impact of this program are the lack of adequate manpower and counseling."

Without denying the need for an expanded administrative staff, one can offer an alternative explanation for the failure to utilize all the available funds. FHA's traditional operating and farm ownership loans were regionally allocated and any funds that were not used in the assigned areas were transferred to other areas. Local officials were therefore anxious to distribute all of these loans first, and only after this was done did they concentrate on processing antipoverty loans. As a result, fewer rural loans were processed than were available.

Eventually this situation changed, as the level of borrowing exceeded new obligational authority during fiscal 1967 and again during the subsequent year. When FHA found by the end of fiscal 1968 that it had almost exhausted the funds available for Economic Opportunity loans, it was forced to discontinue further loans temporarily. To prevent overcommitment of resources, FHA then adopted a formula for allocating funds to regional offices which limited its lending to the 1,230 counties mentioned earlier. The criteria used in selecting these counties were the number and proportion of rural poor in the population, average school attainment, the age distribution of residents, and the condition of rural housing. The 1,230 most deprived counties were declared eligible for Economic Opportunity loans, and all funds were allocated to the states on the basis of the above criteria.

Funding and Operations

The planners of the Economic Opportunity loan program envisaged the creation of a self-sustaining or revolving fund to finance the program. The assumption was that the government would appropriate initial funds but that eventually repayment of loans by borrowers would be sufficient to sustain the program. The continuation of the fund depends, of course, upon the repayment of loans with relatively few defaults.

A total of $93 million was allocated to the rural loan program during its first four years of operation, exclusive of administrative costs (Table 10–2). No attempt was made during this time to put the fund on a strict business basis. The interest charged to borrowers (4.125 percent) was less than the interest FHA had to pay the Treasury. Even the most ardent supporters of the program must concede that if the loan program was to have any future, it would have to be

Table 10–2. Economic Opportunity Fund, Fiscal 1965–68 (Thousands)

	Total	1965	1966	1967	1968
New loan authority	$92,950	$23,950	$33,000	$21,500	$14,500
Loan interest received	3,931	1	398	1,392	2,140
Principal repayment	21,611	150	3,721	7,502	10,238
Additions to fund	—	24,101	37,119	30,394	26,878
Interest paid Treasury	7,026	124	1,300	2,306	3,296
Net additions to fund	—	23,977	35,819	28,088	23,582
Carryover from preceding	—	—	4,314	8,161	5,004
Funds available for loans	—	23,977	40,133	36,249	28,586
Loan level authorized	—	23,950	33,000	33,900	29,000
Total loans	110,829	19,676	31,973	32,246	26,934
Unobligated funds at end of year	—	4,314	8,161	5,004	1,540

Source: Farmers Home Administration, U.S. Department of Agriculture.

subsidized by the government or interest charges would have to be raised appreciably. By the end of fiscal 1968 only $1.5 million were left in the revolving fund. Thus loans for fiscal 1969 required further appropriations if they were to match the previous levels.[6]

Loan Repayment and Delinquency

Part of the problem inherent in the funding and operation of the rural loan program is delinquency. As of mid-1967, advance payments were greater than delinquencies and total repayments were more than the principal matured. Of the $10.5 million that had matured, $1.6 million was delinquent, leaving a delinquency rate of 15 percent. FHA officials estimated that only two-thirds of these delinquencies would prove to be actual losses—or the loss rate would be no more than 10 percent.[7]

Another way of calculating delinquency is by the number of borrowers who are delinquent or slow in paying back their loans. At the close of calendar 1967, one-third of the individual borrowers and 26 percent of the cooperative borrowers were delinquent by one or more payments. The figures indicate that smaller borrowers were most likely to be delinquent. Only 15 percent of all funds were delinquent, which suggests that the larger borrowers were better able to make repayments.

It is fair to assume that the delinquency rate may increase with time. Although 109 percent of the matured principal had been repaid as of June 30, 1967, only 92 percent of the matured principal had been repaid six months later, and only 84 percent by the end of fiscal 1968. A shortage of funds because of the larger than expected increase in delinquency compelled a temporary suspension of loans at the end of fiscal 1968. Perhaps the delinquency rate increases during the life of the loan, so that, for example, delinquency on loans made in 1965 may have been greater in 1968 than in 1967. Either initial expectations were too high or the initial repayments were scheduled at too low a level.

One of the factors in the repayment rates may be that borrowers who were eligible for additional (subsequent) loans have used them to facilitate repayments, making the loans disguised subsidies. There is no way to verify this hypothesis short of a case-by-case examination, but its probable significance can be derived from the statistics on subsequent loans (Table 10-3). Total subsequent or additional loans as of June 30, 1968, were $7.5 million, or 35 percent of total repayments. Subsequent loans had risen from 25 percent of principal repayments in

Table 10–3.   Economic Opportunity Loans, Initial and Subsequent Loans, Fiscal 1965–68

Loans	Total	1965	1966	1967	1968
Number of Loans					
Individual loans to farmers					
Initial	28,375	7,595	8,875	6,960	4,945
Subsequent	5,883	0	1,118	2,492	2,273
Individual loans to non-farmers					
Initial	19,406	3,427	6,552	5,635	3,792
Subsequent	3,005	0	528	1,366	1,111
Coop loans					
Initial	1,160	83	387	362	328
Subsequent	53	0	4	20	29
Total Amount of Loans (Thousands)					
Individual loans to farmers					
Initial	$50,903	$12,660	$14,630	$13,460	$10,153
Subsequent	4,234	0	608	1,829	1,797
Individual loans to non-farmers					
Initial	38,656	6,118	11,719	11,756	9,063
Subsequent	2,341	0	307	1,114	920
Coop loans					
Initial	13,774	942	4,674	3,629	4,530
Subsequent	962	0	34	459	469

Source: Farmers Home Administration, Department of Agriculture.

fiscal 1966 to 46 percent in fiscal 1967. No doubt some of these additional loans were made to borrowers who were unable to make repayments, though legally the subsequent loans were made only for specific purposes. An alternative explanation, favored by FHA and OEO, is that only successful borrowers received the additional loans.

Loans to Individuals

Four years' experience is hardly adequate to indicate trends in a maturing program, but even in this short time span shifts have occurred in the types of loans made under the Economic Opportunity Loan program. Total annual loans to cooperatives have, after an initial slow start, ranged from $4 million to $5 million, accounting for nearly a fifth of the total funds loaned in fiscal 1968. The types of loans made to individuals also changed. During the initial year, loans to farmers accounted for two-thirds of all individual loans. Since then, non-farmers have received an increasing proportion of the funds lent to individuals (Table 10–3).

Individual loans to farmers are made overwhelmingly for agricultural purposes; only 7 percent of the loans to farmers were for non-agricultural purposes. In fiscal 1968, loans were made for such needs as the purchase of livestock, 28 percent; the purchase or refinancing of real estate debts, 28 percent; the purchase of machinery and equipment, 4 percent; operating expenses, 13 percent; construction, repair, and improvement of buildings, 6 percent. The average size of both initial and subsequent loans to farmers has increased but the number of such loans has decreased (Table 10–4).

Loans to non-farmers are unique to the rural loan program. The average initial and subsequent loans made to non-farmers are larger than those to farmers, and this average has been on the increase. Such loans can and have funded almost every type of small enterprise. The major categories of non-farm uses are as follows: purchase of machinery and equipment, 61 percent; operating expenses, 11 percent; construction, repair, and improvement of buildings, 12 percent.

A weakness of the rural loan program has been its emphasis on the farming segment of its clientele. Although loans to individual farmers have decreased slightly as a portion of total loans, some 55 percent of all individual loans have gone to farmers, even though these persons account for only a third of the rural poor. Considering the resources available under the traditional FHA operating loan program, the rural loan program does not significantly increase the funds available to farmers. There seems to be little justification for the priority given to farmers under the Economic Opportunity loan program, unless the older loan program discriminates against poor farmers, and this does not seem to be the case. "Less than adequate farms," according to FHA officials, are getting more than 50 percent

Table 10–4. Average Size of Loan by Type, Fiscal 1965–68

Loan	Total	1965	1966	1967	1968
Individual loans to farmers					
Initial	$1,795	$1,666	$1,652	$1,933	$2,053
Subsequent	719	0	543	733	790
Individual loans to non-farmers					
Initial	1,989	1,785	1,788	2,086	2,390
Subsequent	779	0	581	815	828
Coop loans					
Initial	11,863	11,354	12,077	10,022	13,810
Subsequent	18,150	0	8,500	22,928	16,172

Source: Farmers Home Administration, Department of Agriculture (computed from table 10–3 above).

of the loans under the traditional programs. Whether a poor farmer receives a loan under the old program or the antipoverty program may depend on administrative practices. As already noted, local FHA officials tend to make operating or farm ownership loans early in the fiscal year and to concentrate on rural loans later. Thus traditional FHA loans are probably made to some who could receive rural loans, while later in the year the opposite is the case.

Loans to Cooperatives

Although individual loans have been of much greater quantitative significance, cooperative loans have received the lion's share of publicity, both favorable and unfavorable. As of June 30, 1968, approximately 48,000 families or individuals had received initial loans that averaged about $1,850, and subsequent loans that averaged $800. The 1,160 initial loans made to cooperatives averaged $12,000, and subsequent loans were 50 percent higher (see Table 10–4).

Cooperative loans have been used for the most part to finance the purchase of farm equipment. Altogether, 56 percent of the cooperative loan funds through fiscal 1967 were used for the purchase of equipment, 22 percent for the construction and installation of buildings, and 14 percent for initial operating and management costs.[8]

Because of the difficulty of founding, financing, and maintaining large coops, FHA favors the smaller, unincorporated cooperatives, and about nine of every ten initial loans in fiscal 1968 went to unincorporated cooperatives that boasted an average of five members. Loans to this group averaged $7,500, or $1,500 per member. Initial loans to marketing cooperatives averaged $100,000, but since these cooperatives averaged 159 members, the per capita loan amounted to only half the per capita amount of the unincorporated coops. The Southern Regional Council and other groups have criticized this emphasis on small cooperatives, claiming that such loans offer little hope of meaningful progress.[9] In rebuttal, FHA officials point out that one of every ten cooperative loans was made to finance rural marketing associations whose average membership exceeds 50. They also argue that it would be inviting trouble to make larger loans to new coops before they have had a chance to prove their worth.

In fact, most of the controversy about the rural loan program has focused upon loans to cooperatives. Though cooperatives have a long tradition in American agriculture, critics have contended that the cooperative concept is antithetical to the norms of private ownership and individual initiative. In 1966 some 8,400 agricultural cooperatives with 6.9 million members were in operation and were grossing almost $2.1 billion annually. These data suggest that cooperatives can hardly be considered "un-American"; so less lofty reasons must be found to explain the underlying opposition toward loans to them.

One basis for the opposition to federal support of cooperatives is the doubt that such institutions can provide any meaningful benefit to low-income rural residents. As one administrator put it: "Thirty years ago, a lot of poor farmers in the U.S. used the coop technique to become successful. But they weren't outside the mainstream of society like many Southern Negroes and others in poverty today."[10] As a result, cooperatives made up of low-income rural residents face formidable obstacles, the most critical of which is the lack of managerial talent. Managers must not only possess technical competence, they must also be able to work with a group that is poorly educated and unfamiliar with modern agricultural and/or business practices. Another critical problem is participation. Purchasing and marketing cooperatives are initiated to enhance the market power of the individual buyer and seller; therefore the larger the cooperative, the greater its market power and probability of success. Because many of the rural poor are unwilling to join struggling cooperatives, the chances of adequate internal growth for such small organizations are not good.

But the major opposition to loans to cooperatives has come from sectors of the rural Establishment that see themselves threatened by the concentrated power of the rural poor. Needless to say, advocates hope that coops will help free the poor farmer from dependence on the rural Establishment of creditors, tenant farm owners, and processors. The overt threat is economic, but it goes hand in hand with a social and political challenge to the society that has been built around its economic institutions.

The problems and potentialities of large-scale rural cooperatives are well illustrated by the Southwest Alabama Farmers' Cooperative Association (SWAFCA). This organization of some 800 families was initially led by veterans of the Selma civil rights march, and its membership was almost exclusively Negro. The purpose of the cooperative was to effect economies in the purchase of fertilizers and seed, to help the members diversify into production of vegetables, and to raise the price of farm produce by counteracting the market power of the two major food processors in the area. To initiate the project, SWAFCA submitted a proposal for a $503,000 CAP grant. Local vested interests swung into opposition, and the Alabama congressional delegation intervened against the grant, in the process instigating an FBI investigation of SWAFCA officials. OEO finally made a $400,000 grant to SWAFCA, overriding the governor's veto, but local opposition has continued. Fertilizer plants have refused delivery to coop members; processing plants have discontinued purchases of cucumbers and Southern peas from coop members; and "traffic violations" have delayed SWAFCA delivery trucks and caused spoilage.

Given this environment, SWAFCA's accomplishments have been limited, and perhaps its greatest achievement has been its survival. In fact, it has increased its membership to 1,000 families. SWAFCA has also forced local processors to raise their prices for cucumbers and peas by 50 percent. But the organization's total sale of vegetables was only $52,000 in the first season, or roughly $50 per family. A much larger crop was planted during the next season.

Late in fiscal 1968, FHA approved an $852,000 rural cooperative loan for SWAFCA. However, the loan included provisions for the complete supervision of expenditures, which was unacceptable to SWAFCA. FHA claimed that its local officials supervise expenditures by borrowers as a matter of routine; nonetheless, the loan was refused on the grounds that supervision would give the Establishment and Alabama FHA officials (who were allegedly unsympathetic to SWAFCA) control over the group's affairs.[11] By the middle of June, an agreement was finally reached for an $852,000 loan to SWAFCA. FHA agreed to remove requirements for the attendance of a USDA representative at all meetings of the board of directors and for local FHA supervision of all loans, a move which insured the independence of SWAFCA from the local establishment. SWAFCA's position was further improved on July 17, 1968, by a CAP demonstration grant of $600,000 for a 15-month period.

The large size and liberal terms of SWAFCA's loan do not portend a new orientation of administrative policy, however. SWAFCA was funded as a demonstration project, and the future of large cooperative loans depends to a great extent on its subsequent performance. While FHA was forced by external pressures to refund SWAFCA, OEO officialdom was divided on the merits of supporting controversial coop projects. The administrators of CAP research and demonstration programs favored the funding of coops that challenged existing rural institutions, and their views prevailed over those who advocated greater caution or felt that the cooperatives of marginal farmers had little promise of economic viability.

Not all OEO-funded rural cooperatives involved challenges to the political structure. One promising case is the Livestock Management and Marketing Co-op, operating in 13 northwestern Wisconsin counties and made up of some 700 families. This marketing cooperative for feeder pigs was awarded an initial grant of $178,000, followed by a grant of $123,000 the next year. Several factors suggest promising results: (1) there is little resistance from the Establishment because the population is homogeneous; (2) the LM&M is to be assisted by a successful existing coop and by agricultural experts from the University of Wisconsin; and (3) the success of the earlier coop has shown the very significant economic potential of such an organization.

Another notable project is that of the Migrant Rural Action group (MIRA) in Laredo, Texas, whose purpose is to find permanent employment at a home base for seasonally employed agricultural workers. By providing income payments during the growing season, and lending money for leasing farmlands, this nonprofit corporation hopes to create a cash reserve that will finance expansion of the project and the cooperative purchase of lands. Because local interests are not being hurt by the measure there is little local opposition to the project.

SWAFCA, the best known and largest OEO-funded cooperative, typifies the problems and potentialities of large agricultural purchasing and marketing cooperatives. As noted, their problems include lack of managerial and technical talent, nonparticipation, and the opposition of the local Establishment. But even more significant is the inherently limited potential of such organizations. Farming methods can be improved and market exploitation overcome, but the fact remains that these poorly trained farmers must support themselves on a limited quantity of typically marginal land. There are limits to what training, capital, and market freedom can accomplish, and the record of SWAFCA thus far suggests that this limit may still leave the participants below the poverty threshold.

SWAFCA, LM&M, and MIRA represent three different types of agricultural cooperative projects funded by OEO grants. Because of the government's long experience with agricultural loans and grants, the benefits that will come from these projects are fairly predictable. In general, they do not produce a drastic improvement in income. But the income gains of several hundred dollars a year which can be anticipated from these agricultural cooperatives can be very meaningful, even if they fail to lift the members above the poverty threshold.

Whereas the FHA has been sensitive to the opposition of the local Establishments (often its county organizations were basic components of these Establishments) OEO's demonstration projects have consciously attempted to reorder the social, political, and especially the economic conditions inimical to the poor. In funding cooperative ventures, officials of OEO's demonstration programs sought to change the environment that perpetuated marginal farming rather than work through existing institutions. Given this orientation, the problem has been to find the best way to make these changes, and OEO has experimented by funding a wide variety of demonstration projects. While many of these programs do not involve cooperatives *per se*, the distinction between cooperatives and the community corporations that have been set up to achieve cooperative benefits is frequently semantic.

OEO has also funded rural cooperatives that are engaged in light manufacturing. The latest grant to SWAFCA, for example, provides for the eventual establishment of food processing and packaging plants. But the best-known example of this type of coop is Crawfordsville Enterprises in Taliaferro County, Georgia, With an OEO grant of $212,000, this "community corporation" expanded its garment production and began an industrial silk screen processing operation and a woodworking plant. Along with these "community businesses," the corporation provides credit unions, coop housing, youth programs, and child care.

Crawfordsville Enterprises was faced with the same problems as SWAFCA—a lack of adequate management and the resistance of the local Establishment. The corporation grew out of a bitter school desegregation fight in Crawfordsville and was initially supported by SCLC and the National Council of Negro Women. It was managed by a former Negro teacher, dismissed for his participation in the desegregation struggle, who had no business experience. Lack of adequate management has led to extreme financial difficulties; opposition from the Establishment has also hurt because the garment work must be subcontracted from white-owned firms in the state.

The experience of Crawfordsville Enterprises and other light manufacturing cooperatives suggests that there is less chance of success in such enterprises than in agricultural cooperatives. If a manufacturing venture is successful, the returns are probably greater than those from agricultural enterprises, but they are still not large, because labor-intensive industries that use the unskilled are marginal and necessarily low-paying. Experience would suggest that large-scale agricultural cooperatives are a better investment for government funds than light manufacturing rural cooperatives.

Up to the present time there has been little connection between loans from FHA under Title IIIA and direct OEO funding under other EOA provisions. There is a dearth of evidence as to whether cooperative loans are more productive than individual loans, and specifically whether loans to large cooperatives are more productive than loans to small cooperatives.

The Effect of Economic Opportunity Loans

Like other antipoverty efforts, the rural loan program made early and inflated claims of instant success. A May 1966 press release asserted that non-farm families were increasing their average gross income by $1,800 as a result of loans, farm families were boosting their income by about $1,000, and the average cooperative member was realizing an increase of about $300.[12] In testimony before Congress in November 1967, FHA officials revised these estimates downward, predicting that the average farm borrower would increase his income between $300 and $500 a year while the average non-farm borrower would increase his income from $500 to $700 a year.[13] These later estimates were based on preliminary findings of a then unpublished study of approximately 350 borrowers in Mississippi, South Carolina, and the Missouri-Arkansas Ozarks by the U.S. Department of Agriculture's Economic Research Service. The lower figure is based on the borrower's calculation of income boost within 18 months after securing the loan; the higher figure is based on his expectations for the coming year. A more limited study published by the Economic Research Service on loans to lobster fisherman in Maine has found that expectations averaged twice the realized gains,[14] so the lower figures quoted above are probably the more realistic. Thus net gains to farmers are probably around $300 a year and those to non-farmers around $500 a year—by no means insignificant additions to the $1,891 and $2,366 average annual family incomes for the two groups. However, the loans must be repaid from these increases in income. Since repayment schedules are geared to the use-life of the articles purchased, the earning capacity of the funded item is probably insignificant by the time repayment is complete. As a simple illustration, a farm loan of $2,100 with a seven-year equal increment repayment period would require an average yearly repayment of $300, and when it was repaid it would probably not yield any further income gains. Undoubtedly this oversimplifies the case, but it suggests that the lasting impact of Title IIIA loans is minimal.

The loan program does not seem to be an effective means of combating rural poverty. Needless to say, FHA spokesmen take strong exception to these conclusions. They stress the point that land purchased or refinanced with a loan continues to be a productive asset after the loan is repaid. They also claim that the credit and associated counseling may offer the borrower a head start for achieving economic independence.

Aside from substantive weaknesses, the rural loan program has also been plagued by several administrative shortcomings: (1) the lack of adequate supervision and counseling; (2) the "spreading thin" of the funds; and (3) the emphasis on loans to farmers as opposed to non-farmers, despite the fact that rural loans may offer the only alternative to the latter group and seem to benefit them more than the farmers. But these shortcomings are of little consequence if, even under the best conditions, loans of this sort fail to boost the income of borrowers.

This raises the question of whether the very concept of loans to the rural disadvantaged is a viable one. Do loans result in meaningful increases in productivity which would justify a strict loan program? The tentative answer seems to be no, at least for individual loans. The experience with cooperatives is too limited for even a tentative judgment, and the funding of cooperatives involves noneconomic issues that cannot be measured on cost-benefit bases.

11.

ASSISTANCE TO MIGRANT AND SEASONAL LABORERS

A tar-paper curtain separates the
migrants from the rest of America.

Truman Moore

Legislative Background

One of the few congressional contributions to the 1964 Administration-sponsored antipoverty bill was an explicit provision to aid migrant and seasonal farm laborers (Title IIIB). Executive architects of the legislation had thought that the broad provisions of the Community Action Program were adequate to cover the needs of poor farm laborers (along with other groups of the poor) and that no special provisions would be required. Though this was no doubt correct, a number of liberal congressmen and senators who had for years pressed for legislation to aid seasonal farm laborers, particularly migrant workers, were not content with these assurances.

Until 1966, farm workers were denied protection of the federal minimum wage legislation; they were specifically exempted by the National Labor Relations Act, which protects the right of workers to join unions of their own choosing. Frustrated in repeated attempts to obtain legislation to aid migratory and seasonal farm workers, Representative James Roosevelt of California insisted that the Act's title dealing with aid to submarginal farmers be expanded to include farm laborers. Roosevelt threatened to oppose Title III if provisions were not made for migrant education, day care, sanitation, and housing facilities—proposals which had passed the Senate on several occasions but were stymied in the House. These programs were chosen because they were deemed to be least controversial with opponents of migrant legislation. The sponsors of the OEO legislation left untouched existing legislation which presented obstacles to the right of farm workers to organize, though this legislation was within the domain of the congressional committees that considered the poverty legislation. Health provisions were also excluded so as not to undercut the fairly new 1962 Migrant Health Act, the only migrant legislation passed prior to the Economic Opportunity Act.[1]

The Clientele

More than one of every five poor people is a potential client of the migrant and seasonal farm worker programs. The Department of

Agriculture has estimated that in 1966 there were 351,000 migratory workers and some 2.4 million seasonal farm workers.[2] However, about half of the seasonal laborers worked less than 25 days during the year, receiving the bulk of their income from non-farm work. Thus, they were not covered by OEO's definition of migrant and seasonal farm workers. It is estimated that the target population ranged between 1 and 1.5 million. With the inclusion of family members, the potential clientele would be about 6 million persons, though some OEO estimates put the figure somewhat higher. OEO defines its farm labor clientele to include persons who earn more than half of their income from seasonal agricultural labor, work for more than one employer, and are below the poverty level.[3]

The life of migrant workers has remained virtually the same since John Steinbeck depicted it three decades ago in his classic *The Grapes of Wrath*. Year after year, investigators such as the Senate Subcommittee on Migratory Labor (chaired by Senator Harrison Williams of New Jersey) have documented the continuing plight of migrants, who together with seasonal farm workers comprise the poorest occupational group in the nation.[4] There is little need to further document their low wages (less than $1,600 annual income in 1966, including about $500 from non-farm work), chronic spells of unemployment, miserable housing, scanty education, exclusion from normal community life, and denial of services that most people take for granted.[5] Migrants are truly "at the bottom of the barrel," neglected for too long by nearly every level of government (although a few states and localities had set up special migrant committees or offices).

OEO officials estimate that the migrant and seasonal worker program has distributed its resources equally between migrant and seasonal workers, with growing emphasis on the latter. Mexican-Americans, many of whom have language handicaps, tend to predominate in the migrant streams that travel along the west coast from California, or up from Texas through the Rocky Mountains and the central states. Negroes and Puerto Ricans predominate in the third basic stream, which flows from Florida and Puerto Rico.

Seasonal workers are the rural equivalent of the urban ghetto poor—but often they have even less education and larger families and are older in age. The problem of helping migrant and seasonal workers is paradoxical. On the one hand, mechanization and migration are reducing their number; at the same time, however, relocating displaced farm workers continues to be difficult because of their low educational attainments and lack of salable skills for an urban environment. What is needed is substantial income maintenance to support these people in their rural environment, or else extensive education and training to equip them for other jobs.

Program Development

OEO has funded two types of projects, depending on whether the programs were operated "along the stream" or at "home base." The former provide services in places where the migrants stop to work, or move the projects along with them. "Home base" projects serve migrants where they live during the slack farm season, and seasonal farm workers where they live the year round.

Educational programs account for the bulk of the funds obligated under the migrant and seasonal farm worker program. Initially these programs were divided between remedial education for adults and educational programs for youths, but the latter were transferred to the Office of Education in HEW as part of the Elementary and Secondary Education Act amendments of 1966 (although OEO youth projects continued through fiscal 1967). The adult education program focused on basic prevocational education, including English for Spanish-speaking persons. "Home base" classes offered weekly stipends to heads of households whenever feasible and tended to occupy participants full-time. These classes were suspended during the farming season, when work was available. Stipends were not paid "along the stream" or during the farming season, except at the end of the season to migrants who settled in the states where they had worked.

After Congress "spun off" responsibility for both regular adult basic education and education of migrant children to the Office of Education, OEO officials felt there was still a need of providing secondary education for migrant and seasonal high school dropouts between the ages of seventeen and twenty-two. OEO's solution was to place these youths on college campuses and provide them with residential facilities and education to enable them to complete the equivalent of a high school education and receive the usual high school credentials necessary for a job. This is the High School Equivalency Program (HEP).

Child labor laws are virtually meaningless for farm labor, and during the season many children (even pre-teens) join their parents to work in the fields. Babies and younger children are typically left in locked cars or are cared for by older children who perhaps have had to drop out of school. OEO attempted to provide for the younger children by offering day-care facilities modeled on the Head Start experience. The aim was to provide not merely babysitting facilities but to prepare the children for elementary education.

The rest of the OEO-funded migrant and seasonal farm worker projects provided housing and sanitation facilities. At first the program emphasized temporary (often demountable) units on public lands to house migrant farm laborers and their families. More recently, emphasis has been on permanent housing at "home base." Most of the construction work was performed by the owners, a fact that has minimized cash outlays and involved supervised work experience and training in construction.

The goal of OEO planners has been comprehensive aid to the clients rather than fragmented assistance. According to an OEO publication, top priority should be assigned "to programs aimed at reaching entire families: preschool programs that teach mothers about child development; housing programs which include education for new home owners about community resources; adult education programs that provide citizenship and consumer education as well as literacy and vocational preparation."[6] Given OEO's extremely limited resources and the complexity of the problems faced by agricultural workers, the design of comprehensive projects proved an insuperable task, and many of the projects continued to provide only fragmented assistance.

OEO attempted to set priorities for the projects it was to fund. The agency's rhetoric emphasized "self-help" rather than rendering poverty more "comfortable." The "band aid" approach was shunned; the goal was to achieve a lasting change that would pull the clients out of poverty.[7] But harsh realities made it difficult, if not impossible, to separate stop-gap measures and permanent change. The head of a migrant worker household, for example, could hardly be expected to undertake an effective period of remedial education without income maintenance. Therefore about a third of the total funds available to the migrant and seasonal labor program was allocated for the payment of stipends, reducing the funds available for actual education and training. Of course, the fact that a person undergoes a course of remedial basic education is no guarantee that he will end up improving his economic status. It is estimated that about half of those who undertook full-time training received better-paying jobs, and one of every four went on to enroll in vocational training courses.[8] Given the deep-seated handicaps of migrant workers, supporters of the program claimed that the results were impressive.

In response to OEO's objective of providing comprehensive services to migrant and seasonal farm laborers, Congress in 1967 expanded the program's scope to encompass health and legal services, counseling, and consumer training. Congress also instructed OEO to provide for the immediate needs of migrants and seasonal workers, as well as for long-run rehabilitation. Despite OEO's preference for permanent housing, the amendment specifically included temporary housing and sanitation facilities among the immediate needs that should be met. There was one flaw in the broadened vision of Congress: it failed to provide additional funds for the program. There is a considerable element of truth in the oft quoted statement that more money is spent on migratory birds than on migratory labor!

Steinbeck's image of the Okies still applies to casual farm laborers and particularly to migrant workers of today. They are not usually considered part of the community in which they live or work, and, as already indicated, they are unprotected by most welfare legislation. The community's attitude, as described by one official, is "here today, gone tomorrow—and the faster the better."

Cognizant of the fact that migrant and seasonal laborers are not ordinarily part of a community, the 1967 amendments to the Economic Opportunity Act instructed the administrators of the program "to promote increased community acceptance of migrant and seasonal farm workers and their families (Section 312)." The provision is likely to remain little more than an exhortation, and Congress was silent in prescribing means that would help to achieve this objective.

Aside from their lack of political clout, the migrants' mobility also presents special administrative problems. Neither the federal government (which normally only funds projects) nor the states are structurally equipped to deal with the migrants as they wander from state to state. OEO contracts directly with various private or public organizations for the administration of the migrant and farm labor projects. In the administration of its projects, OEO administrators found that they could not rely upon local CAA's to develop projects for migrant and seasonal labor. Only one of every eight migrant projects funded in fiscal 1968 was administered by a CAA.

Funding and Administration

Level and Type of Funding

Altogether, OEO has allocated some $108 million to the migrant and farm labor program, including some $15 million in CAP funds. The level of funding for fiscal years 1965 through 1968 is shown in Table 11–1. The apparent reduced funding of farm labor programs during fiscal 1968 is misleading and reflects the close relationship between OEO-administered antipoverty programs and those of other agencies. In that year migrant youth programs were transferred from OEO to the Office of Education; the $9 million allocated to these projects was then being provided by the Office of Education under the Elementary and Secondary Education Act.

The funding level provided by Congress for migrant and seasonal farm labor programs was enough to help only a small proportion— possibly 2 to 3 percent—of the target population. Unlike some of their

Table 11–1. *Distribution of Title IIIB Obligations by Function, Fiscal 1965–68*

Functions	1965[a]		1966[a]		1967		1968	
	Dollars (Millions)	Percent	Dollars (Millions)	Percent	Dollars (Millions)	Percent	Dollars (Millions)	Percent
Total	$15.0	100	$35.0	100	$33.0	100	$25.0	100
Education	9.5	63	28.0	80	26.0	79	19.9	80
Adult (including income maintenance stipends)	6.0	40	19.0	54	17.0	52	19.9	80
Youth	3.5	23	9.0	26	9.0	27	—	—
Housing and sanitation	3.5	23	3.0	9	3.0	9	2.3	9
Day care	2.0	13	4.0	11	4.0	12	.7	3
Program administration[b]	n.a.	n.a.	n.a.	n.a.	n.a.	n.a.	2.1	8

Note: Details may not add to totals because of rounding.

Source: Derived from Office of Economic Opportunity data.

[a] Includes CAP funds (Sec. 205): $5 million in fiscal 1965, $9.5 million in fiscal 1966.

[b] Prior to 1968, administrative costs were included with program components.

OEO colleagues, administrators of Title IIIB attempted to keep meaningful data on the number of persons served by their projects—although it is difficult to get firm figures on the actual number of *different* persons served. In fiscal 1967 more than 100,000 persons were estimated to have participated in the program; that is, they were enrolled in educational classes, given day care, or assisted with housing facilities. During fiscal 1968 this figure was doubled.

Adult basic education programs consumed the overwhelming portion of Title IIIB funds. For planning purposes, OEO officials estimated that the annual cost per individual in those programs was $1,500, with two-thirds earmarked for income support and the balance for teachers' salaries and other administrative costs. Projects normally operated six to nine months during the year, and the payment of stipends was largely restricted to heads of households who were enrolled on a full-time basis. In addition, the program enrolled part-time trainees (without stipend) at an annual per capita cost of $300. There was considerable competition for full-time enrollment and qualification for stipends. Part-time enrollees normally received priority for full-time enrollment when "slots" for the latter became available, though national data are not available on overage attendance or length of enrollments. Stipends for full-time participants in the program were decided on an individual project basis but could not exceed MDTA levels, which equal state unemployment insurance benefits plus a maximum of $20 a week for dependents and $10 for expenses.

Because day-care facilities had to be adjusted to the long workday of agricultural laborers, facilities usually had to be provided for 10- to 12-hour days. Where possible, Title IIIB project officials attempted to use the Head Start classes, adding extra hours to meet the needs of the children and their families. For planning purposes, the estimated cost per child was $100 a month—the same as Head Start—and the average estimated stay was three months per year. By fiscal 1968, most day-care facilities for migrant children had been paid for from Elementary and Secondary Education Act funds; Title IIIB funds had been reduced to provide facilities for about 2,000 children.

The initial cost of temporary housing was estimated at $2,000 per unit, with an additional annual cost of $500 for maintenance. Outlays from Title IIIB funds for permanent "self-help" units were not much greater because loans from the Farmers Home Administration to the prospective owners covered most construction costs, and the OEO portion was primarily for technical assistance and stipends.

Though no additional funds were provided, Title IIIB administrators were constrained to carry out the congressional mandate to expand the scope of their program. An example was the funding of

referral centers to advise migrants of available local services and programs.[9] A grant in North Carolina provided, among other things, for
a residential center that offered health care, job placement, and follow-
up services after placement.[10] Plans were also made to expand HEP
to help dropouts finish high school in a residential college setting.
Much of the administrative responsibility for this program was turned
over to a consulting firm, Educational Systems Corporation, which
gave supportive and consultative services to the universities. HEP, like
Upward Bound, provides for residential facilities, but the former's objectives are much more modest than the latter's. HEP attempts to provide enrollees with a high school education and to prepare them for
jobs or vocational training, while the goal of Upward Bound is a college diploma for its participants.

Geographic Allocation

The administrators of the Title IIIB program had maximum latitude in spending the available money, for Congress imposed no criteria for the allocation of funds by states. Though the nearly 100
projects funded by the program in fiscal 1968 were distributed over
a majority of the states, Texas and California accounted for more
than a third of the funds obligated under the program during the first
three years. Florida, New Mexico, Mississippi, Oregon, and Alabama
received some 30 percent of the funds.

Project funding ranged from a few thousand dollars to more than
$6 million. The latter grant was made to the Texas governor's office (in
both fiscal 1966 and 1967) to expand an existing state program that provided school facilities for 18,000 children and more than 4,000 adults
while they were at their home base. The grant was continued during
fiscal 1968, though it was then directed mainly at adult education
inasmuch as children's education was funded under the Elementary
and Secondary Education Act. Another large grant—$3.5 million in
fiscal 1965 and $4.7 million in fiscal 1966—went to the state of Califor-
nia for a variety of programs, but particularly for temporary housing,
which OEO wanted to deemphasize. However, Governor Edmund G.
Brown and his successor, Governor Ronald Reagan, favored the funding of temporary housing, and the Senate Subcommittee on Employment, Manpower, and Poverty supported their views. In subsequent
years California projects continued to receive large amounts, but they
were increasingly directed to private or local agencies. This development was explained by the fact that OEO's relations with Governor
Reagan were markedly less cordial than with his predecessor.

The two major grants to state agencies in Texas and California notwithstanding, fiscal 1966 funds were about evenly divided between public and private nonprofit sponsors of projects. Since that time, OEO has relied increasingly on private sponsors for Title IIIB projects. In fiscal 1968, state and local government agencies received only about a quarter of the funds; the rest of the grants were made to private nonprofit agencies, including religious organizations, educational institutions, and community action agencies.[11] As suggested earlier, community action agencies played a relatively minor role in sponsoring migrant and seasonal farm labor projects. Many private sponsors were organizations that had already worked with migrant labor, and OEO funds made it possible for them to expand their activities.

In addition to discretion in allocating grants geographically and by type of sponsor, OEO officials could purchase necessary services if none could be obtained "free" from existing sources. This enabled OEO to tie in with other agencies or programs to generate additional funds or provide more comprehensive services. In fiscal 1967 it was estimated that the $33 million in OEO grants was matched by $24 million from other federal agencies and $4 million from local governments and private organizations.[12]

Federal Administration

At the federal level, the migrant and seasonal farm labor program remained highly centralized, and project funding was never delegated to regional offices. The program was administered by a special migrant branch in the Office of Special Field Programs, whose jurisdiction also included projects on Indian reservations, in the Commonwealth of Puerto Rico, and in the U.S. territories. Although the Title IIIB program was formally under the Community Action Program, it retained its separate legislative basis and for all practical purposes was separate from the rest of the Community Action Program. As already mentioned, the administrators had considerable flexibility: the projects were not subject to a governor's veto or to allocation formulas, and they did not require local or state contributions. Nonetheless, many local sponsors made contributions "in kind," and some made substantial additions to the federal grants; OEO's loan authority was virtually unused. An attempt in 1967 to empower governors to veto Title IIIB projects failed. Senator George Murphy of California, the sponsor of the amendment, argued that migrant funds had been used to support a CAP project which, Murphy argued, was for all practical purposes the same as a project vetoed by Governor Reagan. One of the charges was that project personnel had helped in unionizing migrant workers.[13]

As in most of its activities, OEO not only encouraged participation on the part of the projects' beneficiaries, but also required that they be included on boards of directors and be hired in nonprofessional roles; some 4,000 were so employed by the end of 1967. Also, as with many OEO-sponsored projects, there are no national data indicating the number of migrants serving on the boards that direct projects, although information is available for many individual projects. There is little doubt, however, that such participation, when it occurred, contributed to the development of social awareness and political leadership among migrant and seasonal farm laborers. These activities were buttressed by "citizenship" courses offered by some of the projects which made participants aware of their rights to unionize and receive welfare programs and stimulated interest in political action, including registration and voting.

Employers of migrant and seasonal farm laborers tolerated the government programs insofar as they helped to improve the status of workers and their families through education and improved housing facilities. Opposition was generated, however, over charges that OEO projects called for the "organizing of migrants into labor unions."[14] No doubt unionization might in many instances be the most effective means of aiding seasonal and farm laborers; however, OEO shunned such help, and some projects specifically prohibited the use of funds for unionization. In the few instances where GAO or other investigators found that funds had been used for unionization, the amounts were minimal and were ordered repaid.[15] But the line of demarcation between "citizenship education" and the exercise of citizen rights is not a sharp one. Many delegate agencies were committed to liberal causes and to the organization of workers as one means of reducing the exploitation of farm labor; therefore Title IIIB funds might have been used to spur the organization of farm laborers. One of the most controversial grants was to an organization headed by Cesar Chavez, who led the Delano, California, grape pickers' strike. The reaction of a grower to this grant is representative of the views held by his colleagues about some of the Title IIIB projects: "They are going to have 31 persons going around being paid to talk up citizenship . . . and one of the rights of citizenship is to join a union and I have no doubt whatever that the money will be used for that purpose."[16] Chavez decided not to use any of the grant money until the strike was resolved, and has thus not spent any OEO funds.

Related Programs

Neglected as the migrant and seasonal farm population has been, Title IIIB projects were not the only efforts aimed at helping them.

Administrators of seasonal farm and migrant labor projects naturally tried to supplement their efforts with other resources from the welfare and training programs initiated under the Economic Opportunity Act or other legislation. Some projects obtained "free" labor from the VISTA volunteers assigned to them, and day-care projects were often grafted onto Head Start facilities at only slight additional cost. Some CAA's extended their services to migrants who happened to come into the area, using their own funds rather than those from Title IIIB. Participants in Title IIIB projects could also be referred to programs funded by other sources.

It does not follow that all those in charge of relevant programs extended enthusiastic cooperation. Each program has its own clientele and may ignore the interests of migrant laborers. For example, partisans of seasonal and migrant labor projects criticized Department of Labor officials for failing to supply adequate vocational training, including basic education from MDTA funds; and Farmers Home Administration officials were faulted for allegedly short-changing migrants in supplying housing by failing to utilize all the available funds earmarked for this purpose.

The friction that developed between MDTA officials and administrators of the Title IIIB project in Coahoma, Mississippi, illustrates the problem of getting clients enrolled in non-OEO projects. In this case the parties had evidently agreed that Title IIIB funds would be used to offer remedial education to seasonal farm workers and that MDTA institutional courses would then train them for employment. The arrangements did not work out, and Title IIIB officials charged their MDTA colleagues with bad faith and unwillingness to train these workers. There were racial overtones to the controversy. State officials were blamed for wanting to train Negroes for jobs they might obtain only upon leaving the state, and national MDTA officials were blamed for not intervening. MDTA spokesmen claimed that the Title IIIB training was not adequate to bring the enrollees up to the standards needed for vocational training. There is no need to assign blame in this case; the point is that in the absence of a special effort to provide for these workers, few officials were willing to assume the burden of delivering the necessary services. The problems of the Coahoma project were apparently due to the failure of the parties to coordinate and/or follow through on their efforts, though state MDTA administrators apparently also lacked enthusiasm for serving the clientele of Title IIIB.[17]

Other complaints against Labor Department officialdom and its state affiliates were that the latter acted as agents for employers and misrepresented working conditions, housing facilities, and the amount of pay on jobs to which farm laborers were referred. The Labor De-

partment rarely received credit for its refusal to refer federally recruited migrant labor to farmers whose housing did not meet the required standards.[18] Nor did many praise Secretary of Labor Willard
Wirtz for his courageous stand in sharply reducing the importation
of *braceros*, although alleged liberality in issuing work permits to
commuting Mexicans was taken up by an OEO legal services agency.
The Secretary of Labor settled the case out of court, promising to use
greater diligence in limiting *bracero* labor.[19]

The Farmers Home Administration also came in for criticism.
Migrant and farm labor spokesmen accused that agency of favoring
well-to-do farmers and discriminating against the poor. There is certainly little evidence that FHA officials utilized all the resources at
their disposal to provide housing and other services to migrant and
seasonal farm laborers. FHA officials appeared to view "self-help"
housing projects as financially unsound and the product of social reformers. "We're not a social agency," an FHA official is reported to
have asserted.[20] And quite apart from "self-help" housing, there is little
evidence, according to spokesmen for migrant labor, that FHA moved
aggressively in using its authority to provide loans and grants for the
construction of conventional housing for farm labor. FHA lent only
about a third of its $44 million level of authorized loans from 1961
through June 1968, and it left unused about a fifth of its $9.5 million
in grant funds.

The Most Effective Way To Help?

Relatively brief experience with the migrant and seasonal farm
labor program emphasizes the difficulties of combating poverty with
extremely limited resources. The stated goal of the antipoverty fighters
is that they are aiming to effectuate "permanent change," not merely
to make poverty more comfortable. But in order to undergo a permanent change, either through education or training, workers and their
families need support during the period of "rehabilitation." Ameliora-
tive measures cannot be separated from the services that will eventually
pull the participants out of poverty. The issue raised by migrant and
seasonal farm laborers is certainly not an unwillingness to work but
whether work can be made available at a wage that will bring them
above the poverty threshold. While the $108 million allocated to Title
IIIB programs during the first four years stressed long-range corrective
measures, more than a third of the money was expended on income
maintenance and temporary housing. Except for outright opponents of
the welfare legislation, few would oppose bolstering the income of
farm laborers who are able to earn only poverty wages despite the fact

that they are performing useful and hard work, and who are striving to improve their economic status by undergoing training.

An assessment of the Title IIIB programs must take for granted the need to spend a significant proportion of the funds for income maintenance. The issue is whether a larger proportion of the funds should have been used for this purpose rather than for measures that are supposed to bring about permanent change. OEO spokesmen have argued that the two approaches may be complementary. They claim, for instance, that the stipends paid to several hundred Negroes on a Holmes County, Mississippi, Title IIIB project gave the participants a measure of economic security that made far-reaching chain events possible. The outside income enabled them to risk registering and voting in a hostile atmosphere, which in turn led to the election in 1967 of Robert Clark, the Holmes County Title IIIB project director, the first Negro member of the Mississippi state legislature in this century. Also, OEO officials optimistically viewed the stipends as a pump-priming device for stimulating economic activity in the area, a claim that is hard to document.

Concerning the "success" of its educational measures aimed at permanent change, OEO, as usual, has not been reticent. In justifying the program before Congress in 1968, OEO officials claimed that 16,530 persons had completed full-time education and rehabilitation programs, that nearly half of them had found "upgraded" jobs, and that another one of every four had entered advanced training. In addition, 1,253 persons had completed high school equivalency programs.[21]

Having presented these figures, OEO officials failed to specify just what constituted the completion of the educational program or the extent to which the 8,000 success cases were "upgraded." No data were presented on their rates of pay, the type of jobs the upgraded individuals found, or the length of time they have held these jobs; nor do we have any idea whether the jobs were found within their area or whether the trainees had to move elsewhere to get them. Nor was information provided about the advanced training that nearly one of every four persons entered. Since the stipends paid by MDTA may exceed the regular income of migrant or seasonal laborers, the advanced training program may have been a subterfuge for income maintenance rather than training for a vocation. Obviously the two are not mutually exclusive, but OEO officials did not attempt to describe the nature of the training to which Title IIIB clients advanced.

There is room to speculate that the 1,253 persons who received GED credentials will most likely move into better jobs. The same might be asserted about the High School Equivalency Program. One of every three who had entered the program the first semester received the high school equivalency certificate, and others were still working for it, but the report to Congress did not indicate the dropout ratio. In the absence of data, no conclusion can be made concerning the success of the program, but few would deny the need to establish institutional arrangements whereby children of migrant families can complete a high school education. The average cost of $3,000 per year appears reasonable. Despite OEO's strained attempt to show Congress the "payoff" in future income, there is no need for a cost-benefit analysis to justify a program that helps migrant children complete high school.

Lack of data frustrates any attempt to evaluate the adult training programs. Testimony published by OEO, aside from referring to the numbers who completed courses, is limited largely to anecdotes. The story of the Oregon trainee who tripled his income upon completion of a welding course even found its way into the President's 1968 manpower message. Heartwarming as this story is, it is not enough to justify a $100 million investment. The justification of the program, therefore, must depend upon a simple faith that people who need help are receiving it.

It is a fact that Title IIIB programs have for the first time created an office in the federal establishment whose sole concern is improving the lot of migrant and seasonal farm workers. No claim can be made that the Farmers Home Administration or other bureau in the Department of Agriculture had championed these groups. OEO has insisted that its special office representing the interests of these laborers means more than simply that "somebody cares." That would hardly feed migrant children or provide them with education and housing. The assumption is that a special office might spur other agencies to extend additional help to migrant and seasonal farm laborers.

Though at this stage it is hard to point to specific cases in which the new office in OEO has mobilized other federal resources, some progress has been made. For example, one wonders if Congress would have provided education for migrant children under the amendments to the Elementary and Secondary Education Act if the Title IIIB projects had not led the way before to the transfer. Probably Title IIIB experience was a factor in the adoption of a "self-help" housing program in the rural portion (Title X) of the 1968 Housing and Urban Development Act (PL 90–448), though it is more likely that it was included as a political counterthrust to the National Home Ownership bill proposals of Senator Charles H. Percy of Illinois which the Administration had opposed. Whatever the cause, the result was authority for a regular self-help program, administered by the Farmers Home Administration, that provides grants and loans at low interest rates to subsidize housing for low- and moderate-income rural families, including migrant and seasonal laborers. But having passed a moderate authorization, Congress failed in 1968 to appropriate funds for the program.

Possibly the most effective governmental assistance for migrant and seasonal farm laborers would be protection of their right to organize and an increase in their statutory minimum wage. Granted, there is no "free lunch": a boost in farm labor wages would unquestionably speed mechanization and reduce the need for farm laborers. It could be argued, however, that this would be no loss considering the level of living that seasonal and particularly migrant farm laborers now endure. The "solution" of reducing the number of farm labor jobs is predicated, of course, on the assumption that jobs would be created for the workers elsewhere.

It is no wonder, then, that OEO has not resolved the basic issue. The question, as stated earlier, is whether such programs should concentrate on helping the migrant and seasonal farm laborers and their families to adjust in the rural environment or whether the programs should concentrate on helping them to move into urban areas. In light of the grave problems of metropolitan areas, a case can be made for buying time and "keeping 'em down the farm," even if mainly through income maintenance measures. Title IIIB projects attempted something more in providing education and training that might be useful either at home or elsewhere.

The danger of concentrating on income maintenance in areas where no economic bases exist is, of course, the creation of a dependent population and discouragement of migration to economically viable areas. Here one must distinguish between the older unskilled illiterates in these areas and the younger people whose life work is ahead of them. For the latter, society should not settle for income maintenance; it must also offer opportunities for education and training for the future, whether through migration or through the development of an economically viable home area.

12.

HELPING THE
ORIGINAL AMERICANS

The Indians had their families with them.... No cry,
no sob, was heard among the assembled crowd;
all was silent. Their calamities were of
ancient date, and they knew them to be irremediable.

Alexis de Tocqueville

The estimated 400,000 Indians who live on 290 federal reservations are another predominantly rural group whose claim to the resources of the antipoverty program is as strong as that of migrant labor. An additional 200,000 to 250,000 Indians live elsewhere, in urban areas or in scattered rural enclaves; some estimates, especially for urban areas, go much higher. Although poverty is no stranger to Indians wherever they reside, federal agencies that deal with Indians as a group serve primarily those on reservations. This chapter's discussion focuses on Economic Opportunity Act programs for Indians residing on federal reservations, with emphasis on CAP efforts.

Legislative Background

Indians have a unique historical and legal relationship to the federal government; it was Chief Justice John Marshall who first enunciated the doctrine that Indians are "wards of the State." Despite the patronizing connotations of this doctrine, the special relationship was based upon the fact that the Indians had ceded vast tracts of valuable land, in return for which the federal government agreed to furnish the services generally provided by local and state governments. This relationship was implicit in the various hearings and task force reports which preceded the passage of the Economic Opportunity Act, though the Act made no special provision for Indians.

Hundreds of millions of dollars have been spent to "care for" Indians over the past century—primarily channeled through the Bureau of Indian Affairs (BIA of the Department of the Interior, and more recently through other federal agencies as well. According to the unofficial summary of an unpublished Presidential Commission report, the government's Indian policies have been subject to violent shifts and contradictions—"assimilation" versus "self-determination," en-

263

couraging migration from the reservations to jobs in the city versus attempts to develop industry and jobs on the reservations.[1] During the discussions that led to the passage of the EOA, various public and private groups underscored the special dimensions of Indian poverty and projected a new administrative point of departure in an attempt to solve them.[2]

In 1967 the Indian reservations, with a total labor force of about 131,000, had an unemployment rate of 38 percent—more than ten times the national average. The average family income was less than a fourth of the comparable national figure. Illiteracy was greater than elsewhere in the nation, and the high school dropout rate was double the national average. In addition to substandard and dilapidated housing for 50,000 families (perhaps 75 percent of the reservation population), Indians suffered very high rates of sickness. Their average life expectancy was forty-four years, compared with sixty-five years for other Americans; the infant mortality rate was ten times the national average.

Given the dimensions of the problem, the 1964 antipoverty hearings focused on methods of approach. The Association on American Indians Affairs, for example, urged that:

> To make these [OEO] projects successful, it will ... be important to work with the communities rather than imposing ... from the outside. Projects should be developed jointly with the Indian tribal councils and ... designed to give key planning roles to the Indian people themselves. This approach would not only safeguard the success of the project but would also provide valuable leadership training for the participants.[3]

That the drafters of the EOA shared the same concern was borne out by Sargent Shriver's testimony:

> We expect broad participation by Indian and tribal communities all across the nation. In every program there must be strong Indian involvement for consent and development.... We expect tribal groups to be in the forefront of developing community action programs.[4]

Even though OEO was not the originator of "self-determination," there is little doubt that OEO's Indian program gave strong impetus to this approach, and OEO pioneered in making grants (or "raw cash" as one admiring BIA official called it) directly to Indian groups for programs more or less of their own choosing.

Goals, Program Development, and Administration

The Indian Community Action Program (ICA) shared the goals of all Title II OEO programs—stimulation of local initiative through the organization of CAA's, rapid development of needed remedial programs, improved delivery of services to the poor, better utilization of existing resources through improved coordination of public and private services, and in the long run improved employment capability and economic well-being.

In view of the extreme poverty on the reservations, the cultural differences, and the unique federal-reservation relationship, perhaps ICA's most important initial objective was to encourage indigenous participation and simultaneously to stimulate leadership development. The federally chartered tribal governments (under the Indian Reorganization Act of 1934), comparable on most reservations to municipal and county governments elsewhere, provided a ready-made apparatus for the rapid creation of CAA's. Although reservations (like other rural communities) were plagued by isolation and the lack of infrastructure, reservation dwellers were more homogeneous and possessed a long history of reliance on federal programs. Within months of the EOA's passage most tribal councils had adopted resolutions authorizing community action agencies, with the tribal councils themselves usually designated as the CAA boards.

As was done for migrant laborers to stimulate and facilitate program development, OEO set up a small Indian Branch within CAP's Office of Special Field Programs. This produced a highly centralized structure under which applicants submitted proposals directly to Washington, bypassing regional and state offices. For all practical purposes, ICA operated separately from the regular CAP program and with considerable flexibility; there was apparently little friction with state governments because the governors never exercised their veto power on ICA projects. For example, grants were not charged against the regular CAP county fund allotments, nor did the program follow any other geographical formula in allocating funds.

OEO assisted further in mid-1965 by creating a consortium of Utah, South Dakota, and Arizona State universities (three others were added later), whose staff provided technical assistance in planning and drafting proposals, organizing the CAA's, and starting their programs, training their staffs, and providing other services as requested.[5]

OEO was not adequately staffed or funded to deal with all the Indian reservations. While tribal lands totaled about 39 million acres, reservations ranged in size from tiny pueblos and rancherias to the huge 14-million-acre Navajo reservation spread across Arizona, New Mexico, and Utah. Ten other reservations had more than a million acres each; these were in Arizona, Washington, South Dakota, Wyoming, and Montana.[6] These eleven reservations accounted for most of the Indian lands but for less than two-fifths of the total reservation population. It was impractical to fund CAA's on all of the small reservations. Using a combination of land and population statistics, OEO set 150 as the number of reservations on which CAA's could be established and funded to provide at least some immediate limited services.[7] By the end of fiscal 1968 there were 63 CAA's serving 129 reservations with a total population of 312,000, about 80 percent of whom were poor.[8] Non-Indians living within reservation boundaries were also served by ICA; and some CAA's served several reservations.

OEO officials claimed in 1968 that 80 percent of the reservation population had been "reached."[9] This was accomplished through various antipoverty activities, such as occasional legal aid, participation in a credit union, systematic skill training programs, community education programs, employment as Head Start or community aides, or participation in the various children's and youth education and health programs.

The size of the CAA's and their grants ranged from small ones with minimal funding, serving a few hundred persons, to the largest one of almost $6 million for the Navajo, which encompassed about a fourth of the total federal reservation population, and which provided a wide variety of services through hundreds of employees.

As for the components in programs requested by reservations, an early OEO-sponsored evaluation of six reservations showed that actual "local" choice or control was not usually as great as had been promised. Applicants soon found that approval could be expedited by choosing "packaged" programs known to have been approved elsewhere, rather than more orginal ones which they might have preferred but which might require a long and difficult decision-making process involving more of the community. The evaluation also expressed concern over tribal councils acting as CAA boards, and questioned whether members of the reservation Establishment would be sympathetic to developing new approaches to the reservation's problems.[10] These criticisms are applicable to many if not most CAA's. Given the choice between carefully conceived plans and "instant action," OEO normally opted for the latter—particularly with reservation CAA's—lest Indians consider OEO another "do nothing" organization.

It was not unusual for small reservations to request an annual budget of a thousand dollars or more per inhabitant. ICA officials soon adopted a formula, based on population and poverty incidence, which granted about $40 annually per person with a minimum of $15,000 per CAA. This funding could encourage local innovation and flexibility on reservations with large populations, but for a small community it meant little more than ability to establish a CAA with a very small staff and modest administrative budget. The smaller, less populous reservations, however, could achieve greater community involvement, while the bigger ones, though they might have more funds, were dispersed and found it harder to obtain total involvement. The funding formula also offered "incentives" to the CAA's that met certain standards of performance by providing extra funds for special additional projects.

Funding and Program Levels

Level of ICA Funding

OEO's funding of reservation CAA's was as diverse as aid to CAA's in other areas. However, the mix reflected the special needs and desires of the reservation clientele. "Local initiative" or "versatile" grants played a more important role on Indian reservations than in other CAA's, accounting for nearly 70 percent of ICA funds during the first four years of OEO (Table 12–1). The other $17.8 million came from CAP national emphasis programs such as Head Start, Legal Services, and Comprehensive Health Centers. Of the national emphasis programs, only Head Start allocated a lump sum to the Indian Branch; other EOA programs channeled their funds and programs directly to the reservations, bypassing OEO's Indian office.

Comparative data on individual ICA components are available only for fiscal years 1967 and 1968.[11] After Head Start, home improvement was the single largest component of ICA, reflecting the critical housing conditions on reservations. Only 25 percent of reservation homes are considered adequate; 21 percent are considered repairable, but 54 percent need replacement. ICA's Home Improvement Program

Table 12–1. *Indian Community Action Obligations, Fiscal 1965–68 (Millions)*

	1965	1966	1967	1968
Total	$3.6	$12.0	$20.1	$22.3
Local Initiative	3.6	10.5	11.7	14.4
Community organization			3.7	3.6
Home improvement			3.6	4.3
Educational development	n.a.	n.a.	2.2	2.5
Health			1.0	.9
Special programs			.7	2.4
Economic development			.5	.7
National Emphasis	—	1.5	8.4	7.9
Head Start	—	1.5	7.7	6.7
Comprehensive Health Centers	—	—	.4	.5
Legal Services	—	—	.3	.7

Source: Office of Economic Opportunity.

(HIP), a variant of "self-help sweat equity" housing, pays stipends to full-time trainees and teaches them construction skills while they build or repair their own homes. According to OEO estimates, these programs provided better housing for 75,000 persons. In fiscal 1968, when housing loans were tight, HIP emphasis switched to repair work. ICA housing grants were frequently tied in with those of other federal agencies, with OEO providing training funds and stipends while HUD, BIA, and the Public Health Service covered costs of materials, equipment, water, and sewage.

ICA also funded a combination of formally structured basic education for adults, remedial and supplementary work for youngsters, and some wide-ranging "community education," including consumer education, citizen participation, and community development. A related educational program of special interest, funded from CAP summer youth program funds, was the Indian Circle held in the summer of 1968, which offered a brief course on Indian history and culture to about 125 high school youngsters from 62 CAA's representing 80 tribes.

Economic and business development was the aim of a small but growing program. Cooperating with other agencies, ICA made grants to 15 reservations for a wide variety of activities aimed at encouraging employers to create jobs on reservations. OEO officials claimed that the grants enabled Indian CAA's to provide "one stop" service for industries wishing to locate on a reservation, through advice about benefits available from all federal agencies and local sources.

Head Start was the largest single item of either versatile or national emphasis funds. All CAA's had a Head Start component, and about 10,000 children were enrolled in the 50 full year and 17 summer Head Start projects in fiscal 1967 and 1968—at a cost of about $1,000 per year per child. Thus, the programs served only slightly more than a third of the estimated 26,000 four- and five-year olds on reservations. (BIA schools do not take children below six.)

A major aspect of the various ICA programs was job creation. At the end of fiscal 1968, CAA staffs employed about 760 professionals and 3,000 nonprofessionals. Included in the latter category were some persons receiving stipends from training programs.

Related OEO Funding

ICA funding accounted for almost two-thirds of the total EOA contribution to Indian reservations. It is estimated that other EOA programs added about $12 million to ICA's $20 million in fiscal 1967. VISTA assigned 255 volunteers to 49 reservations in 1968 at a cost of about $900,000. For the most part, these volunteers were assigned to reservation CAA's. Upward Bound enrolled 1,050 Indian students, or about 4 percent of its total enrollees in 1968, at an estimated cost of $1.4 million. OEO also contributed about a million dollars annually to the University Consortium program, mentioned earlier. Meanwhile, OEO's Research and Demonstration Division funded about $2 million worth of projects for Indians, including a prefabricated housing factory at Rosebud, South Dakota, and the first all-Indian community college at the Navajo school. Five Job Corps centers were located on reservations, and several others in reservation areas, but they served and employed a wide variety of persons and were not limited to Indians. EOA's delegated programs also contributed to reservations: The Department of Labor provided $8.2 million for the Neighborhood Youth Corps during fiscal 1967 and 1968, and an additional $3.2 million for Operation Mainstream; HEW's Work Experience obligated $6.8 million from its start through the end of 1968.

Other Federal Funding

Compared with total federal spending for Indians by all agencies, OEO has been a very junior partner. It contributed about 7 percent ($32 million) of $435 million spent in fiscal 1967. Federal funds for Indian programs, however, increased six-fold between 1952 and 1967. In 1952, BIA administered virtually all Indian program funds; but by 1967, though its budget had tripled, it administered only about half the available funds. Table 12–2 presents estimates of increases during the Johnson Administration. Although the BIA administers more services than any other agency, OEO insists that ICA's modest share has had a disproportionately great impact. It would be foolhardy for

Table 12–2. Estimated Funding for Indian Programs[a], Fiscal 1964 and 1968 (Millions)

	1964	1968
Total	$287.4	$440.2
Department of Interior, Bureau of Indian Affairs	207.8	237.5
Department of Health, Education, and Welfare	77.3	133.5
Public Health Service	65.5	101.7
Office of Education	11.8	31.8
Office of Economic Opportunity (ICA only)[b]	0	22.3
Department of Commerce, Economic Development Administration	2.3	42.0
Department of Labor	n.a.	4.9

[a] Department of Housing and Urban Development not included. In fiscal 1967 this was about $15.1 million; Department of Agriculture also not included.

[b] BIA estimated total OEO funds in fiscal 1967 at $32 million.

Source: Based on estimates used by National Council on Indian Opportunity.

OEO and ICA to claim full credit, but congressional and Administration interest in Indians has increased dramatically, and since OEO came into being several agencies have established "Indian desks" in their Washington offices.

Can OEO Turn the Tide?

In balance, the major contribution of OEO's Indian programs appears to have been to encourage local initiative through direct grants to Indian groups, permitting them to initiate programs and organize their own operational structures. Tribal councils were encouraged to run their own affairs rather than turn for "guidance" to federal officials. Secretary of the Interior Stewart Udall praised OEO for being a needed "gadfly organization" and credited OEO with supplying "an innovative thrust that I don't think . . . [BIA] would have under normal circumstances."[12]

ICA spokesmen have claimed that its activities (and the resulting jobs) have encouraged young trained Indians to return to the reservations. The hope is that they, as well as some nonprofessionals who gained experience in CAA jobs, will remain to run for tribal offices or for other governing boards (for example, housing authorities) which are developing; even if they do not aspire to tribal office, these people would be of value as staff with other agencies or private firms working on the reservations. While ICA has not supplied quantitative support for its claims, it may be speculated that experience on CAA staffs, boards, and training programs has contributed to a higher level of participation in community affairs. More apparent is ICA's contribution to breaking up the service monopoly historically held by the Bureau of Indian Affairs, and its role in accelerating fundamental changes in federal funding practices by promoting direct contracting by Indians themselves.

In the absence of any follow-up data, it is not at all certain that ICA is producing a lasting economic impact, or that it is providing a stepping stone to regular employment and higher income. The task of lifting appreciable numbers of Indians out of poverty is clearly beyond the scope of ICA's limited funds. One doubts if the task is even within the reach of the present level of federal expenditure for Indians. Until the nation adopts a comprehensive program supported by adequate funds and actively involving Indian leadership, significant progress toward the elimination of the poverty in which our "first Americans" have too long been living is very unlikely.

Part IV

Job Corps

13.

THE JOB CORPS

*...assist the reduced fellowman...so that he may
earn an honest livelihood...*

Moses Ben Maimon

The Mission

The Job Corps was created as part of the Economic Opportunity
Act to prepare youths, aged sixteen through twenty one, "for the responsibility of citizenship and to increase [their] employability...by
providing them in rural and urban residential centers with education, vocational education, useful work directed toward conservation
of natural resources, and other appropriate activities" (Section 101).
The assumption underlying this mission was that many youths from
impoverished homes must be removed from their home environment
before they could be rehabilitated through training and education.

Although the antecedents of the Job Corps may be traced back
to the Civilian Conservation Corps of the thirties, the contrasts between the two institutions are more significant than the similarities.
The CCC was a product of the Great Depression, when deprivation
and need were widespread, and its 1.5 million enrollees represented
a broad cross section of the population. It was terminated when the
armed forces absorbed the bulk of its clients and acute labor shortages
developed from wartime conditions. The Job Corps, on the other hand,
focuses upon the special needs of a small minority of youths who,
because of educational deficiency and debilitating environment, are
at a competitive disadvantage in the labor market. The CCC was
essentially a job creation program (although the term did not come
into vogue until three decades later) which emphasized conservation
work. The Job Corps stresses the needs of the individual members,
although the work experience of enrollees in conservation centers is
also devoted to "useful social work."

The idea of reviving residential centers for disadvantaged youth
was advanced by Senator Hubert Humphrey in 1957. Although a bill
authorizing conservation camps for youth passed the Senate two years
later, the bill was not even taken up by the appropriate House committee, and it attracted scant support. By 1963, however, youth unemployment was recognized as a pressing national problem which was
not responding to over-all improvements in economic conditions. In

273

that year a coalition of conservationists and welfare organizations expanded the proposed rural conservation bill to include federally supported job creation programs in urban areas. The expanded bill, which included the basic features of the Job Corps and the Neighborhood Youth Corps, was again approved by the Senate. In the House, the Education and Labor Committee approved the measure but the Committee on Rules prevented it from reaching the floor. The opposition included segregationists as well as opponents of welfare legislation. (The two were not, of course, mutually exclusive groups, but the fact that the proposed camps were to be racially integrated added force to the coalition.)

In January 1964 the publication of *One-Third of a Nation* by the President's Task Force on Manpower Conservation confirmed that the armed forces annually rejected one out of three potential draftees because of mental and physical deficiencies; most of the rejectees came from impoverished homes. This publication gave impetus to the proposed program, which was included as part of the Administration's antipoverty bill.

The 1964 Administration proposal differed substantially from the 1963 bill. While the earlier bill emphasized conservation work, the antipoverty bill stressed the establishment of residential centers where youth could receive educational and vocational training. Although the 1964 bill did not preclude conservation centers (in deference to the conservation interests), it was intentionally vague so as to permit maximum flexibility in administration. Under pressure from the conservation groups, Administration witnesses who testified on the Economic Opportunity bill indicated that they would establish two types of camps: urban centers emphasizing vocational training for youths with a sixth-grade level or better reading achievement, and conservation centers emphasizing basic education and work experience for enrollees with more acute educational deficiencies Sargent Shriver distinguished between the two types of centers as follows: "Let us say after six months or a year in the conservation corps [the] boy had reached the levels [of education] indicated ... he then could be transferred into the educational centers ... and get further training so that he could get a skill."[1] The expressed objective of the Job Corps has been that of "taking people where they are and advancing them as far as they can go in the time allotted."[2]

The main opposition to the Job Corps was directed against the establishment of conservation centers. It was argued that conservation work would add little to the employability of the youth and that whatever conservation work might be performed would not justify the high cost of maintaining the centers. The conservation lobbyists, needless to say, were not dissuaded. Unwilling to leave the size of the conservation component to the discretion of program administrators, they succeeded in persuading Congress to specify that 40 percent of the male Job Corps enrollees be assigned to conservation centers.

The Universe

It is difficult to estimate the size of the Job Corps' potential clientele. Over-all economic conditions, as well as the attractiveness of residential centers to potential enrollees, would be the determinants. In 1967 there were about 1 million out-of-school unmarried youths from poor families, and most of them were eligible to enroll in the Job Corps. Even under ideal conditions, the majority of these potential candidates might not have been interested in residential centers, or even required such costly training. In fact, the Job Corps had to maintain a continuous promotional effort to fill the available facilities, which by mid-1967 could accommodate a maximum of 43,000 youths.

It must be left to speculation whether the difficulties in attracting enrollees were caused by a lack of interest on the part of potential clients, the quality of training and education offered in the centers, or an inability to "reach" the youths. In large part the problem may be traced to the decision of the Job Corps administrators to stress the needs of the most poorly educated, those who needed the Job Corps facilities most desperately. The Corps could have avoided a great deal of criticism and unfavorable publicity if its administrators had decided to attract the "cream" of the disadvantaged youths. But whether they could have filled their quotas by "creaming" is also open to speculation since the expanding labor market and the armed forces provided ample opportunities in most areas for "good," well-motivated youths. The initial negative image of the Job Corps, which still persists, may also have hindered recruiting. It is probable, therefore, that the Job Corps offered little attraction to youths who were able to obtain jobs on their own.

The record of the Job Corps is clear: it tried to attract youths who had difficulty finding employment even in a tight labor market. Two of every five enrollees (according to May 1968 statistics) had completed eight years of education or less; and actual educational achievement was much lower than the formal education would indicate. This has not varied much since the second year of the Job Corps. Reading and arithmetic comprehension for half of the enrollees was at about the fifth-grade level; nearly one of every three was unable to read a simple sentence or solve a third-grade arithmetic problem. Three of every five came from broken homes, and two of every five from families on relief (Table 13–1).

Ethnic Mix

A major problem of the Job Corps has been the continuous increase in the proportion of Negro and other nonwhite enrollees, a factor which has contributed to the tensions experienced in centers and to the early departure of some enrollees. During the first year of the Job Corps, whites constituted a majority of the enrollees. By July 1967, the ethnic distribution of Job Corps enrollment was:

Caucasian 32.3%
Negro 58.5%
Other 9.2%

The ethnic distribution did not vary much by type of center.

Even a very experienced and knowledgeable staff might have found the problems of achieving the proper balance between discipline and freedom within the centers difficult, if not impossible. Inducing southern whites, for example, to live with Negroes in racially integrated dormitories on a voluntary basis and motivating both racial groups to train and learn together on an equal basis is certainly no mean accomplishment, even for an expert in social psychology. Few of the Job Corps staff members, at least in the early days, were

Table 13–1. Corpsmen Characteristics as of May 1, 1968

| Education and Family Background | Total | Men | | Women |
		Urban Centers	Conservation Centers	
Highest grade completed (%)				
8 grades or less	38	33	51	24
9 to 10	42	50	38	38
11 to 12	20	17	11	38
Median educational attainment				
Reading	5.2	6.0	3.6	6.3
Arithmetic	5.2	6.3	3.6	6.1
Family (%)				
Broken home	60	n.a.	n.a.	n.a.
Unemployed head of family	63	n.a.	n.a.	n.a.
On relief	39	n.a.	n.a.	n.a.

Source: Job Corps, Office of Economic Opportunity.

fully prepared to handle such problems. But they learned quickly. Plagued by strife and violence during the first two years, the centers have recorded few racial incidents since then.

Understandably, Job Corps spokesmen have been hesitant to speak publicly about the danger that the Job Corps might become a segregated institution. When queried about the problem in late 1966, an OEO spokesman commented that the racial problem was "not quite as acute at this point as it might have been."[3] Nevertheless, it appears that the Job Corps officials were concerned about the declining white enrollment, and in the spring of 1967 they instituted a special drive to enroll youths from Appalachia, a region of predominantly white population. During the following year these special efforts stabilized white enrollment at about a third of the total Job Corps population.

Age Mix

Another continuing operational difficulty was the decline in the age of enrollees. By mid-1967, sixteen- and seventeen-year-olds constituted 57 percent of the total enrollment. The age distribution at that time was:

16 years	30.3%	19 years	12.9%
17	26.4	20	7.6
18	18.6	21	2.7

The problem was twofold: the youngest enrollees tended to drop out early—only 10 percent of the sixteen- and seventeen-year-olds stayed in the centers six months or longer—and many found that child labor laws or arbitrary age requirements prevented them from utilizing whatever training they had received. Conscious of the problems created by the changing age composition of enrollees and the difficulty of keeping the younger ones in the centers, policy-shapers attempted to remedy the situation. Several proposals were considered. It was thought that assigning the younger enrollees to centers close to their homes would increase home visits and alleviate problems of homesickness. Another alternative was to concentrate the sixteen- and seventeen-year-olds in special centers and use older corpsmen in these centers in leadership roles and for performing chores the younger ones were not permitted to do by law (such as driving vehicles and handling certain equipment). A third alternative was to secure commitments that enrollees would stay in the centers for at least a year, and then design special educational and training curricula that would be suitable for these longer periods. A fourth and probably the most promising alternative was to convert some of the conservation centers to experimental institutions that would stress education and prepare sixteen- and seventeen-year-old enrollees for the equivalent of a high school education, and those who were properly motivated, for further educational advancement.

Other pressures seemed to intervene, however, and Job Corps operations were not sufficiently altered to make the centers more attractive to younger enrollees. Little progress had been made in checking the disturbingly high dropout rate among this group. Designing ways and means to keep, as well as educate and train, the younger enrollees remains a crucial problem for the Job Corps.

Program Administration and Operation

Although the director of the Office of Economic Opportunity was charged by law with responsibility for administering the programs created under the Act, he was also authorized to delegate their administration to established federal agencies. Secretary of Labor Willard Wirtz sought jurisdiction of the Job Corps, pressing the Labor Department's claim for the administration of all training and job creation programs. However, OEO Director Shriver decided to retain this program in his office. It was reported that he expected the program to be innovative and highly visible (the latter anticipation was fully realized, though doubtless not in the way the director desired). It is also probable that OEO decided to keep the Job Corps in order to round out its operational responsibilities, especially since the Neighborhood Youth Corps was to be delegated to the Labor Department. The competing claims for the Job Corps were resolved by the President, who sided with OEO.

By mid-1967 the Job Corps had reached its peak, operating 123 centers with a total enrollment of 42,000. The administrative challenge of such a venture was formidable, and budgetary constraints forced OEO to retrench on enrollment during the following year and to close 16 centers. A year later, total enrollment dropped to 32,600 and 300 demonstration projects were discontinued (Table 13–2).

Urban Centers

To operate the urban centers, the Job Corps turned to private contractors. In May 1967 universities or nonprofit organizations operated only seven of the 28 urban centers. Private firms—including such corporate giants as General Electric, IBM, Litton Industries, RCA, and Westinghouse—operated the remaining 21 urban centers.

Table 13–2. Job Corps Capacity and Enrollment, May 30, 1968

Type of Center	Active Centers	Available Spaces	Enrollment
Total	109	35,599	32,954
Men (urban)	6	11,650	10,350
Women (urban)	18	9,065	9,200
Conservation (federal)	75	13,255	12,080
Conservation (state)	7	1,205	1,040
Demonstration	3	424	284

Source: Job Corps, Office of Economic Opportunity.

OEO welcomed this corporate involvement because it gave the Job Corps and the other divisions of the war on poverty an image of respectability and acceptance by the business community. Corporate involvement resulted from a mixture of "do-goodism" and the more traditional business interest. Though profits were small, contractors took no financial risk; they operated on a cost-plus-fixed-fee basis. Moreover, operation of a center offered an opportunity to enter the expanding educational and training market; the centers could serve as subsidized laboratories for developing and testing new techniques and know-how. And in late 1964, when the initial contracts were negotiated, some corporations viewed the activity as a hedge against slackening defense expenditures though their interest in the program was maintained as defense needs expanded in the following three years. The operation of centers also offered occasional side benefits. For example, Litton Systems, Inc., which operates the Parks Center in Pleasanton, California, purchased $350,000 worth of educational material from a sister division—material and equipment which, the General Accounting Office has charged, "by and large have not been effectively utilized, and a major portion appears of questionable use to Job Corpsmen."[4] Such "waste," however, can in part be attributed to the experimental nature of the educational programs, and it should not overshadow the social responsibility aspect of corporate involvement. The small profits involved could hardly justify prestigious corporations putting "their names and resources on the line by operating Job Corps camps."[5] It just happened that social responsibility and sound business motives complemented each other in the operation of Job Corps centers.

Initially, it appeared that corporations were better equipped than educational institutions to run the centers; indeed, universities seemed to be the greatest failures in administering centers. Commenting upon a university-operated center that was beset by troubles, including a riot, an observer noted that the contractor "has been excessively cautious and slow in buying equipment for the enrollees. Food and food services were inadequate with 600 being fed in a dining hall that accommodated only 160 at a time."[6] In the same vein, a Job Corps official stated that "on balance, private corporations have the techniques educational groups lack in tackling large organizational problems like setting up the basic structure without having to run through a faculty committee."[7] Unencumbered by the red tape so common to institutions of higher learning, the corporations "got the show on the road" in minimum time.

However, the talent to organize a restaurant or operate a center's facilities does not necessarily include the ability to motivate, train, and educate deficiently prepared youth. John H. Rubel, vice president of Litton Industries and the man who first suggested that Shriver contact corporations to operate centers, is reported to have said: "I think of the Job Corps as a complex transforming machine with many internal parts. The input—the raw material—that is fed into this machine is people. The output is people. It is the function of this machine to transform these people."[8] There is no evidence that such a machine has yet been fashioned. Corporations, traditionally engaged in personnel training and the development of complex defense systems, were expected to have little trouble developing new approaches and techniques for educating and training the disadvantaged, but it does not appear that the corporations have lived up to these expectations. The high cost of running the centers has forced the Job Corps to cut its operating expenses and to reduce the budgets for research and development in education and training. And because of such budget constraints, corporate contractors have attracted few proven top-level educators or administrators. Four of the 16 centers closed because of budget limitations were urban centers run by private corporations; this may be indicative of long-run weaknesses in corporate-managed urban centers as compared with government-operated conservation centers.

Perhaps the most successful contractor has been the Texas Education Foundation, an independent, nonprofit corporation established by the state of Texas to operate the Gary Job Corps Center. The success of the Gary Center, whose enrollment of 3,000 makes it the largest urban center, was largely due to the interest of Governor John B. Connally. The Texas governor mobilized outstanding state educators to administer the center, and business leaders to help develop curricula and place corpsmen. An interesting point is that the Gary Center was run by the same educational establishment that presumably had failed to educate the youths in school. The experience of Gary suggests that, given more adequate support (including money) from businesses and the community at large, the educational system might do better in serving the disadvantaged.

Conservation Centers

Because the Job Corps delegated responsibility for the operation of conservation centers to the Departments of Agriculture and Interior, these centers were unique among the federally supported manpower programs in that they were operated directly by federal agencies. The two departments assumed day-to-day responsibility for their administration and operated them on a reimbursible basis. The Job Corps retained the authority to formulate policy and develop training and educational curricula.

The Job Corps has avoided contracting with states to operate centers, though the Economic Opportunity Act authorized such contracts. In May 1968 only 7 of the 82 conservation centers, with a total enrollment of 1,040, were operated by state agencies. None of the urban centers was operated by a state agency, though the Gary Center was run by a state-established nonprofit corporation. Job Corps officials admitted that they had not solicited state participation, but noted that states were free to submit proposals the same as any other potential contractor. It is clear, however, that the states received little or no encouragement to apply.

Girl Problems

In addition to operating centers for men, the law required that residential centers be established for women. The Administration's original proposal had limited the Job Corps to men on the theory that they would be the future family breadwinners, and that returns on money invested in training girls would be short-lived because they would soon marry and assume family responsibilities. Congresswoman Edith Green insisted, however, that the high unemployment rate among nonwhite teenage girls justified the inclusion of women in the Job Corps. Deficiently educated girls brought up in deprived homes, it was further argued, are likely to raise children who will remain in poverty. Thus the Job Corps experience should help future mothers break the cycle of poverty, even if they do not continue as lifetime wage earners. Congress accepted the Green amendment and opened the Job Corps to women.

This decision resulted in operational problems for the Job Corps. Though the women did not necessarily cause any more difficulties than the men, a number of factors hindered efficient operation of women's centers. Female enrollees could not, of course, be assigned to conservation centers where the training emphasis was on physical labor. At the same time, and on professional advice, OEO decided to limit women's centers to a few hundred enrollees. This condition conflicted with the desires of private contractors who operated urban centers and favored larger units to achieve economies of scale and provide diversified training, It was also difficult to find suitable sites for women's centers, in view of the early decision to locate them in urban areas. Thus the Job Corps resorted either to renovating old hotels or to seeking adequate facilities in YWCA's.

Aside from the administrative obstacles, it appears that Job Corps officials were less than enthusiastic about the women's Job Corps program. In addition to the breadwinner argument, they were evidently influenced by the Moynihan thesis concerning the deterioration of the Negro family.[9] This thesis suggested that the cohesiveness of Negro families could be strengthened by improving the educational attainment of the Negro boy and enhancing his employability. It was therefore concluded that the limited resources of the Job Corps should be directed largely to males, the majority of whom were Negro.

Not satisfied with the slow progress of the Job Corps in enrolling women, Congresswoman Green succeeded in 1966 in amending the Act to require that women enrollees constitute 23 percent of the total enrollment. As a result, the Job Corps did a lot of "girl chasing" during the latter part of fiscal 1967 to live up to the congressional injunction. As late as May 4, 1967, women accounted for only 17.3 percent of total enrollment; but by midyear the Job Corps had enrolled enough women to meet the statutory requirement. In the process, the Corps was forced to utilize abandoned military facilities and to discard its earlier decision to limit women's centers to only a few hundred girls. Enrollment in several of the older centers was expanded and a new center in Poland Spring, Maine, was opened with a capacity in excess of 1,100. In addition, a men's center in Oregon was converted into a women's center. In 1967 Congress instructed OEO to take immediate steps to expand women's participation to 50 percent of the total Job Corps enrollment. The equal-enrollment requirement was reflected in the February 1968 closing of 16 men's centers; no women's centers were closed, and no closings were even contemplated.

Size and Location of Centers

Job Corps centers ranged in size from less than 100 enrollees to 3,000. The National Association of Training and Juvenile Agencies and the American Psychiatric Association recommended that a 150-bed facility would provide maximum individual attention and avoid the dangers of institutional rigidity. The Job Corps has generally followed this norm for conservation centers, whose capacity ranges from 100 to 250. But budget considerations have made the 150-bed standard impractical for urban centers. The capacity of male urban centers has varied from 600 to 3,000, and women's centers from 300 to 1,100.

To obtain the best of both worlds—gaining economies of scale while meeting the individual needs of corpsmen—the larger urban centers have experimented with small subdivisions or communities within a center, based on the vocational interests of the enrollees. This practice parallels the experience of a number of universities which have created small communities within the larger institution.

Closely related to a center's capacity is the question of its location. Having decided not to encourage state operation of centers, the Job Corps had to locate most conservation and urban centers on federally owned lands confined largely to sparsely populated areas in the western states. Since corpsmen depended upon neighboring towns and cities for much of their recreation and leisure-time activity, the relative isolation of many conservation centers has been unfortunate. This remains a problem of the Job Corps; and if it continues, the Job Corps may be forced to abandon the more isolated centers in favor of those near urban areas.

Because urban centers for men were located on abandoned military installations, the Job Corps had to accept whatever sites were available. Some selections proved unfortunate because the communities, or at least influential sectors of their population, did not welcome the corpsmen in their midst. This symbolized the inherent tension between community and center—reminiscent of town-and-gown problems—except that in the case of the Job Corps these frictions were accentuated. For example, the 1,500 or more corpsmen at the Custer Center in Michigan found that they were not welcome in the nearby cities of Kalamazoo and Battle Creek. After several incidents and one riot, both cities were placed off limits to corpsmen, who then had to travel 100 miles or more for recreation. Similar problems developed in New Bedford, Massachusetts, where the Rodman Center was located. In this case, as in several others, the city fathers unanimously requested the closing of the center after clashes between corpsmen and local youth, but reversed themselves as a result of an apparently successful community relations campaign instituted by the center director and OEO. The experience of Rodman was typical.[10] With the passage of time, most of the centers and communities have learned to coexist.

Locational difficulties related to community relations continued to be a problem, however. Despite OEO claims that community relations had improved, Custer and Rodman were two of the four urban centers that were closed in February 1968. According to one source: "On the basis of experience, Job Corps now feels that they made some errors in the location of some centers. All of the centers to be closed shared one or more of the following disadvantages: a northern location in a very cold climate; relative isolation from major urban centers, from transportation centers, and from Negro communities."[11]

Some communities were so unchivalrous as to oppose the establishment of women's centers. Several sites chosen during the early days of the Job Corps reflected lack of experience or poor judgment on the part of the administrators—such as the selection of St. Petersburg, Florida, as the site for a women's center. The hotel-center chosen was in the midst of a residential hotel area that was populated mostly by retired persons who were not happy about the youngsters, particularly when local swains came calling and the noise decibels rose above the old people's threshold of tolerance. The mayor and other community leaders declared that they supported the Job Corps in principle, but not in the midst of a hotel district catering to retired guests. Although public criticism of the center was directed at the boisterous activities of its residents and their visitors, another objection, normally not voiced publicly, was the center's racially integrated population. After repeated community protests, the Job Corps moved from the "hostile environment" before its lease expired. The St. Petersburg experience was unique, for it was the only case in which the Job Corps was forced to close a center in direct response to community demand. Even there, however, the community did not speak with one voice, and some residents favored continuation of the center.

During its first year of operation the Job Corps suffered from an extremely bad press, and every incident that involved a corpsman appeared to merit national attention. For example, the Job Corps was even blamed for polluting caves in Kentucky; the conservation center near Mammoth Cave National Park was attacked by the National Speleological Society for spoiling the underground wilderness. Like the opponents in St. Petersburg, the members of the society declared that they did not object to the Job Corps as such, they just wanted it moved somewhere else.

Although the Job Corps had disciplinary problems—including fights, stabbings, and even riots—most of the incidents hardly merited national publicity. Some of the unfavorable publicity resulted from the failure of the Job Corps and its contractors to prepare the communities in advance for their new neighbors—an oversight that was understandable during the early days when there was little time for this kind of

groundwork. As the Job Corps matured, it tried to overcome these
initial difficulties, and in 1967 OEO sponsored an amendment which
gave statutory force to these efforts. The amendment required OEO
"to establish a mutually beneficial relationship between Job Corps
centers and surrounding or nearby communities."

Costs

Underlying much of the discontent with the Job Corps was the
undeniably high cost of the experiment. The funds allocated to the
Corps during its first four years of operation totaled $989 million,
divided as follows:

> Fiscal 1965 .... $183 million
> Fiscal 1966 .... $310 million
> Fiscal 1967 .... $211 million
> Fiscal 1968 .... $285 million

Opponents were quick and persistent in exploiting the fact that
the total annual cost per enrollee was more than $8,000 in 1967, stress-
ing that the cost to the taxpayer supporting a corpsman was higher
than the cost to parents supporting a child at the best American colleges. Pundits and congressmen entered into the debate, and the
Congressional Record carried a detailed analysis of the comparative
costs of supporting a student for a year at Harvard University and an
enrollee in a Job Corps center. The fascination with this subject might
deserve the close study of social psychologists, but it was as useful as
the debates about the number of angels who can dance on the head
of a pin. Few raised questions about the relevancy of the comparison.
When Dr. Otis Singletary, former director of the Job Corps, was confronted with the unfavorable cost comparison between the Job Corps
and Harvard, he offered to pay personally for any Job Corps enrollee
accepted by Harvard. The offer, to no one's surprise, was not taken up.

Regrettably, the Job Corps added to the confusion over costs by
being less than candid with the public and with Congress. Its failure
to explain the reasons for the high costs added to the impression that
there were grounds for the charge that the centers were "country clubs
for juvenile delinquents." Most cases in which the Job Corps spent
public funds on "frill" activities were attributable to inexperience or
to errors of judgment on the part of some center personnel. Providing
enrollees with bus transportation to attend a dance several hundred
miles from their center may be classified in this category. There was
also room to question some of the regular practices, such as the payment of corpsmen's transportation costs for home visits during the

Christmas season and legal fees for those who became involved in brushes with the law.[12] The armed forces are not as generous with their enlisted men.

Conscious of the widespread attacks upon the cost of maintaining the Job Corps, OEO has trimmed its costs to the point at which further belt tightening could not be effected without damaging the training and education of enrollees. The maintenance of residential centers that provide education and training is a costly affair, and the program, if it is to continue, must be judged on its merits and not on the hopes that the expenditures per enrollee will decline. In response to public criticisms of the high cost of operating the centers and the sniping by officials of competing federally supported programs, Congress in 1966 imposed an expenditure ceiling of $7,500 during fiscal 1967 for each Job Corps enrollee. The amount was reduced to $6,900 for the subsequent year. Though Congress may get credit for cutting the costs, the action was unnecessary because the Job Corps had already taken steps to eliminate some of the more expensive training programs, to reduce the number of training occupations, and to eliminate most of the "frills."

A breakdown of the annual cost per enrollee is presented in Table 13-3. Total annual costs per enrollee in established centers (those in operation more than nine months) averaged roughly $8,100, ranging from nearly $7,400 for conservation centers to $9,600 for women's centers. Although the 1967 average cost exceeded the statutory limitation by nearly $600, the Job Corps did not ignore the limitation imposed by Congress. Excluded by law from the $7,500 limitation were overhead costs for enrollee recruitment, screening, placement, and Job Corps headquarters and regional expenses (which averaged $600 a year per enrollee), the cost of amortizing the $141 million capital investment ($600 per enrollee), and the cost of materials expended on conservation work ($854 per conservation center enrollee).

The rationale for excluding the last item is persuasive. The materials were utilized on useful public works and therefore do not represent a real training cost. Indeed, a case could be made—as the Job Corps did—for subtracting the value of the work performed on public projects from conservation center enrollee expenditures. The rationale for the exclusion of the overhead and amortization costs is less convincing and appears to be an arbitrary decision on the part of Congress. A calculation of true costs cannot ignore these expenditures.

Many difficult considerations obscure the true cost per enrollee of operating the Job Corps. The dropout rate during the first 30 days, though decreasing, stood at 20 percent in the first quarter of fiscal 1968. It could be argued that for those who stay such a short time the

Table 13–3. Job Corps Annual Cost per Enrollee, Fiscal 1967

Category	Average	Men's Urban Centers	Women's Urban Centers	Conservation Centers (Federal)
Total	$8,077	$8,737	$9,602	$7,357
Enrollee Expense	*2,790*	*2,639*	*2,642*	*2,958*
Pay & allowances	1,188	1,220	1,150	1,170
Travel	324	267	248	396
Clothing	278	233	227	328
Subsistence	464	367	383	564
Medical & dental care	252	178	354	296
Educational supplies	78	90	104	62
Vocational supplies	155	301	123	34
Recreation	107	108	96	108
Less Receipts[a]	−56	−125	−43	—
Operations & Maintenance	*1,115*	*1,441*	*1,956*	*807*
Center administration	340	409	468	256
Center maintenance	176	179	254	158
Utilities & fuel	128	128	119	131
Communications	77	73	105	75
Motor vehicle costs	112	42	31	187
General-purpose equipment	11	179	16	—
Legal, accounting, & insurance costs	6	9	22	—
Lease costs	27	—	293	—
Contractors' fees	118	220	299	—
Contractors' expenses	120	202	349	—
Center Staff Expense	*2,969*	*3,454*	*3,801*	*2,389*
Educational personnel	435	401	627	429
Vocational personnel	271	479	358	72
Safety & recreational personnel	139	209	272	52
Guidance & counseling	691	716	819	646
Management personnel	1,001	1,420	1,396	561
Medical & dental personnel	108	157	198	48
Work project personnel	235	—	—	484
Staff travel	77	53	121	91
Miscellaneous	12	19	10	6
Overhead[b]	603	603	603	603
Capital Costs[b, c]	600	600	600	600

[a] Includes payments made by visitors for lodging and other receipts.

[b] Breakdown by types of center not available.

[c] Amortization costs calculated independently and not based on Job Corps estimates.

Source: Job Corps, Office of Economic Opportunity.

Job Corps experience has little positive impact and may actually represent a setback. Early studies of wage earnings showed that those who stayed less than three months actually earned less money six months after termination than a control group which did not join the Job Corps and had been in the labor force an equal time. Spokesmen for the Job Corps insist, however, that even a short stay is not a total loss since the enrollees receive counseling and medical treatment and are fed and housed. Job Corps officials also maintain that average annual costs exaggerate the true investment per enrollee because most corpsmen complete their course of study in less than a year. This claim that the prescribed curriculum can be mastered by deficiently educated youth in less than a year raises questions about the quality and quantity of the education and training offered at the centers.

However the costs may be measured, there are limits to further belt tightening. The 1967 amendment requiring equal representation of the sexes will increase costs. In fiscal 1967, women's centers had a statutory cost of $8,400 compared to the men's average of $6,900, but the higher cost of operating centers for women did not reflect higher living standards. Almost a third of the total annual differential between female and male urban centers was accounted for by lease costs, inasmuch as no rental was paid for the male centers, which are located on government property. Economies of size accounted for most of the balance. At any rate, increasing the percentage of women in the Job Corps will put upward pressures on average annual costs per enrollee.

The higher average costs of female urban centers have important policy implications. Some advocates of residential centers opposed the Job Corps because of its policy of sending youths far from home, frequently to isolated areas. According to this view, it would be better to place the youths in small residential centers, preferably in the communities in which they live. If such a policy is adopted, however, the cost of male Job Corps centers is likely to rise significantly since many such centers would have to be leased from private concerns and would be too small for economical operation.

Screening of Candidates

Could the cost per Job Corps enrollee be justified if enrollment were limited to youths whose needs could not be met by a less costly alternative program and if the enrollees remained long enough to benefit from their experience? The evidence on neither point is conclusive.

The record of the Job Corps is clear: at no time was there an attempt to "cream" applicants, a common feature of other federally supported training programs. The Job Corps extended its welcome to all youths from impoverished families. The agency was even willing to take chances with youths convicted of a felony if an appropriate review board decided that an applicant was willing to conform to Job Corps standards. It does not follow, however, that Job Corps enrollees were carefully screened or that adequate care was taken to offer alternative programs for applicants when appropriate. At first the screening of enrollees was necessarily haphazard and chaotic. Although now improved, it still leaves much to be desired. Pressures to meet quotas result in occasional "pushing" of Job Corps, reminiscent of the "specials" offered in department stores.

Many of the Job Corps difficulties were caused by the Office of Economic Opportunity. Even before it opened its first center, the Corps had embarked on an extensive national advertising campaign to interest young people. Concerned that the Job Corps could not attract an adequate number of enrollees and that the potential clientele would have to be sold on the idea, interested youths were invited to complete "opportunity cards" indicating an interest. The response of about a quarter of a million youths was better than even the most enthusiastic advocates had hoped. Though many of those who responded were neither qualified nor really interested in the Job Corps, a large proportion were potential candidates. It took the Job Corps several months to respond to the deluge of inquiries, some of which were never acknowledged. When the campaign started, the Job Corps had facilities for only a few hundred.

Under the circumstances, it is hard to understand the need for the extensive advance publicity. Indeed, knowledgeable advisers cautioned Shriver not to embark upon the campaign, and the Job Corps disappointed many potential clients even before it opened for business. The performance also antagonized some of the program's best friends. For example, Congressman William F. Ryan of New York, a consistent advocate of the antipoverty war, complained publicly that as of June 1, 1965, 1,600 New York youths had applied but only two had been selected for the Job Corps.[13]

To screen the applicants, the Job Corps turned to several agencies. Most of the screening of men was delegated to the United States Employment Service (USES) and its affiliated state agencies. In addition, 14 community action agencies were designated to undertake the job in their communities. The task of screening women was turned over to Women in Community Service (WICS), a volunteer agency whose members were the National Council of Catholic Women, the National Council of Negro Women, the National Council of Jewish Women, and the United Church Women. As the recruitment of girls was stepped up to meet the statutory requirement, WICS could not meet its quota and the USES was asked to provide half of the female enrollees. In addition, the Job Corps expanded its contracts for outreach and screening with community action agencies, urban leagues, and the AFL–CIO Appalachian Council. During fiscal 1967 the USES accounted for almost three-fourths of the 96,000 youths who were screened and referred, and the proportion was about the same for the first half of fiscal 1968. Earlier plans to rely upon sources other than USES for screening did not materialize, and the USES accounted for a slightly higher proportion of all Job Corps screening and referral during fiscal 1967 and 1968 than in the first two years.

The screening agencies were reimbursed for the cost, which averaged $73 per qualified youth screened and referred to the Job Corps in fiscal 1967. The costs ranged from $83 per person for USES to less than half that amount for WICS, whose members not only screened the candidates for women's centers but also provided numerous volunteer services for the selectees, including clothing and other needs.

Having little previous contact with such youth, most of the local employment services were poorly prepared to screen Job Corps enrollees. Some counselors oversold the Job Corps in order to fulfill their quotas. A study of former Job Corps enrollees showed that half of them felt they had not been given a true picture of "what the Job Corps would be like."[14] The major complaint was that they hadn't received the training or money promised by the counselors. Although there was considerable room for misunderstanding about the former, disappointment over allowances is more difficult to explain and would suggest that applicants were misinformed by the screeners.

During the first two years the Job Corps experienced difficulty in filling its available capacity; but by the spring of 1967, with expanded recruitment activities, OEO expressed confidence that it had licked this problem. Diverse factors contributed to the difficulty in recruiting enrollees. OEO underestimated the rate of enrollee turnover and consequently planned for a lower level of recruitment than the needs indicated. Aside from the initial ineffectiveness of local employment offices, extraneous factors complicated the job of recruiting. Expanding job opportunities and increases in military manpower needs provided alternative opportunities. Congressional action, or more precisely inaction, further complicated recruitment plans. During the summer of 1966 OEO was prevented from planning the future size of the Job Corps pending congressional approval of the authorized enrollment level. The law, when passed, allowed the Job Corps to expand to a capacity of 45,000. Finally, continued attacks on the Job Corps marred its image and probably discouraged many potential applicants.

Altogether, only one of every seven youths interviewed by the screening agencies ended up in the Job Corps. The vast majority of those interviewed either showed no interest in enrolling, or were referred to other programs, or received no help at all. Of those who indicated interest in joining a center and who qualified on the basis of income and age, nearly one of every eight was rejected during 1966. Previous behavior patterns accounted for the bulk of the rejections. About three of every ten who were selected never reached a center because they had lost interest between the time of the interview and their notification of acceptance, and a few were never assigned to a center. With experience, the Job Corps has succeeded in reducing the time between the initial interview and the final acceptance from an average of six weeks to less than three. Another two or three weeks usually elapsed before a youth was assigned and scheduled to arrive at the center.

Center Experience

Away from Home

In the spring of 1967 the average enrollee had to travel nearly a thousand miles to reach a Job Corps center. The distance between homes and training centers has been a point of controversy, and in 1966 Congress specified that wherever feasible youths should be placed in centers within their own regions. As a result, the average distance enrollees had to travel to centers was reduced from 1,300 miles to 943 miles between June 1966 and April 1967. Compared with the total cost of the program, the savings realized by placing enrollees closer to home were minuscle. The concern of Congress over this issue was apparently not shared by the enrollees themselves. A survey by Louis Harris and Associates found that almost as many enrollees preferred to be far away from home as those who preferred to be sent to a center close by.[15]

A more significant issue is whether enrollees should be placed in centers within commuting distance of their homes, if such centers are available. At first the Job Corps made a conscious effort to remove youths from their homes to preclude weekend visits, on the theory that frequent contacts with the pre-enrollment environment would interfere with the enrollee's rehabilitation. More recently, however, the Job Corps has softened this policy, and some agency spokesmen have even argued in favor of placing younger enrollees near their homes. The agency continues to insist that corpswomen not be placed within 50 miles of their home. The explanation is that removal from the home environment helps the enrollee to concentrate on her studies by reducing distractions from home problems. This position was presented by the Job Corps to the Senate Committee on Labor and Public Welfare without explaining the reasons for differentiating between male and female enrollees.

Some educators have questioned the assumption that it is necessary to remove youths from their home environments so that they may benefit from the education and training provided by the centers. Professor Francis P. Purcell of Rutgers University, a chief critic of the Job Corps whose views have received national attention, has argued that the Corps has "relied on the rather naive belief that removing young men from their home communities would enable those youths to partake of middle-class education." Instead, he advocated that "the Job Corps use existing educational facilities and create new ones within the area where the youngsters live."[16] Purcell's conclusion was that the centers had the opposite effect upon enrollees than that anticipated by the Job Corps because "paramilitary" camp life may encourage antisocial behavior. Evaluating the first six months' experience of the Kilmer Center, Purcell and a number of his colleagues at Rutgers concluded: "It should never be thought that removing youth from their homes and communities is other than a stop-gap solution to youth employment problems. Indeed, such act may be socially debilitating, and produce extremely undesirable results."[17]

Needless to say, spokesmen for the Job Corps responded that the educators' findings had no basis in fact, and they questioned the appropriateness of describing life in a center as "regimented" or "paramilitary." It would be more correct, in the view of these officials, to compare the centers to school-like dormitories where the student body participates in developing rules of behavior. The new environment, they conclude, is beneficial to the future development of enrollees.

Educational Gains

Since the average beginning corpsman's level of mathematical and verbal achievement is roughly equivalent to the fifth-grade norm and since about one in every five has a reading level below that of third grade, improvement of his basic education is vital if he is to improve his employability. At times such basic improvement is necessary before he can even begin to receive vocational training. The question of educational gains is at the heart of any analysis of the benefits to the Job Corps experience.

The Job Corps claimed that "the average Corpsmember progressed in arithmetic one and three-fourths times faster than the school norm, and in reading one and one-fourth times the average public school rate."[18] Its study indicated that the educational progress of corpsmen varied widely by type of center. Men in urban centers made the greatest progress, followed by those in conservation centers; women showed the least achievement. The explanation for the latter fact was that "many of the girls had higher entry scores and were not kept in programs all the time they were in a center." There were also wide variations among individual centers. The Job Corps found that the median educational gains of enrollees in five high-performance conservation centers "was nearly three times the public school norm in reading and exactly three times the norm in arithmetic. These rates of gain are nearly twice as great as the Job Corps average."[19]

OEO was quick to publicize the results of this study and to pronounce the educational attainments of the Job Corps a success. But three reservations, or comments, are in order. First, as Job Corps officials themselves admit: "Some of the 'gain' is simply the recovery of skills once possessed but lost through disuse."[20] Second, the gap between the best and worst centers of each type, and between the types themselves, indicate that optimal educational programs have yet to be adopted in the great majority of centers. Third, because educational programs apparently do not continue past a basic level, they yield the long-term or initially better-trained corpsman little benefit.

In the absence of any reliable standards for comparison, it is difficult to appraise the educational gains claimed by the Job Corps. However, a more recent set of data generated by the Corps (but not yet released) presents a much less favorable picture. These data (shown in the first two columns of Table 13–4) are a compilation of the mean gains measured in terms of school years completed for corpsmen over varying lengths of training.

By weighting the mean gains in each training-time category by the percentage of terminees in each category since the beginning of the Job Corps, the average gain should be represented by the sum of the weighted means. Since data were not available on the percentage of terminees in each training-time category over the history of the Corps, percentages were calculated from the records of terminees in the first quarter of fiscal 1968. These results suggest that the average corpsman raised his reading ability by about one-third of a grade. For men's centers the gains indicated in the published studies were more than twice those shown in Table 13–4. Women's progress at the centers was lower than that of male enrollees according to both studies.

The Job Corps has maintained that the unpublished data contained some technical flaws and are not as reliable as the publicized data. Careful evaluation of these arguments suggests that the actual achievements of corpsmen are somewhere in between the two esti-

Table 13–4.   Job Corps Grade Gain Scores as of November 30, 1967

Months of Training	Mean Gain Verbal	Mean Gain Math	Percent of Terminees in Category (1st Quarter, '68)	Weighted Mean Verbal	Weighted Mean Math
	Men's Urban Centers				
0– 3	.21	.36	.397	.084	.141
4– 6	.32	.54	.228	.073	.123
7– 9	.50	.66	.194	.097	.128
10–12	.50	.73	.079	.040	.058
13–15	.73	1.00	.053	.039	.053
16–18	.81	.99	.023	.018	.023
over 18	.97	1.20	.026	.025	.031
			Average Gain:	.376	.557
	Women's Centers				
0– 3	.08	.08	.321	.026	.026
4– 6	.20	.32	.290	.058	.093
7– 9	.18	.74	.185	.033	.137
10–12	.20	.56	.103	.021	.058
13–15	.50	.88	.053	.026	.047
16–18	.70	.48	.025	.019	.022
over 18	.69	.88	.023	.016	.020
			Average Gain:	.199	.403
	Conservation Centers				
0– 3	.17	.22	.557	.095	.122
4– 6	.34	.17	.202	.069	.034
7– 9	.50	.30	.107	.053	.032
10–12	.68	.39	.056	.038	.022
13–15	.54	.68	.035	.019	.024
16–18	.67	1.00	.028	.019	.028
over 18	.84	.33	.015	.013	.005
			Average Gain:	.306	.267

Source: Job Corps, Office of Economic Opportunity.

mates. The most valid conclusion seems to be that Job Corps educational gains are probably not greater than public school norms but that they are probably better than the gain rates corpsmen maintained in public school.

Vocational Education

It is even more difficult to assess the quality of vocational training received in the centers, and in the absence of standards, the impressions and views of former enrollees and their employers must suffice. According to a survey by Patricia A. Goldman, prepared for the Chamber of Commerce of the United States, employers thought that four of every five former corpsmen in their employ had received satisfactory to excellent training in centers. The views of the employers were corroborated by 90 percent of the former corpsmen, who, according to the survey, said that the training was "excellent" or "good." And nearly the same proportion considered the entire program "great" or "good." "I had only one chance in life," was a typical response, "and found it was in the Job Corps." Nevertheless, nearly half of the corpsmen felt that the skill training they received was of no help to them in obtaining the skills used on their jobs.[21]

The duration of training, rather than its quality, in part explains why many corpsmen found the training no help in obtaining a job. A survey by Louis Harris and Associates of enrollees who left the Job Corps in August 1966 found that the longer a youth stayed in the Job Corps, the more likely he was to use the training he received at the center: 42 percent of those who stayed longer than six months used their Job Corps training, compared with only 5 percent of those who stayed less than three months.[22]

A serious weakness of the Job Corps has been that from the beginning it decided to "go it alone," without involving the vocational education establishment and state vocational education institutions, even though a number of states had previously operated vocational residential centers. Spokesmen for the Job Corps have recognized that closer cooperation with state vocational authorities could have broadened support for the program and added to its professional capability. The involvement of state institutions might also have ameliorated some of the tension between the centers and their neighboring communities. State-operated centers could also have provided for experimenting with new and different program approaches. According to an unpublished report submitted by the Office of Economic Opportunity to the Senate Committee on Labor and Public Welfare: "There is great flexibility for innovation and experimental approaches in program content and in management. If this flexibility is properly exploited, many valuable lessons of potentially wide application throughout Job Corps and other similar programs may result." Nevertheless, the Job Corps has done little to achieve a rapprochement with state vocational authorities; less than 3 percent of the Job Corps enrollment were in state related conservation centers by mid-1967.

Proposals to place the Job Corps in the Vocational Education Division of the Office of Education present inherent problems despite the indicated advantages. Since the residential centers would be operated by state vocational authorities, it is likely that some would not acquiesce in establishing racially integrated residential centers. Although few Job Corps centers were located in the southeastern states, where the problem is most acute, youths from these areas can enroll in centers outside their state or region. State operation of residential centers would intensify problems of integration and probably preclude some youths from enrolling. Experience has shown that federal proscription of racial discrimination does not solve the problem. The vocational education establishment might also lack experience in handling the special problems of operating residential centers for disadvantaged youth. The Job Corps has gained considerable expertise in this area.

Although there is a need to expand the base of support for the Job Corps and to involve more vocational educators in its operations, transferring the Corps to HEW is a doubtful solution. On the other hand, ignoring the capability of state and local vocational authorities in the operation of the centers has been a serious shortcoming of the Job Corps. The issue is not a new one. In the spring of 1966 the Advisory Commission on Intergovernmental Relations recommended that OEO "take positive steps to interest states in acting as prime or supporting contractors for Job Corps facilities."[23] The commission's recommendations were ignored by OEO. It was left to Congress to force closer cooperation between the Job Corps and related state institutions in 1967.

Duration of Stay

The benefits of vocational and basic education are directly related to length of training, and thus the retention rate of the Job Corps is crucial to its success. A study conducted for the Job Corps by Louis Harris and Associates found that six months after they left the Corps, 56 percent of the former corpsmen thought they were better off as a result of their experience, 16 percent thought they were worse off, and the balance either were not sure about the impact of the experience or thought it had made no difference. Significantly, those who remained in the corps for longer periods of time gave a more favorable evaluation. Three of every four corpsmen who stayed in the Job Corps for more than six months thought they were "better off," compared with 44 percent of those who stayed in a center for less than three months. The Harris study concluded:

> There is clear evidence that a successful stay in the Job Corps can improve a youth's chances. The graduates and those in centers over six months have not only improved their employment situation and their pay rate more than the other groups, but they also sensed this improvement. Whether these groups will maintain their advantage in the future is a question that, at this point, cannot be answered.[24]

Additional discussion of the correlation between length of stay and wage and employment levels by no means definitively answers Harris' question, but subsequent data indicate that the advantage over the short-term enrollee tends to narrow.

The record of the Job Corps leaves much to be desired when the Corps is judged on its ability to retain enrollees. The law authorized a two-year enrollment and gave the OEO director discretionary power to allow a youth to remain at a center even longer. Experience clearly indicates either that the authorized length of stay in the Job Corps was excessive or that centers failed to hold youths for a sufficient length of time. Only one of every nine corpsmembers remained in a center for as long as one year. Indeed, the Job Corps curriculum was designed to allow a youth to complete his course of training in nine months or less.

The decision to "graduate" youths from the Job Corps after this short period was based on pragmatic considerations: few enrollees indicated an interest in staying longer, and the Job Corps has even had difficulty in retaining them long enough to complete this abbreviated course of study and training. Thus the "quickie graduation" served a double purpose: it established a reachable goal for some enrollees, and it provided the Job Corps with a justification for calculating costs per enrollee on less than an annual basis in response to widespread criticism of the high cost.

Job Corps spokesmen have argued that its low retention rates were largely due to lack of experience in the center staffs. This was true. Although during fiscal 1966 half of the enrollees departed within two months, the median length of stay doubled the following year and continued to improve during fiscal 1968. Retention rates are still low, however. The mean length of stay for terminees in fiscal 1967 was 5.3 months; but 22 percent terminated within the first month, 43 percent within the first three months, and only 34 percent stayed longer than six months (Table 13–5). For the first quarter of fiscal

Table 13–5.   Length of Time Spent in Job Corps, Fiscal 1966 and 1967

Duration	1966	1967
Median	2.0 months	3.9 months
Average	3.3	5.3
Less than 1 month	33%	22%
1 to 1.9	17	11
2 to 2.9	13	10
3 to 5.9	18	24
6 to 8.9	12	15
9 to 11.9	5	8
12 to 17.9	2	10
18 and over	—	1

Source: Job Corps, Office of Economic Opportunity.

1968, both the median and the average lengths of stay had improved to 4.2 and 5.6 months respectively.

A special retention problem is found among younger corpsmen. For sixteen- and seventeen-year-old terminees in 1967 the average stay was only 3.9 and 4.4 months respectively, compared to 5.3 and 5.4 months for nineteen- and twenty-year-olds. While the centers' percentage of sixteen- and seventeen-year-olds was 40 percent in the first quarter of fiscal 1968, they constituted 57 percent of all arrivals. Not only do the younger enrollees tend to drop out more quickly, child labor laws and arbitrary age restrictions prevent them from securing employment in many of the trades for which they were trained. This is reflected in the higher percentages of unplaced terminees among sixteen- and seventeen-year-olds and the lower starting wages of younger terminees (Table 13–6).

To provide incentives for enrollees to extend their stay, the director of OEO exercised discretionary authority to raise the basic monthly allowance from $30 to $50. Relatively few enrollees received the maximum authorized rates, though an increasing proportion received increases above the minimum (Table 13–7).

Two measures were introduced in the EOA amendments of 1967 to encourage longer duration of stay. Personal allowances were limited to $35 per month during the first six months of enrollment and to $50 per month thereafter. Enrollees had also received readjustment allowances of up to $50 per month upon termination from the corps, but according to the amendments this allowance should be paid only to enrollees who had served at least 90 days in the Corps.

Placement Record

In the final analysis, the effectiveness of the Job Corps will be measured in terms of the education and the training it provides enrollees, and the lasting impact of the experience. Additional benefits

Table 13–6. Selected Data of 1967 Job Corps Terminees by Age

	Age at Termination						
	16	17	18	19	20	21	22
30-day terminees (%)	19.1	17.8	16.1	16.0	15.9	15.6	5.0
Length of stay (months)	3.9	4.4	4.9	5.3	5.4	6.0	8.0
Unemployed terminees (%)	60.1	54.7	50.5	49.1	47.8	47.4	41.7
Starting wage (dollars)	1.41	1.50	1.57	1.57	1.61	1.62	1.82

Source: Job Corps, Office of Economic Opportunity.

Table 13–7.   Allowance Distribution among Job Corps Enrollees

Monthly Pay	May 1967	January 1968
$30	74%	64%
35	11	18
40	8	11
45	4	4
50	3	3
Mean monthly pay	$32.60	$33.20

Source: Job Corps, Office of Economic Opportunity.

may accrue to enrollees, including social development and family stability resulting from a higher income and additional education.[25] Unfortunately, these benefits cannot be measured at this time; in fact, longitudinal studies over many years would be required to gain insights into the extent of these additional effects.

As of October 1, 1967, nearly 110,000 youths had enrolled in and left the Job Corps. In an attempt to fulfill the congressional requirement to gather follow-up information about the employment and earnings records of former corpsmembers, OEO contracted with Louis Harris and Associates to conduct periodic sample follow-up studies. As a result of information collected under these contracts, data are now available for terminees who left centers around August 1966— about their status prior to enrolling in the Job Corps, upon leaving the centers, and at six-month intervals during the succeeding 18 months.[26] Another study was performed for November 1966 terminees, yielding data prior to their enrollment, at termination, and 6 and 12 months later.[27] An attempt was also made to design a control group for the August 1966 terminees by studying "no-shows"—applicants who had been accepted but never entered the program.[28] In addition, a special study was devoted to dropouts.[29]

Basing its conclusions on the early sample studies, OEO estimated that 70 percent were either working, in the military, or enrolled in school, and that the balance was "not placed." Characteristically, OEO does not use the term "unemployed" in connection with former corpsmembers.[30] Similarly, the OEO claim was far too sweeping and generalized. Of more importance than the aggregate figures are the specific details the sample studies yielded on various aspects of the Job Corps placement record, possibly the most comprehensive follow-up data available for any federally supported manpower program (Table 13–8).

Despite this comprehensiveness the data from these studies must be used with caution. Shortcomings in the original as well as in the follow-up samples make it reasonable to conclude that the findings

Table 13–8. *Labor Force Status of August 1966 Job Corps Terminees before Entering and upon Leaving Job Corps and 6 and 12 Months after Termination*[a]

Terminees	Working				Unemployed				In School and Other[b]			
	Before Entering Job Corps	Upon Leaving Job Corps	6 Months Later	12 Months Later	Before Entering Job Corps	Upon Leaving Job Corps	6 Months Later	12 Months Later	Before Entering Job Corps	Upon Leaving Job Corps	6 Months Later	12 Months Later
Total	58%	60%	57%	58%	32%	27%	36%	37%	10%	15%	12%	7%
Graduates	61	59	66	62	29	26	28	32	10	16	9	3
Dropouts	56	61	52	56	34	27	40	39	10	14	13	7
Discharges	56	51	55	54	30	36	37	39	14	16	10	8
Sex												
Men	59	61	57	58	31	26	37	36	10	15	11	8
Women	38	43	51	56	50	40	29	45	12	18	23	5
Race												
Negro	61	62	58	53	29	27	35	40	10	13	9	8
White	52	57	54	63	37	28	39	33	11	17	14	8
Length of Time in Job Corps												
Less than 3 months	50	59	49	52	38	27	43	43	12	17	15	6
3 to 6 months	61	61	56	56	28	25	36	38	11	17	12	9
More than 6 months	58	60	69	66	34	32	27	28	8	10	8	7
Age												
Under 18 years	44	48	44	44	38	28	45	50	18	26	17	10
18 to 19 years	56	62	60	59	33	26	34	33	11	14	10	10
20 years and over	68	65	61	61	28	33	34	36	4	3	9	4

[a] Figures may add up to more than 100 percent because some enrollees were both in school and working during the various periods.

[b] Most were in school. Data do not include former corpsmen who entered military service. If, in the follow-ups, those in the military were included, the over-all figures would be for the 6 months and 12 months respectively: working, 53% and 50%; in school, 10% and 3%; in the military, 7% and 15%; unemployed, 34% and 32%; and other, 1% and 2%.

Source: Louis Harris and Associates, *A Study of August 1966 Terminations from the Job Corps* (March 1967) and *A Study of the Status of August 1966 Job Corps Terminees—12 Months after Termination* (October 1967) (revision).

may not only tend to overestimate the total Job Corps achievements but that the findings from the later follow-up data may be particularly "iffy." The problem with the 12- and 18-month follow-ups is mainly that of a shrinking sample, which became less and less reliable because so many interviewees were "lost"—868 were interviewed for the 6-month follow-up but only 430 for the 18-month follow-up. Use of the 18-month follow-up data is further hampered because they are not completely comparable with the information obtained in earlier surveys.

A major finding (for the August 1966 terminees), as suggested earlier, appears to be a positive correlation between the employment status of former corpsmembers and the time they spent in the Job Corps, although the advantage of the long-term stayers over the short-term stayers seems to have narrowed considerably with the passage of time. Harris observed in his six-month follow-up that "the longer a corpsman stays in the Job Corps, the more likely he is to have worked since leaving the center and the less likely he is to have changed jobs. Longer exposure to the Job Corps thus leads to higher employment and greater job stability."[31]

Job Corps graduates and those who stayed longer than six months —as contrasted with those who stayed less than six months—usually displayed advantages in securing employment after leaving the Corps, although that advantage was not manifested immediately upon leaving the Corps. Six months after termination, over two-thirds of those who remained more than six months were employed. In contrast, less than half of those who remained less than three months had jobs, and only a little over half of those who stayed three to six months. In addition, the rate of employment for the long-term stayers was higher for such individuals than it had been before they entered the Corps.

That the immediate effect of a longer stay in the Job Corps on securing employment was not greater probably reflected the limited assistance the centers offered these youths upon completion of their Job Corps career. Only 6 percent of the youths who obtained jobs immediately upon leaving the centers in August 1966 reported that they had secured employment through the Job Corps. As might be expected, the Job Corps exerted a greater effort for those with longer stays. State employment agencies also exerted greater effort for these, placing 28 percent of those who were in centers more than six months but only 12 percent of those who stayed less than three months.[32]

While both the level and the amount of increase in employment of those who remained over six months became more pronounced six months after they left the Job Corps—up 11 percentage points over preentry as contrasted with only two points immediately after leaving the Corps—the employment rate of corpsmembers who stayed less than three months declined six months later, even though it had temporarily gone up immediately after they left the Corps. Apparently, a short stay in the Job Corps had little lasting effect, and these corpsmembers lost ground a short time after returning to their old environment. It would therefore appear that enrollment of less than three months brought limited, if any, advantage to the corpsmen.

With the passage of time, however, the picture apparently changed. Although the long-term stayers continued to have a higher rate of employment than the short-term stayers, the difference narrowed so that 18 months after corpsmen left the centers, it appeared insignificant—only 3 percentage points higher. (The shortcomings of the 18 month data must be remembered here.)

Differences in the employment record of ex-corpsmembers were also noticeable for other categories than length of stay. Age categories, for example, showed a major difference. Those who were under eighteen years when they entered the Job Corps tended to find less employment than those who were over eighteen, both prior to Job Corps entry and in the months after their stay. This could be expected, of course, in view of the higher unemployment rate of younger workers and the operation of the "aging vat" process. A longer stay in the Corps, however, could offset the handicap of younger age: sixteen- and seventeen-year-old enrollees who remained in centers long enough to graduate had an unemployment level of 34 percent compared with a 45 percent unemployment rate of younger trainees who stayed less than three months.[33]

Women showed greater employment gains than men but lost their early advantage within 18 months after leaving centers, by which time less than half were employed. The drop is apparently accounted for by a temporary or permanent departure from a job because of pregnancy and marriage. Negroes did not do as well as whites; the proportion of black employed fell to about half at 18 months while the whites rose to over two-thirds employed. Harris feels this reflects "the pervasiveness of the national problem of discrimination." As might be expected, the percentage of ex-trainees who went into the military continued to rise as an increasing proportion reached draft age. Six months after termination, 7 percent went into the military; after 12 months this percentage rose to 15, and by 18 months it was almost a fifth.

The hourly pay rates of the former corpsmembers are another aspect of assessing the Job Corps. Again, graduates and those who stayed in the centers longer than six months had higher wage levels and made much greater gains than dropouts or dischargees (Table 13–9). Although prior to enrollment the graduates and dropouts had

Table 13–9.   Average Hourly Wage Rates for August 1966 Job Corps Terminees

Terminees	Pre-Job Corps	After Termination		Net Improvement from Pre-Job Corps
		12 months	18 months	
Men	$1.23	$1.80	$1.90	$ .67
Graduates	1.24	1.92	2.12	.88
Dropouts[a]	1.21	1.69	1.80	.59
Dischargees	1.19	1.79	1.84	.65
Negro	1.23	1.82	1.85	.62
White	1.23	1.82	1.98	.75
Conservation centers	1.21	1.69	1.86	.65
Urban centers	1.26	1.91	1.94	.68
Women	1.14	1.37	1.67	.53

[a] Defined here as those in the Job Corps less than three months.

Source: Louis Harris and Associates, *A Study of the Status of August 1966 Job Corps Terminees 18 Months after Termination* (March 1968), p. 3.

similar wage rates, the average hourly wage gain of the men with the longer stay was 88 cents after 18 months, compared with 59 cents for dropouts. Women showed less improvement than men, possibly reflecting discrimination against the fairer sex in the labor market rather than Job Corps performance, and whites improved more than Negroes. A special breakdown by age showed that length of stay outweighed the lower-age handicap: the younger graduates earned 19 cents an hour more after 18 months than either the younger or the older corpsmen who stayed for the shorter time.[34]

An Assessment

This analysis of Job Corps achievements has been based largely on the data gathered by the surveys of Louis Harris and Associates, particularly those for the August 1966 terminees. The August 1966 terminees were used rather than the November 1966 terminees because a longer series of follow-up data was available. There are, however, substantial differences in the trends between the two groups. No attempt has been made here to summarize or identify the reasons for the discrepancies between the two sets of data. If we assume that the information supplied by the former trainees is accurate, the over-all results would still be subject to reservations because of the previously mentioned shortcomings in both the original and the follow-up samples.

In further assessing the achievements of the Job Corps, it does not follow that the improved employment and wage levels of former trainees were necessarily the result of Job Corps training and education. Improvement could be the result of other factors: a changing labor market, increased military demand, and especially the aging process, inasmuch as the employability of youths increases as they mature. Also, there is evidence for the importance of exogenous factors in the survey of "no-shows" mentioned earlier.[35] Since the "no-shows" displayed characteristics similar to those of youths who entered the Job Corps, it is reasonable to consider them an appropriate control group.

Both groups increased their level and amount of employment, but these were *higher* for the "no-shows" than for corpsmembers. Sixty percent of the former were employed and 27 percent were unemployed six months after their failure to enter the Job Corps; of the August 1966 terminees only 57 percent were employed and 36 percent were unemployed six months later.[36] This would seem to indicate that, relatively, employability was not increased by the Job Corps experience.

As for wages, the differences between the "no-shows" and the ex-corpsmembers (August 1966 terminees) were quite small. Table 13–10 shows that the average improvement of corpsmembers' wages over preentry levels, compared with the improvement of the "no-shows," was only 9 cents more an hour for graduates and 4 cents *less* an hour for dropouts, with a weighted average hourly advantage of 1 cent for both categories. Thus dropouts were comparatively worse off after leaving the program, and Job Corps "results" on wages can be questioned on the basis of the six-month-later wage gain.

It would be a mistake, however, to conclude from these "no-show" data that the Job Corps had no impact. When the record is analyzed in terms of length of stay—namely, for those who stayed more than six months—the value of the Job Corps experience itself appears to have been significant, and it would be a grievous mistake

Table 13–10.   Average Hourly Wage for August 1966 Job Corps Terminees and "No–Shows" from 1966

Wage Variables	Graduates	Dropouts	"No–Shows"
Pre-Job Corps wage	$1.14	$1.19	$1.17
Wage 6 months after termination	1.48	1.40	1.42
Wage gain	.34	.21	.25
Terminees' net improvement compared with "no-shows"	.09	−.04	
Weighted average improvement		.01	

Source: Louis Harris and Associates, *A Study of August 1966 Terminations from the Job Corps* (March 1967) and *A Study of Job Corps "No–Shows": Accepted Applicants Who Did Not Go to a Training Center* (February 1967).

to underestimate it. Those who remained in the Job Corps for more than six months did better than the "no-shows," and were the only group to do so. They earned more than the "no-shows"—$1.50 per hour compared with $1.42 per hour, and a greater proportion found jobs—69 percent versus 60 percent.[37]

There were many other instances (already discussed) in which those who stayed six months or more did better than those who stayed a shorter time. Apparently six months represented the crucial cut-off period needed to make the Job Corps experience a "success," even though the most recent data seem to indicate that those with shorter stays tend to "catch up" with the passage of time. Unfortunately, as has been pointed out, a major problem of the Job Corps has been its inability to keep enrollees in the centers long enough to affect their future employability.

Some observers have argued, upon examination of the pre-employment record of former corpsmen, that youths who remained in the Job Corps for six months or longer could possibly have made it on their own, without the aid of the Corps. Fifty-eight percent of this group were employed prior to entering the Job Corps and 34 percent were unemployed; while of those who stayed less than three months, 50 percent were employed prior to entering the Job Corps and 38 percent were unemployed. Thus the group that stayed the longest demonstrated increased employability from the very start.

The argument is not persuasive. It can be argued that boys who qualify for Harvard (or Muddy Gulch) University could also make it on their own. The need is to establish institutional arrangements that will help eligible Job Corps candidates acquire a basic education and the rudiments of a trade, in turn helping them gain employment and advance at a pace commensurate with their ability and motivation.

Viability of the Job Corps

Considerable progress has been made by the Job Corps during its first three years of operation. Discipline in the centers has been improved as a result of more effective screening and the experience gained by administrators, counselors, and teachers. The enrollees' duration of stay has been lengthened; curricula have been developed; and relations between the centers and surrounding communities have improved. However, much remains to be done before the future of the Job Corps as a viable institution is insured.

Screening processes need improvement to insure that enrollment is limited to those whose needs cannot be met by less costly alternative programs. Vocational training must make greater use of the vocational training community and reject the "go it alone" policy. Trainees must be encouraged to stay longer. For youths who have stayed long enough to complete an assigned course of study, the experience appears to have been meaningful and to have helped them gain employment at a higher wage level than they might otherwise have realized. Although follow-up data seem to indicate that the advantage of the longer over the shorter stay is narrowing, too few corpsmen remain in centers long enough so that the education and training they receive is meaningful in the outside world.

Despite the current vogue of "the culture of poverty," studies have indicated that the aspirations of corpsmen are not very different from those of middle-class youth. Four of every five corpsmen stated that they enrolled in a center to "learn a trade" and more than half said they wanted to "get an education."[38] Based on his extensive studies of the aspirations of youths from impoverished homes, Dr. David Gottlieb concluded that "lower income youth do in fact seek a better life, a life which has the dimensions of what we come to identify with the middle-class."[39] Not surprisingly, he found that poor youths find this goal elusive.

The Job Corps is one institution with the potential of helping disadvantaged youths bridge the gap between aspiration and reality. The harsh fact is that it has helped only a minority of those who sought its aid, despite the relatively ample resources that were allocated to it. The future of the Job Corps as a viable institution therefore remains in doubt and will depend upon its ability to perform the Herculean tasks of efficiently operating residential centers where poor youths will remain long enough to gain an experience meaningful to their futures, and of persuading the dominant sectors of the population that the effort is worth the investment.

Part V

Poverty Is Here to Stay: Is OEO?

14.

POVERTY IS HERE TO STAY: IS OEO?

A decent provision for the poor is the true test of civilization.

Samuel Johnson

The Economic Opportunity Act sought to remedy the causes of poverty rather than merely to mitigate its symptoms. Its goal was not to ease the burdens of poverty by providing cash benefits but to offer the poor the opportunity to lift themselves out of poverty. In practice, income support was often a necessary adjunct to "rehabilitation," but the thrust of the EOA programs was essentially one of self-help.

The various Economic Opportunity Act efforts have in one way or another helped millions; and new approaches were tried for age-old problems. However, because of the orientation, these efforts bypassed many who could not benefit from the self-help approach, and they failed to reach additional millions because of limited funds. Even for those who were helped, the assistance was frequently minor, and there was rarely immediate or perceptible improvement. Thus, though poverty sharply declined during the years of the Great Society, the most ardent friends of the EOA would not credit its programs with contributing much to this improvement.

An Evaluator's Lot

The uncertain impact of the EOA programs is not necessarily a reflection of their worth but rather a recognition that there are no reliable measurements that one can use to make conclusive judgments about program effectiveness. Since it takes time for opportunities to be realized and effects to be felt, most EOA programs are still too new to permit appraisal of their value as antipoverty tools. For example, the first participants in Head Start have barely reached their tenth birthday, and it would be premature to anticipate the lasting impact of the children's experience in the antipoverty program. If Head Start is to produce long-term results, society will have to provide other compensatory opportunities as the children progress in their school careers.

An evaluator finds it hard to determine which programs have been successful enough to warrant expansion and which could be cut back or eliminated without undue loss. The dearth of reliable data, mentioned earlier, adds to the evaluator's difficulties. But even if the results of a program were measurable and quantified so as to determine its effectiveness, consideration would have to be given to its relationship to the total antipoverty effort. Thus, while the Job Corps may be expensive and produce few successful graduates, it could be the only measure to help some enrollees. And the selection of priorities and the rejection of existing programs must remain largely a matter of value judgment and gut feeling, all model building and computer-generated data notwithstanding. Formulas have yet to be devised which permit "scientific" judgment about the relative superiority of a million dollars expended on locally planned and designed cultural projects for the poor compared with an equal amount for a job creation project devised in Washington. If self-determination is an essential ingredient in combating poverty, then locally planned and administered programs might have an added intrinsic value that should be properly considered and weighted in evaluating antipoverty efforts. An effective antipoverty design might include apparent inefficiencies and "frills" which in the long run could prove effective in motivating the poor.

The difficulties of evaluating the EOA programs and comparing their effectiveness does not mean that once a program has started it should continue indefinitely. The worth of specific programs can be assessed, and judgments on their effectiveness can be made, in light of explicitly stated assumptions. Thus Upward Bound is a poor program if securing maximum feasible participation by parents and community action agencies is considered a higher priority than helping youths from poor homes to enter college. Legal Services may be important to instill dignity and self-reliance in the poor and to help protect their rights, even if some legal aid activities do not have any bearing on raising the income of clients. VISTA can be criticized for frittering away much of its resources on a lot of small projects in many large cities, but there is no way to measure the total impact of the "good works" performed on hundreds of VISTA projects. Rural loans appear to be a poor investment if the goal is achieving economic independence, but it may be an acceptable means of providing income maintenance under the guise of self-help. In assisting rural migrant and seasonal labor, OEO could not decide whether its programs should concentrate on "keeping 'em down on the farm" or on aiding farm laborers to move into urban areas where the jobs are. Similar issues remained unresolved in Indian assistance programs. The significance of participatory democracy as an antipoverty tool is impossible to measure. Participation of the poor is closely intertwined with other forces that operate slowly and by indirection.

It is not surprising, therefore, that the General Accounting Office, after spending more than a year on a detailed examination of the Economic Opportunity Act programs, despaired of carrying out its mandate to recommend to Congress the future direction of the Act. The GAO report, while evaluating individual programs, did not indicate priorities. The Senate Subcommittee on Employment, Manpower, and Poverty undertook a similar exercise in 1967 but also failed to spell out program priorities.

The public may demand a more definitive judgment about the impact of the Economic Opportunity Act, and Congress must determine again the future scope of the legislation and the magnitude of its programs. Given the immensity of the needs and the paucity of funds, this evaluator would conclude that the funds expended on EOA self-help programs have been a worthwhile investment, but this is only a subjective testimonial, and proof is lacking. However, available evidence mixed with a dose of value judgment indicates the need for expansion of some programs and the curtailment of others.

The adage that "an ounce of prevention is worth a pound of cure" seems to be the case with the EOA programs. On the basis of cost effectiveness criteria, the birth control program appears to be the best investment of antipoverty dollars. Economic consideratons are not enough, however; opposition to this program has come from another quarter. Thus, OEO has rationalized its timidity in funding birth control projects on the ground that excessive zeal in this area would bring criticism upon the agency and place its other programs in jeopardy. The argument does not appear persuasive in light of the demonstrated effectiveness and increased public acceptance of the birth control program. Efforts to prevent poverty with "the pill" should be substantially increased.

OEO programs have contributed important insights about approaches to the solution of old social problems. The Head Start experience has indicated that we start public education too late, at least for children from poor families. By the time they reach public school age, many of these children are already "retarded" compared with children raised in a more favorable environment. There is evidence that these disadvantages can be overcome, or at least minimized, by providing child development programs at age three and earlier. But even this popular program has its detractors. Some cautious scholars have warned about the "fade-out" effects of a short summer program. The failure of the program to leave lasting results should not be surprising, since it is unrealistic to expect the debilitating effects of living in poverty for four or five years to be overcome by an eight-week summer project. This suggests the need for universal nursery and kindergarten, supplemented by nutritional and health programs, for all poor children.

Recommendations for retrenchment are more difficult. Obviously there is fat in almost all EOA programs, but it is more pronounced in the Job Corps than in the others. President Nixon joined in a favorite pastime of OEO critics when he condemned the Job Corps as being too expensive an effort. The President's criticism was not merely campaign rhetoric, though he exaggerated the annual cost per enrollee in Job Corps centers. With the wisdom of hindsight it can be concluded that much of the billion dollars allocated to the Job Corps during its first four years could have been more wisely spent elsewhere, particularly the funds expended on conservation and women's centers. At an annual cost of $7,400 per youth, it is difficult to justify assigning enrollees to conservation work; the Job Corps should concentrate instead on the needs of the youth. Another statutory provision requiring that Job Corps enrollment be equally divided between the sexes also needs reexamination. It is not that females should be given less consideration than males, but experience shows that they do not utilize Job Corps training. Past performance does not seem to justify the expenditures, and the savings from reducing the scale of the program should be allocated to other programs.

After four years of experience it is also time for OEO to take a hard look at the community action programs. A good place to start is with the decision to spread CAP funds among more than a thousand areas. While the poor, regardless of where they live, deserve OEO help, it does not follow that OEO can reach them all. With current funds, CAP can expend only about $45 a year per poor person. While it may be difficult for OEO officials to exclude poor people from CAP just because they reside in the "wrong" place (where there are few poor people), the cause of antipoverty is not served by spreading CAP's meagre resources thin. At the local level, some CAA's might better concentrate on designing effective new systems for delivering services to the poor than on rhetoric favoring transformation of society. Neighborhood centers have been a useful rediscovery of CAP, but CAA's have not had the muscle or the know-how to secure from old-line agencies in the communities cooperation in the delivery of vital services.

Restructuring OEO

Whatever the allocation of funds within and between programs, a question that remains unanswered is whether the Office of Economic Opportunity is the proper mechanism for administering antipoverty dollars. Should OEO survive, or should its resources be allocated to other agencies? If the elimination of poverty is to remain a prime national goal, then there is room, indeed a necessity, to include in the federal establishment an agency dedicated to its realization.

Experience indicates some basic faults in the initial design, however. The Act charged OEO with two distinct responsibilities: (1) planning, coordinating, and mobilizing antipoverty efforts; and (2) operating several programs established under the Act. OEO assumed direct responsibility for operation of the Job Corps, Community Action Program, migrant and seasonal labor programs, and VISTA, while delegating administration of the remaining programs to other federal agencies. Even advocates of OEO cannot claim that the agency has made a serious effort to plan and monitor federal antipoverty efforts and to mobilize federal, state, and local resources to aid the poor. Preoccupied with day-to-day operational responsibilities, OEO is another illustration of Senator Jacob K. Javits' observation: "Program operations drive out planning and innovation."

Congress recognized these failures and tried to remedy them. However, congressional attempts to secure information about OEO's long-range planning have been frustrated. What planning was done has been pigeonholed within the federal executive establishment and has been unavailable to the public because of "executive privilege." The Johnson Administration apparently decided that neither Congress nor the public was ready to be exposed to grand plans aimed at eradicating poverty by huge federal expenditures. Congress also sought to strengthen the capability of the executive branch to coordinate antipoverty efforts by empowering the cabinet-level Economic Opportunity Council, which has this role, to hire its own staff; but President Johnson ignored this legislative initiative. As a result, the Great Society's effort to coordinate antipoverty programs was assigned to a special assistant in the White House, who performed the task on a part-time basis. In the claims for budget allocation, OEO was just another agency in the Executive branch and had little influence on setting priorities.

In the Nixon Administration, coordination of federal antipoverty efforts is apparently to be carried out by the Urban Affairs Council in the Executive Office of the President. While it is too early to pass judgment on this arrangement, experience with welfare programs argues against this mechanism if antipoverty efforts are to remain a major goal of the administration. The Urban Affairs Council will be concerned with the numerous pressing problems of our cities, and in its jurisdiction are measures which help all sectors of the population. Experience has shown that institutions that serve the rich and the poor normally tend to ignore the needs of the poor and aid their more affluent clients. Even with the best intentions, it is likely that before too long the Urban Affairs Council will focus upon the needs of the majority and will ignore the poor, who have little political clout. The case for funding special programs in aid of the poor and for establishing a special council in the Executive Office of the President charged with the responsibility of planning, coordinating, and evaluating antipoverty efforts is persuasive. If added prestige is desired, it might help to require the advice and consent of the Senate in appointing the members of such a council. This idea was first proposed by the Republican Opportunity Crusade of 1967. President Nixon has apparently chosen to ignore the proposal, as did his predecessor.

Once the planning, coordinating, and evaluating functions of OEO are separated from its operating responsibilities, the scope of the reconstituted agency must be determined. There is little to be said for continuing the present arrangement whereby OEO indefinitely delegates programs to other agencies. Once a program is entrusted to another agency and appropriate guidelines have been established that guarantee the rights of the poor under the measure, OEO's responsibility should cease. Funneling funds through OEO complicates, rather than solves, administrative problems. Thus the manpower programs under Title IB of the Economic Opportunity Act could be transferred altogether to the Labor Department, and a revised Job Corps might be added as part of a comprehensive manpower package. This would leave OEO with a number of operating responsibilities.

The present organization of CAP is a product of happenstance, and the role of CAA's in Model Cities is ambiguous. As programs evolved, CAP assumed certain responsibilities and funded selected activities while it neglected or delegated others. A sound arrangement would be to transfer all proven and established programs to other agencies for administration. OEO (or whatever the antipoverty agency might be called) could then focus its resources on demonstration and experimental projects, transferring successful ones and abandoning those falling short of their mark. CAP has proven a useful tool in developing and testing innovative approaches and in nourishing participation by the poor, even if it was not "maximum." There are signs, however, that it is growing less flexible with age. If CAP becomes another bureaucracy with a specified set of functions, its major contribution will diminish. If it is to remain a viable agency it should concentrate on experimental programs in aid of the poor.

One experimental program that is an excellent candidate to be added as a major CAP effort is support of community development corporations. CAP has already funded a few such projects; given additional funds, it could experiment with more community-based development programs. Where feasible, experimental community-centered projects that are aimed at the rehabilitation of slum areas or at helping their poor residents should be part of the community action program. The challenge to the federal community action agency would be to encourage and fund worthwhile programs and to continue only those that gain acceptability. If it fails in this mission, it may as well wither away.

Consideration should also be given to overhauling the distribution and allocation of community action funds. The federal government does not operate community action agencies; its role should be to fund activities of these agencies within broad guidelines and not to dictate operational details. The experience of OEO has indicated that funding on a project-by-project basis is wasteful and tends to impose federal judgments on details best left to the communities. OEO practice has led to a proliferation of disjointed projects and efforts, frequently just for the sake of encouraging participation, without improving services to the poor. Conceptually, it would appear that OEO can best discharge its responsibilities to a community by providing the funds, leaving the community to decide the structure of their organizations as well as the programs they undertake.

This begs the question of the role of the state, city halls, court houses, and community groups in administering CAP funds. In rural areas, states will have to play an important part since smaller rural communities rarely possess the technical expertise and institutions needed to develop viable programs. But in urban areas, a case can be made for direct funding to city hall or local groups, although state agencies control significant sources of funds and vital services. On balance, it appears desirable to include the states as partners in a federal effort. Since there is also a need for funding specific experimental projects, and for helping communities where states are recalcitrant, it might be practical to distribute a fixed percentage, say 70 percent, of total funds to states on the basis of predetermined formulas, using the remainder for experimental projects or for direct help where states or communities fail to carry out federal objectives.

The states would then be faced with choosing between city halls and local community groups to administer their funds. This is not as difficult a choice as one might expect from the image of constant friction between CAA's and city halls. This friction was more a creation of the mass media looking for the man-bites-dog story than a reflection of reality. Where conflicts did exist, they have usually been resolved. Some communities have created semi-public or private community action agencies, others have operated through their elected officials; but in most cases at least a moderately successful accommodation has evolved, and there is no apparent reason to disturb this arrangement.

What Would It Take To Eliminate Poverty?

The discussion thus far has been limited to the EOA programs. However, Congress and the Nixon Administration do not have to

settle for merely streamlining the administration of the 1964 antipoverty law and improving program operations. Society could raise its
sights and focus on the elimination of poverty, an undertaking that
would require a sustained effort involving allocation of vast resources.
It would call not only for expansion of self-help programs but also
for income maintenance programs. The crucial question is whether
the American people consider the elimination of poverty a high
priority goal.

Few would disagree that the United States has the capacity to
raise the income of all its poor above the poverty threshold. The
aggregate poverty gap of the 22 million poor in 1967 was "only" $10
billion, based on current poverty income criteria. Latest available
data would support a poverty threshold about one-third higher than
that used by the government. A plan that would guarantee a poverty-
threshold income for all, with realistic incentives to keep the poor
and near-poor wage earners in the labor force, might carry an annual
price tag of $20 billion to $25 billion.

Whatever the income deficit of the poor, an effective antipoverty
effort must provide more than income maintenance. Since the government has assumed the responsibility of providing many social
services which are currently taken for granted, raising the income of
the poor would not reduce this responsibility. In addition, the services
provided by EOA programs would have to be radically expanded if
the antipoverty effort were to be accelerated.

Over a century ago it was decided that free schooling would be
made available to all. While publicly supported education has con-
tinually expanded, little attention has been given to lowering the
entry age. With present funds, Head Start can provide year-round
facilities for one of every fifteen poor children and for one in five
during the summer months. Universal Head Start is only a first step.
Considerably more needs to be done to improve the quality of education throughout the primary and secondary schools, particularly in
poverty areas. Since a college sheepskin is possibly the best insurance
against poverty, children from poor homes with the required intellectual capacity would benefit from special help in getting into college
and from financial assistance in remaining there.

While additional expenditures for education will undoubtedly
prepare more students for work, there will remain many youths who
will fail in school—or, some would say, whom school fails—and they
will need remedial education, prevocational training, and employment
opportunities. There is a need for expanded community skill centers
to make remedial training accessible to all, and residential facilities
must also be provided to homeless youths or those in isolated rural
areas.

There is also a variety of community services, some of which are provided by OEO funds. Health care is increasingly becoming a responsibility of government. The government's health care bill for the poor is already about $10 billion per year and rising rapidly. Considering the vast expansion of medical services in aid of the poor in recent years, the most crucial public policy consideration is a more efficient utilization of the resources allocated to health programs. OEO's neighborhood health centers offer one example of a promising effort to improve the delivery of health services to the poor. Finally, planned parenthood and birth control programs need additional funds from the present, or in any expanded, war on poverty.

Although this discussion focuses on the development of human resources, environmental factors cannot be ignored. The housing needs of the poor require no elaboration, and the physical rehabilitation of our cities goes hand-in-hand with investment in human resources. Metropolitan problems are not exclusively those of income, jobs, and welfare services.

This oversimplified catalogue of programs for fighting poverty would cost about $20 billion, so that the annual bill for an effective antipoverty war would be in the vicinity of $40 billion, about equally divided between income maintenance and outlays for goods and services. The nation could afford these expenditures without added taxes by utilizing the additional revenue generated by normal economic growth. This assumes, however, that a major proportion of the extra taxes collected by the federal government in the 1970's would be allocated to aid the poor, and that other national programs would remain at about their present level or expand only slightly.

There is little evidence that the American people are willing to assign a top priority to a real war on poverty. Realism would dictate that in the years immediately ahead it would be more useful to concentrate on a gradual expansion of the modest antipoverty efforts initiated by the Great Society and to make the best use of on-going efforts and resources. Admittedly, in the long run this piecemeal approach will involve greater costs than an "unconditional war on poverty." The application of a systems approach should be helpful. The task of Head Start and compensatory education becomes increasingly difficult if the child is brought up in a family where the father is unemployed or the family lives on a dollar a day per person, the level of relief provided in the majority of states. It would be unthinkable to send a soldier to fight in Vietnam without providing him with ammunition, housing, medical aid, and a myriad of other supportive services. We should apply the same standards to the domestic war. However, given the current climate, talk about the imminent elimination of poverty is indulgence in exhortation rather than a practical guide for action.

As long as society continues grudgingly to provide help to the poor, as manifested by the poor laws over the centuries, we must settle for improving the administrative efficiency of the 1964 poor law and augmenting its operations. Therefore, the continuance in the federal Establishment of an agency whose sole mission is to help the poor and to help design new exits from poverty is appropriate. For the foreseeable future it appears that the biblical admonition that "the poor shall never cease out of the land" will hold for our society.

Notes

Chapter 1

1. Dr. Roger H. Davidson collaborated in the research on this chapter; his version was published in John Bibby and Roger Davidson, *On Capitol Hill: Studies in the Legislative Process* (New York: Holt, Rinehart & Winston, 1967), pp. 219–51. Another account of the Economic Opportunity Act's legislative history is presented in James L. Sundquist, *Politics and Policy* (Washington: The Brookings Institution), pp. 111–54.

2. Alfred Marshall, *Principles of Economics* 3d ed.; London: Macmillan & Co., Ltd., 1895), p. 2.

3. Quoted in Herman P. Miller, *Poverty: American Style* (Belmont, Calif.: Wadsworth Publishing Co., 1966), p. 5.

4. Statement made in 1909; quoted in *Encyclopaedia Britannica* (1950 ed.), 18:220.

5. George H. Dunne, S.J., ed., *Poverty in Plenty* (New York: P. J. Kenedy & Sons, 1964), p. 122.

6. U.S. Congress, Senate Committee on Commerce, *The Speeches of Senator John F. Kennedy, Presidential Campaign of 1960*, 87th Cong., 1st sess., S. Rept. 994 (Washington: Government Printing Office, 1961), part I, p. 18.

7. Herman P. Miller, *Rich Man, Poor Man* (New York: Thomas Y. Crowell Company, 1964), p. 37.

8. John K. Galbraith, *The Affluent Society* (Boston: Houghton Mifflin Company, 1958), p. 73.

9. U.S. Congress, Joint Committee on the Economic Report, *Low-Income Families and Economic Stability*, 81st Cong., 2d sess., S. Doc. 146 (Washington: Government Printing Office, 1950); *idem*, Subcommittee on Low-Income Families, *Low-Income Families*, Hearings, November 18, 19, 21, 22, 23, 1955, 84th Cong., 1st sess. (Washington: Government Printing Office, 1955).

10. The Douglas campaign to aid economically depressed areas is summarized in Sar A. Levitan, *Federal Aid to Depressed Areas* (Baltimore: The Johns Hopkins Press, 1964).

11. New York State, Governor's Message to the Legislature, January 30, 1957.

12. U.S. Congress, Senate Special Committee on Unemployment Problems . . ., *Report on Unemployment Problems*, 86th Cong., 2d sess., S. Rept. 1206 (Washington: Government Printing Office, 1960). This committee also printed nine volumes of hearings; a compendium on unemployment problems, *Readings in Unemployment* (Washington: Government Printing Office, 1960); and a volume of essays, *Studies in Unemployment* (Washington: Government Printing Office, 1960).

13. *Ibid.*, Joint Economic Committee, *Low-Income Population and Economic Growth*, 86th Cong., 1st sess., Study Paper 12, December 16, 1959 (Washington: Government Printing Office, 1959).

14. James Morgan, David Martin, Wilbur J. Cohen, and Harvey Brazer, *Income and Welfare in the United States* (Study by the Survey Research Center, Institute for Social Research, University of Michigan) (New York: McGraw-Hill Book Company, 1962); and Conference on Economic Progress, *Poverty and Deprivation in the United States* (Washington: The Conference, 1962).

15. Dwight MacDonald, "Our Invisible Poor," *The New Yorker*, January 19, 1963, pp. 82–92.

16. Galbraith, *The Affluent Society*, p. 328.

17. Herman P. Miller, "Is the Income Gap Closed? 'No!'" *New York Times Magazine*, November 11, 1962.

18. Communications Workers of America, *Proceedings of the 25th Annual Convention, 1963*, p. 141.

19. Homer Bigart, "Kentucky Miners: A Grim Winter," *New York Times*, October 20, 1963.

20. Walter W. Heller, "American Poverty: Its Causes and Cures," address delivered at the Seventh Annual Public Affairs Forum, Indiana State College, Indiana, Pa., March 25, 1965, p. 4.

21. Quoted in Peter Marris and Martin Rein, *Dilemmas of Social Reform: Poverty and Community Action in the United States* (New York: Atherton Press, 1967), p. 43.

22. Roger H. Davidson, "Poverty and the New Federalism," in Sar A. Levitan and Irving H. Siegel, eds., *Dimensions of Manpower Policy: Programs and Research* (Baltimore: The Johns Hopkins Press, 1966), pp. 61–80.

23. Public Law 880, 84th Cong., "Social Security Amendments of 1956," Title XI, sec. 331.

24. Daniel P. Moynihan, "What Is 'Community Action'?" *Public Interest*, no. 5 (Fall 1966), pp. 3–8.

25. Murray Kempton, "The Essential Sargent Shriver," *New Republic*, March 28, 1964, p. 13.

26. *Ibid.*

27. "Poverty U.S.A.," *Newsweek*, February 17, 1964, p. 38.

28. Kempton, "The Essential Sargent Shriver," p. 13.

29. President's Task Force on Manpower Conservation, *One-Third of a Nation* (Washington: Government Printing Office, 1964).

30. Quoted in Lillian Rubin, "Maximum Feasible Participation: The Origins, Implications, and Present Status," *Poverty and Human Resources Abstracts*, November–December 1967, p. 6.

31. U.S. Congress, House Committee on Education and Labor, *Poverty in the United States*, 88th Cong., 2d sess. (Washington: Government Printing Office, 1964).

32. *Ibid., Hearings on Poverty*, 88th Cong., 2d sess. (Washington: Government Printing Office, 1964), part I, p. 22.

33. *Ibid.*, p. 58.

34. *Ibid.*, part III, p. 1150.

35. *Congressional Record* (daily ed.), August 8, 1964, p. 18042.

36. *Congressional Quarterly, 1964 Almanac* (Washington: Congressional Quarterly Service, 1965), p. 226.

37. *Congressional Record* (daily ed.), July 31, 1964, pp. 16209–11.

38. *Ibid.*, p. 16212.

39. *Ibid.*, p. 16213.

40. U.S. Congress, House Committee on Education and Labor, *Economic Opportunity Act of 1964*, 88th Cong., 1st sess., H. Rept. 1458 (Washington: Government Printing Office), p. 19.

41. *Ibid., Hearings on Poverty*, 88th Cong., 2d sess. (Washington: Government Printing Office, 1964), part I, p. 530.

42. *Congressional Record* (daily ed.), July 23, 1964, p. 16203.

Chapter 2

1. Recommendation of Manpower and Employment Conference, National Association for Community Development, December 1965.

2. A discussion of CAMPS is found in Garth L. Mangum, *MDTA: Foundation of a Manpower Policy* (Baltimore: The Johns Hopkins Press, 1968), pp. 71–75.

3. James L. Sundquist, "Issues of Organization and Coordination," U.S. Congress, Senate Committee on Labor and Public Welfare, Subcommittee on Employment, Manpower, and Poverty, *Examination of the War on Poverty, Staff and Consultant Reports*, 90th Cong., 1st sess. (Washington: Government Printing Office, 1967), III, 787.

4. *Ibid.*, p. 788.

5. U.S. Congress, Senate Committee on Labor and Public Welfare, Subcommittee on Employment, Manpower, and Poverty, *Economic Opportunity Amendments of 1967*, Report 563, 90th Cong., 1st sess. (Washington: Government Printing Office, 1967), p. 6. A fuller discussion of manpower coordination is presented by Sar A. Levitan and Garth L. Mangum in *Federal Training and Work Programs in the Sixties* (Ann Arbor, Mich.: The Institute of Labor and Industrial Relations, The University of Michigan, 1969), chapter 9.

6. Robert Walters, "Poverty Agency Shifts Power to Regional Units," *Washington Evening Star*, December 9, 1965.

7. Commencement address at The University of Michigan, Ann Arbor, May 22, 1964. A discussion of "creative federalism" is presented by Roger H. Davidson, "Poverty and the New Federalism," in Sar A. Levitan and Irving H. Siegel, eds., *Dimensions of Manpower Policy* (Baltimore: The Johns Hopkins Press, 1966), pp. 61–80.

8. Address of R. Sargent Shriver at Governors' Conference, 57th Annual Meeting, Minneapolis, July 28, 1965.

9. "New Force Focuses on Urban Ills," *Business Week* (June 24, 1967), p. 75.

10. See above, n. 3, vol. VIII.

11. Ray Reed, "Wallace Vetoes a Poverty Grant," *New York Times*, May 13, 1965.

12. *Congressional Record* (daily ed.), August 17, 1965, pp. 18888–89 (Senate) and September 15, 1965, pp. 23073–78 (House).

13. *Ibid.*, October 4, 1967, p. S14147.

14. Terry Sanford, "Poverty's Challenge to the States," *Law and Contemporary Problems* (Duke University School of Law [Winter 1966]), p. 7.

15. U.S. Congress, Senate Committee on Labor and Public Welfare, Subcommittee on Employment, Manpower, and Poverty, *Examination of the War on Poverty, Hearings*, 90th Cong., 1st sess. (Washington: Government Printing Office, 1967), part 1, p. 104. For an opposing view, see Paul Ylvisaker's testimony, pp. 138–57.

16. *Ibid.*, House Committee on Education and Labor, *Hearings on Economic Opportunity Act*, 88th Cong., 2d sess. (Washington: Government Printing Office, 1964), part 2, pp. 822 and 790.

17. See above, n. 3, pp. 801–2.

18. Robert Walters, "Mayors Can Have Veto over Poverty Programs," *Washington Evening Star*, March 23, 1966.

19. Eve Edstrom, "Powell Would Halt War on Poverty Rather than Give Veto to Mayors," *Washington Post*, March 28, 1966.

20. OEO, Community Action Program, *Organizing Communities for Action under the 1967 Amendments*, February 1968.

21. Eve Edstrom, "OEO 'Guide' Is Blasted on 3 Fronts," *Washington Post*, February 14, 1968.

22. Jonathan Spivak, "Poverty Planners Fear Program's Switch to Public Control May Spur Bitter Battles," *Wall Street Journal*, February 12, 1968.

23. See above, n. 15, part 9, pp. 2711–12.

24. "On Relief, Wages, Jobs," letter to the editor of the *Washington Post*, February 2, 1968, and Jonathan Spivak, "Replacing Welfare," *Wall Street Journal*, October 11, 1968.

25. For accounts of the inspection function during Haddad's tenure, see Joseph A. Loftus in the *New York Times*, August 1, 1965, and Walter Pincus in the *Washington Evening Star*, August 11, 1965.

26. Edgar May, *The Wasted Americans* (New York: Harper and Row, 1964).

27. "Poverty Program: Dim Issue" (a *Monitor* survey), *Christian Science Monitor*, June 22, 1966.

28. Address at the National Conference on Poverty in the Southwest, Tucson, Ariz., January 25, 1965.

29. *Congressional Record* (daily ed.), August 5, 6, 7, 1964, pp. 17610–52, 17672–739, 17932–18025.

30. U.S. Congress, Senate Committee on Labor and Public Welfare, *Economic*

Opportunity Amendments of 1965, Report 599, 89th Cong., 1st sess. (Washington: Government Printing Office, 1965), p. 68.

31. Richard L. Lyons, "Shriver Says Hot Line Helps in Peace Corps, War on Poverty," *Washington Post*, April 27, 1965.

32. Public Law 89–309, October 31, 1965.

33. See above, n. 30, pp. 59–60.

34. *Congressional Record* (daily ed.), July 28, 1965, p. A4157, and August 18, 1965, p. 20076.

35. U.S. Congress, House Committee on Education and Labor, *Examination of the War on Poverty Program*, 89th Cong., 1st sess. (Washington: Government Printing Office, 1965), pp. 30–32.

36. *Ibid., Economic Opportunity Act*, Report on H.R. 10440, Report 1458, 88th Cong., 2d sess. (Washington: Government Printing Office, 1964), p. 11.

37. *Congressional Record* (daily ed.), August 6, 1964, pp. 17674–76.

38. Section 124(a)(3). This identical provision also appears in the Higher Education Act of 1965 P.L. 89–329), Section 441(a)(2)(B).

39. The suit was filed by Protestants and Other Americans United for Separation of Church and State (POAU), *New York Times*, August 2, 1965.

40. *Poverty*, a statement by the Interreligious Committee against Poverty (Washington, 1967), p. 3.

41. Austin C. Wehrwein, "Shriver Calls on Social Workers to Help Antipoverty Campaign," *New York Times*, December 3, 1965.

42. Address to the American Public Welfare Association, Chicago, Ill., December 2, 1965.

43. Task Force on Economic Growth and Opportunity, U.S. Chamber of Commerce, *The Concept of Poverty; Poverty: The Sick, Disabled and Aged*; and *The Disadvantaged Poor* (Washington: The Chamber, 1965 and 1966).

44. Dennis Duggan, "Blue Chips Sign Up in War on Poverty," *New York Herald Tribune*, February 28, 1965.

45. Stephen Kurzman, "Private Enterprise Participation in the Antipoverty Program," (see above n. 3; I: 89–148); and William C. Selover, "The Other War on Poverty: Stepping into Aid-to-Poor Gaps," *Christian Science Monitor*, December 28, 1966.

46. John McHale, "Big Business Enlists for the War on Poverty," *Trans-Action* (May–June 1965), pp. 3–9.

47. Paul Hencke, "Is War on Poverty Becoming War on Business?" *Nation's Business*, March 1966, pp. 40 ff.; and Shirley Scheibla, *Poverty Is Where the Money Is* (New Rochelle, N.Y.: Arlington House, 1968), chapters 12 and 13.

48. AFL–CIO, *Labor's Role in the War on Poverty* (Washington: AFL–CIO, 1965), p. 1.

49. "The War on Poverty," statement of the AFL–CIO Executive Council, Bal Harbour, Fla., February 1967.

50. William C. Selover, "Labor Leaders Find Active Role in Fight against Poverty," *Christian Science Monitor*, January 5, 1967.

51. *Ibid.*

52. Quoted in Donald Pfarrer, "NAACP Polled: Poverty War Is More 'White Paternalism,'" *Washington Evening Star*, June 29, 1965.

53. *Baltimore Sun*, December 1, 1965.

54. OEO Press Release 67–203, August 3, 1967; and Stuart Auerbach, "Hate School Got U.S. Aid, Police Say," *Washington Post*, August 4, 1967.

55. Editorial, "Farmer, Powell and the OEO," *New York Times*, July 9, 1965.

56. Accounts of the history of the proposal are found in Joseph A. Loftus, "Doomed Literacy Drive," *New York Times*, July 6, 1966; and Ernest A. Ostro, "Suddenly, A Project to Teach Illiterates Was Dead," *Washington Evening Star*, August 23, 1966.

57. Gerald Grant, "OEO Denies Politics Stalled Farmer Feud," *Washington Post*, July 5, 1966.

58. National Advisory Council on Economic Opportunity, *Focus on Community Action* (Washington: Government Printing Office, 1968).

59. Robert Walters, "Poor Get Top Poverty Advisory Role," *Washington Evening Star*, January 23, 1966.

60. U.S. Congress, Senate Committee on Appropriations, *Supplemental Appropriations for Fiscal Year 1968*, 90th Cong., 1st sess. (Washington: Government Printing Office, 1968), p. 3.

61. See above, n. 15, part 1, p. 134.

62. U.S. Congress, House Appropriations Committee, *Hearings on Supplemental Appropriation Bill, 1967*, 89th Cong., 2d sess. (Washington: Government Printing Office, 1966), p. 40.

63. *Ibid.*, *Hearings on Supplemental Appropriation Bill, 1968*, 90th Cong., 1st sess. (Washington: Government Printing Office, 1967), p. 141.

64. Erwin Knoll and Jules Witcover, "Maximum Feasible Publicity: The War on Poverty's Campaign to Capture the Press," *Columbia Journalism Review* (Fall 1966), p. 40.

65. Section 602(i). The agency was explicitly exempted from the normal statutory restrictions on public information functions by federal agencies (United States Code, Section 4154 of Title 39).

66. See above, n. 64, p. 34.

67. See above, n. 5, S. Rept. 563, p. 193.

68. See above, n. 64, p. 35.

69. Republican National Committee press release, July 8, 1966, p. 1 (italics in original). The GOP report, "The Alleviation of Poverty," was prepared by its Task Force on the Functions of Federal, State, and Local Governments, a group chaired by Congressman Robert Taft, Jr., of Ohio.

70. OEO press release, July 8, 1966.

71. Willard Edwards, "OEO Uses Poverty Funds to Belittle GOP, Ford Says," *Chicago Tribune*, July 14, 1966.

72. U.S. Congress, House Committee on Education and Labor, *Economic Opportunity Act Amendments of 1967*, Hearings, 90th Cong., 1st sess. (Washington: Government Printing Office, 1967), part 2, pp. 874–75, 880–81.

73. John Kenneth Galbraith, *The Affluent Society* (Boston: Houghton Mifflin Company, 1958), p. 328.

74. Joseph A. Loftus, "How the Poverty Bill Was Saved in the House," *New York Times*, December 25, 1967.

75. William C. Selover, "Antipoverty Program Stumbles in Congress," *Christian Science Monitor*, October 12, 1967.

76. Richard L. Lyons, "City Hall Amendment Key to OEO Victory," *Washington Post*, November 19, 1967.

77. William Greider, "Poverty Bill Boosts Perkins' Esteem," *Louisville Courier-Journal*, November 21, 1967.

78. Guest editorial by Rep. Albert H. Quie in *Rochester* (Minnesota) *Post-Bulletin*, January 13, 1968.

79. Joseph W. Sullivan, "House GOP 'Activism' Takes a Drubbing," *Wall Street Journal*, November 17, 1967; and Tom Littlewood, "Poverty Bill Fight Highlights Rivalry in the GOP," *Chicago Sun-Times*, November 19, 1967.

Chapter 3

1. U.S. Congress, House Committee on Education and Labor, *Hearings on Economic Opportunity Act*, 88th Cong., 2nd sess. (Washington: Government Printing Office, 1964), part 1, p. 304.

2. Peter Marris and Martin Rein, *Dilemmas of Social Reform* (New York: Atherton Press, 1967), pp. 132–36.

3. *Hearings on Economic Opportunity Act*, p. 332.

4. *Ibid.*, p. 332.

324 NOTES

5. *Ibid.*, p. 333.
6. *Ibid.*, II, 728.
7. *Ibid.*, p. 768.
8. *Ibid.*, p. 822.
9. Lillian Rubin, "Maximum Feasible Participation," *Poverty and Human Resources Abstracts* (November–December 1967), p. 6.
10. Office of Economic Opportunity, Memorandum from the Director, "Involvement of the Poor in All OEO Programs," September 9, 1966.
11. American Arbitration Association, *Representation Election and Voter Participation in Community Action Programs under OEO*, June 15, 1966 (mimeographed), pp. 8–11.
12. Joseph A. Loftus, "Election of Poor May be Ended," *New York Times*, March 9, 1966.
13. Jules Witcover and Erwin Knoll, "Politics and the Poor," *Reporter* (December 30, 1965), pp. 23–26; and Barbara Carter, "Sargent Shriver and the Role of the Poor," *Reporter*, (May 5, 1966), pp. 17–20.
14. U.S. Conference of Mayors, *Economic Opportunity in Cities* (Washington: The Conference, January 1966), p. 26. Italics in original.
15. William C. Selover, "U.S. Poor Gain Foothold in Local Programs," *Christian Science Monitor*, August 2, 1966.
16. Nan Robertson, "Should the Poor Lead the Poor?" *New York Times*, March 22, 1966.
17. U.S. Congress, Senate Committee on Labor and Public Welfare, Subcommittee on Employment, Manpower, and Poverty, *Examination of the War on Poverty, Hearings*, 90th Cong., 1st sess. (Washington: Government Printing Office, 1967), IV, 902.
18. Leroy F. Aarons, "Moynihan on Social Reform," *Washington Post*, December 26, 1968.
19. Kenneth Clark, Testimony before the U.S. Congress. Senate. Senate Subcommittee on Employment, Manpower, and Poverty, *Examination of the War on Poverty, Hearings*, 90th Cong. 1st sess. (Washington: Government Printing Office, 1967), part 1, p. 294.
20. *Ibid.*, p. 296.
21. *Ibid.*, p. 391.
22. S. M. Miller, "The Future of Maximum Feasible Participation," Conference of the Columbia School of Social Work, May 4, 1968 (mimeographed).
23. "Poverty Referendums Defeated in Elections," *Economic Opportunity Report* (November 14, 1966), p. A-2.
24. John Barnett, "Profile of Poverty: Program Cutbacks Hurt Those Who Might be Helped Most," *Wall Street Journal*, March 21, 1967.
25. John H. Clark, *Community Action Program*, "A New Fix on Community Action," September 25, 1968 (mimeographed), p. 7.
26. Kirschner Associates, "A Description and Evaluation of Neighborhood Centers," a report for the Office of Economic Opportunity, 1966 (mimeographed), pp. 22–23.
27. *Ibid.*, p. 22.
28. Daniel Yankelovitch, "The Community Action Program," summary of a research report prepared for the Office of Economic Opportunity, April 1967 (mimeographed), p. 19.

Chapter 4

1. Julius Richmond, "For the Child of Poverty," *American Child* (Spring 1966), pp. 5–10.
2. U.S. Congress, House Committee on Education and Labor, *Hearings on the Economic Opportunity Act of 1964* (Washington: Government Printing Office, 1964), part III, p. 1337.

3. "Improving the Opportunities and Achievements of the Children of the Poor," memorandum by Dr. Robert Cooke to Sargent Shriver (mimeographed). The undated memo was prepared in January 1965 and is a blueprint of Head Start.

4. Mark R. Arnold, "Opportunity Knocks for Pre-Schoolers in Slums," *National Observer*, May 24, 1965.

5. U.S. Congress, House Committee on Education and Labor, *Economic Opportunity Act Amendments of 1967* (Washington: Government Printing Office, 1967), part 2, pp. 1413–14.

6. Maya Pines, "Slum Children Must Make Up for Lost Time," *New York Times Magazine*, October 15, 1967.

7. U.S. Department of Commerce, Bureau of the Census, "Project Head Start: One Percent Sample Summarizations of Summer 1965 and Summer 1966 Head Start Program" and "Five Percent Sample of 1965–66 Program."

8. *Los Angeles Times*, October 21, 1966.

9. Gerald Grant, "Head Start: Not Enough," *Progressive Magazine*, 31, no. 3 (March 1967): 31.

10. OEO, Community Action Program, "National Summary—Health Report, Summer 1966 Head Start," April 24, 1967.

11. American Academy of Pediatrics, "AAP Launches Head Start Medical Consultation Program," *Newsletter*, October 10, 1967, p. 1.

12. Ellen Hoffman, "Head Start Rules Scored by Educators," *Washington Post*, December 11, 1966.

13. Ellen Hoffman, "Head Start Revises Its Guidelines after Protest by Schools," *Washington Post*, January 5, 1967.

14. William C. Selover, "Shriver Turnabout on Poverty Project Criticized," *Christian Science Monitor*, October 19, 1966; and Patrick Young, "Why There's a Big Fuss in a Pre-School Program," *National Observer*, October 10, 1966.

15. OEO, Community Action Program, *How to Apply for Head Start Child Development Programs* (September 1966).

16. "Next Year's Head Start," *Washington Post*, January 31, 1967.

17. *Philadelphia Inquirer*, June 5, 1966.

18. OEO, Community Action Program, Community Action Program Memorandum no. 21 (February 28, 1966).

19. U.S. Congress, House Committee on Education and Labor, *1966 Amendments to the Economic Opportunity Act of 1964* (Washington: Government Printing Office, 1966), part 1, pp. 195–208.

20. U.S. Department of Health, Education, and Welfare, Office of Education, *The States Report: The First Year of Title I* (Washington: Government Printing Office, 1967).

21. *Ibid., Summer Education for Children of Poverty*, Report of the National Advisory Council on the Education of Disadvantaged Children (Washington: Government Printing Office, 1966), pp. 39–40.

22. Joe D. Waggonner, *Congressional Record* (daily ed.), November 13, 1967, p. H15091.

23. *Congressional Record* (daily ed.), July 30, 1968, pp. S9789–95, and October 1, 1968, p. S11769.

24. U.S. Congress, Senate Committee on Labor and Public Welfare, "Memorandum from Office of Education and OEO on Cooperation," *Amendments to the Economic Opportunity Act of 1964* (Washington: Government Printing Office, 1966), pp. 71–72.

25. "D.C. Summer Head Start," *Washington Evening Star*, June 16, 1967; and OEO, Community Action Program press release 66–6, "Miami Receives $2 Million Head Start Grant," January 21, 1966, and press release 66–99, "Los Angeles Receives $4 Million Head Start Grant," January 19, 1966.

26. OEO press release 66–340, "OEO Expresses Concern over Segregation in Head Start," May 20, 1966.

27. OEO press release 65–1594, "Freedom of Choice Disallowed for Head Start," December 8, 1965.

28. See above, n. 15.

29. See above, n. 19, part 2, pp. 1133–41.

30. Max Wolff and Annie Stein, "Six Months Later: A Comparison of Children Who Had Head Start, Summer 1965, with Their Classmates in Kindergarten" (August 18, 1966) (mimeographed).

31. James S. Coleman *et al.*, Office of Education, U.S. Department of Health, Education, and Welfare, *Equality in Educational Opportunity* (Washington: Government Printing Office, 1966), pp. 491–522.

32. Harold W. Watts and David L. Horner, *The Educational Benefits of Head Start: A Quantitative Analysis* (Madison: Institute for Research on Poverty, University of Wisconsin, 1968), p. 24.

33. S. M. Miller, "Strategy for Change," *American Child* (Spring 1966), pp. 22–24.

34. Edmund Gordon, "What Did We Learn?," *ibid.*, pp. 11–13.

35. Frank Riessman, "The New Pre-School Mythology: Child-centered Radicalism," *ibid.*, pp. 19–21.

36. National Advisory Council on the Education of Disadvantaged Children, Report of January 31, 1967 (mimeographed).

37. See above, n. 20, p. 105.

38. Susan Jacoby, "Hansen Shifts on Parent Council Plan," *Washington Post*, June 24, 1967.

39. *Washington Post*, June 24, 1967.

40. Lucia Johnson, "Preschool Too Late, Warns OEO," *Christian Science Monitor*, August 16, 1968.

41. "Address to School Administrators in San Diego," *Washington Post*, December 7, 1966.

42. Memorandum of Understanding between OEO and HEW Relative to the Administration of the Follow-Through Program, June 26, 1967.

43. OEO Congressional Presentation C–19, April 1967 (mimeographed).

Chapter 5

1. OEO press release 65–1250, "Upward Bound Program Launched," October 6, 1965.

2. *Ibid.*, press release 65–573, "Shriver Opens War on Talent Waste," June 16, 1965.

3. U.S. Congress, House Committee on Education and Labor, *Hearings on Economic Opportunity Amendments of 1967*, 90th Cong., 1st sess. (Washington: Government Printing Office, 1967), p. 1117.

4. *Report of the National Advisory Commission on Civil Disorders* (Washington: Government Printing Office, 1968), p. 250.

5. Higher Education Act of 1965, Title IV, section 408.

6. Representative Edith Green, *Congressional Record* (daily ed.), July 24, 1968, p. H7414, and October 1, 1968, p. S11746.

7. OEO, Community Action Program, *Upward Bound Guidelines, 1968–69*, p. 8.

8. David E. Hunt and Robert H. Hardt, *National Profile of 1967 Upward Bound Students* (Syracuse University, Youth Development Center, October 31, 1967).

9. Jerrold K. Footlick, "Upward Bound Brings Unusual Type of Student to the Campus," *National Observer*, August 15, 1966.

10. Thomas Billings, "Remarks to American Educational Research Association," *Congressional Record* (daily ed.), March 5, 1968, p. E1565.

11. OEO, Community Action Program, *Upward Bound Guidelines, 1968–69*, pp. 10–11.

12. *Ibid.*, press release 68–42, "Upward Bound Graduates Prove Their Worth," April 19, 1968.

13. Educational Associates, Inc., *Upward Bound, 1967 Class Profile Report* (Washington: EAI, 1968), pp. 40–41.

14. U.S. Department of Health, Education, and Welfare, *1967 Annual Report* (Washington: Government Printing Office, 1968), pp. 161–62.

15. Educational Associates, Inc., "Financial Assistance for Upward Bound Students" (June 1968) (mimeographed), p. 10.

16. U.S. Congress, Senate Committee on Labor and Public Welfare, Subcommittee on Employment, Manpower, and Poverty, *Examination of the War on Poverty* (Washington: Government Printing Office, 1967), III, 825.

17. David E. Hunt and Robert H. Hardt, *Characterization of 1966 Summer Upward Bound Programs* (Syracuse University, Youth Development Center, January 1967).

18. Billings, "Remarks to AERA," pp. E1565–66.

Chapter 6

1. A. Kenneth Pye, "The Role of Legal Services in the Antipoverty Program," *Law and Contemporary Problems* (Winter 1966), p. 211.

2. National Legal Aid and Defender Association, *1966 Summary of Conference Proceedings* (Chicago: The Association, 1966), p. 45.

3. *Idem.*, "Summary of Data on Legal Aid Offices in Communities of 100,000 and Over for the Year 1965" (mimeographed).

4. Jerome E. Carlin and Jan Howard, "Legal Representation and Class Justice," *UCLA Law Review* (1965), p. 417.

5. *Ibid.*, p. 410, n. 8 (estimate for 1964).

6. *Annual Report of the President of the National Legal Aid and Defender Association* (September 1964).

7. OEO press release 67–51, "Law Reform Should Be Top Goal of Legal Services," March 18, 1967.

8. 372 U.S. 335 (1963).

9. Peter Marris and Martin Rein, *Dilemmas of Social Reform* (New York: Atherton Press, 1967), pp. 57–58, 187–88.

10. "The War on Poverty: A Civilian Perspective," *Yale Law Journal* (July 1964), pp. 1316–41.

11. Statement of the NLADA executive committee in December 1964, cited in Frandel, "Experiments in Serving the Indigent," *American Bar Association Journal* (1965), p. 460.

12. Pye, "The Role of Legal Services in the Antipoverty Program," pp. 220–21.

13. Address by Theodore M. Berry, director, OEO, Community Action Program, to the National Conference on Law and Poverty, June 25, 1965, *Law and Poverty: 1965* (Washington: Government Printing Office, 1965), pp. 127–28.

14. U.S. Congress, Senate Subcommittee on Employment, Manpower, and Poverty, *Hearings on Amendments to the Economic Opportunity Act*, 89th Cong. 2d sess. (Washington: Government Printing Office, 1966), p. 282.

15. Address by Shriver to the ABA 1965 Convention, "Shriver Eases Bar Fears on Legal Aid to Poor," *Washington Evening Star*, August 12, 1965.

16. Letter of Al J. Cone, ATLA vice president, to National Legal Aid and Defender Association, January 30, 1966.

17. Address by Theodore M. Berry (see n. 13), p. 171.

18. *Ibid.*, pp. 126–44.

19. Jane Handler, Neighborhood Legal Services, U. S. Department of Health, Education, and Welfare (Washington: Government Printing Office, 1966), p. 21.

20. Peter L. Zimroth, "Group Legal Services and the Constitution," *Yale Law Journal* (April 1967), p. 966; and *idem*, "Neighborhood Law Offices: The New Wave in Legal Services for the Poor," *Harvard Law Review* (Fall 1967), p. 805.

21. Fred Graham, "Judicare—or How to Get a Free Divorce," *New York Times*, September 4, 1966. Also see "Connecticut Bar Plans Aid to Poor," *New York Times*, December 26, 1965.

22. U.S. Congress, Senate Subcommittee on Employment, Manpower, and Poverty, *Hearings on Examination of the War on Poverty*, 90th Cong., 1st sess. (Washington: Government Printing Office, 1967), part 9, pp. 2916–77.

23. Patrick Young, "Legal Help for the Poor," *National Observer*, August 21, 1967.

24. 384 U.S. 436 (1966).

25. 387 U.S. 1 (1967).

26. OEO, Legal Services Program, *National Guidelines for Legal Services Programs*, p. 23.

27. John L. Kane, Jr., "Defenders—Stepchildren to OEO?" *Legal Aid Briefcase* (April, 1966).

28. U.S. Congress, House Committee on Education and Labor, *Hearings on Economic Opportunity Act Amendments of 1967*, 90th Cong., 1st sess. (Washington: Government Printing Office, 1967), part 2, pp. 927–29.

29. *Ibid.*, p. 914.

30. Daniel H. Lowenstein and Michael J. Waggoner, "Neighborhood Law Offices Notes," *Harvard Law Review* (February 1967), pp. 805–50, 811–12.

31. Jerry Landauer, "Legal Aid Skirmish in Poverty War," *Wall Street Journal*, November 8, 1967.

32. "CRLA Brings Dramatic Test Cases," Legal Services, *Law in Action* (October 1967), p. 1.

33. Dana Bulen, in *Congressional Record* (daily ed.), November 14, 1967, p. A5585.

34. *Congressional Record* (daily ed.), p. S14271.

35. "OEO Law Program Defended," letter to *Los Angeles Times*, October 18, 1967.

36. See above, n. 13, pp. 9–14; Allison Dunham, "Consumer Credit Problems of the Poor—Legal Assistance as an Aid in Law Reform."

37. Martin Mayer, "The Idea of Justice and the Poor," *Public Interest* (Summer 1967), p. 104.

38. Address by Earl Johnson, Jr., to the Harvard Conference on Law and Poverty, Harvard Law School, Cambridge, Mass., March 17, 1967 (mimeographed).

39. The Ford Foundation, . . . *And Justice for All* (New York: The Foundation, 1967), p. 6.

40. Edgar S. and Jean C. Cahn, "What Price Justice: The Civilian Perspective Revisited," *Notre Dame Law Review* (1966), pp. 927–60.

Chapter 7

1. U. S. Department of Health, Education, and Welfare, *Delivery of Health Services for the Poor* (Washington: The Department, December 1967).

2. H. Jack Geiger, "The Neighborhood Health Center," *Archives of Environmental Health* (June 1967), pp. 912–16.

3. Lisbeth Bamberger (Schorr), "Health Care and Poverty," *Bulletin of the New York Academy of Medicine* (December 1966), pp. 1140–49.

4. U.S. Congress, Senate Committee on Appropriations, *Departments of Labor and HEW and Related Agencies Appropriation Bill, 1969*, 90th Cong., 2d sess., Rept. No. 1484 (Washington: Government Printing Office, 1968), p. 86.

5. OEO, Community Action Program, *Guidelines [to] Healthright Programs* (Washington: Government Printing Office, 1968), pp. 3–4.

6. OEO, Community Action Program, "Manpower Development in Comprehensive Health Services Programs" (December 1967) (mimeographed).

7. U.S. Congress, House Committee on Education and Labor, *Hearings on Economic Opportunity Act of 1967*, 90th Cong., 1st sess. (Washington: Government Printing Office, 1967), part 4, p. 3488.

8. U.S. Department of Health, Education, and Welfare, *Delivery of Health Services for the Poor*, pp. 49–66.

9. U.S. Congress, House Committee on Education and Labor, *Hearings on 1967 Amendments to the Economic Opportunity Act*, 90th Cong., 1st sess. (Washington: Government Printing Office, 1967), part 2, p. 873.

10. A joint statement of the Department of Health, Education, and Welfare and

the Office of Economic Opportunity, *Coordinated Funding of Health Services* (Washington: Government Printing Office, May 2, 1967), p. 2.

11. U.S. Congress, Senate Committee on Labor and Public Welfare, *Examination of the War on Poverty*, 90th Cong., 1st sess. (Washington: Government Printing Office, 1967), part 9, p. 2893.

12. Dick Kirschten, "AMA Shuns Realities of Slum Health Programs," *Chicago Sun Times*, July 2, 1967.

13. Donald Ganson, "Doctors Bid AMA Push Aid in Slums," *New York Times*, December 16, 1967.

14. OEO, Community Action Program, Health Services Office, Memorandum to Project Directors of Comprehensive Health Services, October 25, 1967.

15. *Ibid.*

16. "OEO Is Here to Stay, So—," *Pharmacy News* (April–May 1968); reprinted in *Congressional Record* (daily ed.), June 6, 1968, pp. S7805–6.

17. Louise Hutchinson, "OEO Is Urged to Close Its Pharmacies," *Chicago Tribune*, July 10, 1968; and address by Willard B. Simmons, "Pharmacy, Patriotism, Politics, Poverty," in *Congressional Record* (daily ed.), September 26, 1968, pp. S11511–12.

18. Edward M. Kennedy, in *Congressional Record* (daily ed.), October 3, 1967, pp. S14040–43.

19. *Report of the National Advisory Commission on Health Manpower* (Washington: Government Printing Office, November 1967), I, 37.

20. Memorandum of the Surgeon General to the Bureau and regional health directors, November 7, 1967.

Chapter 8

1. Frederick S. Jaffe, *Family Planning and Rural Poverty: An Approach to Programming of Services*, report prepared for National Advisory Commission on Rural Poverty (New York: Planned Parenthood–World Population, 1968), p. 5.

2. Harold L. Sheppard, *Effects of Family Planning on Poverty in the United States* (Kalamazoo, Mich.: W. E. Upjohn Institute for Employment Research, October 1967), p. 16.

3. National Academy of Sciences–National Research Council, *The Growth of U.S. Population* (Washington: The Academy, 1965), p. 10.

4. Mollie Orshansky, "Who's Who Among the Poor: A Demographic View of Poverty," *Social Security Bulletin* (July 1965), pp. 14–15.

5. Walter Smart, Walter Rybeck, and Howard E. Shuman, *The Large Poor Family —A Housing Gap*, report prepared for the consideration of the National Commission on Urban Problems (Washington: Government Printing Office, 1968), p. 2.

6. Wilbur J. Cohen, "Ending Poverty, A Will and a Way," address presented at Georgetown University, Washington, D.C., August 31, 1968.

7. Message to Congress on "Domestic Health and Education," March 1, 1966.

8. OEO, VISTA, *VISTA Volunteer Handbook* (Washington: OEO, 1968), pp. 22–23. the Eleventh Annual Meeting, Western Section, Operations Research Society of America, Las Vegas, September 30, 1965.

9. OEO, Community Action Program memorandum 37, "Revised Special Conditions Governing Family Planning Projects and Activities," May 27, 1966.

10. Hobart Rowen, "Economic Impact: OEO's Failure on Birth Issue," *Washington Post*, October 17, 1965.

11. Rowland Evans and Robert Novak, "Inside Report: Birth Control Blunders," *Washington Post*, June 3, 1966.

12. U.S. Congress, Senate Committee on Labor and Public Welfare, *Amendments to the Economic Opportunity Act of 1964*, 89th Cong., 2d sess. (Washington: Government Printing Office, 1966), p. 98.

13. OEO press release, "Omnibus Family Planning Programs Set in Los Angeles," September 17, 1968.

14. Robert Osterman and Mark R. Arnold, *"The Pill" and Its Impact* (Silver Spring, Md.: *National Observer*, Newsbook, 1967), p. 92.

Chapter 9

1. United Community Funds and Councils of America, Institute of Community Studies, *Voluntarism and Human Welfare* (New York: The Institute, January 1968), p. 3.
2. Mark R. Arnold, "VISTA Fights Low Priorities to Get at Poverty," *National Observer*, May 31, 1965.
3. U.S. Congress, House Committee on Education and Labor, *Economic Opportunity Act of 1964*, H. Rept. 1458, 88th Cong., 2d sess. (Washington: Government Printing Office, 1964), p. 37.
4. Joseph A. Loftus, "VISTA Gains Recruits as the Peace Corps Lags," *New York Times*, July 4, 1968.
5. OEO press release, "VISTA Exceeds Volunteer Goal," July 7, 1968.
6. U.S. Congress, Senate Committee on Labor and Public Welfare, *Examination of the War on Poverty: Analysis of VISTA* (Washington: Government Printing Office, 1967), part X, pp. 3221–23.
7. *Ibid.*, House Committee on Education and Labor, *Economic Opportunity Act Amendments of 1967*, 90th Cong., 1st sess. (Washington: Government Printing Office, 1967), p. 837.
8. OEO, VISTA, *VISTA Volunteer Handbook* (Washington: OEO, 1968), pp. 22–23.
9. U.S. Congress, House Committee on Appropriations, *Hearings on Office of Economic Opportunity Appropriations for 1969*, 90th Cong., 2d sess. (Washington: Government Printing Office, 1968), p. 495.

Chapter 10

1. "Rural Poverty: Is Migration the Cure?" *New Generation* (Summer 1968), pp. 20–32.
2. Robert A. Levine, "Thrust of Rural Programs," memo to Bertrand Harding, June 8, 1967 (mimeographed).
3. U.S. Department of Agriculture, Farmers Home Administration, "Economic Opportunity Loans Program: Summary of Progress," April 26, 1968, p. 5.
4. Robert Maynod, "Alabama Negro Exodus Laid to Bias in U.S. Loans," *Washington Post*, April 30, 1968.
5. Robert Beardwood, "The Southern Roots of Urban Crisis," *Fortune*, August 1968; reprinted in *Congressional Record* (daily ed.), August 2, 1968, p. S10095.
6. U.S. Department of Agriculture, Farmers Home Administration, "Supervised Credit as an Antipoverty Program: The First Four-Year Record," November 5, 1968 (mimeographed).
7. U.S. Congress, House Committee on Appropriations, *Hearings on Supplemental Appropriation Bill, 1968*, 90th Cong., 1st sess. (Washington: Government Printing Office, 1967), pp. 253–56. Adjusted data used here.
8. U.S. Department of Agriculture, Farmers Home Administration, "EO Rural Loans Program, Summary and Progress," April 26, 1968.
9. "Small Co-op Drawbacks Pointed Out," *Washington Post*, April 14, 1966, p. 68.
10. Quoted in Burt Schorr, "Federally Aided Co-ops in South Lift Earnings of Farmers, Fisherman," *Wall Street Journal*, May 15, 1968.
11. Michael Miles, "Black Cooperatives," *New Republic*, September 21, 1968, p. 22.
12. U.S. Department of Agriculture press release, "Freeman Reports on Economic Opportunity Loan Program Survey," May 9, 1966.
13. U.S. Congress, House Committee on Appropriations, *Hearings on Supplemental Appropriations Bill, 1968*, 90th Cong., 1st sess. (Washington: Government Printing Office, 1967), p. 255.
14. U.S. Department of Agriculture, Economic Research Service, *Effects of Economic Opportunity Loans on Lobster Fishermen in Maine, 1965–67*, Rept. 136, July 1968.

Chapter 11

1. U.S. Congress, Senate Committee on Labor and Public Welfare, *Economic Opportunity Act of 1964*, Rept. 1218, 88th Cong., 2d sess. (Washington: Government Printing Office, 1964), pp. 30–32; and House Committee on Education and Labor, *Economic Opportunity Act*, Rept. 1458, 88th Cong., 2d sess. (Washington: Government Printing Office, 1964), pp. 24–27.

2. U.S. Department of Agriculture, Economic Research Service, *The Hired Farm Working Force of 1966*, Rept. 20 (Washington: Government Printing Office, 1967).

3. OEO, Farmers Home Administration, "Programs for Migratory and Seasonal Farm Workers Fact Sheet," M-16, March 1967.

4. U.S. Congress, Senate Subcommittee on Migratory Labor, Committee on Labor and Public Welfare, *The Migratory Farm Labor Problem in the United States*, Rept. 1549, 89th Cong., 2d sess., August 30, 1966; Rept. 71, 90th Cong., 1st sess., March 15, 1967; Rept. 1006, 90th Cong., 2d sess., February 19, 1968 (Washington: Government Printing Office).

5. U.S. Department of Agriculture, Economic Research Service, *Domestic Migratory Farm Workers: Personal and Economic Characteristics*, Rept. 121 (Washington: Government Printing Office, 1967).

6. OEO, Special Field Programs, "Summary Fiscal Year 1966 Activities," *Traveler*, a newsletter for migrant and seasonal farm workers (November 1966).

7. U.S. Congress, Senate Committee on Labor and Public Welfare, *Examination of the War on Poverty*, Hearings, 90th Cong., 1st sess. (Washington: Government Printing Office, 1967), part 9, p. 2989.

8. *Ibid.*, House Committee on Appropriations, *Departments of Labor, and Health, Education, and Welfare Appropriations for 1969*, Hearings, 90th Cong., 2d sess. (Washington: Government Printing Office, 1968), part 6, p. 332.

9. OEO press release, "Manpower Evaluation and Development Institute," May 16, 1968.

10. OEO press release, "North Carolina Migrants and Seasonal Farm Workers in Four Counties to Benefit from OEO Program," April 26, 1968.

11. U.S. Congress, House Committee on Appropriations, *Department of Labor, and Health, Education, and Welfare Appropriations for 1969*, p. 327.

12. *Ibid.*, p. 330.

13. *Congressional Record* (daily ed.), October 4, 1967, p. S14141.

14. U.S. Congress, House Committee on Education and Labor, *Economic Opportunity Act Amendments of 1967*, Hearings, 90th Cong., 1st sess. (Washington: Government Printing Office, 1967), part 2, p. 1093.

15. *Ibid.*, pp. 1092–93, and part 4, pp. 2645–64.

16. Haynes Johnson, "Washington Gets Involved in a Strike," *Washington Evening Star*, February 4, 1966.

17. Nick Kotz, "In the Deep South, the Enemy is Poverty," *Minneapolis Tribune*, series that began May 14, 1967.

18. Hank Burchard, "Bad Labor Camps Dog Virginia Shore Farms," *Washington Post*, March 3, 1968.

19. A brief discussion of this case is presented in chapter 6.

20. Nick Kotz, "In the Deep South, The Enemy is Poverty."

21. U.S. Congress, House Committee on Appropriations, *Departments of Labor, and Health, Education, and Welfare Appropriations for 1969*, p. 333.

Chapter 12

1. Herbert E. Striner, "Toward A Fundamental Program for the Training, Employment and Economic Equality of the American Indian" (Kalamazoo, Mich.: W. E. Upjohn Institute for Employment Research, March 1968).

2. U.S. Congress, Senate Committee on Labor and Public Welfare, *Hearings on*

Economic Opportunity Act of 1964, 88th Cong., 2d sess. (Washington: Government Printing Office, 1964), p. 137 ff. See also the later Message to Congress, *Goals and Programs for the American Indian*, The White House, March 6, 1968.

3. U.S. Congress, House Committee on Education and Labor, *Hearings on Economic Opportunity Act of 1964* (Washington: Government Printing Office, 1964), part 2, p. 1055.

4. See above, note 2, pp. 137–38.

5. University Consortium, *Indian Reservation Community Action and the Role of the Three University Consortium in Providing Technical Assistance and Training*, March 15, 1966; 1968 Progress Report of Indian Community Action Projects. (These reports were available through OEO.)

6. U.S. Department of Interior, Bureau of Indian Affairs, *Answers to Your Questions about American Indians* (Washington: Government Printing Office, May 1968); and Bureau of Indian Affairs, *U.S. Indian Population (1962) and Land (1963)*, November 1963 (mimeographed).

7. U.S. Congress, House Committee on Education and Labor, *Hearings on Economic Opportunity Act Amendments of 1967*, 90th Cong., 1st sess. (Washington: Government Printing Office, 1967), part 2, pp. 1069–70.

8. Office of Economic Opportunity, *Indian Opportunities: A Summary of Indian Participation in OEO Programs*, undated but prepared in 1966. An additional annual summary, same title, appeared in 1967 (also undated).

9. U.S. Congress, House Committee on Appropriations, *Departments of Labor and Health, Education, and Welfare Appropriations for 1969* (Washington: Government Printing Office, 1968), part 6, p. 305.

10. Human Sciences Research, Inc., *A Comprehensive Evaluation of OEO Community Action Programs on Six Selected American Indian Reservations* (McLean, Virginia), September 1966; and U.S. Congress, House Committee on Education and Labor, *Economic Opportunity Act Amendments of 1967, Hearings* (Washington: Government Printing Office, 1967), part 5, pp. 3995–98.

11. See above, note 9, pp. 303–14.

12. See above, note 7, part 2, pp. 1555–56 and 1581.

Chapter 13

1. U.S. Congress, Senate Committee on Labor and Public Welfare, *Hearings on the Economic Opportunity Act of 1964*, 88th Cong., 2d sess. (Washington: Government Printing Office, 1964), part 1, p. 147.

2. *Ibid.*, p. 148.

3. Robert Walters, "De Facto Segregation Feared in Job Corps," *Washington Evening Star*, December 29, 1966.

4. Comptroller General of the United States, "Review of Selected Program Activities at the Parks Job Corps Center" (November 1967) (mimeographed), p. 56.

5. "Out of the Job Corps into a Job," *Business Week*, January 29, 1966, p. 32.

6. Joseph A. Loftus, "Job Corps Finds Kentucky Camp Is Still Deficient," *New York Times*, November 3, 1965.

7. Mark R. Arnold, "Trying Two Approaches in Job Corps Training," *National Observer*, February 21, 1966.

8. David Barnett, "Industry's Role in Poverty War," *New York World Journal Tribune*, September 27, 1966.

9. U.S. Department of Labor, Office of Policy Planning and Research [Daniel P. Moynihan], *The Negro Family: The Case for National Action* (Washington: The Department, March 1965).

10. OEO, Job Corps, *Community Relations Reports* (June 1967), and Joseph A. Loftus, "Job Corps Bases Gain Acceptance," *New York Times*, April 6, 1967.

11. OEO, Job Corps, "Job Corps to Close 16 Centers," *Economic Opportunity Report* (February 5, 1968), p. 3.

12. OEO press release, "Job Corps Enrollees Pay One-Fourth of Cost for Legal Defense," September 10, 1968.

13. "Lag in Job Corps Assailed by Ryan," *New York Times*, June 2, 1965.

14. Louis A. Harris and Associates, *A Study of Job Corps Non-Graduate Terminations* (January 1967), reprinted in *Hearings on Economic Opportunity Amendments of 1967*, 90th Cong., 1st sess. (Washington: Government Printing Office, 1967), part 1, p. 155; and *A Study of August 1966 Terminations from the Job Corps* (March 1967), in U.S. Congress, House Committee on Education and Labor, *Hearings on Economic Opportunity Amendments of 1967*, 90th Cong., 1st sess. (Washington: Government Printing Office, 1967), part 1, p. 364.

15. Louis Harris and Associates, *A Study of August 1966 Terminations from the Job Corps*, p. 369.

16. "What's Wrong with the Job Corps?" an interview with Professor Francis P. Purcell in *U.S. News and World Report* (December 27, 1965), p. 54.

17. Rutgers Advisory Committee "Interim Report on the Kilmer Job Corps Center" (September 30, 1965), p. 57. This report was never published, and some of the members of the advisory committee disassociated themselves from its conclusions.

18. OEO, Job Corps, "Educational Gains" (assessment and research reports No. 5) (January 1967) (mimeographed), p. 4.

19. *Ibid.*

20. OEO, Job Corps, "Status Report No. 3: The Job Corps Evaluation" (May 15, 1967) (mimeographed), p. 4.

21. The Chamber of Commerce of the United States, *Youth and the War on Poverty* (Washington: The Chamber, 1966), pp. 46–48.

22. Louis Harris and Associates, *A Study of August 1966 Terminations from the Job Corps*, p. 419.

23. Advisory Commission on Intergovernmental Relations, *Intergovernmental Relations in the Poverty Program* (Washington: Government Printing Office, April 1966), p. 187.

24. Louis Harris and Associates, *A Study of August 1966 Terminations from the Job Corps*, p. 435.

25. Glen G. Cain, "Benefit-Cost Estimate of Job Corps" (for Office of Economic Opportunity) (May 22, 1967) (mimeographed), pp. 13–14.

26. Louis Harris and Associates, *A Study of August 1966 Terminations from the Job Corps*, pp. 337–469.

27. Louis Harris and Associates, *A Study of the Status of August 1966 Job Corps Terminees 12 Months after Termination* (October 1967).

28. Louis Harris and Associates, *A Study of the Status of August 1966 Job Corps Terminees 18 Months after Termination* (March 1968).

29. Louis Harris and Associates, *A Continuing Study of Job Corps Terminations: Wave II—Initial Interview with Terminations from August 15, 1966 to December 15, 1966* (May 1967), printed in *Hearings on Economic Opportunity Amendments of 1967*, 90th Cong., 1st sess. (Washington: Government Printing Office, 1967), part 1, pp. 471–500.

30. OEO press release, "Progress Report by Job Corps Director," June 11, 1967.

31. Louis Harris and Associates, *A Study of August 1966 Terminations from the Job Corps*, p. 411.

32. *Ibid.*, p. 420.

33. Louis Harris and Associates, *A Study of Job Corps Non-Graduate Terminations* (January 1967), reprinted in *Hearings on Economic Opportunity Amendments of 1967*, 90th Cong., 1st sess. (Washington: Government Printing Office, 1967), part 1, pp. 123–239.

34. Louis Harris and Associates, *A Study of the Status of August 1966 Job Corps Terminees 18 Months after Termination*, p. 5.

35. Louis Harris and Associates, *A Study of Job Corps "No-Shows": Accepted Applicants Who Did Not Go to a Training Center* (February 1967), printed in

Hearings on Economic Opportunity Amendments of 1967, 90th Cong., 1st sess. (Washington: Government Printing Office, 1967), part 1, pp. 241–336.

36. Louis Harris and Associates, *A Study of August 1966 Terminations from the Job Corps*, p. 412.

37. *Ibid.*, pp. 412 and 424.

38. *Ibid.*, p. 368.

39. David Gottlieb, "Poor Youth Do Want to Be Middle-Class But It's Not Easy," paper delivered at the 61st Annual Meeting of the American Sociological Association, Miami Beach, Fla., August 30, 1966 (mimeographed), p. 20.

LIST OF TABLES

INDEX

A

Aarons, Leroy F., 324
Accelerated Public Works Act, 14
Adult basic education, 52; delegated to HEW, 50, 56; in migrant-seasonal workers program, 253; not in original EOA, 44; transferred to EOA, 31
Advisory Commission on Intergovernmental Relations: on Job Corps, 296
AFL–CIO support of OEO, 85
Agricultural cooperatives, 239–40, 242
Agriculture, Department of: farm loan programs, 229, 244; operate conservation Job Corps centers, 281; poverty administration claims, 23; 1963 poverty proposals, 18, 36
Alinsky, Saul, 115
American Academy of Pediatrics, 144
American Arbitration Association: analyzes CAA elections, 114
American Bankers' Association, 90
American Bar Association: endorses CAP legal services, 180; on professional ethics, 182
American Bar Foundation, 178
American Council for Education Committee, 168
American Council on Education: origin of Upward Bound, 165
American Dental Association, 201
American Indians. See Indians
American Jewish Congress, 81
American Medical Association: on OEO health programs, 200–201
American Psychiatric Association: recommended Job Corps center size, 283
American Public Health Association, 205
American Public Welfare Association: Shriver's 1965 speech to, 82
American Rescue Workers, 215
American Trial Lawyers' Association: reluctant support of OEO legal services, 181
Appalachia: and Job Corps youth, 277
Area Redevelopment Act, 13–14
Area Redevelopment Administration: overextension of, 23–24; planning experience, 119
Arizona State University, 265
Arnold, Mark R., 325, 329, 330, 332
Association of American Indian Affairs, 264
Auerbach, Stuart, 322
Ayres, William A., 98

B

Baker, Donald M., 78
Bakersfield, Calif.: refused OEO funds, 120
Baltimore County, Md.: refused OEO funds, 120
Bamberger, Lisbeth, 328
Barnett, David, 332
Barnett, John, 324
Battle Creek, Mich.: Job Corps opposition, 283
Beardwood, Robert, 330
Beirne, Joseph, 15
Berry, Theodore M., 112
Bigart, Homer, 320
Billings, Thomas, 171, 326
Birth control programs: cost effectiveness, 207, 311; cost requirements, 212; OEO's timid approach, 209–10; public acceptance of, 311; and quality of human life, 213; See also Family Planning
Black Arts Theatre: controversial HARYOU project, 87
Bookbinder, Hyman, 33, 88; on "maximum feasible participation," 112
Boone, Richard, 34, 36
"Bosses and bollweevil amendment," 66
Boutin, Bernard L., 65–66
British legal aid system, 183
Bronfenbrenner, Urie, 135
Brown, Edmund G., 254
Bulen, Dana, 328
Burchard, Hank, 331
Bureau of the Budget, 70; opposes OEO, 27–28; studies federal expenditures on poor, 9–10
Burns, Arthur F., 12
Burroughs Corporation, 84
Business and Labor Advisory Councils, 89
Businessmen: anti-OEO feelings, 84–85; OEO support, 83–84; See also Job Corps

C

Cahn, Edgar S. and Jean C. See Legal Services program
Cain, Glen G., 333
California's Compensatory Education Act, 156
California grape pickers' strike, 256

California Rural Legal Assistance, 186–87
Cannon, William B., 17, 20
Capp, Al, 96
Capron, William M., 17
Carey, Hugh L., 45
Carlin, Jerome E., 327
Cash assistance programs, 4–6
Cavanagh, Mayor Jerome, 63
Census Bureau Head Start survey, 159
Chamber of Commerce, U.S., 90, 294–95
Chasen, Robert, 84
Chavez, Cesar, 256
Child and parent centers, 162
Child Development Group of Mississippi (CDGM), 147–48
Child labor laws: and farm labor, 249; and Job Corps terminees, 277
Child welfare programs, 7
Children's Bureau, HEW: Denver health center, 200; family planning grants, 212
Church-state controversy: EOA program effect on, 21, 44–45; President Kennedy's position on, 80–81
Citizens Volunteer Corps: assists VISTA, 218–19
Civil rights movement: role in poverty war, 14–15, 86–88
Civilian Conservation Corps, 273. See also Job Corps
Clark, John H., 324
Clark, Joseph S., 68, 101, 117
Clark, Kenneth B., 117, 324
Clark, Robert, 259
Cohen, Wilbur J., 16, 208, 329
Coleman, James S., 326
College students: federal assistance to, expanded, 133, 173–74; VISTA volunteers, 217
Columbia Point Public Housing Development: Boston model health center, 193–94
Commerce, Department of: poverty administration claims, 23–24
Communications Workers of America, 15–16
Community Action Agency (CAA): conclusions, 131; local government support, 64; local innovative projects, 124; nonprofessionals in, 129; and old-line agencies, 312; poor participation in, 115–16; "success stories" of, 127–28; VISTA volunteers, 220. See also CAP; EOA; OEO
—administration: 50, 113; boards, 113–14; centralization vs. decentralization, 125; Green amendment, 66; number,

64; objective strained, 122–23; salary structure, 79
Community Action Program (CAP): bureaucracy in, 314; experimental programs of, 314; mayors' opposition to, 111, 115; reexamination of, 312. See also CAA; EOA; OEO.
—administration: federal role in, 119–20; local mismanagement of funds, 58; regionalization, 58; subordinate government role, 60, 315
—concept, 20–21, 119–20, 131; catch-all projects to aid poor, 109; controversy over, 117–18, 135; restructuring social services, 63–64; role of poor, 35–36, 131; strategy, 109
—funding: distribution of funds, 120–22, 315; Head Start proportion, 152; versatile funds, 127
—origins: agencies, 21, 24–25, 37; concept not understood by Congress, 44; drafting legislation, 34–37, 110; "gray areas influence," 19; Heller-Gordon memo on, 24–25; name, 20
Community development corporations, 127, 314–15
Community Representation Advisory Council, 89
Community Work and Training Bill, 31
Comprehensive health services, 200; OEO concept, 193; OEO Indian program, 267–68
Conference of Mayors, U.S., 65–66, 115
Conference on Economic Progress, 13
Conference on Law and Poverty, 188
Congress: cuts Research and Demonstration funding, 126; EOA committee assignment, 38–39; economy in social legislation, 103; funding OEO, 90–91, 93; future poverty legislation, 311; liberal 89th, 92; OEO review, 101; on education for migrants, 249; on Job Corps, 286, 290; on national emphasis, 124; on VISTA, 216–17. See also House of Representatives committees; Senate committees and subcommittees
Connally, Governor John B., 280–81
Conservation centers. See Job Corps
Conservation lobbies and EOA legislation, 44, 275
Conway, Jack, 76
Cooperatives: buying programs, 221; limited potential of, 242; loans to, 231, 239; major opposition to, 240
Cost-benefit analysis: of birth control, 207, 311; of VISTA, 223. See also individual programs

Designed by Edward D. King.
Composed in Baskerville by Monotype Composition Company, Inc.
Printed offset by Universal Lithographers, Inc., on 50-lb Warren's 1854.
Bound by Moore and Company in Riverside Vellum, RV-3443.